www.wadsworth.com

wadsworth.com is the World Wide Web site for Wadsworth Publishing Company and is your direct source to dozens of online resources.

At *wadsworth.com* you can find out about supplements, demonstration software, and student resources. You can also send e-mail to many of our authors and preview new publications and exciting new technologies.

wadsworth.com
Changing the way the world learns®

CONTEMPORARY ISSUES IN CRIME AND JUSTICE SERIES

Todd Clear, Series Editor

The Color of Justice

Race, Ethnicity, and Crime in America

Second Edition

SAMUEL WALKER
University of Nebraska at Omaha

CASSIA SPOHN
University of Nebraska at Omaha

MIRIAM DeLONE
University of Nebraska at Omaha

Australia • Canada • Denmark • Japan • Mexico • New Zealand
Philippines • Puerto Rico • Singapore • South Africa • Spain
United Kingdom • United States

Executive Editor, Criminal Justice: Sabra Horne
Senior Development Editor: Dan Alpert
Assistant Editor: Shannon Ryan
Editorial Assistant: Ann Tsai
Marketing Manager: Christine Henry
Marketing Assistant: Ken Baird
Project Editor: Jennie Redwitz
Print Buyer: Karen Hunt
Permissions Editor: Bob Kauser

Production Service: Sarah Kimnach, nSight, Inc.
Copy Editor: Teresa Horton
Illustrator: Samantha Stanko
Cover Designer: Bill Stanton
Cover Image: t/k
Cover Printer: Webcom Limited
Compositor: Pre-Press Company, Inc.
Printer/Binder: Webcom Limited

Printed in Canada
1 2 3 4 5 6 7 03 02 01 00 99

**Library of Congress
Cataloging-in-Publication Data**

Walker, Samuel
    The color of justice : race, ethnicity, and
crime in America / Samuel Walker, Cassia
Spohn, Miriam DeLone. — 2nd ed.
        p.   cm.
    Includes bibliographical references and
index.
    ISBN 0-534-52362-5 (alk. paper)
    1. Discrimination in criminal justice ad-
ministration—United States. 2. Race discrimination—United States. 3. Ethnicity—United
States. 4. Social structure—United States.
5. Minorities—Crimes against—United States.
6. Police misconduct—United States. 7. United
States—Race relations. 8. United States—
Social conditions. I. Spohn, Cassia. II. DeLone,
Miriam. III. Title.
HV9950.W33   1999
346'.089'00973—dc21   99-35878

For more information contact
Wadsworth/Thomson Learning
10 Davis Drive
Belmont, CA 94002-3098
USA
www.wadsworth.com

International Headquarters
Thomson Learning
290 Harbor Drive, 2nd Floor
Stamford, CT 06902-7477
USA

UK/Europe/Middle East
Thomson Learning
Berkshire House
168-173 High Holborn
London WC1V 7AA
United Kingdom

Asia
Thomson Learning
60 Albert Street #15-01
Albert Complex
Singapore 189969

Canada
Nelson/Thomson Learning
1120 Birchmount Road
Scarborough, Ontario M1K 5G4
Canada

Contents

Preface

Since the first edition of *The Color of Justice* was published, issues of race and ethnicity with respect to crime have, if anything, become even more prominent in American political life. The president of the United States appointed a special commission to create a national dialogue on race in response to an apparent worsening of race relations across the country. The question of racial profiling—that is, police making traffic stops solely on the basis of drivers' race—has emerged as a national controversy. And allegations of racial disparity in sentencing, particularly with respect to the death penalty, have not abated.

Our decision to write this book also reflects the fact that all three of us have addressed questions of race, ethnicity, and crime for many years, both in research and in our teaching. It seemed natural to combine our experience, our insights, and our ideas into one book.

More immediately, this book originated over dinner with our former editor at Wadsworth, Brian Gore. Brian listened to our ideas and encouraged us to write this book. We would like to thank Brian for his immediate and enthusiastic interest in the project. Sabra Horne, our current editor, has also enthusiatically supported our work. Jennie Redwitz shepherded the book through production in an extremely efficient manner and was a pleasure to work with.

The following reviewers contributed their expertise in the early stages of the book's creation: George S. Bridges, University of Washington; Robert G. Huckabee, Indiana State University; Martha A. Myers, University of Georgia;

Gregory D. Russell, California State University, Chico; and Mary Ann Zager, Northeastern University.

For their helpful suggestions on the Second Edition, we thank the following reviewers: Orie A. Brown, California State University, Fresno; James G. Fox, Buffalo State College; Marianne O. Nielson, Northern Arizona University; Katheryn Russell, University of Maryland; Jill Shelley, Northern Kentucky University; and Marjorie Zatz, Arizona State University.

We would like to thank Greg DeLone for suggesting the title of this book. We would also like to thank Erika Frenzel for compiling the Index.

Samuel Walker
Cassia Spohn
Miriam DeLone

1

Race, Ethnicity, and Crime

The Present Crisis

Nearly one hundred years ago, the great African American scholar W. E. B. Du Bois declared, "The problem of the twentieth century is the problem of the color line."[1] By that he meant that racism and racial discrimination were the central problems facing modern society.

Much the same can be said about crime and justice in American society today. Nearly every problem related to criminal justice issues involves matters of race and ethnicity:

- Half of all the prisoners in the United States (49.4 percent in 1996) are African American, despite the fact that blacks represent only 12 percent of the U.S. population. Even more alarming, the incarceration *rate* for African American men is seven times the rate for white men (3,250 per 100,000 compared with 461 per 100,000).[2]

- Hispanics were 17.5 percent of all prisoners in 1996, up from only 10.9 percent in 1985.[3]

- About 40 percent of the people currently on death row and 53 percent of all the people executed since 1930 are African American.

- The 1992 riot that devastated Los Angeles, leaving more than fifty people dead and over $750 million worth of property destroyed, was an expression of outrage over perceived racial injustice: An all-white jury had acquitted four white police officers of beating Rodney King, an African American.[4]

■ Eighty percent of African American high school students in one survey said they had been stopped by the police; 62 percent of those said the police treated them with disrespect. Sixty percent of the Hispanic high school students had been stopped by the police, and 63 percent of those said the police were disrespectful.[5]

■ Since the mid-1960s, crime has been a central issue in U.S. politics. For many white Americans, the crime issue is an expression of racial fears: fear of victimization by African American offenders, fear of racial integration of neighborhoods.

In short, on both sides of the color line there is suspicion and fear: a sense of injustice on the part of racial minorities and fear of black crime on the part of whites. American society is deeply polarized over the issues of crime, justice, and race.

This polarization of attitudes toward crime is especially strong with respect to the death penalty. In 1996, 77.2 percent of whites favored the death penalty, compared with only 58.6 percent of African Americans and 61 percent of Hispanics.[6]

Even though African Americans are more likely to be the victims of crime, whites also express high levels of fear of crime. For many whites, crime is a code word for fears of social change. A study of community crime control efforts in Chicago, for example, found that neighborhood organizations usually were formed in response to perceived changes in the racial composition of their neighborhoods.[7]

THE SCOPE OF THIS BOOK

This book offers a comprehensive, critical, and balanced examination of the issues of crime and justice with respect to race and ethnicity. We believe that none of the existing books on the subject is completely adequate.[8]

First, none of the previous books or articles offers a comprehensive treatment of all criminal justice issues. There are many excellent articles on particular topics, such as the death penalty or police use of deadly force, but none covers the full range of topics in a complete and critical fashion. As a result, there are often no discussions of whether relatively more discrimination exists at one point in the justice system than at others. For example, is there more discrimination by the police in making arrest decisions than, say, by prosecutors in charging? In a report to President Bill Clinton's Initiative on Race, Christopher Stone, Director of the Vera Institute of Justice, concluded that our knowledge about most criminal justice issues is "uneven."[9] There are many important questions about which we just do not have good information.

Second, the treatment of race and ethnicity in introductory criminal justice textbooks is very weak. They do not identify race and ethnicity as a major issue and fail to incorporate important literature on police misconduct, felony sentencing, the employment of racial minorities, and other important topics.[10]

Third, few books or articles discuss all racial and ethnic groups. Most focus entirely on African Americans. As Coramae Richey Mann pointed out, "the available studies focus primarily on African Americans and neglect other racial minorities."[11] There is relatively little research on Hispanic Americans and almost none on Native Americans or Asian Americans.[12]

It is increasingly clear to us that there are important differences between the experiences of different racial and ethnic groups with respect to crime and justice. A contextual approach emphasizes the unique historical, political, and economic circumstances of each group. Alfredo Mirandé, author of *Gringo Justice,* argued that historically "a double standard of justice" has existed, one for white Americans and one for Chicanos.[13] Marianne O. Nielsen, meanwhile, argues that the subject of Native Americans and criminal justice "cannot be understood without recognizing that it is just one of many interrelated issues that face native peoples today," including "political power, land, economic development, [and] individual despair."[14]

Consequently, there are no useful comparisons of the experiences of different groups. We do not know, for example, whether Hispanic Americans are treated worse, better, or about the same as African Americans. We have chosen to title this book *The Color of Justice* because it covers all people of color.

Fourth, many of the books on the subject do not offer a sufficiently critical perspective. The handling of the evidence is often superficial, ignoring many of the complexities related to specific issues. Too often authors rely only on evidence that supports their preconceptions. We disagree with William Wilbanks's argument that racism in the criminal justice system is a "myth."[15] We also reject Christopher Stone's conclusion, in his report to the President's Initiative on Race, that is the data suggest "strong reason for optimism" about race and criminal justice.[16]

We believe that the problem of race, ethnicity, and crime is serious and in some important respects getting worse. Many people believe that race relations in the United States have worsened in recent years. In response to this perception, President Bill Clinton established a special President's Initiative on Race in 1997 to create a national dialogue on the subject. The activities of the President's panel, however, became embroiled in controversy, indicating the depth of the divisions in public opinion.

Finally, as Hawkins pointed out, American sociologists and criminologists have done a very poor job of studying the relationship of race, ethnicity, and crime. In particular, there is an absence of solid theoretical work that would provide a comprehensive explanation for this extremely important phenomenon. The main reason for this, according to Hawkins, is that "public discourse about both crime and race in the United States has always been an ideological and political mine field."[17] On the one side have been racist theories of biological determinism that attribute high rates of crime among racial and ethnic minorities to genetic inferiority. On the other side, the mainstream of U.S.

criminology has reacted by downplaying racial differences and emphasizing the inadequacy of official crime data. The extreme sensitivity of the subject has tended to discourage rather than stimulate the development of theoretical studies of race, ethnicity, and crime.

The Color of Justice has several objectives. First, it seeks to synthesize the best and most recent research on the relevant topics: the patterns of criminal behavior and victimization, police practices, court processing and sentencing, the death penalty, and prisons and other correctional programs.

Second, it offers an interpretation of what the existing research means. Is there systematic discrimination in the criminal justice system? If so, where does it exist? How serious is it? What are the causes? Have any reforms succeeded in reducing it?

Third, *The Color of Justice* offers a multiracial and multiethnic view of crime and justice issues. The United States is a multicultural society, with many different races, ethnic groups, and cultural lifestyles. Unfortunately, most of the research has ignored the rich diversity of contemporary society. There is a great deal of research on African Americans and criminal justice but relatively little on Hispanics, Native Americans, and Asian Americans. In addition, much of the criminal justice research confuses race and ethnicity.

Finally, *The Color of Justice* does not attempt to offer a comprehensive theory of the relationship of race, ethnicity, and crime. Although Hawkins makes a persuasive case for the need for such a theory, this book has a more limited objective. It seeks to lay the groundwork for a comprehensive theory by emphasizing the general pattern in the administration of justice with respect to race and ethnicity. We feel that the available evidence permits us to draw some conclusions about that subject. The development of a comprehensive theory will have to be the subject of a future book.

GOALS OF THE CHAPTER

As an introduction to the book, Chapter 1 provides a foundation for a discussion of race, ethnicity, and crime involving several basic issues. The first is the subject of race and ethnicity itself. When we speak of race and ethnicity, what are we talking about? The second is the issue of discrimination. When we talk about disparities or discrimination in the justice system, what exactly do we mean? What is the difference between these two concepts? What difference does it make with respect to our interpretation of the criminal justice system?

The first section of this chapter describes the racial and ethnic categories used in the United States. It also discusses the quality of data on race and ethnicity reported by the different criminal justice agencies.

The second section examines the distribution of racial and ethnic groups in the United States. The uneven distribution of racial and ethnic minority groups means that race and ethnicity have a very different impact on the criminal justice systems in various parts of the country.

A third section addresses the distinction between disparity and discrimination. One of the central controversies in criminal justice is whether the overrepresentation of racial minorities in the justice system is the result of discrimination or whether it represents disparities that can be explained by other factors.

THE COLORS OF AMERICA:
RACIAL AND ETHNIC CATEGORIES

The United States is a multiracial, multiethnic society. In 1996 the population was 82.8 percent white, 12.6 percent African American, 0.8 percent Native American, and 2.9 percent Asian or Pacific Islander. Meanwhile, 10.7 percent of the population was Hispanic. These figures represent significant changes from just twenty years earlier, and demographers are predicting steady changes in the immediate future. As Figure 1.1 indicates, Hispanics are the fastest growing racial or ethnic group in the United States, increasing from 6.4 percent of the population in 1980 to an estimated 24.5 percent by the year 2050.[18]

Racial and Ethnic Categories

Race and ethnicity are extremely complex and controversial subjects. The categories we use are problematic and do not necessarily reflect the reality of American life.

Race Traditionally, race referred to the "major biological divisions of mankind," which are distinguished by color of skin, color and texture of hair, bodily proportions, and other physical features.[19] The traditional approach identifies three major racial groups: Caucasian, Negroid, and Mongoloid.

Few experts on the subject today accept the strict biological definition of race. Because of intermarriage and evolution over time, it is virtually impossible to identify exclusive racial categories. Scientists have not been able to determine meaningful differences between people who are referred to as white, black, and Asian. Yinger maintained that "we cannot accept the widespread belief that there are a few clearly distinct and nearly immutable races. Change and intermixture are continuous."[20]

Anthropologists and sociologists regard the concept of race as "primarily a social construct."[21] That is to say, groups define themselves and have labels applied to them by other groups. The politically and culturally dominant group in any society generally defines the labels that are applied to other groups. Racial designations have changed over the centuries as a result of changes in both political power and racial attitudes. Yinger argued that the critical categories for social analysis are the "socially visible 'racial' lines, based on beliefs about race and on administrative and political classifications, rather than genetic differences."[22]

A good example of the politics of racial categories is the history of the classification and labeling of African American people in the United States.

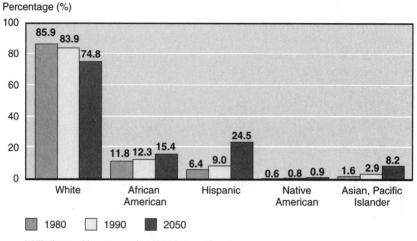

FIGURE 1.1 Changing Population of the United States, 1980, 1990, 2050 (estimated).

Bureau of the Census, *Statistical Abstract of the United States: 1993*, Tables 18, 10.

Historically, the attitudes of whites—and official policy—embodied the racist "drop of blood" theory: Anyone with the slightest African ancestry was defined as "black," even when a majority of that person's ancestors were white or Caucasian.[23] Following this approach, many data sets in the past used the categories of "white" and "nonwhite." The federal government today prohibits the use of the "nonwhite" label.[24]

The problem with traditional racial categories is obvious when we look at U.S. society. Many people have mixed ancestry. What, for example, is the "race" of a child whose father is African American and whose mother is white? Or a child whose mother is Japanese American and whose father is white? Or a child whose mother is Native American and whose father is Hispanic? Many "white" Americans have some ancestors who were African American or Native American. Few African Americans have ancestries that are purely African.

These are not abstract questions; they have very real, and often cruel, human meaning. An article in *The New Yorker* magazine highlighted the case of Susan Graham of Roswell, Georgia, who complained, "When I received my 1990 census form, I realized that there was no race category for my children." She is white and her husband African American. She called the Census Bureau and was finally told that children should take the race of their mother. No rational reason was given about why the race of her husband, the children's father, should be arbitrarily ignored. Then, when she enrolled the children in kindergarten, the school classified them as "black." Thus, she pointed out, "my child has been white on the United States census, black at school, and multiracial at home—all at the same time."[27]

Focus on an Issue
The Bell Curve Controversy: Race and IQ

A national storm of controversy erupted in the fall of 1994 over a book entitled *The Bell Curve*.[25] Authors Richard J. Herrnstein and Charles Murray argued that success in life is determined largely by IQ: The smarter people succeed, and those with lower intelligence, as measured by standard IQ tests, fail and end up at the bottom of the social scale. The authors contended that those at the low end of the IQ scale do poorly in school and are more likely to be unemployed, receive welfare, and commit crime.

The most provocative and controversial parts of their thesis are the points that intelligence is inherited and that there are significant differences in intelligence between races. The authors cited data indicating that Asian Americans consistently score higher on IQ tests than white European Americans who, in turn, score higher than African Americans. Herrnstein and Murray were very clear about the policy implications of their argument. Because intelligence is mainly inherited, social programs designed to improve the performance of poor children, such as Head Start, are doomed to failure and should be abandoned.

The Bell Curve was attacked by psychologists, anthropologists, and sociologists, among others.[26] Critics disputed the authors' assumptions that there is some entity called "intelligence" that is inherited and that IQ tests are a valid measure of intellectual capacity. They also disputed their handling of the evidence regarding intelligence tests, the impact of environmental factors as opposed to inherited factors, and the effect of programs such as Head Start. There is evidence, for example, that Head Start does improve IQ test scores, as well as children's later success in life.

This book is not the place for a full-scale critique of *The Bell Curve*, although we do reject its basic argument. One point is relevant to the discussion in this chapter, however. Herrnstein and Murray argued that there are basic, inherited differences in intelligence between races. We reject that argument on the grounds that the vast majority of anthropologists and sociologists do not accept the idea of separate races as distinct biological entities. If there are no scientifically valid racial differences, the basic argument of *The Bell Curve* falls apart.

This problem has some direct implications for criminal justice data. What if the National Crime Victimization Survey (NCVS) calls the Graham household? Is their household classified as "white" or "black"? What if one of their children were the victim of a robbery? Would the NCVS record that as a "white" or "black" victimization?

As these examples suggest, the complex multicultural reality of U.S. society means that the categories used by government agencies such as the Census Bureau are "illogical."[28]

Many people have protested the requirement of having to choose one or another racial category. The Association of Multi Ethnic Americans (AMEA) was established to fight for the right of people with mixed heritage to acknowledge their full identity. AMEA proclaimed victory in October 1997

Focus on an Issue

The Impact of a "Multicultural" Category

In preparation for the 2000 Census, the federal government debated the idea of creating a new "multicultural" category. Ultimately, the OMB rejected the idea.[30] But what if we did create such a category for the census and other official forms? What difference would it make? Would the census be more accurate? What would be the impact on American life? On criminal justice in particular?

The main argument in favor of a multicultural category is that it would more accurately reflect the reality of American life, where many people in fact have mixed racial and ethnic heritages. A multicultural category would solve the dilemma of the family in which the parents are of different races. Their children (and their children's children) would not have to choose only one part of their heritage. When the NCVS surveyed such a family, it would not have to force the household into one or the other category.

Yet, a new multicultural category would also create serious problems. Government agencies (along with innumerable private organizations) identify people by race and ethnicity for a reason. Discrimination against racial and ethnic minorities is both a historic fact and contemporary reality. Because discrimination violates the basic values of U.S. society, we have enacted laws designed to eliminate it: the 1964 Civil Rights Act, the 1965 Voting Rights Act, and others. *Brown v. Board of Education* (1954) and many other court decisions have declared racial segregation and discrimination unconstitutional.

To enforce these laws and court decisions, it becomes necessary to count people by race and ethnicity. We have to know how many white, African Ameri-

can, and Hispanic employees a company has to determine whether it is complying with or violating Title VII of the 1964 Civil Rights Act. Without data we cannot enforce the law. The OMB specifically cited this reason when it rejected the proposal for a multicultural category.[31] In a powerful argument against the multicultural category, Christine B. Hickman argued that "However imperfect the census may be, it is our main yardstick for measuring the progress we as a society have made toward ending racism. We tamper with it at our peril."[32]

By the same token, we need to know the race and ethnicity of people caught up in the criminal justice system. If we do not know the race of people sentenced to death, we cannot tell whether there is discrimination in the application of the death penalty. Similarly, we need to know the race and ethnicity of people arrested if we are to determine whether arrest discrimination exists.

The Dilemma

This leaves us with a real dilemma. The existing categories are admittedly arbitrary, yet abolishing them would have serious consequences. Classifying people by race and ethnicity, and keeping accurate records on what happens to whom, is not something done for the convenience of academic researchers. It is a practice dictated by the needs of enforcing our civil rights laws.

You Decide

What would you recommend? Should we adopt a new "multicultural" category? Should we eliminate all racial and ethnic designations? Or should we continue current practice? You decide.

when the Office of Management and Budget (OMB) adopted new federal guidelines allowing people to identify themselves in terms of more than just one race.[29]

Most of the data in this book use the racial categories established by the federal OMB in Directive 15 and required for use by all federal agencies including the Census Bureau. In October 1997, OMB issued revised guidelines, replacing the ones that had been in use since 1977. In a historic change, OMB now permits individuals to identify themselves in terms of more than one racial group. (The U.S. Census classifies people on the basis of self-identification.) In addition, OMB revised the names used for some racial groups.[33]

The new categories are: (1) American Indian or Alaska Native, (2) Asian, (3) Black or African American, (4) Hispanic or Latino, (5) Native Hawaiian or Other Pacific Islander, and (6) white. Previously, OMB used only the term *black;* the new category is *Black or African American.* Persons may also identify themselves as Haitian or Negro. Previously, only the term *Hispanic* was used. The new guidelines used *Hispanic or Latino.* The OMB considered but rejected a proposal to use *Native American* and retained the old term *American Indian.*

OMB Racial and Ethnic Group Definitions The OMB defines a black or African American person as anyone "having origins in any of the black racial groups of Africa." It defines a white person as anyone "having origins in any of the original peoples of Europe, the Middle East, or North Africa." Accordingly, a person who is from Morocco or Iran is classified as "white," and someone from Nigeria or Tanzania is classified as "black."

The category of American Indians includes Alaska Natives and "original peoples of North and South America (including Central America)." Asian includes people from the Far East, Southeast Asia, or the Indian subcontinent. Pacific Islanders are no longer in the same category with Asians and are now included with Native Hawaiians in a separate category.

The OMB concedes that the racial and ethnic categories it created "are not anthropologically or scientifically based." Instead, they represent "a social-political construct." Most important, OMB warns that the categories "should not be interpreted as being primarily biological or genetic in reference."[34]

In the 1990 Census, in fact, an estimated 43 percent of all Hispanics identified themselves as "other" race.[35] As we have already noted, there is a growing problem with people whose parents are of different races. As the Population Reference Bureau put it, "Many Americans with multicultural and multiethnic parentage do not really fit into any" of the major categories.[36]

Ethnicity Ethnicity is not the same thing as race. *Ethnicity* refers to differences between groups of people based on cultural customs, such as language, religion, foodways, family patterns, and other characteristics. Among white Americans, for example, there are distinct ethnic groups based primarily on country of origin: Irish Americans, Italian Americans, Polish Americans, and so on.[37] Yinger used a three-part definition of ethnicity: (1) The group is perceived by others to be different with respect to such factors as language, religion, race, ancestral homeland, and other cultural elements; (2) the group perceives itself to be different with respect to these factors; and (3) members of the group "participate in shared activities built around their (real or mythical) common origin and culture."[38]

The Hispanic or Latino category is extremely complex. First, Hispanic is an ethnic designation, and individuals may belong to any racial category. Thus, some Hispanics identify themselves as white, others consider themselves African American, and some identify as Native Americans. In the 1990 census, 43 percent of Hispanics categorized themselves as "other." In the past, government agencies generally classified Hispanics as white. As a result, most criminal justice data sets do not provide good longitudinal data on Hispanics.

Second, the Hispanic American population is extremely diverse with respect to place of origin, which includes Mexico, Puerto Rico, Cuba, Central America, South America, and others.[39] The traditional distinctions are not entirely logical. Mexico and Cuba are countries, whereas Central America and South America are regions consisting of several nations.

Mexican Americans are the largest single group within the Hispanic community, comprising about 60 percent of the total. Puerto Ricans are the second largest (12.2 percent), and Cubans are third (4.4 percent).[40]

Minority Groups The term *minorities* is widely used as a label for people of color. The United Nations defines minority groups as "those nondominant groups in a population which possess and wish to preserve stable ethnic, religious or linguistic traditions or characteristics markedly different from those of the rest of the population."[41] The noted sociologist Louis Wirth added the element of discrimination to this definition: Minorities "are singled out from the others in the society in which they live for differential and unequal treatment, and who therefore regard themselves as objects of collective discrimination."[42]

Use of the term *minority* is increasingly criticized. Among other things, it has a pejorative connotation, suggesting "less than." The new OMB guidelines for the Census and other federal agencies specifically "do *not* identify or designate certain population groups as 'minority groups'."[43] Many people today prefer to use the term *people of color.*

The Politics of Racial and Ethnic Labels

There has always been great controversy over what term should be used to designate different racial and ethnic groups. The term *African American,* for example, is relatively new, and became widely used only in the 1980s. It has begun to replace *black* as the preferred designation, which replaced *Negro* in the 1960s. Negro, in turn, replaced *colored* about twenty-five years earlier. The leading African American civil rights organization is the National Association for the Advancement of Colored People (NAACP), founded in 1909. Ironically, *colored* replaced *African* much earlier. In some respects, then, we have come full circle in the past 150 years. As John Hope Franklin, the distinguished African American historian and Chair of the President's Initiative on Race, pointed out in the seventh edition of his classic history of African Americans, *From Slavery to Freedom,* the subjects of his book have been referred to by "three distinct names . . . even during the lifetime of this book."[44]

Preferred labels can change quickly in a short period of time. The term African American, for example, replaced black as the preferred label among African Americans in just five years (although a majority say that it does not matter).[45]

The controversy over the proper label is political in the sense that it often involves a power struggle between different racial and ethnic groups. It is not just a matter of which label but who chooses that label. Wolf argued that "the function of racial categories within industrial capitalism is exclusionary."[46] The power to control one's own label represents an important element of police power and autonomy. Having to accept a label placed on you by another group is an indication of powerlessness.

Black emerged as the preferred term in the late 1960s as part of an assertion of pride in blackness and a quest for power by African Americans themselves. As a political statement, the African American community was saying to the majority white community, "This is how we choose to describe ourselves." To be forced to bear a label imposed by someone else is a badge of inferiority and powerlessness. In a similar fashion, the term *African American* emerged in the 1980s through a process of self-designation on the part of the African American community.

In this book, we use the term *African American.* It emerged as the preferred term by spokespersons for the African American community, and has been adopted by OMB for the 2000 Census (and can be used along with black, Negro, and Haitian). It is also consistent with terms commonly used for other groups. We routinely refer to Irish Americans, Polish Americans, and Chinese Americans, for instance, using the country of origin as the primary descriptor. It makes sense, therefore, to designate people whose continent of origin is Africa as African Americans. The term *black* refers to a color, which is an imprecise descriptor for a group of people whose members range in skin color from a very light yellow to a very dark brown.

There is a similar controversy over the proper term for Hispanic Americans. Not everyone, including some leaders of the community itself, prefers this term. Some prefer Latino, and others use Chicano. A 1994 Gallup Poll found that 62 percent of Hispanics preferred that term; only 10 percent preferred Latino, and 24 percent said that it did not matter.[47] Some white Americans incorrectly refer to Hispanics as Mexican Americans, ignoring the many people who have a different country of origin. The OMB has accepted the term Latino, and the 2000 Census uses the category of Hispanic or Latino.

In this book we use the term *Hispanic.* It is more comprehensive than other terms and includes all of the different countries of origin.

We use the term *Native Americans* to designate those people who have historically been referred to as American Indians. The term *Indians,* after all, originated through a misunderstanding, as the first European explorers of the Americas mistakenly thought they had landed in Asia.

The term *Anglo* is widely used as a term for whites, but it is not an accurate descriptor. Only a minority of white Americans traces ancestry back to the British Isles. The pejorative term *WASP* (white, Anglo-Saxon Protestant) is also inaccurate because many white Americans are Catholic, Jewish, or members of some other religious group. Therefore, in this book we use the term *white*.

Actually, however, the term white is as inaccurate as black. People who are commonly referred to as white include a wide range of skin colors, from very pale white to a dark olive or brown. The term *Caucasian* may actually be more accurate.

The Quality of Criminal
Justice Data on Race and Ethnicity

Serious analysis of the racial and ethnic dimensions of crime and justice requires good data. Unfortunately, the official data reported by criminal justice agencies are not always reliable.

The first problem is that many important subjects have not been researched at all. The majority of the published research to date involves African Americans. Although there are important gaps and much remains to be done, we do have a reasonably good sense of how African Americans fare at the hands of the police, prosecutors, judges, and correctional officials. Hispanic Americans, however, have been neglected.[48] Even less research is available on Native Americans[49] and Asian Americans. Overall, the body of literature is very small, and many important subjects have not been researched at all. Consequently, we are not able to discuss many important subjects in detail in this book (e.g., the patterns of police arrest of Hispanics compared with whites and African Americans).

A second problem involves the quality of the data. Criminal justice agencies do not always use the same racial and ethnic categories. The problem is particularly acute with respect to Hispanic Americans. Many criminal justice agencies collect data only on race and use the U.S. Census categories of white and black, including Hispanics as whites. This approach, however, masks potentially important differences between Hispanics and non-Hispanic whites. This has important implications for analyzing the nature and extent of disparities in the criminal justice system. If we assume that Hispanics are arrested at a higher rate than non-Hispanic whites (and a recent report finds that they are stopped by the police at a much higher rate than the other two groups,[50]) the available data not only eliminate Hispanics as a separate group but also raise the overall non-Hispanic arrest rate. This result would narrow the gap between whites and African Americans and understate the real extent of racial disparities in arrest.

Some data systems use the categories of white and nonwhite. This approach incorrectly treats all people of color as members of the same race. As noted earlier, OMB prohibits government agencies from using the term *nonwhite*.

The Uniform Crime Reports (UCR) data are useless with respect to many important issues related to race, ethnicity, and crime. First, the data used to create the Crime Index, "crimes known to police," do not include data on race and therefore do not tell us anything about rates of offending. Second, the data on arrests utilize the categories of white, black, American Indian or Alaska Native, and Asian or Pacific Islander. There is no separate category for Hispanics.

With respect to Native Americans, LaFree pointed out that they "fall under the jurisdiction of a complex combination of native and nonnative legal entities" that render the arrest data "problematic."[51] Snyder-Joy characterizes the Native American justice system as "a jurisdictional maze" in which jurisdiction over various criminal acts is divided among federal, state, and tribal governments.[52] It is not clear, for example, that all tribal police agencies report arrest data to the UCR system. Thus, Native American arrests are probably significantly undercounted.

Finally, the Federal Bureau of Investigation (FBI) changed the categories for Asian Americans over the years, making longitudinal analysis impossible.

The appendices in the *Sourcebook of Criminal Justice Statistics* reveal a lack of consistency in the use of the Hispanic designation among criminal justice agencies.[53] In the National Corrections Reporting Program, for example, Colorado, Illinois, Minnesota, New York, Oklahoma, and Texas record Hispanic prison inmates as "unknown" race. Ohio records Native Americans and Asian Americans as "unknown" race. California, Michigan, and Oklahoma classify only Mexican Americans as Hispanic, apparently classifying people from Puerto Rico, Cuba, and South America as non-Hispanic.

Another problem is that the criminal justice officials responsible for classifying persons may be poorly trained and may rely on their own stereotypes about race and ethnicity. The race of a person arrested is determined by the arresting officer and indicated on the original arrest report. In the Justice Department's Juvenile Court Statistics, race is "determined by the youth or by court personnel."[54] We are not entirely sure that all of these personnel designate people accurately.

In short, the official data reported by criminal justice agencies are very problematic, which creates tremendous difficulties when we try to assess the fate of different groups at the hands of the criminal justice system. The disparities that we know to exist today could be greater or smaller, depending on how people were classified. We need to be sensitive to these data problems as we discuss the various aspects of the criminal justice system in the chapters ahead.

THE GEOGRAPHY OF
RACIAL AND ETHNIC JUSTICE

Because of two factors, the "geography of justice" in the United States varies across the country. First, the primary responsibility for criminal justice lies with city, county, and state governments. The federal government plays a very small role in the total picture of criminal justice. Second, the major racial and ethnic minority groups are not evenly distributed across the country.[55] As a result, salience of race and ethnicity varies from jurisdiction to jurisdiction.

Although the United States as a whole is becoming more diverse, most of this diversity is concentrated in a few regions and metropolitan areas. One study concluded that "most communities lack true racial and ethnic diversity."[56] In 1996 only 745 of the 3,142 counties had a white population that was below the national average. Only 21 metropolitan areas qualified as true "melting pots" (with the percentage of whites below the national average, and at least two minority groups with a greater percentage than their national average).

More than half of all racial and ethnic minorities live in just five states (California, Texas, New York, Florida, and Illinois), with 20 percent in California alone. More than half (52.3 percent) of the African American population is located in the seventeen states in the Southeast. The other major concentration is in the big cities of the North and Midwest. For example, African Americans represent 76 percent of the population of Detroit, 67 percent of Atlanta, and 46 percent of Cleveland.[57]

The distribution of the Hispanic population is even more complex. More than half (52 percent) live in just two states, Texas and California. About 83 percent of these people are Mexican Americans. Puerto Rican Americans are concentrated on the East Coast, with almost 60 percent living in New York and New Jersey. About 67 percent of all Cuban Americans live in Florida.

Native Americans are also heavily concentrated. Just under half (45 percent) live in four states: Oklahoma, Arizona, New Mexico, and California.[58]

The uneven distribution of the major racial and ethnic groups is extremely important for criminal justice. Crime is primarily the responsibility of state and local governments. Thus, racial and ethnic issues are especially salient in those cities where racial minorities are heavily concentrated. For example, the context of policing is very different in Detroit, which is 76 percent African American, compared with Minneapolis, where African Americans are only 13 percent of the population. Similarly, Hispanic issues are far more significant in San Antonio, which is 55 percent Hispanic, than in many other cities where very few Hispanics live.

The concentration of racial and ethnic minority groups in certain cities and counties has important implications for political power and the control of criminal justice agencies. Mayors, for example, appoint police chiefs. In recent years, African Americans have served as mayors of most of the major cities: New York, Los Angeles, Chicago, Philadelphia, Detroit, Atlanta, Washington, D.C., and others. There have also been African American police chiefs or commissioners in each of these cities. In 1992 Chicago appointed Matthew Rodriguez superintendent of police, the first Hispanic to head one of the country's six largest police departments.

The concentration of African Americans in the Southeast has at least two important effects. On the one hand, this concentration gives this group a certain degree of political power that translates into elected African American sheriffs and mayors (who may appoint African American police chiefs). For instance, by 1990 the population of Mississippi was 35 percent African American and the state had 751 elected African American officials, more than any other state, including 8 elected sheriffs.[59]

DISPARITY VERSUS DISCRIMINATION

Perhaps the most important question with respect to race and ethnicity is whether there is discrimination in the criminal justice system. Many people argue that it is pervasive, whereas others believe that intentional discrimination does not exist. Mann presents "a minority perspective" on the administration of justice emphasizing discrimination against people of color.[60] Wilbanks, on the other hand, argues that the idea of systematic racism in the criminal justice system is a "myth."[61]

Debates over the existence of racial discrimination in the criminal justice system are often muddled and unproductive because of confusion over the meaning of discrimination. It is, therefore, important to make two important distinctions. First, there is a significant difference between disparity and discrimination. Second, discrimination can take different forms and involve different degrees of seriousness. Box 1.1 offers a schematic diagram of the various forms of discrimination, ranging from total, systematic discrimination to perfect justice.

Disparity refers to a difference, but one that does not necessarily involve discrimination. Look around your classroom. If you are in a conventional college program, almost all of the students will be relatively young (e.g., between the ages of eighteen and twenty-five). This represents a disparity in age compared with the general population. There are no children, few middle-aged people, and probably no elderly students. This is not a result of discrimination, however. These groups are not enrolled in the class mainly because the typical life course is to attend college immediately after high school. The age disparity, therefore, is the result of factors other than discrimination.

The example of education illustrates the point that a disparity is a difference that can be explained by legitimate factors. In criminal justice, the crucial distinction is between legal and extralegal factors. *Legal factors* include the seriousness of the offense or an offender's prior criminal record. These are considered legitimate bases for decisions by criminal justice officials because they relate to an individual's criminal behavior. *Extralegal factors* include race, ethnicity, gender, social class, or lifestyle. They are not legitimate bases for arrest, prosecution, or sentencing because they involve group membership and are unrelated to a person's criminal behavior. It would be illegitimate, for example, for a judge to sentence all male burglars to prison but place all female burglars on probation, despite the fact that women committed the same kind of burglary and had prior records similar to many of the men. Similarly, it would be illegitimate for a judge to sentence all unemployed persons to prison but grant probation to all employed persons.

BOX 1.1   Discrimination–Disparity Continuum

Systematic Discrimination	Institutionalized Discrimination	Contextual Discrimination	Individual Acts of Discrimination	Pure Justice

Definitions

   Systematic discrimination—Discrimination at all stages of the criminal justice system, at all times, and all places.

   Institutionalized discrimination—Racial and ethnic disparities in outcomes that are the result of the application of racially neutral factors such as prior criminal record, employment status, demeanor, etc.

   Contextual discrimination—Discrimination found in particular contexts or circumstances (e.g., certain regions, particular crimes, special victim-offender relationships).

   Individual acts of discrimination—Discrimination that results from the acts of particular individuals but is not characteristic of entire agencies or the criminal justice system as a whole.

   Pure Justice—No racial or ethnic discrimination at all.

Discrimination is a difference based on differential treatment of groups without reference to an individual's behavior or qualifications. A few examples of employment illustrate the point.

Until the 1960s most Southern police departments did not hire African American officers. The few that did, meanwhile, did not allow them to arrest whites. Many Northern police departments, meanwhile, did not assign African American officers to white neighborhoods.[62] These practices represented differential treatment based on race; in short, discrimination. Also during that time period, airlines only hired young women as flight attendants. This approach also represented a difference in treatment based on gender rather than individual qualifications. (The flight attendants were also automatically terminated if they married; because no male employees were fired for being married, this practice represented a form of sexual discrimination.)[63]

African Americans were excluded from serving on juries because they were illegally disenfranchised as voters and, therefore, were not on jury lists.[64] This practice represented racial discrimination in jury selection. But let's imagine a rural county in the northwestern United States where there are no African American residents. The absence of African Americans from juries would represent a racial disparity but not discrimination. Consider another hypothetical case. Imagine that a police department arrested only African Americans for suspected felonies and never arrested a white person. That situation would represent racial discrimination in arrest.

The questions we deal with in the real world, of course, are not quite so simple. There are, in fact, racial disparities in jury selection and arrest: African

Americans are less likely to serve on juries, and more African Americans are arrested than whites. The question is whether these differences represent a disparity or discrimination.

It is also important to remember that the word discrimination has at least two different meanings. One has a positive connotation. When we describe someone as a "discriminating gourmet" or a "discriminating music lover," we mean that he or she has good taste and chooses only the best. The person discriminates against bad food and music. The other meaning of discrimination has a negative connotation. We say that someone "discriminates against racial minorities." This statement means that the person makes invidious distinctions based on negative judgments about an entire group of people. That is, the person discriminates against all African Americans without reference to a particular person's qualities (e.g., ability, education, or experience).

The Discrimination–Disparity Continuum

To help clarify the debate over this issue, let's review Box 1.1. *Systematic discrimination* means that discrimination occurs at all stages of the criminal justice system, in all places, and at all times. That is to say, there is discrimination in arrest, prosecution, and sentencing (stages); in all parts of the country (places); and without any significant variation over time.

Institutionalized discrimination involves disparities in outcomes (e.g., more African Americans than whites are sentenced to prison) that result from established (institutionalized) policies. Such policies do not directly involve race. As Georges-Abeyie explained, "The key issue is result, not intent. Institutionalized racism is often the legacy of overt racism, of de facto practices that often get codified, and thus sanctioned by de jure mechanisms."[65]

A local criminal court, for example, has a bail policy granting pretrial release to defendants who are currently employed. This policy is based on the reasonable assumption that an employed person has a greater stake in the community and is less likely to flee than the unemployed person.[66] The policy discriminates against the unemployed, and, because racial minorities are disproportionately represented among the unemployed, they are more likely to be denied bail. Thus, the bail policy has a race effect: a racial disparity in the outcomes that is the result of a criterion unrelated to race. The racial disparity exists not because any judge holds a prejudice but because judges apply the rules consistently.

Employment discrimination law recognizes the phenomenon of institutionalized discrimination with reference to "disparate impact." A particular hiring policy may be illegal if it has a particularly heavy impact on a particular group and is not demonstrably job-related. In policing, for example, police departments formerly did not hire people who were shorter than 5'6". This standard had a disparate impact on women, Hispanics, and Asian Americans and is no longer used.

Contextual discrimination involves discrimination in certain situations or contexts. One example is the victim–offender relationship. As we will see in Chapter 8, the odds that the death penalty will be given are greatest when an

African American murders a white person, whereas there is almost no chance of a death sentence when a white person murders an African American.[67] This factor has been found in the context of other felony sentencing as well. It also appears that drug enforcement has a much heavier impact on African Americans and Hispanics than routine police work.[68]

Organizational factors represent another contextual variable. Some police departments encourage aggressive patrol activities (e.g., frequent stops and frisks). The Kerner Commission found that "aggressive preventive patrol" aggravated tensions between the police and racial minority communities.[69] Thus, departments with different patrol policies may have less conflict with minority communities. Some police departments have very bad records in terms of use of physical force, but others have taken steps to curb misconduct.

Individual discrimination involves acts of discrimination by particular justice officials: one police officer is biased in making arrests, although others in the department are not; one judge sentences minorities very harshly, although other judges in the same court do not. These are discriminatory acts, but they do not represent general patterns of how the criminal justice system operates.

Finally, at the far end of the spectrum in Box 1.1 is the condition we label pure justice. This means that there is no discrimination at any time or place in the criminal justice system.

In a controversial analysis of the administration of justice, Wilbanks argued that the idea of a racist criminal justice system is a "myth." He claimed that "there is racial prejudice and discrimination within the criminal justice system" but denied that "the system is characterized by racial prejudice and discrimination."[70] Using our discrimination–disparity continuum, Wilbanks falls somewhere in the area of contextual discrimination and individual discrimination. Mann, on the other hand, argued that there is systematic discrimination: "The law and the legal system has perpetuated and continues to maintain an ingrained system of injustice for people of color."[71]

This book takes a position on the issue of disparities versus discrimination. Rather than announce it here, however, we prefer to develop it in each chapter based on the evidence related to that particular subject. A summary of all the evidence is presented in the final chapter.

A THEORETICAL PERSPECTIVE ON RACE, ETHNICITY, AND CRIME

There are many different theories of crime and criminal justice. We believe that the available evidence on race, ethnicity, and crime is best explained by a theoretical perspective known as *conflict theory*.

The basic premise of conflict theory is that the law is used to maintain the power of the dominant group in society and to control the behavior of individuals who threaten that power.[72] A classic illustration of conflict theory involves the law of vagrancy. Vagrancy involves merely being out in public with little or no money and no clear "purpose" for being there. Vagrancy is something only engaged in by the poor. To make vagrancy a criminal act and to enforce vagrancy laws is a means by which the powerful attempt to control the poor.

Conflict theory explains racial disparities in the administration of justice as products of broader patterns of social, economic, and political inequality in U.S. society. These inequalities are the result of prejudicial attitudes on the part of the white majority and discrimination against minorities in employment, education, housing, and other aspects of society. These inequalities are explored in detail in Chapter 3. Conflict theory explains the overrepresentation of racial and ethnic minorities in arrest, prosecution, imprisonment, and capital punishment as both the product of these inequalities and an expression of prejudice against minorities.

Conflict theory has often been oversimplified by both advocates and opponents. Considerable research has found certain "anomalies" in which racial minorities are not always treated more harshly than whites. For example, there are certain situations in which African American suspects are less likely to be arrested than white suspects. Hawkins argued that these anomalies can be explained through a revised and more sophisticated conflict theory that takes into account relevant contingencies.[73]

One contingency is crime type. Hawkins claimed that African Americans might be treated more leniently for some crimes because officials believe that these crimes are "more normal or appropriate for some racial and social class groups than for others."[74] In the South during the Segregation Era, for example, African Americans often were not arrested for certain crimes, particularly crimes against other African Americans. The dominant white power structure viewed this behavior as "appropriate" for African Americans. The fact that minority offenders were being treated leniently in these situations is consistent with conflict theory because the outcomes represent a racist view of racial minorities as essentially "childlike" people who cannot control their behavior.

A second contingency identified by Hawkins involves the race of the offender relative to the race of the victim. Much research has found that the criminal justice system responds more harshly when the offender is a minority and the victim is white, particularly in rape and potential death penalty murder cases. According to conflict theory, such crimes are viewed as challenges to the pattern of racial dominance in society. The same crime is not perceived as a threat when it is intraracial (e.g., white offender and white victim, African American offender and African American victim). A relatively lenient response to crimes by minorities against minorities or crimes in which a racial or ethnic minority is the victim is explained by conflict theory in terms of a devaluing of the lives of minority victims.

There may also be important contingencies based on geographic region. It may be that crimes by racial minorities are treated more harshly when they represent a relatively large percentage of the population and therefore are perceived as a social and political threat. At the same time, some research on imprisonment has found that the disparity between white and African American incarceration rates is greatest in states with small minority populations.[75] In this context, minorities have little political power.

Alternative Theories

Conflict theory is a sociological explanation of criminal behavior and the administration of justice in that it holds that social factors explain which kinds of behavior are defined as criminal; which people commit crime; and how crimes are investigated, prosecuted, and punished. Sociological explanations of crime are alternatives to biological, psychological, and economic explanations. These other factors may contribute in some way to explaining crime but, according to the sociological perspective, they do not provide an adequate general theory of crime.[76]

Conflict theory also differs from other sociological theories of crime. Consensus theory holds that all groups in society share the same values and that criminal behavior can be explained by individual acts of deviance. Conflict theory does not see consensus in society regarding the goals or operation of the criminal justice system. Conflict theory also differs from Marxist theory, even though there are some areas of agreement.

Conflict theory and Marxist theory both emphasize differences in power between groups. Conflict theory, however, does not hold that there is a rigid class structure with a ruling class. Instead, it is consistent with a pluralistic view of society in which there are different centers of power—business and labor, farmers and consumers, government officials and the news media, religious organizations, public interest groups, and so forth—although they are not necessarily equal. The pluralistic view also allows for changes in the relative power of different groups.

SUMMARY

The question of race and ethnicity is a central issue in American criminal justice—perhaps the central issue. The starting point for this book is the overrepresentation of racial and ethnic minorities in the criminal justice system.

This chapter has attempted to set the framework for a critical analysis of this fact about contemporary American society. We have learned that the subject is extremely complex. First, the categories of race and ethnicity are extremely problematic. Much of the data we use are not as refined as we would like. Second, we have learned that there is much controversy over the issue of discrimination. An important distinction exists between disparity and discrimination. Also, there are different kinds of discrimination. Finally, we have indicated the theoretical perspective about crime and criminal justice that guides the chapters that follow.

DISCUSSION QUESTIONS

1. What is the difference between *race* and *ethnicity*? Give some examples that illustrate the differences.

2. When social scientists say that the concept of race is a "social construct," what exactly do they mean?

3. Do you think the U.S. Census should have a category of "multicultural" for race and ethnicity? Explain why or why not. Would it make a difference in the accuracy of the Census? Would it make a difference to you?

4. Explain the difference between discrimination and disparity. Give one example from some other area of life.

NOTES

1. W. E. B. DuBois, *The Souls of Black Folk* (Chicago: McClurg, 1903), p. 13.

2. Bureau of Justice Statistics, *Prisoners in 1997* (Washington, D.C.: U.S. Government Printing Office, 1998), p. 9.

3. Ibid.

4. Mark Baldassare, ed., *The Los Angeles Riots: Lessons for the Urban Future* (Boulder, CO: Westview, 1994).

5. Warren Friedman and Marsha Hott, *Young People and the Police: Respect, Fear and the Future of Community Policing in Chicago* (Chicago: Chicago Alliance for Neighborhood Safety, 1995), p. 111.

6. Bureau of Justice Statistics, *Sourcebook of Criminal Justice Statistics, 1996* (Washington, D.C.: U.S. Government Printing Office, 1997), p. 161.

7. Dennis Rosenbaum, D. A. Lewis, and J. Grant, "Neighborhood-Based Crime Prevention: Assessing the Efficacy of Community Organizing in Chicago," in *Community Crime Prevention: Does It Work?*, ed. Dennis Rosenbaum (Newbury Park, CA: Sage, 1986), pp. 109–136.

8. See, for example, Michael Tonry, *Malign Neglect* (New York: Oxford University Press, 1994); Coramae Richey Mann, *Unequal Justice* (Bloomington: Indiana University Press, 1988); Ronald Barri Flowers, *Minorities and Criminality* (Westport, CT: Greenwood, 1988); William Wilbanks, *The Myth of a Racist Criminal Justice System* (Monterey, CA: Brooks/Cole, 1987); Joan Petersilia, *Racial Disparities in the Criminal Justice System* (Santa Monica, CA: Rand, 1983); National Minority Advisory Council on Criminal Justice, *The Inequality of Justice: A Report on Crime and the Administration of Justice in the Minority Community* (Washington, D.C.: U.S. Government Printing Office, 1982); Elton Long, James Long, Wilmer Leon, and Paul B. Weston, *American Minorities: The Justice Issue* (Englewood Cliffs, NJ: Prentice-Hall, 1975).

9. Christopher Stone, "Race, Crime, and the Administration of Justice: A Summary of the Available Facts," paper presented to the Advisory Board of the President's Initiative on Race, May 19, 1998.

10. Samuel Walker and Molly Brown, "A Pale Reflection of Reality: The Neglect of Racial and Ethnic Minorities in Introductory Criminal Justice Textbooks," *Journal of Criminal Justice Education* 6 (Spring 1995): 61–83.

11. Mann, *Unequal Justice*, p. viii.

12. National Minority Advisory Council on Criminal Justice, *The Inequality of Justice*, Chap. 2, "Impact of Criminal Justice on Hispanic-Americans"; Chap. 3, "Impact of Crime and Criminal Justice on American Indians"; Chap. 4, "Impact of Crime and Criminal Justice on Asian-Americans."

13. Alfredo Mirandé, *Gringo Justice* (Notre Dame, IN: Notre Dame, 1987), p. ix.

14. Marianne O. Nielsen, "Contextualization for Native American Crime and Criminal Justice Involvement," in *Native Americans, Crime, and Justice*, ed. Marianne O. Nielsen and Robert A. Silverman (Boulder, CO: Westview, 1996), p. 10.

15. Wilbanks, *The Myth of a Racist Criminal Justice System*.

16. Stone, "Race, Crime, and the Administration of Justice."

17. Darnell F. Hawkins, "Ethnicity, Race, and Crime: A Review of Selected Studies," in *Ethnicity, Race, and Crime,* ed. D. F. Hawkins (Albany: State University of New York Press, 1995), p. 40.

18. Bureau of the Census, *Statistical Abstract of the United States, 1997* (Washington, D.C.: U.S. Government Printing Office, 1997), p. 14.

19. The concept of race is both problematic and controversial. For a starting point, see Ashley Montagu, *Statement on Race,* 3d ed. (New York: Oxford University Press, 1972), which includes the text of and commentary on four United Nations statements on race.

20. J. Milton Yinger, *Ethnicity: Source of Strength? Source of Conflict?* (Albany: State University of New York Press, 1994), p. 19.

21. Paul R. Spickard, "The Illogic of American Racial Categories," in *Racially Mixed People in America,* ed. Marla P. Root (Newbury Park, CA: Sage, 1992), p. 18.

22. Yinger, *Ethnicity,* p. 20.

23. Christine B. Hickman, "The Devil and the One Drop Rule: Racial Categories, African Americans, and the U.S. Census," *Michigan Law Review* 95 (March 1997): 1161–1265.

24. U.S. Office of Management and Budget, Directive 15, *Race and Ethnic Standards for Federal Statistics and Administrative Reporting,* OMB Circular No. A-46 (1974), rev. 1977 (Washington, D.C.: U.S. Government Printing Office, 1977).

25. Richard J. Herrnstein and Charles Murray, *The Bell Curve: Intelligence and Class Structure in American Life* (New York: Free Press, 1994).

26. Steven Fraser, *The Bell Curve Wars* (New York: Free Press, 1995).

27. Lawrence Wright, "One Drop of Blood," *The New Yorker* (July 25, 1994), p. 47.

28. Ibid.

29. Source: AMEA Website: www.ameasite.org

30. U.S. Office of Management and Budget, "Revisions to the Standards for the Classification of Federal Data on Race and Ethnicity," *Federal Register* 62 (October 30, 1997): 368–374.

31. Ibid.

32. Hickman, "The Devil and the One Drop Rule," p. 1264.

33. U.S. Office of Management and Budget, "Revisions to the Standards for the Classification of Federal Data on Race and Ethnicity," p. 368–374.

34. Ibid.

35. William P. O'Hare, "America's Minorities—The Demographics of Diversity," *Population Bulletin,* Vol. 47, No. 4 (Washington, D.C.: Population Reference Bureau, 1992).

36. Ibid.

37. James Paul Allen and Eugene James Turner, *We the People: An Atlas of America's Ethnic Diversity* (New York: Macmillan, 1988).

38. Yinger, *Ethnicity,* pp. 3–4.

39. Allen and Turner, *We the People,* pp. 153–176.

40. Bureau of the Census, *Statistical Abstract of the United States, 1997,* p. 21, Table 30.

41. Quoted in Yinger, *Ethnicity,* p. 21.

42. Louis Wirth, "The Problem of Minority Groups," in *The Science of Man in the World Crisis,* ed. Ralph Linton (New York: Columbia University Press, 1945).

43. U.S. Office of Management and Budget, Directive 15.

44. John Hope Franklin and Alfred A. Moss, Jr., *From Slavery to Freedom: A History of African Americans,* 7th ed. (New York: Knopf, 1994), p. xix.

45. George Gallup, Jr., *The Gallup Poll Monthly* (August 1994), p. 30.

46. Eric R. Wolf, *Europe and the People Without History* (Berkeley: University of California Press, 1982), pp. 380–381.

47. Gallup, *The Gallup Poll Monthly,* p. 34.

48. Mirandé, *Gringo Justice.*

49. Nielsen and Silverman, eds., *Native Americans, Crime, and Justice.*

50. Bureau of Justice Statistics, *Police Use of Force* (Washington, D.C.: U.S. Government Printing Office, 1997).

51. Gary LaFree, "Race and Crime Trends in the United States, 1946–1990," in *Ethnicity, Race, and Crime,* pp. 173–174.

52. Zoann K. Snyder-Joy, "Self-Determination and American Indian Justice: Tribal Versus Federal Jurisdiction on Indian Lands," in *Ethnicity, Race, and Crime,* p. 310.

53. Bureau of Justice Statistics, *Sourcebook of Criminal Justice Statistics, 1997* (Washington, D.C.: U.S. Government Printing Office, 1998).

54. Ibid., p. 746.

55. Allen and Turner, *We the People.*

56. William H. Frey, "The Diversity Myth," *American Demographics* 20 (June 1998): 41.

57. O'Hare, "America's Minorities," p. 21; Bureau of the Census, *Statistical Abstract of the United States 1997,* p. 286, Tables 458, 459.

58. Allen and Turner, *We the People.*

59. Bureau of the Census, *Statistical Abstract of the United States 1997,* p. 286, Tables 458, 459.

60. Mann, *Unequal Justice,* pp. vii–xiv.

61. Wilbanks, *The Myth of a Racist Criminal Justice System.*

62. W. Marvin Dulaney, *Black Police in America* (Bloomington: Indiana University Press, 1996).

63. Peter B. Bloch and Deborah Anderson, *Policewomen on Patrol: Final Report* (Washington, D.C.: Police Foundation, 1974); *United Airlines v. Evans,* 433 U.S. 553 (1977).

64. Gunnar Myrdal, *An American Dilemma* (New York: Harper & Brothers, 1944), pp. 499, 524, 549.

65. D. E. Georges-Abeyie, "Criminal Justice Processing of Non-White Minorities," in *Racism, Empiricism, and Criminal Justice,*

ed. B. D. MacLean and D. Milovanovic (Vancouver: Collective, 1990), p. 28.

66. Wayne H. Thomas, Jr., *Bail Reform in America* (Berkeley: University of California Press, 1976), pp. 20–22.

67. David C. Baldus, George G. Woodworth, and Charles A. Pulaski, *Equal Justice and the Death Penalty: A Legal and Empirical Analysis* (Boston: Northeastern University Press, 1990).

68. Jerome G. Miller, *Search and Destroy: African-American Males in the Criminal Justice System* (New York: Cambridge University Press, 1996).

69. Kerner Commission, *Report of the National Advisory Commission on Civil Disorders* (New York: Bantam Books, 1968), p. 304.

70. Wilbanks, *The Myth of a Racist Criminal Justice System.*

71. Mann, *Unequal Justice,* p. 160.

72. Richard Quinney, *The Social Reality of Crime* (Boston: Little, Brown, 1970).

73. Darnell F. Hawkins, "Beyond Anomalies: Rethinking the Conflict Perspective on Race and Criminal Punishment," *Social Forces* 65 (March 1987): 719–745.

74. Ibid.

75. Alfred Blumstein, "Prison Populations: A System Out of Control?" in *Crime and Justice: A Review of Research,* ed. Michael Tonry and Norval Morris, Vol. 10 (Chicago: University of Chicago Press, 1988), p. 253.

76. Freda Adler, Gerhard O. W. Mueller, and William S. Laufer, *Criminology,* 2d ed. (New York: McGraw-Hill, 1995).

2

🛠

Victims and Offenders

Myths and Realities
About Crime

On Wednesday, April 19, 1989, at 10:05 P.M., "a 28-year old investment banker, jogging through Central Park, was attacked by a group of teenagers. They kicked and beat her, smashed in her head with a pipe and raped her."[1] The offenders were later identified as minority youth in East Harlem. The New York Times reported that "the attack sparked angry cries for vengeance and increased police patrol, partly, some have argued, because those charged in the attack were minority group teenagers and the victim was an affluent white woman."[2]

Does this incident reflect a "typical" criminal event? Many people believe that it does: a white victim falling prey to the violence of minority gang activity. However, the evidence suggests that it is not a typical criminal event. First, more than 80 percent of crimes reported to the police are property crimes.[3] Second, a disproportionate number of crime victims are minorities. Third, interracial (between-race) crimes are the exception, not the rule. Finally, not all group activity is gang activity, not all gang actions are criminal, and not all gang members are racial or ethnic minorities.

An article in the New York Times several weeks after the well-publicized event described here helps put this victimization in perspective. A total of twenty-nine rapes were reported in the city that week (April 16–22, 1989), with seventeen African American female victims, seven Hispanics, three whites, and two Asians.[4] Thus, the typical rape victim was in fact a minority female. Although the twenty-nine reports from the New York City Police Department did not indicate the race of the offender, other sources, including the national victimization data discussed later in this chapter, demonstrate that rape is predominantly an intraracial (within-race) crime.[5]

GOALS OF THE CHAPTER

In this chapter we describe the context of crime in the United States. We use several different sources of data to paint a picture of the typical crime victim and the typical offender. We compare victimization rates for racial minorities and whites, focusing on both household victimization and personal victimization. We also compare offending rates for racial minorities and whites, focusing on crime by both adults and juveniles. We then present statistics to document the fact that crime is an intraracial, rather than an interracial, event, but we also spend time discussing a specific occurrence of interracial crime, hate crime. We end the chapter with a discussion of ethnic youth gangs and their role in crime in the United States.

PICTURE OF THE TYPICAL VICTIM

Our perceptions of crime are shaped to a large extent by the highly publicized crimes featured on the nightly news and sensationalized in newspapers. We read about young African American or Hispanic males who sexually assault, rob, and murder whites, and we assume that these crimes are typical. We assume that the typical crime is a violent crime, that the typical victim is white, and that the typical offender is African American or Hispanic. As Silberman observed, this topic is difficult to address:

> In the end, there is no escaping the question of race and crime. To say this is to risk, almost guarantee, giving offense; it is impossible to talk honestly about the role of race in American life without offending and angering both whites and blacks—and Hispanic browns and Native American reds as well. The truth is terrible, on all sides; and we are all too accustomed to the soothing euphemisms and inflammatory rhetoric with which the subject is cloaked.[6]

In short, compelling evidence suggests that the arguably prominent picture of crime, criminal, and victim just described is at best incomplete and at worst inaccurate, particularly as it concerns race and ethnicity of crime victims. Recent victimization data, in fact, reveal that racial minorities are more likely than whites in most circumstances to be victimized by crime.

In the sections that follow, we use victimization data to paint a picture of the typical crime victim. We begin by discussing the National Crime Victimization Survey, the source of most data on criminal victimization in the United States. We then compare the household victimization rates of African Americans and whites, as well as Hispanics and non-Hispanics. Personal victimization rates (property and violent offense) are then compared for African Americans and whites. We conclude with a discussion of homicide victimization rates.

The National Crime Victimization Survey

The most systematic source of victimization information is the National Crime Victimization Survey (NCVS).[7] The survey, which began in 1973, is conducted by the Bureau of Census for the Bureau of Justice Statistics (BJS).[8] Survey data are used to produce annual estimates of the number and rate of personal and household victimizations for the nation as a whole and for various subgroups of the population.

The Census operates with a sampling frame of 43,000 households (totaling approximately 80,000 respondents in 1997) at a six-month interval to ask whether household members have been the victims of selected major crimes during the preceding six months. Information is collected from persons age twelve and older who are members of the household selected. The sample is chosen on the basis of the most recent census data to be representative of the nation as a whole.

Members of selected households are contacted either in person or by phone every six months for three years. Household questionnaires are completed to describe the demographic characteristics of the household (income, number of members, etc.). The race and ethnicity of the adult completing the household questionnaire is recorded from self-report information as the race and ethnicity of the household. Incident questionnaires are completed for both household offenses and personal victimizations. The designated head of the household is questioned about the incidence of household burglary, household larceny, and motor vehicle theft. Personal victimization incident questionnaires are administered to household members age twelve and older, probing them to relay any victimizations of rape, robbery, assault, and personal larceny. Those who report victimizations to interviewers are asked a series of follow-up questions about the nature of the crime and the response to the crime. Those who report personal victimizations are also asked to describe the offender and their relationship (if any) with the offender. Some sample personal victimization questions are as follows:

> During the last six months . . .
>
> Did anyone beat you up, attack you or hit you with something such as a rock or a bottle?
>
> Did anyone take something directly from you by using force, such as by a stickup, mugging or threat?
>
> Was anything stolen from you while you were away from home, for instance at work, in a theater or restaurant, or while traveling?

In many ways, the NCVS produces a more complete picture of crime and the characteristics of those who are victimized by crime than official police records. For one thing, respondents are asked about victimizations not reported to the police. In addition, the survey includes questions designed to elicit detailed information concerning the victim, the characteristics of the offender(s), and the context of the victimization. This information is used to calculate age-, sex-, and race-specific estimates of victimization. In addition, estimates of interracial and intraracial crime can be calculated.

The NCVS also has several limitations. For example, it does not cover commercial crime, kidnapping, or homicide; the estimates produced are for the nation as a whole, central city compared to suburban areas, but not for states or local jurisdictions; homeless people are not interviewed; and responses are susceptible to memory loss and interviewer bias. In addition, the information on race is limited to white, African American, and other, whereas ethnicity is limited to Hispanic and non-Hispanic, with the latter being available for selected issues only. It is important to remember that Hispanics may be of any race (see Chapter 1). NCVS designations are determined by Census categories, so the Hispanic category includes all individuals of Spanish origin (Mexican American, Chicano, Mexican, Puerto Rican, Cuban, Central or South American) regardless of racial identity.

Household Victimization

As noted, the NCVS questions the designated head of household about crimes against the household—burglary, household larceny, and motor vehicle theft. It is clear that household victimization rates vary by race and ethnicity, indicating African American households are more vulnerable than white households, and Hispanic households are more vulnerable than non-Hispanic ones.[9]

In 1997, households headed by African Americans had a higher victimization rate than white households (see Figure 2.1) for all designated household offenses (292.0 per 1,000 households compared to 242.3 per 1,000 households). This general pattern also characterized each of the three household crimes. That is, the rate for African American households exceeded the rate for white households for burglary (62.5 compared to 42.3)and household larceny (205.3 compared to 188.1). The greatest disparity was present in motor vehicle theft rates, with African American households victimized at a rate more than twice that of white households (24.1 compared to 11.9).

The BJS also estimates that victimization rates for Hispanic households are markedly higher than the victimization rates for non-Hispanic households.[10] Figure 2.2 shows higher rates for Hispanics for all household crimes combined (329.4 per 1,000 households compared to 240.8 per 1,000 households). Burglary and household larceny rates indicate that Hispanic-headed households have higher victimization rates than non-Hispanic ones (60.9 compared to 43.2; 289.9 compared to 185.2), with motor vehicle theft reflecting the greatest disparity, with rates twice as high for Hispanic households (29.5 compared to 12.5).

The Effect of Urbanization The racial differences in household victimization rates discussed thus far are differences for the United States as a whole.

Rate per 1,000 households

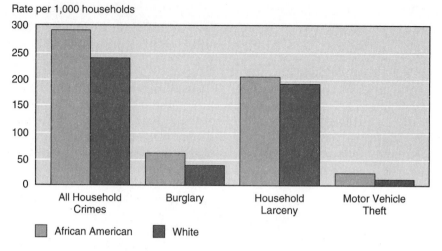

FIGURE 2.1 Victimization Rates, by Head of Household, 1997

Bureau of Justice Statistics, *Criminal Victimization in the United States, 1997* (Washington, D.C.: U.S. Government Printing Office, 1999).

Rate per 1,000 households

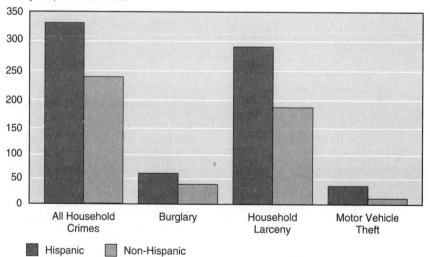

FIGURE 2.2 Victimization Rates, by Ethnicity of Head of Household, 1994

Bureau of Justice Statistics, *Criminal Victimization in the United States, 1994* (Washington, D.C.: U.S. Government Printing Office, 1996).

These patterns vary, however, depending on the degree of urbanization.[11] Household victimization rates are higher for all groups in the central city sections of a metropolis, with the overall victimization rates remaining higher for African American households than for white households.

The emerging familiar pattern of African American households having higher victimization rates than white households does reverse under some circumstances.[12] Specifically, suburban area data reflect higher victimization rates for white households for both burglary and household larceny. Rural area victimization rates are more similar for white and African American households, with African Americans having substantially higher rates only for motor vehicle theft.

Personal Victimization

In addition to questioning the head of the household about crimes against the household, the NCVS interviewers ask all household members over the age of twelve whether they themselves have been the victim of an act of rape (worded as sexual assault), robbery, assault, or theft within the past six months. This information is then used to estimate victimization rates for the nation as a whole and for the various subgroups in the population.

Consistent with the pattern of racial disparity in household victimizations, these estimates reveal that African Americans are more likely than either whites or members of "other" racial groups to be the victims of personal crimes. As shown in Table 2.1, the overall victimization rate (which combines crimes of violence and personal theft) for African Americans is 52.3 per 1,000 persons in the population over age twelve, 39.7 for whites, and 29.3 for other races.

The racial differences are much larger for crimes of violence than for crimes of theft. In particular, African Americans are nearly twice as likely as whites to be the victims of robbery aggravated assaults and clearly more likely to be the victims of aggravated assault than whites or other races. On the other hand, the victimization rates are more similar for simple assaults and crimes of theft. Little can be said about differences in reported rape victimizations.

Table 2.1 also displays personal victimization rates by ethnicity. Overall, Hispanics have slightly higher victimization rates than non-Hispanics (48.5 per 1,000 persons compared to 39.9). While Hispanics are almost twice as likely to be the victim of robbery than non-Hispanics, aggravated and simple assault rates are similar between the groups.

The Effects of Gender and Location The data presented in Table 2.2 factor gender and location into the race-specific personal victimization rates discussed earlier and offers an even more complex picture of criminal victimization. Note that victimization rates are highest for all groups in the urban areas. We present all personal victimization rates, all crimes of violence, robbery, and aggravated assault. We leave out personal theft rates and simple assaults given that these offenses reveal little variation across groups.

As noted earlier, African American males have the highest personal crime victimization rate, but this general pattern does vary under certain circum-

Table 2.1 Personal Victimization Rates[a] by Type of Crime and by Race and Ethnicity of Victims, 1997

	RACE			ETHNICITY	
	White	African American	Other	Hispanic	Non-Hispanic
Crimes of violence	38.3	49.0	28.0	43.1	38.3
Rape	1.4	1.6	1.1	1.5	1.4
Robbery	3.8	7.4	5.0	7.3	3.9
Assault	33.1	39.9	21.9	34.3	33.0
Aggravated	8.2	12.2	6.1	10.4	8.3
Simple	24.9	27.4	15.8	24.0	24.7
Crimes of theft	1.4	3.3	1.3	2.4	1.5
Total	39.7	52.3	29.3	48.5	39.9

[a]Victimization rates per 1,000 persons age twelve and older.

SOURCE: Bureau of Justice Statistics, U.S. Department of Justice, *Criminal Victimization in the United States, 1997* (Washington, D.C.: U.S. Government Printing Office).

Table 2.2 Personal Victimization Rates[a] by Race and Gender of Victims, Location, and Type of Crime

	All Personal Crimes	Crimes of Violence	Robbery	Aggravated Assault
All areas				
African American female	60.1	56.2	10.3	13.3
African American male	71.7	68.5	18.5	20.6
White female	43.1	40.7	3.2	17.4
White male	60.4	58.6	6.5	14.6
Urban				
African American female	70.6	64.6	12.3	14.1
African American male	94.2	89.9	25.0	26.7
White female	53.7	49.0	5.1	9.4
White male	77.7	74.8	12.6	18.4
Suburban				
African American female	60.4	58.0	11.3	14.7
African American male	53.3	51.0	16.1	13.1
White female	43.3	40.9	3.2	7.0
White male	61.0	58.9	5.4	14.7
Rural				
African American female	28.1	28.1	2.8	8.1
African American male	40.0	38.2	4.8	15.6
White female	33.5	33.0	1.5	6.2
White male	45.0	44.5	3.3	11.1

[a]Victimization rates per 1,000 persons age twelve and older.

SOURCE: Bureau of Justice Statistics, *Criminal Victimization in the United States, 1994* (Washington D.C.: Department of Justice).

BOX 2.1   American Indians and Violent Crimes

Information on the victimization rates of American Indians is difficult to compile. This group represents approximately 1 percent of the population. Given that incidence of victimization in the general population is a rare event, documenting a rare event in a small population is challenging. The BJS has combined a number of data sources and pooled a number of years to reveal a picture of American Indian (nonfatal) violent victimization at twice the rate of the general population, exceeding the victimization rates of African Americans in for both categories of assault.[13]

In contrast to the general intra-racial victimization patterns of white and African American crime, American Indians report that seven of ten violent offenses are of someone they perceive to be of a different race.[14]

stances. Although robbery rates stay highest for African American males regardless of urbanization, white male victimization rates are close to or even exceed that of African American males in other victimization categories in suburban and rural areas.

African American female personal victimization rates are consistently higher than white female rates in urban and suburban areas, but not rural areas. However, the personal violence victimization rate for rural white females seems to be fueled by simple assaults (not shown), as robbery rates and aggravated assault rates remain higher for African American females. Although victimization rates are often expected to be lower for females, in many cases, African American female personal victimization rates are closer to the rates of African American males than white females. That is, African American female victimization rates often match or exceed the rates recorded for white males. This situation is more likely in robbery offenses and less likely in rural areas.

Trends in Household and Personal Victimization

A review of NCVS data from 1973 to 1997 indicates that most of the general patterns of victimization noted here have not changed over time. The household victimization data for these years illustrate that property crime rates for rates for African American households consistently exceed the rates for white households. Similarly, rates of robbery and aggravated assault for African Americans are repeatedly higher, as simple assault rates remain similar. Although personal theft rates are characterized by a convergence of rates for these two groups over time, African American rates remain somewhat higher.

Lifetime Likelihood of Victimization

Although annual victimization rates are important indicators of the likelihood of victimization, they "do not convey the full impact of crime as it affects people."[15] To gauge the impact of crime, we must consider not just the odds of

Table 2.3 Lifetime Likelihood of Victimization[a]

	African Americans	Whites
Violent Crimes	87%	82%
Robbery	51	27
Assault	73	74
Rape (females only)	11	8
Personal Theft	99	99

[a]Percentage of persons who will experience one or more victimizations starting at twelve years of age.

SOURCE: Bureau of Justice Statistics, U.S. Department of Justice, *Lifetime Likelihood of Victimization* (Washington, D.C.: U.S. Government Printing Office, 1987).

being victimized within the next few weeks or months, but the possibility of being robbed, raped, assaulted, or burglarized at some time in our lives. Even though the odds of being victimized during any twelve-month period are low, the odds of ever being victimized may be high. Although only 16 out of 10,000 women are rape victims annually, for example, the lifetime likelihood of being raped is much greater: Nearly one out of every twelve females (and one out of every nine black females) will be the victim of a rape at some time during her life.[16]

The BJS used annual victimization rates for 1975 through 1984 to calculate lifetime victimization rates. These rates, presented in Table 2.3, indicate that about five out of six people will be victims of a violent crime at least once during their lives and that nearly everyone will be the victim of a personal theft at least once. There is no difference in the African American and white rates for personal theft, and only a slight difference in the rates for violent crimes.

For the individual crimes of violence, the lifetime likelihood of being assaulted is nearly identical for African Americans and whites: About three of every four persons, regardless of race, will be assaulted at some time during their lives. There are, on the other hand, large racial differences for robbery, with African Americans almost twice as likely as whites to be robbed. The lifetime likelihood of rape is also somewhat higher for African American females than for white females. Thus, for the two most serious (nonmurder) violent crimes, the likelihood of victimization is much higher for African Americans than for whites.

Homicide Victimization Rates

The largest and most striking racial differences in victimization are for the crime of homicide. In fact, all of the data on homicide point to the same conclusion: African Americans, and particularly African American males, face a much greater risk of death by homicide than do whites.

Although the NCVS does not produce estimates of homicide victimization rates, there are a number of other sources of data. A partial picture is available from the Supplemental Homicide Reports submitted by law enforcement agencies to the FBI as part of the Uniform Crime Reports (UCR)

Program. This information is collected when available for single-victim/ single-offender homicides. These data reveal that a disproportionate number of homicide victims are African American. In 1997, African Americans constituted only 12 percent of the population, but nearly 50 percent of all homicide victims.[17]

The race and sex differences in the likelihood of death by homicide are revealed more clearly by comparing the rates of death by homicide (per 100,000 population) for various subgroups of the population.[18] These data reveal that homicide is a more significant risk factor for African Americans than for whites. Although homicide rates have decreased among all groups since the early 1990s, the homicide rate in 1997 for African Americans (26.6 per 100,000 specified population) remained seven times the rate for whites (3.9 per 100,000). Even more striking, the rate for African American males was nearly eight times the rate for white males and was twenty-four times the rate for white females. The rate for African American females exceeded the rate for white females, appearing closer to that of white males.

We noted earlier that young African American ales are particularly likely to be victims of robbery and assault. The same is true of homicide. In fact, in 1997 the homicide rate for African American males between eighteen and twenty-four years old was an astounding 143.4 per 100,000 young black males in the population. In other words, young African American males made up only 1 percent of the population, but represented 18 percent of the victims of homicide. In contrast, the rate for young white males in this age group was 15.1 per 100,000. That is, 8 percent of the U.S. population made up approximately 10 percent of the victims of homicide. Among young males the homicide rate for African Americans was nearly ten times the rate for whites.

Summary: A Picture of the Typical Crime Victim

The victimization data presented in the preceding sections reveal that African Americans and Hispanics are more likely than whites and non-Hispanics to be victims of household and personal crimes. These racial and ethnic differences are particularly striking for violent crimes, especially robbery. African Americans—especially young African American males—also face a much greater risk of death by homicide than whites. It thus seems fair to conclude that in the United States, the typical crime victim is a racial minority.

PICTURE OF THE TYPICAL OFFENDER

For many people the term crime evokes an image of a young African American males who is armed with a handgun and commits a robbery, rape, or murder. In the minds of many Americans, crime is synonymous with black crime.

It is easy to see why the average American believes that the typical offender is African American. The crimes that receive the most attention—from the media, from politicians, and from criminal justice policymakers—are "street crimes" such as murder, robbery, and rape. These are precisely the crimes for

---

BOX 2.2   Victimization of Young African American Males[19]

Although African Americans generally have higher rates of personal victimization than whites, young African American males are particularly at risk. In 1992, the violent victimization rate for African American males age sixteen to nineteen was double the rate for white males and three times the rate for white females. The majority of these incidents involved serious violent crimes—rapes, robberies, and aggravated assaults. One out of every fourteen African American young males age twelve to fifteen was the victim of a violent crime in 1992; for those age sixteen to nineteen the rate was one out of six; for those age twenty to twenty-four the rate was one out of eight. Young African American males also were more likely to be victims of crimes involving weapons, particularly handguns. From 1987 to 1992 the average annual rate of handgun victimization was 39.7 (per 1,000 population) for African Americans in the sixteen-to-nineteen age group, 29.4 for those in the twenty-to-twenty-four age group. The comparable rates for white males were 9.5 (sixteen to nineteen) and 9.2 (twenty to twenty-four).

---

which African Americans are arrested at a disproportionately high rate. In 1997, for example, 56 percent of those arrested for murder, 55 percent of those arrested for robbery, and 40 percent of those arrested for rape were African American.

Arrest rates for serious violent crimes, of course, do not tell the whole story. Although violent crimes may be the crimes we fear most, they are not the crimes that occur most frequently. Moreover, arrest rates do not necessarily present an accurate picture of offending. Many crimes are not reported to the police and many of those reported do not result in an arrest.

In this section we use a number of criminal justice data sources to paint a picture of the typical criminal offender. We summarize the offender data presented in official police records, victimization reports, and self-report surveys. Because each of these data sources varies both in terms of the offender information captured and the "point of contact" with the offender, the picture of the typical offender that each produces also differs somewhat. We note these discrepancies and summarize the results of research designed to reconcile them.

Official Arrest Statistics

Annual data on arrests are produced by the UCR system, which has been administered by the FBI since 1930. Today, the program compiles reports from more than 16,000 law enforcement agencies across the country representing 95 percent of the total U.S. population. The annual report, Crime in the United States, offers detailed information from local, state, and federal law enforcement agencies on crime counts and rates, as well as arrest information.

Focus on an Issue

The Creation of Victims and Offenders of Color

Silberman made the following observation on the common misconceptions of race and crime:[20]

> For most of their history in this country . . . blacks were victims, not initiators, of violence. In the Old South, violence against blacks was omnipresent—sanctioned both by customs and by law. Whites were free to use any methods, up to and including murder, to control "their Negros." . . . There was little blacks could do to protect themselves. To strike back at whites, or merely to display anger or insufficient deference, was not just to risk one's own neck, but to place the whole community in danger. It was equally dangerous, or at best pointless, to appeal to the law.

Indeed, the purpose of the Fourteenth Amendment to the U.S. Constitution following the Civil War was to create a situation of full citizenship for former slaves. One of the implications of this newfound status of citizenship was that African Americans were formally conferred the status of victim and offender in the eyes of the law. Prior to this time, actions of assault, rape, and theft against slaves and by slaves were handled informally, or even as civil matters. Even African American offenders were not necessarily viewed as subject to formal criminal trial and adjudication, especially if the "victims" were also slaves.

One frequently retold example of a slave's lack of status as a citizen is the case of Margaret Garner. This female slave escaped with her children to Ohio from a Kentucky plantation in 1855. Once discovered by her master, who was given the right of retrieval under federal law, she responded to the threat of capture by taking the life of one of her children and attempting to do so to her other children. Outrage at her actions led to the rather unprecedented call for the intervention of the formal justice of the U.S. judicial system. The legal issue of citizenship complicated this situation. In short, the slave could not be tried for murder, as she was not a citizen and the victim of the murder was not a citizen, either. The issues were merely of a civil nature. Although most would agree the child was a victim, she was not so in the eyes of the law. Garner could only be tried in a civil forum for her destructive actions to the master's property. This case became the foundation for the story *Beloved* first in a novel by Toni Morrison and later in a movie of the same title.[21]

Problems With UCR Data The information on offenders gleaned from the UCR is incomplete and potentially misleading due to the fact that it includes only offenders whose crimes result in arrest. The UCR data exclude offenders whose crimes are not reported to the police, as well as offenders whose crimes do not lead to arrest. A second limitation is that the UCR reports include arrest statistics for four racial groups (white, African American, Native American, and Asian), but do not present any information by ethnicity (Hispanic versus non-Hispanic).

Focus on an Issue

A Proposal to Eliminate Race from UCR Reports

In October 1993, a group of mayors, led by Minneapolis Mayor Donald Fraser, sent a letter to the U.S. Attorney General's office asking that the design of the UCR be changed to eliminate race from the reporting of arrest data. The mayors were concerned about the misuse of racial data from crime statistics. They charged that the current reporting policies "perpetuate racism in American society" and contribute to the general perception "that there is a causal relationship between race and criminality." Critics of the proposal argued that race data are essential to battling street crime, because they reveal who the perpetrators are.

Although the federal policy of reporting race in arrest statistics has not changed, Fraser was instrumental in pushing a similar request through the Minnesota Bureau of Investigation. The final result in Minnesota was the following disclaimer in state crime publications: "Racial and ethnic data must be treated with caution . . . [E]xisting research on crime has generally shown that racial or ethnic identity is not predictive of criminal behavior within data which has been controlled for social and economic factors." This statement warns that descriptive data are not sufficient for causal analysis and should not be used as the sole indication of the role of race and criminality for the formation of public policy.

Using inductive reasoning, the overrepresentation of minority race groups in arrest data can be suggestive of at least two causal inferences: Certain racial groups are characterized by differential offending rates, and arrest data are reflective of differential arrest patterns targeted at minorities. What steps must a researcher take to move beyond descriptions of racial disparity in arrest data to an exploration of causal explanations for racial patterns evident in arrest data?

A substantial proportion of crimes is not reported to the police. In fact, the NCVS reveals that fewer than half of all victimizations are reported to the police.[22] Factors that influence the decision to report a crime include the seriousness of the crime and the relationship between the victim and the offender. Violent crimes are more likely than property crimes to be reported, as are crimes committed by friends or relatives rather than strangers.[23]

Victimization surveys reveal that victims often fail to report crimes to the police because of a belief that nothing could be done, the event was not important enough, the police would not want to be bothered, or it was a private matter.[24] Failure to report also might be based on the victim's fear of self-incrimination or embarrassment due to criminal justice proceedings that result in publicity or cross-examination.[25]

The NCVS indicates that the likelihood of reporting a crime to the police also varies by race. African Americans are slightly more likely than whites to report crimes of theft and violence to the police, and Hispanics are substantially less likely to report victimizations to the police than non-Hispanics.[26] Hindelang found that victims of rape and robbery were more likely to report the victimization to the police if there was an African American offender.[27]

Even if the victim does decide to report the crime to the police there is no guarantee that the report will result in an arrest. The police may decide that the report is unfounded; in this case, an official report is not filed and the incident is not counted as an offense known to the police. Furthermore, even if the police do file an official report, they may be unwilling or unable to make an arrest. In 1997 fewer than 25 percent of all index crimes were cleared by the police; the clearance rate for serious crimes ranged from 15 percent for burglary to 65 percent for murder.[28]

Police officer and offender interactions also may influence the inclination to make an arrest and cultural traditions may influence police–citizen interactions. For instance, Asian communities often handle delinquent acts informally, whereas other communities would report them to the police.[29] Hispanic cultural traditions may increase the likelihood of arrest if the Hispanic tradition of showing respect for an officer by avoiding direct eye contact is interpreted as insincerity.[30] African Americans who appear hostile or aggressive also may face a greater likelihood of arrest.[31]

The fact that many reported crimes do not lead to an arrest, coupled with the fact that police decision making is highly discretionary, suggests that we should exercise caution in drawing conclusions about the characteristics of those who commit crime based on the characteristics of those who are arrested. To the extent that police decision making reflects stereotypes about crime or racially prejudiced attitudes, the picture of the typical offender that emerges from official arrest statistics may be racially distorted. If police target enforcement efforts in minority communities or concentrate on crimes committed by racial minorities, then obviously racial minorities will be overrepresented in arrest statistics.

A final limitation of UCR offender information centers around the information not included in these arrest reports. The UCR arrest information fails to offer a full picture of the white offender entering the criminal justice system. Specifically, additional sources of data present the white offender as typical in the case of many economic, political, and organized crime offenses. Russell, in detailing the results of her "search for white crime" in media and academic sources, supported the view that the occupational (white-collar) crimes for which whites are consistently overrepresented may not elicit the same level of fear as the street crimes highlighted in the UCR, but nonetheless these crimes have a high monetary and moral cost.[32]

Arrest Data The arrest data presented in Table 2.4 reveal that the public perception of the typical criminal offender as an African American is generally inaccurate. Examination of the arrest statistics for all offenses, for instance, reveals that the typical offender is white; more than two thirds (67.6 percent) of those arrested in 1997 were white, fewer than one third (30.4 percent) were African

---

BOX 2.3   The Operationalization of Race in Criminal Justice Data

The concept of race is measured—operationalized—in a number of ways, depending on the discipline and depending on the research question. Most biologists and anthropologists recognize the difficulties with using traditional race categories (white, black, red, yellow) as an effective means of classifying populations, and most social scientists rely on administrative definitions for record keeping, empirical analysis, and theory testing. Given these conditions, however, the term *race* still carries the connotation of an objective measurement with a biological or genetic basis. The origin of recording of race in the UCR can be traced to a practice that has no formal theoretical or policy relevance. From available accounts, this information was recorded because it was "available" and may be a side effect of efforts to legitimize fingerprint identification. Currently, the UCR manual gives detailed information on the definitions for index offenses and Part Two offenses, as well as specific instructions about the founding of crimes and the counting rules for multiple offenses. What is lacking, however, are specific instructions on the recording of race information.

Categories are expected to reflect Census Department rules and regulations, but no information is provided to inform the actual collection of these data. Administrative and Census definitions provided by local law enforcement agencies on agency arrest forms are calculated and reported,

but no guidelines for governing the source of the information are given. Thus, some arrest records forwarded to the FBI will reflect self-reporting by the arrested, whereas others will reflect observations of police personnel. Some police arrest reports use black, white, Native American, and Asian, whereas many use an "other" category. Still others use Hispanic in the race category, rather than a separate ethnicity. Given that the FBI does not currently request or report ethnicity in the UCR, much information is lost. Ongoing implementation of an incident-based reporting system may be calibrated to assess this measurement dilemma.

The NCVS attempts to collect race and ethnicity information consistent with Census definitions. Given their sampling procedures, information is collapsed into merely Black, White, and other. An attempt is made to acknowledge one ethnicity, Hispanic, and this is compared to non-Hispanic. Household information reflects the self-reported race of the individual with sufficient knowledge (and interest) in answering demographic questions about the family and the household incident questions. However, no multiracial household category is available. For personal offenses the race and ethnicity information is available as self-report information from the respondent reporting a victimization. However, the offender race information is based on victim perception of the offender.[33]

American, and fewer than 3 percent were Native American or Asian. Similarly, more than half of those arrested for violent crimes and nearly two thirds of those arrested for property crimes were white. In fact, the only crimes for which the typical offender was African American were murder, robbery, and gambling.

Examination of the percentage of all arrests involving members of each racial group must be done in the context of the distribution of each group in

Table 2.4 Percentage Distribution of Arrests by Race, 1997

	% White	% African American	% American Indian	% Asian
Total	67.1	30.4	1.3	1.2
Part One crimes	62.7	34.7	1.1	1.5
Murder and non-negligent manslaughter	41.9	56.4	.7	1.0
Forcible rape	58.2	39.7	1.1	1.0
Robbery	41.2	57.1	.6	1.2
Aggravated assault	61.2	36.6	1.0	1.1
Burglary	68.0	29.6	1.0	1.3
Larceny-theft	64.7	32.4	1.2	1.7
Motor vehicle theft	58.1	39.0	1.1	1.8
Arson	73.2	24.9	.8	1.1
Violent crime	56.8	41.1	.9	1.1
Property crime	64.8	32.4	1.2	1.7
Part Two crimes				
Other assaults	62.6	35.1	1.3	1.0
Forgery and counterfeiting	66.0	32.2	.6	1.2
Fraud	68.1	30.7	.5	.7
Embezzlement	63.2	34.8	.5	1.5
Stolen property; buying, receiving, possessing	56.9	41.1	.8	1.1
Vandalism	73.0	24.7	1.3	1.0
Weapons: carrying, possessing, etc.	58.7	39.6	.7	1.0
Prostitution and commercialized vice	57.9	40.4	.5	1.2
Sex offenses (except forcible rape and prostitution)	74.0	23.6	1.2	1.2
Drug abuse violations	62.0	36.8	.5	.7
Gambling	28.9	67.1	.5	3.5
Offenses against family and children	66.0	31.1	1.0	1.9
DUI	86.3	10.9	1.5	1.3
Liquor laws	83.5	12.5	3.1	.9
Drunkenness	80.3	16.9	2.3	.4
Disorderly conduct	62.1	35.9	1.4	.7
Vagrancy	51.5	46.3	1.9	.3
All other offenses (except traffic)	63.0	34.6	1.2	1.2
Suspicion	64.0	33.9	1.5	.6
Curfew and loitering law violations	74.8	22.6	1.3	1.3
Runaways	77.2	18.1	1.1	3.6

SOURCE: Bureau of Justice Statistics, *Crime in the United States, 1997* (Washington, D.C.: U.S. Department of Justice, 1998).

the population. In 1997 whites comprised approximately 84 percent of the U.S. population, African Americans comprised 12 percent, Asians comprised 3 percent, and Native Americans comprised less than 1 percent. The appropriate comparison, then, is the percentage in each racial group arrested in relation to that group's representation in the general population.

Thus, although whites are the persons most often arrested in crime categories reported in the UCR, it appears that African Americans are arrested at a disproportionately high rate for all offenses except driving under the influence and liquor law violations. The summary combined rate for all offenses indicates that the arrest rate for African Americans is two and a half times higher than would be predicted by their representation in the population. The disproportion is even larger for violent crimes: For these serious offenses the arrest rate for African Americans is more than three times what would be predicted.

Among the individual offenses, the degree of African American overrepresentation varies. The largest disparities are found for robbery and murder. The arrest rate for African Americans is nearly five times what we would expect for murder and robbery. The differences also are pronounced for rape, motor vehicle theft, suspicion, gambling, vagrancy, stolen property offenses, and weapons offenses.

Table 2.4 also presents arrest statistics for Native Americans and Asians. Although the overall pattern for Native American arrest figures is a slight overrepresentation compared to their representation in the population (1.3 percent arrested versus 0.8 percent in the population), the pattern across crimes is more erratic. For Part One crimes, most arrests are for larceny-theft, with the arrest figures for all other offenses similar to or lower than what is expected.

Native Americans are overrepresented in several Part Two offenses, including other vagrancy, driving under the influence, liquor law violations, and drunkenness. They are underrepresented in arrest figures for murder, robbery, fraud, embezzlement, receiving stolen property, prostitution/commercialized vice, gambling, and drug abuse violations.

Caution is required when interpreting Native American arrest figures, as arrests made by tribal police and federal agencies are not recorded in UCR data. Using information from the Bureau of Indian Affairs, Peak and Spencer[34] found that although UCR statistics revealed lower than expected homicide arrest rates for Native Americans, homicide rates were nine times higher than expected across the 207 reservations reporting.

For overall figures and each index offense, Asian Americans are underrepresented in UCR arrest data. The notable exception to the pattern of underrepresentation is the Part Two offense of gambling. Although 1997 data reveal 3.5 percent of arrests are of Asians, UCR arrest figures have been as high as 6.7 percent. The arrest rate for this offense is twice what is expected given the representation of Asians in the population. These figures do not speak to the gang problems in many Asian communities. This topic is addressed in a later section.

Juvenile Arrests The UCR arrest data also are available by age.[35] The overrepresentation of African Americans for violent crimes is very similar for adults (defined as offenders age eighteen and older) and juveniles. For example, slightly over 50 percent of adult and juvenile homicide arrests in 1997 were African Americans; for robbery the figures were over 50 percent, as well. For serious property crimes, on the other hand, the overrepresentation of African Americans was greater for adults than for juveniles. The overrepresentation of whites in the category of liquor law violations is even more pronounced for juveniles. The percentages are nearly identical for Native American and Asian juvenile and adult offenders, but African Americans account for almost all youth gambling arrests.

Perceptions of Offenders by Victims

Clearly African Americans are arrested at a disproportionately high rate. The problem, of course, is that we do not know the degree to which arrest statistics accurately reflect offending. As already noted, not all crimes are reported to the police and not all of those that are reported lead to an arrest.

One way to check the accuracy of arrest statistics is to examine data on offenders produced by the NCVS. Respondents who report a "face-to-face" encounter with an offender are asked to indicate the race of the offender. If the percentage of victims who report being robbed by an African American matches the percentage of African Americans who are arrested for robbery, we can have greater confidence in the validity of the arrest statistics. We can be more confident that differences in the likelihood of arrest reflect differences in offending.

If, on the other hand, the percentage of victims who report being robbed by an African American is substantially smaller than the percentage of African Americans who are arrested for robbery, we can conclude that at least some of the disproportion in the arrest rate reflects what Hindelang referred to as *selection bias* in the criminal justice system. As Hindelang noted, "If there are substantial biases in the UCR data for *any* reason, we would expect, to the extent that victimization survey reports are unbiased, to find large discrepancies between UCR arrest data and victimization survey reports on racial characteristics of offenders."[36]

Problems with NCVS Offender Data There are obvious problems in relying on victims' "perceptions" of the race of the offender. Respondents who report a victimization are asked if the offender was white, black, or some other race. These perceptions are of questionable validity because victimizations often occur quickly and involve the element of shock. In addition, victim memory is subject to decay over time and to retroactive reconstruction to fit the popular conception of a criminal offender. If a victim believes that the typical criminal is African American, this may influence his or her perception of the race of the offender.

There is another problem in relying on victims' perceptions of offender race. To the extent that these perceptions are based on skin color, they may be unreliable indicators of the race of offenders whose self-identification reflects their lineage or heritage rather than the color of their skin. Thus, individuals may appear in different racial groupings in victimization reports than they do on a police arrest report. A light-skinned offender who identifies himself as Hispanic and whose race is thus recorded as "other" in arrest data might show up in victimization data as white. If this occurs with any frequency, it obviously will affect the picture of the offender that emerges from victimization data.

Perceptions of Offenders With these caveats in mind, we present the NCVS data on the perceived race of the offender for single-offender violent victimizations. As Table 2.5 shows, although the typical offender for all of the crimes except robbery is white (or is perceived to be white), African Americans are overrepresented as offenders for all of the offenses. The most notable disproportion revealed by Table 2.5 is for robbery, with more than half (51.1 percent) of the offenders in single-offender robberies identified as African American. Also, African Americans also are overrepresented as offenders for rape, aggravated assault, and simple assault.

We argued earlier that one way to check the accuracy of arrest statistics is to compare the race of offenders arrested for various crimes with victims' perceptions of the race of the offender. These comparisons are found in Table 2.6. There is a relatively close match in the figures for white offenders for three offenses, with a noticeable gap in the rape comparison, suggesting that whites may be underrepresented in arrest data. For African Americans, on the other hand, the pattern is more consistent. That is, African Americans are represented in arrest figures in much higher proportions than the perception of offenders from victim interviews suggests.[37] These comparisons indicate that the racial disproportion found in arrest rates for these offenses cannot be used to resolve the dilemma of differential arrest rates by race versus a higher rate of offending among African Americans. It may be reasonably argued that such evidence actually suggests the presence of both differentially high offending rates by African Americans for serious violent offenses and the presence of differentially high arrest rates for African Americans, particularly for rape offenses.

Hindelang used early victimization data to determine which of these explanations was more likely. His initial comparison of 1974 arrest statistics with victimization data for rape, robbery, aggravated assault, and simple assault revealed some evidence of "differential selection for criminal justice processing"[38] for two of the offenses examined. For rape and aggravated assault, the percentage of African American offenders in the victimization data was smaller (9 percentage points for rape, 11 percentage points for aggravated assault) than the proportion found in UCR arrest statistics.

However, once Hindelang controlled for victimizations that were reported to the police, the discrepancies disappeared and the proportions of offenders identified as African American and white were strikingly similar. Hindelang concluded that "it is difficult to argue [from these data] that blacks are no more likely than whites to be involved in the common law crimes of robbery, forcible rape, assault."[39]

Table 2.5 Perceived Race of Offender for Single-Offender Crimes of Violence

| | PERCEIVED RACE OF THE OFFENDER | | |
Type of Crime	White	African American	Other
All crimes of violence	64.3%	25.3%	8.8%
Rape	68.0	20.6	9.0
Robbery	34.9	51.1	10.1
Assault	66.9	23.0	8.6
Aggravated	57.0	30.4	10.7
Simple	70.0	20.8	8.0

SOURCE: Bureau of Justice Statistics, *Criminal Victimization in the United States, 1994* (Washington, D.C.: U.S. Department of Justice, 1996).

Table 2.6 A Comparison of UCR and NCVS Data on Offender Race[a]

| | WHITES | | AFRICAN AMERICANS | |
	Arrested	Perceived	Arrested	Perceived
Rape	55.6	68.0	42.4	20.6
Robbery	38.7	34.9	59.5	51.1
Aggravated assault	59.6	57.0	38.4	30.4
Simple assault	63.0	70.0	33.1	20.8

[a]Percentage of whites and African Americans arrested in 1995 compared to percentage of those who reported being victimized in 1994 who perceived offender (in single-offender victimizations) to be white or African American.

Hindelang's analysis of victimizations reported to the police also revealed a pattern of differential reporting by victims. Specifically, Hindelang found that for rape and robbery, those victimized by African Americans were more likely than those victimized by whites to report the crime to the police. Hindelang suggested that this is a form of selection bias—victim-based selection bias.

Hindelang concluded his comparison of UCR arrest rates and victimization survey data by separating the elements of criminal justice system selection bias, victim-based selection bias, and differential offending rates. He argued that both forms of selection bias were present, but that each was outweighed by the overwhelming evidence of differential involvement of African Americans in offending.

Self-Report Surveys

Self-report surveys are another way to paint a picture of the criminal offender. These surveys question respondents about their participation in criminal or delinquent behavior. Emerging in the 1950s, the self-report format remains a popular source of data for those searching for descriptions and causes of criminal behavior. One of the advantages of asking people about their behavior is that it gives a less distorted picture of the offender than an official record because it is free of the alleged biases of the criminal justice system. However, it is not at all clear that self-report survey results provide a more accurate description of the criminal offender.[40]

Problems with Self-Report Surveys One of the major weaknesses of the self-report format is that there is no single design used. Moreover, different surveys focus on different aspects of criminal behavior. Not all self-report surveys ask the same questions or use the same or similar populations, and very few follow the same group over time. Typically, the sample population is youth from school settings or institutionalized groups.

In addition to the problems of inconsistent format and noncomparable samples, self-report surveys suffer from a variety of other limitations. The accuracy of self-report data is influenced by the respondents' honesty and memory and by interviewer bias.

One of the most confounding limitations in criminal justice data sets is present with self-report surveys: The comparisons are overwhelmingly comparisons of African Americans and whites. Little can be said about Native Americans, Asian Americans, or Hispanic Americans. Some studies suffer from the additional limitation of homogenous samples with insufficient racial representation, making it difficult to draw conclusions about how many members of a racial group commit delinquent activity (prevalence) and how frequently racial minorities commit crime (incidence).

Although self-report surveys generally are assumed to be reliable and valid, this assumption has been shown to be less tenable for certain subgroups of offenders.[41] Specifically, it has been shown that there is differential validity for white and African American respondents. *Validity* is the idea that, as a researcher, you are measuring what you think you are measuring. Reverse record checks (matching self-report answers with police records) have shown that there is greater concurrence between respondent answers and official police arrest records for white respondents than for African American respondents.[42] This indicates that African American respondents tend to underreport some offending behavior.

Elliot et al. cautioned against a simplistic interpretation of these findings.[43] They found that African American respondents are more likely to underreport index-type offenses than less serious offenses. Therefore, they suggested that this finding might indicate the differential validity of official police records rather than the differential validity of the self-report measures by race. An example of differential validity of police records would occur if police report the clearly serious offenses for whites and African Americans, but report the less serious offenses for African Americans only. In short, most self-report researchers conclude that racial comparisons must be made with caution.

Characteristics of Offenders Typically, juvenile self-report surveys record demographic data and ask questions about the frequency of certain delinquent activities in the past year. The delinquent activities included range in seriousness from skipping class to drinking liquor, stealing something worth more than $50, stealing a car, or assaulting another person.[44]

Early self-report studies conducted before 1980 found little difference in delinquency rates across race (African American and white only). Later, more refined self-report designs have produced results that challenge the initial assumption of similar patterns of delinquency.[45] Some research findings indicate that African American males are more likely than white males to report serious criminal behavior (prevalence). Moreover, a larger portion of African Americans than whites report a high frequency of serious delinquency (incidence).[46]

Perhaps the most recent and comprehensive analysis of the race and prevalence and race and incidence issues was done by Huizinga and Elliot[47] with six waves of the National Youth Survey (NYS) data. This self-report survey is a longitudinal study that began in 1976 using a national panel design. This study offers the only national assessment of individual offending rates based on self-report studies for a six-year period.

Huizinga and Elliot explored whether African American youth have a higher prevalence of offending than whites and whether a higher incidence of offending by African Americans can explain differential arrest rates. Their analysis revealed few consistent racial differences across the years studied, either in the proportion of African American and white youth engaging in delinquent behavior or the frequency with which African American and white offenders commit delinquent acts. Contrary to Hindelang, they suggested that the differential selection bias hypothesis cannot be readily dismissed, as the differential presence of youth in the criminal justice system cannot be explained entirely by differential offending rates.

Drug Offenders A prevalent image in the news and entertainment media is the image of the drug user as a racial or ethnic minority. In particular, arrest data for nonalcoholic drug abuse violations reflect an overrepresentation of African Americans and the overrepresentation of Native Americans for alcohol-related offenses. A more comprehensive picture of the drug user emerges from self-report data that ask respondents to indicate their use of and prevalence of use behavior for particular drugs. In a recent report on the use of drugs among people of color, the National Institutes of Health (NIH) summarized the current body of research as indicating:

- African American youth report less alcohol use than white youth and report similar prevalence levels for use of illicit drugs compared to other racial and ethnic groups. (NIH did note research suggesting that African Americans experience higher rates of drug-related health problems than users from other race/ethnicity groups).

- Asian/Pacific Islander youth responding to sporadic state-level surveys and several years of pooled national data consistently report less drug use than other non-Asian populations.

- Native American youth begin using a variety of drugs (not limited to alcohol) at an earlier age than white youth. Inhalant use is twice as high among Native American youth.

- Hispanics are found to have a higher reported use of illicit drugs than non–Hispanic whites.[48]

In short, there is no clear picture of the typical drug user or abuser. Additional race differences are evident in results from a recent school-based survey by the Centers for Disease Control and Prevention that indicate that self-reported lifetime crack use is highest among Hispanic students, followed by lower percentages for whites and even lower percentages for African Americans. However, the National Household Survey on Drug Abuse data reveal the disturbing observation that a far greater number of African American and Hispanic youth (approximately one third) reported seeing people sell drugs in the neighborhood occasionally or more often than did whites (less than 10 percent).

Summary: A Picture of the Typical Criminal Offender

The image of the typical offender that emerges from the data examined here conflicts somewhat with the image in the minds of most Americans. If by the phrase *typical offender* we mean the offender who shows up most frequently in arrest statistics, then for all crimes except murder and robbery the typical offender is white, not African American.

As we have shown, focusing on the number of persons arrested is somewhat misleading. It is clear from the data discussed thus far that African Americans are arrested at a disproportionately high rate. This conclusion applies to property crime as well as violent crime. It applies to juveniles as well as adults. Moreover, victimization data suggest that African Americans may have higher offending rates for serious violent crime. However, examinations of victim perception of offender with official arrest data reveal that some of the overrepresentation of African American offenders may well reflect selection bias on the part of criminal justice officials, but this dilemma remains unsettled.

If part of the view of the typical criminal offender is that the typical drug offender is a minority, we have shown that self-report data from youth populations in the United States reveal that people of color do not have consistently higher drug use rates than whites. This picture varies slightly by type of drug, with Hispanic youth showing higher rates of use with some drugs and American Indian youth with other drugs. However, there is little evidence of differential patterns of higher use rates among African Americans compared with other racial groups.

CRIME AS AN INTRARACIAL EVENT

In the minds of many Americans, the term *crime* conjures up an image of an act of violence against a white victim by a black offender. In the preceding sections we demonstrated the inaccuracy of these perceptions of victims and offenders; we illustrated that the typical victim is a racial minority and that the typical offender, for all but a few crimes, is white. We now turn to a discussion of crime as an intraracial event.

The National Crime Victimization Survey

Few criminal justice data sources, including the NCVS, offer comprehensive information on the racial makeup of the victim—offender dyad. Recall that the NCVS asks victims about their perceptions of the offender's race in crimes of violence and data presented distinguish among only African Americans, whites, and "others" (victims' perceptions of the offender as Hispanic are not available).

With these limitations in mind, NCVS data on the race of the victim and the perceived race of the offender in single-offender violent victimizations can be examined.[49] These data indicate that almost all violent crimes by white offenders were committed against white victims (73 percent). This pattern also characterized the individual crimes of robbery and assault. The typical white offender, in other words, commits a crime against another white person.

This intraracial pattern of violent crime perceived to be committed by African Americans is also reported by African American victims. However, African American robbery offenders, depending on the type of robbery, are roughly as likely to have white victims as African American victims.

UCR Homicide Reports

Another source of data on the victim—offender pair is the Supplemental Homicide Report. Contrary to the popular belief, 1997 UCR Supplemental Homicide Reports reveal that homicide is essentially an interracial event. Specifically, 94 percent of African American murder victims were slain by other African Americans and 85 percent of white victims were killed by other whites.[50] The small percentage of intraracial homicides are more likely to occur with young victims and young offenders, and they are slightly more like to be black-on-white offenses than white-on-black offenses.

Summary

The general pattern revealed by the data discussed here is one in which white offenders consistently victimize whites, whereas African American offenders, and particularly African American males, more frequently victimize both African Americans and whites. As noted, the politicizing of black criminality continues, while the emergence of and subsequent focus on racial hoaxes persists.[52]

Some researchers have challenged the assertion that crime is predominantly intraracial,[53] pointing to the fact that a white person has a greater likelihood of being victimized by an African American offender than an African American has of being victimized by a white offender. Although this is true, it

---

Focus on an Issue
The Politicization of Interracial Crime

Willie Horton played an important role in the 1988 presidential campaign. He was featured in campaign ads and frequently mentioned in speeches given by the Republican candidate and his supporters. By the end of the campaign, Willie Horton was a household name.

Horton was a convicted murderer from Massachusetts. While serving a lengthy prison term, he became eligible for a furlough program and occasionally was allowed to leave the prison for short periods of time. On one such trip, he fled to Maryland, where he committed a brutal rape. Horton was African American; his victim was white.

George Bush, the Republican candidate, used Horton to portray Michael Dukakis, the Democratic nominee for president, as "soft on crime." Although Dukakis played no part in the decision to allow Horton out on furlough, he had been governor of Massachusetts at the time.

Critics of the Republicans' tactics disputed their claim that the "Willie Horton incident" was simply being used to illustrate what was wrong with the U.S. criminal justice system. They charged that it was no coincidence that Horton was black and his victim white. They charged that the campaign ads featuring Horton's picture had racist overtones and that use of the incident exemplified political pandering to public fears and stereotypes about crime.

Focus on an Issue
Politicizing Black-On-Black Crime

Much attention has been devoted to "black-on-black" crime . . . . It is not unusual to see in the written press or to hear in the electronic media stories depicting the evils of living in the black community. [This] has occurred with such frequency that some individuals now associate black people with criminality. Simply put, it has become fashionable to discern between crime and black-on-black crime. Rarely does one read or hear about white crime or "white-on-white" crime. This is troubling when one considers that most crimes, including serious violent crimes, are committed by and against whites as well as blacks.[51]

---

does not logically challenge the assertion that crime is predominantly an intraracial event. Remember that the NCVS reveals that the typical offender is white, not African American. In fact, recent NCVS estimates indicate that 2,810,900 single-offender personal victimizations involved white offenders, compared to only 1,280,250 involving African American offenders.[54]

When comparing race of offender and race of victim for all crimes of violence, we can see that there were 2,726,573 crimes involving white offenders and white victims, 614,520 involving African American offenders and African American victims, 84,327 involving white offenders and African American victims, and 665,730 involving African American offenders and white victims. In other words, only 18 percent of these crimes of violence were interracial crimes.

CRIME AS AN INTERRACIAL (HATE) EVENT

Not all interracial criminal events are considered hate crimes. The term *hate crime* (or *bias crime*) is most often defined as a common law offense that contains an element of prejudice based on the race, ethnicity, national origin, religion, or sexual orientation of the victim. Generally, hate crime legislation is enacted in the form of enhancement penalties for common law offenses (ranging from assault to vandalism) that have an element of prejudice. Justifications for the creation of such legislation include the symbolic message that certain actions are exceptionally damaging to an individual when they are "provoked" by the status of race and ethnicity and that such actions are damaging to the general community and should be condemned.

The FBI has been mandated to collect information on hate crime in the United States.[55] In 1997, the FBI received 8,049 reports of hate crimes (with 10,225 victims), from 11,211 agencies, representing 85 percent of the U.S. population.[56] Most offenses involved individuals, and the remaining offenses were against a business, institutions, or society as a whole. Nearly 60 percent of offenses involved race bias, with another 10 percent reflecting bias based on ethnicity or national origin. The most common bias offense is crimes against persons.

The victims of race and ethnic bias crimes are reflective of all race categories. African Americans and Hispanics are the most common victims, with Asian and mixed-race victims being overrepresented as well. White victims are not overrepresented in relation to their presence in the population, but are the second largest group of hate crime victims.

Offender information is provided by victim reports to the police rather than arrest information. In this information whites are most often identified as suspected offenders, but each victim race category reflects a suspected offender from each of the offender race categories. That is, all race groups have individuals who have been victimized by bias crimes and all race groups have individuals who are suspected offenders of bias crimes. Information on the trends of victimization and offending in bias crime events is limited, but patterns for both whites and African Americans are beginning to emerge.[57] Whites are most likely to be victimized by African Americans, and Native American offenders (although rare) are more likely to victimize whites than other race groups. African Americans are more often victimized by whites, and the Asian offender is more likely to victimize African Americans than other race groups.

Jacobs[58] argued that hate crime statutes create a law unlikely to deter and its implementation will widen social division. He also argued that hate crime legislation represents an ill-advised insertion of the civil rights paradigm into the criminal law. Specifically, he reasoned that civil rights legislation is an attempt to extend "positive rights and opportunities to minorities and women . . . directed at the conduct of government officials and private persons who govern, regulate, or sell goods and services. By contrast, hate crime law deals with conduct that is already criminal and with wrongdoers who are already criminals."[59] He concluded that the "possibility that criminals can be threatened into not discriminating in their choice of crime victims is slight."[60]

ETHNIC YOUTH GANGS

In the minds of most Americans, the words *gang, race,* and *crime* are inextricably linked. Recall the incident described at the beginning of this chapter—a woman raped and attacked by a group of minority teenagers in Central Park. The media labeled these youth a "gang." This designation, however, was challenged by those who argued that the teenagers involved in the incident were not organized, had no gang identity, and behaved more like a mob than a gang.[61]

A comprehensive review of recent research on ethnic youth gangs is beyond the scope of this chapter. Instead, we discuss some of the prevailing myths about gangs and gang membership and summarize research on ethnic gang activities. Although there is no universally accepted definition of a gang, the term is generally used to refer to a group of young people who recognize some sort of organized membership and leadership, and who, in addition, are involved in criminal activity.[62]

Gang Myths and Realities

We have shown that popular perceptions of crime, crime victims, and criminal offenders often are inaccurate. Many of the prevailing beliefs about gangs are similarly mistaken. In the sections that follow, we discuss some of the myths surrounding gangs and gang activity. We show that although there is an element of truth in each of these myths, there also are a number of inaccuracies.

Myth 1: Gangs are only found in large cities. It is important to understand that the gang phenomenon is not a homogeneous one. Although many gangs are located in urban areas, gangs are increasingly found in suburban[63] and rural communities, as well as Indian reservations.[64]

Myth 2: All gang members are African American and belong either to the Bloods or Crips. The Bloods and the Crips are predominantly African American and are very widely known. These two gangs are heavily involved in illegal drug activities and are characterized by a confederation of local gangs that stretch across the country.[65] They are not, however, exclusively African American.

Mydans[66] provided examples of well-to-do white youth joining California Crips and Bloods.

Although members of the racial minority groups we focus on in this book are overrepresented in gangs, they do not comprise the entire gang problem. In a recent review of the juvenile gang literature, Covey, Menard, and Franzese[67] documented the existence of African American, Hispanic, Asian, and white gangs. (It is somewhat misleading to categorize gangs as Hispanic or Asian. These terms are very broad and mask the variety within each group. In reality, gangs are ethnically specific by nationality. There are Puerto Rican, Cuban, Mexican American, Vietnamese, Cambodian, Korean, Chinese, and Japanese gangs.)

The earliest gangs in the United States actually were composed of white ethnic youth from Eastern European counties.[68] Currently, white ethnic gangs are not as prevalent. Covey et al.[69] argued that "the relative absence of white ethnic gangs in official studies may be a product of a number of factors including the difficulty of identifying them[70] and biases in reporting and public perception."[71] Many of the white ethnic groups that do exist are characterized by white supremacist activities or satanism.

Myth 3: All gangs are involved in selling drugs and drug trafficking. Many, but not all, gangs are involved in illegal drug activities. Moreover, at least some of these gangs existed before they began selling drugs. It is possible that gangs have been exploited because of their structure and organization to sell drugs, and that this lucrative activity serves as a reason for recruitment and expansion.

Drug use is common in most gangs, but the emphasis placed on drug sales varies by the character and social organization of the gang.[72] Many researchers challenge the idea that selling drugs is usually an organized gang activity involving all gang members.[73] In their study of Denver youth, Esbensen and Huizinga[74] distinguished between a gang involved in drug activity and individual gang members selling drugs. They found that 80 percent of the respondents said that their gangs were involved in drug sales, but only 28 percent admitted to selling drugs themselves. In short, although gang members were found to be more active in drug-related crimes (use and sales) than nongang youth, not all gang members sold drugs.

Related to the myth that all gang members sell drugs is the notion that drugs and violence are inextricably linked. In fact, there is a complex relationship between drugs and violence in gangs. Fagan found that, regardless of the level of drug dealing within a gang, violent behaviors still occurred, with the majority of incidents unrelated to drug sales.[75] He concluded that "for gang members, violence is not an inevitable consequence of involvement in drug use and dealing."[76] Curry and Decker also noted the prevalence of violence in gang activity, pointing out that much of this violence is also intraracial.[77]

Myth 4: Gangs are the result of poverty and a growing underclass. It is overly simplistic to attribute the existence of gangs solely to poverty. Gangs exist for a variety of reasons: the growth of the underclass,[78] the disintegration of the African American and Hispanic family,[79] poverty,[80] difficulty assimilating into

American culture,[81] marginality,[82] political and religious reasons,[83] and general rebellion against adult and conventional society.[84] However, Curry and Decker did argue that gang formation and gang delinquency are more likely to be explained at the community level rather than at the individual level.[85]

Myth 5: All gang members are male. Although it is true that males are overrepresented in gang membership, there are female gang members. The early sociological literature on gangs only discussed males; females who accompanied male gang members were often described in terms of an "auxiliary"—present, but not a formal part of the criminal activity.

More recent studies have found both fully active female gang members and a few solely female gangs. Researchers estimate that females represent between 10 percent[86] and 25 percent[87] of all gang members. Campbell identified several all-female gangs in New York City. The Sandman Ladies, for example, were Puerto Rican females with a biker image. The Sex Girls were African American and Hispanic females who were involved in drug dealing.

The presence of female gang members differs by ethnicity as well. Females are found in Hispanic gangs, African American gangs, and white ethnic gangs, but appear to be conspicuously absent in both journalistic and scholarly accounts of Asian American gangs.[88]

Varieties of Ethnic Gangs

We already noted that, contrary to popular wisdom, all gang members are not African Americans. There are Hispanic, Asian, and white gangs as well as African American gangs.

Covey et al. stated that "[ethnicity] is not the only way to understand gangs, but gangs are organized along ethnic lines, and it would be a mistake to ignore ethnicity as a variable that may affect the nature of juvenile gangs."[89] Most ethnic gangs reflect a mixture of their members' culture of origin and the American "host" culture; indeed, many gangs form as the result of a clash between the two cultures.

African American The most widely known African American gangs are the Bloods and the Crips. Each gang has unique "colors" and sign language to reinforce gang identity. It is believed that these gangs are really "national confederations of local gangs" in U.S. cities.[90] They are characteristically very territorial and are linked to drug distribution.

Other African American gangs exist across the United States. Researchers have identified many big-city African American gangs that are oriented toward property crime rather than drug sales.[91] In addition, African American gangs have formed around the tenets of Islam, with corresponding political agendas.[92]

American Indian The circumstances among which American Indian youth are becoming part of the gang culture in the United States include the emerging presence of gangs in the semisovereign tribal lands throughout the country and as members of gangs located in urban and rural nonreservation areas.

Specifically, the Navajo nation has documented the presence of youth gangs of tribal members, recently reporting the presence of more than fifty gangs with nearly 1,000 members on the reservation.[93] These gangs often take names from more established urban gangs such as Crips and Bloods, and are characterized by violence, but appear to be less coordinated.[94]

Asian As previously stated, there are a variety of Asian ethnic gangs. Most Asian gang researchers attribute the formation of these gangs, at least in part, to feelings of alienation because of difficulty assimilating into U.S. culture.[95] Similarities between Asian gangs include an emphasis on economic activity and a pattern of intraracial victimization. Asian gangs are found primarily in coastal cities such as New York, San Francisco, Boston, and Portland, which have large Asian immigrant populations.[96]

The origins of Chinese American gangs can be traced to the early 1890s and the secret "Tong" societies.[97] Chinese American gang activity increased with the relaxation of immigration laws in the mid-1960s.[98] The research on Chinese American gangs shows a commitment to violence for its own sake (gang warfare) and as a means for attaining income (robbery, burglary, extortion, protection).[99] Chin[100] noted that, generally, the structure of Chinese American gangs is very hierarchical; he also explained that gang members may participate in legitimate business, establish drug distribution and sale networks, and form national and international networks.

Vietnamese American gang activity is not as structured as that of Chinese American gangs. The rise in gang activity for this ethnic group can also be tied to an influx in immigration. Overall, Vietnamese American gang activity is less violent, typically economically oriented, and most likely to target other Vietnamese Americans.[101]

Hispanic Hispanic gangs have identifiable core concerns: brotherhood/ sisterhood, machismo, and loyalty to the *barrio* (neighborhood).[102] Many Hispanic gangs have adult as well as juvenile members,[103] and gang members may be involved in the use and sale of drugs. The importance of machismo may explain the emphasis of many Hispanic gangs on violence, even intragang violence.

White The white ethnic gangs—composed of Irish, Polish, and Italian youth— identified by researchers earlier in this century are less evident in today's cities. Contemporary white ethnic gangs are most often associated with rebellion against adult society, suburban settings, and a focus on white supremacist or satanist ideals.

"Skinheads" may be the most well-known example of a white ethnic gang. Covey et al. described them in this way: "Skinhead gangs usually consist of European American youths who are non-Hispanic, non-Jewish, Protestant, working class, low income, clean shaven and militantly racist and white supremacist."[104] Skinheads have been located in cities in every region of the country and have been linked to adult domestic terrorist organizations such as the White Aryan Resistance and other Neo-Nazi movements. Skinheads are unique in the sense that they use violence not to protect turf, protect a drug market, or commit robberies, but rather "for the explicit purpose of promoting political change by instilling fear in innocent people."[105]

"Stoner" gangs, another form of white ethnic gangs, are characterized by an emphasis on satanic rituals. This doctrine is supplemented by territoriality and the heavy use of drugs.[106]

In recognizing the racial nature of gangs, it is important to clarify the role of racism in the formation of gangs. Most gangs are racially and ethnically homogenous. Some researchers argue that this situation is merely reflective of the racial and ethnic composition of neighborhoods and primary friendships. That is, "where schools and neighborhoods are racially and ethnically mixed, gangs tend to be racially and ethnically mixed."[107]

Although violent conflicts do occur between and within ethnic gangs, violence is seldom the reason for gang formation. Racism as a social phenomenon that creates oppressive conditions can contribute to gang formation. However, individual racism explains very little in terms of the formation of gangs or the decision to join gangs. Skinhead membership is a notable exception, being almost exclusively a function of individual racism.[108]

CONCLUSION

We began this chapter with a description of the sexual assault of a white woman by a group of minority youth in New York City's Central Park. We argued that incidents like this shape perceptions of crime in the United States. In the minds of many Americans, the typical crime is an act of violence involving a white victim and an African American offender.

We have used a variety of data sources to illustrate the inaccuracy of these perceptions. We have shown that the typical victim of both household and personal crime is African American or Hispanic, and we have demonstrated that this pattern is particularly striking for crimes of violence. We have demonstrated that although the typical offender for all crimes except murder and robbery is white, African Americans are arrested at a disproportionately high rate. We also have shown that although most crimes involve an offender and victim of the same race, interracial crime in the form of hate crime is of concern. Finally, we have attempted to dispel some of the myths surrounding race, drug use, gangs, and crime.

The information provided in this chapter might raise as many questions as it answers. Although we have attempted to paint an accurate picture of crime in the United States, we are hampered by limitations inherent in existing data sources. Some criminal events are not defined as crimes by the victims, many of those that are defined as crimes are not reported to the police, and many of those reported to the police do not lead to an arrest. There is no data set, in other words, that provides information on all crimes that occur.

We have attempted to address this problem by using several different sources of data. We believe that we can have greater confidence in the conclusions we reach if two or more distinct types of data point in the same direction. The fact that both NCVS data and data from the Supplemental Homicide Reports consistently reveal that racial minorities are more likely than whites to fall victim to crime, for example, lends credence to the conclusion that the typical crime victim is African American or Hispanic. Similarly, the fact that a variety of data sources suggest that crime is an intraracial event enhances our confidence in this conclusion.

We have less confidence in our conclusions concerning the racial makeup of the offender population. Although it is obvious that African Americans are arrested at a disproportionately high rate, particularly for murder and robbery, it is not clear that this reflects differential offending rather than selective enforcement of the law. Arrest statistics and victimization data both indicate that although African Americans have higher rates of offending than whites, comparisons also seem to suggest the presence of differential selection bias in arrest data. In addition, some self-report studies suggest that there are few, if any, racial differences in offending. We suggest that this discrepancy limits our ability to draw definitive conclusions about the meaning of the disproportionately high arrest rates for African Americans.

One final caveat seems appropriate. The conclusions we reach about victims and offenders are based primarily on descriptive data; they are based primarily on percentages, rates, and trends over time. These data are appropriate for describing the typical victim and the typical offender, but are not sufficient for drawing conclusions concerning causality. The data we have examined in this chapter can tell us that the African American arrest rate is higher than the white arrest rate, but they cannot tell us why this is so. We address issues of causation in subsequent chapters.

DISCUSSION QUESTIONS

1. The descriptive information in UCR arrest data depicts an overrepresentation of African America offenders for most violent and property crimes. What are the possible explanations for such disparity? What must a researcher include in a study of "why people commit crime" to advance beyond disparity to test for causal explanations?

2. "Should hate be a crime?" What arguments can be made to support the use of sentencing enhancement penalties for hate crimes? What arguments can be made to oppose such statutes? Are hate crime laws likely to reduce crime?

3. If most youth gangs are racially and ethnically homogenous, should law enforcement use race and ethnic specific strategies to fight the formation and activities of such gangs? Or, should law enforcement strategies be racially and ethnically neutral? What dilemmas are created for police departments who pursue each of these strategies? Is the likely result institutional or contextual discrimination?

NOTES

1. *New York Times* (May 29, 1989), p. 28.

2. Ibid., p. 25.

3. According to UCR index crime totals for 1997, nearly 90 percent of crimes were property crimes. It is believed that rapes are severely underreported, but similar arguments can be made for property crimes, especially fraud. Even if the rape numbers are low, the numbers of violent criminal events do not overshadow property crime.

4. *New York Times* (May 29, 1989), p. 25.

5. Robert M. O'Brien, "The Interracial Nature of Violent Crimes: A Reexamination," *American Journal of Sociology* 92 (1987): 817–835.

6. Charles Silberman, *Criminal Violence, Criminal Justice* (New York: Random House, 1978), pp. 117–118.

7. The National Crime Survey (NCS) was recently renamed the National Crime Victimization Survey (NCVS) to clearly emphasize the focus of measuring victimizations.

8. The Bureau of Justice Statistics was formerly the National Criminal Justice and Information Service of the Law Enforcement Assistance Administration.

9. Bureau of Justice Statistics, U.S. Department of Justice, *Criminal Victimization in the United States, 1997* (Washington, D.C.: U.S. Government Printing Office, 1999).

10. Ibid.

11. Bureau of Justice Statistics, U.S. Department of Justice, *Criminal Victimization in the United States, 1994* (Washington, D.C.: U.S. Government Printing Office, 1996).

12. Ibid.

13. Lawrence A. Greenfeld and Steven K. Smith, American Indians and Crime (Washington, D.C.: Bureau of Justice Statistics, 1999).

14. Ibid.

15. Bureau of Justice Statistics, U.S. Department of Justice, *Lifetime Likelihood of Victimization* (Washington, D.C.: U.S. Department of Justice, 1987), p. 1.

16. Ibid., p. 3.

17. Percentages reflect 11,250 single-offender homicides.

18. U.S. Bureau of the Census, *Statistical Abstract of the United States: 1994* (Washington, D.C.: U.S. Government Printing Office, 1994), Table 128.

19. Bureau of Justice Statistics, *Young Black Male Victims* (Washington, D.C.: U.S. Department of Justice, 1994).

20. Silberman, *Criminal Violence, Criminal Justice.*

21. Steven Weisenburger, *Modern Medea* (New York: Hill & Wang, 1998); Toni Morrison, *Beloved: A Novel* (New York: Plume, 1988).

22. Bureau of Justice Statistics, U.S. Department of Justice, *Criminal Victimization in the United States, 1997.*

23. Ibid.

24. Ibid.

25. D. L. Decker, D. Shichor, and R. M. O'Brien, *Urban Structure and Victimization* (Lexington, MA: D.C. Heath, 1982), p. 27.

26. U.S. Department of Justice, *Criminal Victimization in the United States, 1992* (Washington, D.C.: U.S. Government Printing Office, 1994).

27. Michael J. Hindelang, "Race and Involvement in Common Law Personal Crimes," *American Sociological Review* 43 (1978): 93–109.

28. U.S. Department of Justice, Federal Bureau of Investigation, *Crime in the United States, 1997* (Washington, D.C.: U.S. Government Printing Office, 1998).

29. John Huey-Long Song, "Attitudes of Chinese Immigrants and Vietnamese Refugees Toward Law Enforcement in the United States," *Justice Quarterly* 9 (1992): 703–719.

30. Margorie Zatz, "Pleas, Priors and Prison: Racial/Ethnic Differences in Sentencing," *Social Science Research* 14 (1985): 169–193.

31. Donald Black, "The Social Organization of Arrest," in *The Manners and Customs of the Police,* ed. Donald Black (New York: Academic Press, 1980), pp. 85–108.

32. Katheryn K. Russell, *The Color of Crime* (New York: New York University Press, 1998).

33. Paul Knepper, "Race, Racism and Crime Statistics," *Southern Law Review* 24 (1996): 71–112.

34. K. Peak and J. Spencer, "Crime in Indian Country: Another Trail of Tears," *Journal of Criminal Justice* 15 (1987): 485–494.

35. U.S. Department of Justice, Federal Bureau of Investigation, *Crime in the United States, 1997,* Table 43.

36. Hindelang, "Race and Involvement in Common Law Personal Crimes," p. 93.

37. Granted, the robbery arrest figures do include commercial offenses, but we are not looking at the volume of offenses, but rather the demographics of who is arrested.

38. Hindelang, "Race and Involvement in Common Law Personal Crimes," p. 99.

39. Hindelang, "Race and Involvement in Common Law Personal Crimes," pp. 100–101.

40. Gwynn Nettler, *Explaining Crime,* 3d ed. (New York: McGraw-Hill, 1984).

41. Patrick G. Jackson, "Sources of Data" in *Measurement Issues in Criminology,* ed. Kimberly Kempf (New York: Springer-Verlag, 1990).

42. Michael Hindelang, Travis Hirschi, and Joseph G. Weis, *Measuring Delinquency* (Beverly Hills, CA: Sage, 1981); Delbert Elliot, David Huizinga, Brian Knowles, and Rachelle Canter, *The Prevalence and Incidence of Delinquent Behavior: 1976–1980: National Estimates of Delinquent Behavior by Sex, Race, Social Class and Other Selected Variables* (Boulder, CO: Behavioral Research Institute, 1983); Robert M. O'Brien, *Crime and Victimization Data* (Beverly Hills, CA: Sage, 1985).

43. Elliot et al., *The Prevalence and Incidence of Delinquent Behavior.*

44. National Youth Survey questionnaire in O'Brien, *Crime and Victimization Data.*

45. O'Brien, *Crime and Victimization Data.*

46. Delbert Elliot and S. S. Ageton, "Reconciling Race and Class Differences in Self-Reported and Official Measures of Delinquency," *American Sociological Review*

45 (1980): 95–110; Hindelang et al., *Measuring Delinquency.*

47. David Huizinga and Delbert S. Elliot, "Juvenile Offenders: Prevalence, Offender Incidence, and Arrest Rates by Race," *Crime and Delinquency* 33 (1987): 206–223.

48. National Institute of Health, *Drug Use Among Racial/Ethnic Minorities,* Report No. 95–3888 (Washington, D.C.: Author, 1995).

49. Bureau of Justice Statistics, U.S. Department of Justice, *Criminal Victimization in the United States, 1994.*

50. Ibid.

51. Robert Bing, "Politicizing Black-on-Black Crime: A Critique of Terminological Preference," in *Black-on-Black Crime,* ed. P. Ray Kedia (Bristol, IN: Wyndham Hall Press, 1994).

52. Katheryn K. Russell, *The Color of Crime* (New York: New York University Press, 1998).

53. William Wilbanks, "Is Violent Crime Intraracial?" *Crime and Delinquency* 31 (1985): 117–128.

54. U.S. Department of Justice, *Criminal Victimization in the United States, 1992.*

55. Hate Crimes Act of 1990.

56. Note that although data collection is mandatory, participation by law enforcement agencies is voluntary. Hate Crime Statistics, 1997, UCR.

57. Hate Crime Statistics, 1997, UCR.

58. James Jacobs, "Should Hate Be a Crime?" *Public Interest* 1993 (1993): 3–14.

59. Ibid., p. 11.

60. Ibid., pp. 11–12.

61. A. K. Cohen, "Foreword and Overview," in *Gangs in America,* ed. C. Ronald Huff (Newbury Park, CA: Sage, 1990).

62. Herbert C. Covey, Scott Menard, and Robert J. Franzese, *Juvenile Gangs* (Springfield, IL: Charles C. Thomas, 1992).

63. J. W. C. Johnstone, "Youth Gangs and Black Suburbs," *Pacific Sociological Review* 24 (1991): 355–375; E. G. Dolan and S. Finney, *Youth Gangs* (New York: Simon & Schuster, 1984).

64. *Omaha World Herald* (September 18, 1997).

65. Covey et al., *Juvenile Gangs*, p. 52.

66. S. Mydans, "Not Just the Inner City: Well to Do Join Gangs," *New York Times* National (April 10, 1990), p. A-7.

67. Covey et al., *Juvenile Gangs*.

68. F. Thrasher *The Gang* (Chicago: University of Chicago Press, 1927).

69. Covey et al., *Juvenile Gangs*, p. 64.

70. C. J. Friedman, F. Mann, and H. Aldeman, "Juvenile Street Gangs the Victimization of Youth," *Adolescence* 11 (1976): 527–533.

71. William J. Chambliss, "The Saints and The Roughnecks," *Society* 11 (1973): 341–355.

72. Ronald C. Huff ("Youth Gangs and Public Policy," *Crime and Delinquency* 35 [1989]: 528–537) identified three gang types: hedonistic, instrumental, or predatory. Jeffrey Fagan ("The Social Organization of Drug Use and Drug Dealing Among Urban Gangs," *Criminology* 27 [1989]: 633–666) identified four: social gangs, party gangs, serious delinquents, and organized gangs.

73. Malcomb W. Klein, Cheryl Maxson, and Lea C. Cunningham, " 'Crack,' Street Gangs and Violence," *Criminology* 29 (1991): 623–650; Scott H. Decker and Barrick Van Winkle, "Slinging Dope: The Role of Gangs and Gang Members in Drug Sales" *Justice Quarterly* 11 (1994): 583–604.

74. Finn-Aage Esbensen and David Huizinga, "Gangs, Drugs and Delinquency," *Criminology* 31 (1993): 565–590.

75. Fagan, "The Social Organization of Drug Use."

76. Ibid.

77. David G. Curry and Scott H. Decker, *Confronting Gangs: Crime and Community* (Los Angeles: Roxbury, 1998).

78. J. M. Hagedorn, *People and Folks* (Chicago: Lake View Press, 1989); Huff, *Gangs in America*.

79. W. K. Brown, "Graffiti, Identity, and the Delinquent Gang," *International Journal of Offender Therapy and Comparative Criminology* 22 (1978): 39–45.

80. Johnstone, "Youth Gangs and Black Suburbs."

81. Thrasher, *The Gang;* J. D. Moore and Vigil R. Garcia, "Residence and Territoriality in Chicano Gangs," *Social Problems* 31 (1983): 182–194; Ko-Lin Chin, Jeffrey Fagan, and Robert J. Kelly, "Patterns of Chinese Gang Extortion," *Justice Quarterly* 9 (1992): 625–646; Calvin Toy, "A Short History of Asian Gangs in San Francisco," *Justice Quarterly* 9 (1992): 645–665.

82. Mary G. Harris, *Cholas: Latino Girls in Gangs* (New York: AMS, 1988); James D. Vigil, *Barrio Gangs* (Austin: University of Texas Press, 1988).

83. A. Campbell, *Girls in the Gang: A Report From New York City* (Oxford, England: Basil Blackwell, 1984); Dolan and Finney, *Youth Gangs.*

84. J. F. Short and F. L. Strodbeck,. *Group Process and Gang Delinquency* (Chicago: University of Chicago Press, 1965).

85. Curry and Decker, *Confronting Gangs.*

86. Mydans, "Not Just the Inner City."

87. Esbensen and Huizinga, "Gangs, Drugs, and Delinquency"; Jeffrey Fagan, "Social Process of Delinquency and Drug Use Among Urban Gangs," in *Gangs in America*, ed. Ronald Huff (Newbury Park, CA: Sage, 1990); Anne Campbell, *The Girls in the Gang* 2d ed. (Cambridge, MA: Basil Blackwell, 1991).

88. Covey et al., *Juvenile Gangs.*

89. Ibid., p. 49.

90. Ibid., p. 52.

91. C. Ronald Huff, "Youth Gangs and Public Policy" *Crime and Delinquency* 35 (1989): 524–537; Campbell, *Girls in the Gang.*

92. Campbell, *Girls in the Gang.*

93. *Omaha World Herald* (September 18, 1997).

94. Ibid.

95. James D. Vigil and S. C. Yun, "Vietnamese Youth Gangs in Southern California," in *Gangs in America;* Chin et al., "Patterns of Chinese Gang Extortion"; Toy, "A Short History."

96. Covey et al., *Juvenile Gangs*, p. 67.

97. Ibid.

98. Chin et al., "Patterns of Chinese Gang Extortion"; Toy, "A Short History."

99. Chin et al., "Patterns of Chinese Gang Extortion."

100. K. Chin, "Chinese Gangs and Extortion," in *Gangs in America*.

101. Vigil and Yun, "Vietnamese Youth Gangs."

102. Covey et al., *Juvenile Gangs*.

103. Ibid.

104. Ibid., p. 65.

105. Mark S. Hamm, *American Skinheads* (Westport, CT: Praeger, 1994), p. 62.

106. I. A. Spergel, "Youth Gangs: Continuity and Change," in "Patterns of Chinese Gang Extortion" in *Crime and Delinquency: An Annual Review of Research, Vol 12* (Chicago: University of Chicago Press, 1990).

107. Covey et al., *Juvenile Gangs*.

108. Hamm, *American Skinheads*.

3

⚐

Race, Ethnicity, Social Structure, and Crime

In 1968 the Kerner Commission warned that "our Nation is moving toward two societies, one black, one white—separate and unequal."[1] Twenty-four years later, political scientist Andrew Hacker published a book on U.S. race relations entitled *Two Nations: Black and White, Separate, Hostile, Unequal.*[2] Hacker's subtitle says that the Kerner Commission's dire warning has come true: Instead of moving toward greater equality and opportunity, since the 1960s we have moved backward. In response to this perceived problem, President Bill Clinton established a special commission in 1997 to create a national dialogue on race relations.

GOALS OF THE CHAPTER

Race discrimination and social and economic inequality have a direct impact on crime and criminal justice, accounting for many of the racial disparities in the criminal justice system. The goals of this chapter are to examine the broader structure of American society with respect to race and ethnicity and to analyze the relationship between social structure and crime. As we learned in Chapter 2, racial and ethnic minorities are disproportionately involved in the criminal justice system, both as crime victims and offenders. In very general terms, there are two possible explanations for this overrepresentation. One is discrimination in the criminal justice system. We explore the data related to this issue in Chapters 4, 5, 6, and 7. The other explanation involves structural inequalities in American society. This chapter examines the relationship among race and ethnicity, the social structure, and crime.

We should first define what we mean by social structure. *Social structure* refers to any general social circumstance, such as religion or income level, that shapes peoples' lives. The analysis of social structure reveals patterned relationships between groups of people that form the basic contours of society. The patterned relationships are related to employment, income, residence, education, religion, gender, and race and ethnicity. In combination, these factors explain a person's circumstances in life, relationships with other groups, attitudes and behaviors on most issues, and prospects for the future.

This chapter explores three distinct issues related to the relationship among inequality, race and ethnicity, and crime:

1. *The extent of racial and ethnic inequality.* The first issue we examine is the nature and extent of inequality in American society with respect to the economic status of racial and ethnic minorities. What is the economic status of racial and ethnic minorities compared with whites? Is the gap between whites and minorities narrowing or growing?

2. *Inequality and crime.* The second issue is the relationship between inequality and crime. In what ways is inequality associated with crime? To what extent do the leading theories of crime help to explain the relationship between inequality and crime?

3. *The impact of the civil rights movement.* The third issue is the impact of efforts designed to reduce inequality. Have civil rights laws effectively eliminated discrimination in employment, housing, and other areas of U.S. life? If Hacker is right that the United States is "two nations: separate, hostile, [and] unequal," how do we explain the failure of the national effort to eliminate discrimination? At the same time, have various economic programs designed to increase economic opportunity—from the War on Poverty in the 1960s to Reaganomics in the 1980s—achieved their goals and reduced poverty? If not, how do we explain the persistence of economic inequality?

ECONOMIC INEQUALITY

The first important issue is the nature and extent of inequality in the United States. The data indicate three important patterns: (1) a large gap between rich and poor, without regard to race or ethnicity; (2) a large economic gap between white Americans and ethnic and racial minorities; and (3) the growth of the very poor—a group some analysts call an underclass—in the past twenty years. The standard measures of economic inequality are income, wealth, unemployment, and poverty status. All of these measures indicate deep

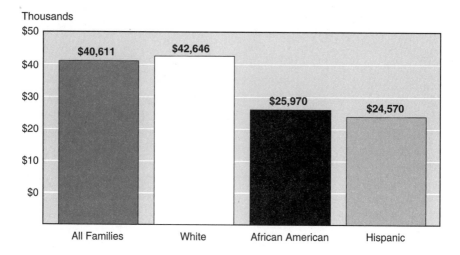

Thousands

FIGURE 3.1 Median Family Income, 1995

and persistent inequality both in society generally and with respect to race and ethnicity.

Income

In 1995 the median income for all families in the United States was $40,611. For white families the median income was $42,646, but it was only $25,970 for African American families and $24,570 for Hispanic families (see Figure 3.1). Thus, the median family income for African Americans is 61 percent of that for white Americans and for Hispanics it is 58 percent of that for white families.[3] African Americans made significant progress relative to whites in the 1950s and 1960s, but then stagnated in the 1970s. The National Research Council concluded, "Since the early 1970s, the economic status of blacks relative to whites has, on average, stagnated or deteriorated."[4]

The median family income figures mask significant differences *within* racial and ethnic groups. One of the most significant developments over the past forty years has been the growth of an African American middle class.[5] This is the result of two factors. First, the civil rights movement opened the door to employment for racial and ethnic minorities in many job categories from which they previously had been excluded, notably white-collar, service, and professional-level jobs. At the same time, the changing structure of the U.S. economy has been characterized by tremendous growth in the white-collar sector. An increasing number of African Americans and Hispanics have been able to take advantage of these new opportunities. At the same time, however, the percentage of African Americans among the very poor has also increased. Thus, among racial and ethnic minorities there is a greater gap between the middle class and the poorest now than at any other time in our history.

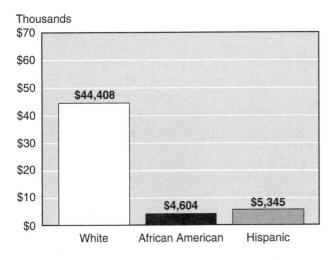

Thousands

FIGURE 3.2 Median Family Net Worth, 1991

Wealth

The data on family wealth reveal an even larger gap between whites and minorities. The distinction between income and wealth is important. *Income* measures how much a person or family earns in any given period. *Wealth,* on the other hand, measures all of their accumulated assets: home, cars, savings, stocks, and so forth. The family that owns a house, for example, has far more wealth than the family that rents. The 1991 median wealth of white families was $44,408, compared with only $4,604 for African Americans and $5,345 for Hispanics (see Figure 3.2).[6]

The reasons for the huge wealth gap are easy to understand. Middle-class people are able to save each month; the poor are not. These savings are used to buy a house, stocks, or other investments. The family's net wealth increases as the value of their home rises. Affluent whites, moreover, usually buy houses in neighborhoods where property values are rising rapidly. Lower-middle-class families, regardless of race, are often able to buy homes only in neighborhoods where property values are stagnant. As a result, their wealth does not increase very much. The poor, of course, are not able to save or invest anything, and they continually fall behind everyone else in terms of wealth.

Wealth plays an important role in perpetuating inequality. It cushions a family against temporary hard times, such as the loss of a job. The lower-middle-class person who is laid off, even temporarily, may lose his or her home; as a result, the family slides down the economic scale. Wealth is also transferred to the next generation. Families with savings can afford to send their children to private colleges and graduate or professional schools. They can also help their children buy their first home by giving or loaning them all or part of the down payment. Finally, when they die, their children inherit their estate in the form of cash, stock, or property. Poor and even many lower-middle-class families are not able to help their children in any of these ways.

Unemployment

In 1996, the official unemployment rate for the United States was 5.4 percent. Because of the booming economy in the 1990s, this was the lowest it had been since the early 1970s. It is worth noting that the crime rate in the late 1990s was the lowest it had been since the 1960s. The unemployment rate for whites in 1996 was 4.7 percent, compared with 10.5 for African Americans and 8.9 for Hispanic Americans. The African American unemployment rate has been consistently twice as high as the white rate for decades (and for some years in the 1980s the gap was even wider).[7] Thus, even though African Americans benefit from economic good times, they have not been able to overcome their relative disadvantage with respect to the unemployment rate.

The official data on unemployment tell only part of the story, however. First, there are serious problems with the official unemployment rate, just as there are problems with the official crime rate. The official unemployment rate counts only those people who are actively seeking employment. It does not count three important groups: (1) discouraged workers who have given up and are not looking for work; (2) part-time employees who want full-time jobs but cannot find them; and (3) workers in the "underground economy," who are paid in cash to avoid paying taxes and Social Security withholding. Many economists believe that racial minorities are disproportionately represented among those not counted by the official unemployment rate.[8]

Equally important, the official unemployment rate is much higher for teenagers than for older people. The unemployment rate for all Americans in 1996 was 5.4 percent, but it was 16.7 percent for people between the ages of sixteen and nineteen—and slightly higher for sixteen- to nineteen-year-old men (18.1 percent) than for women in that age group (15.2 percent). The unemployment rate for African American teenagers between the ages of sixteen and nineteen was 33.6 percent. Among Hispanics in that age group it was 23.6 percent.

The unemployment rate data reveal important differences within the Hispanic community related to national origins. In 1995, the unemployment rate for Puerto Rican Hispanic men was 11.4 percent, compared with 9.0 percent for Mexican-origin and only 7.6 percent for Cuban-origin Americans.[9]

As several of the theories of crime explain (see later), the teenage unemployment rate is particularly important in terms of crime. The peak years of criminal activity for index crimes are between the ages of fourteen and twenty-four. Official arrest data indicate that involvement in crime peaks at age eighteen for violent crimes and at age sixteen for property crimes. The lack of meaningful job opportunities for teenagers is an important factor in the high rates of crime. The persistently higher rates of unemployment for African

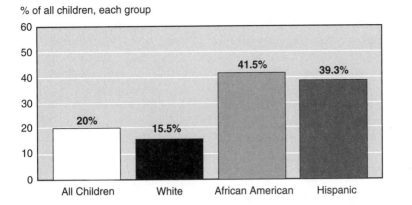

% of all children, each group

FIGURE 3.3 Percentage of Children Below the Poverty Line, 1995

American and Hispanic teenagers help explain their higher rates of criminal activity compared with whites.

Poverty Status

Yet another measure of economic status is the percentage of families in poverty. The federal government first developed an official definition of poverty in 1964 designed to reflect the minimum amount of income needed for an adequate standard of living. In 1995 the official poverty line was $7,763 for a single person and $15,569 for a family of four.[10] In 1995, 13.8 percent of all Americans were below the poverty line. The percentage has fluctuated over time, from 22.2 percent in 1960 to 11.4 percent in 1978. In 1995, 11.2 percent of all whites were below the poverty line, compared with 29.3 percent of African Americans and 30.3 percent of Hispanics.

The most disturbing aspect of the poverty figures is the percentage of children under the age of eighteen living below the poverty line (see Figure 3.3). In 1995, 41.5 percent of all African American children and 39.3 percent of all Hispanic children were living in poverty, compared with only 15.5 percent of white children.[11] Because childhood poverty status is associated with so many other social problems—inadequate nutrition, single-parent households, low educational achievement, high risk of crime victimization, high rate of involvement in crime—the data suggest a grim future for a very large percentage of racial and ethnic minority children.

Human and Social Capital

Sociologists and economists have been concerned about the transmission of inequality from one generation to the next.[12] This problem can be understood not just in economic terms, but with reference to noneconomic resources, referred to as human capital and social capital.

Human capital includes values, habits, and outlook, which in turn shape behavior. Sociologists and psychologists generally agree that the family is the primary unit for transmitting values to children. These values include self-respect, self-reliance, hard work, and respect for other people. If a family is dysfunctional, these values are not effectively transmitted to the children. The condition of poverty is generally associated with single-parent families, which are less able to transmit positive values.

Social capital includes associations and networks that are useful for individual achievement. With respect to employment, one important form of social capital is having family, friends, or neighbors who are able to offer jobs (e.g., in a small family business) or personal referral to someone who is able to offer a job. This process is often referred to as *networking,* and is generally recognized as extremely important in finding jobs and advancing careers. In extremely poor neighborhoods, however, there are few people with jobs to offer or with family or friends who can make good job references. Criminologist Elliot Currie illustrated the point by citing a comparative study of juvenile delinquents who graduated from the Lyman School in Massachusetts and the Wiltwyck School in New York in the 1950s. The predominantly white Lyman graduates often had personal connections who helped them find good employment. One graduate explained: "I fooled around a lot when I was a kid . . . . But then I got an uncle on the [police] force. When I was twenty he got me my first job as a traffic man."[13] The predominantly African American and Hispanic graduates of Wiltwyck did not have similar personal resources. As a result, they recidivated into criminal activity at a much higher rate.

In short, conditions of extreme poverty diminish the human and social capital that young people possess, and as a consequence these conditions contribute to higher rates of criminal activity.

Progress, Stagnation, or Regression?
The Debate over the Status of African America

In a comprehensive survey of U.S. race relations, the National Research Council concluded, "The status of black Americans today can be characterized as a glass that is half full." Despite considerable progress in race relations since the 1960s, there remain "persisting disparities between black and white Americans." Although civil rights laws and economic change have allowed "a substantial fraction of blacks to enter the mainstream of American life," the majority of African Americans have not achieved social or economic equality with whites.[14] Hispanics, Native Americans, and other racial and ethnic minorities experience similar inequalities in social and economic status.

Not everyone agrees with this pessimistic assessment, however. In *America in Black and White: One Nation Indivisible,* Stephan and Abigail Thernstrom argue that African Americans have made remarkable progress since the 1940s, economically, socially, and politically. "The signs of progress are all around us," they observed, "although we now take that progress for granted."[15] Using

Gunnar Myrdal's classic study of U.S. race relations, *An American Dilemma* (1944), as their baseline, they found that the percentage of African American families in poverty fell from 87 percent in 1940 to 26 percent in 1995. The number of African Americans enrolled in college increased thirty-fold in the same period, rising from 45,000 students in 1940 to 1.4 million in the late 1990s. Whereas 60 percent of employed African American women worked as domestics in 1940, today more than half are in white-collar jobs. The number of black elected officials rose from a national total of only 103 in 1960 to 8,406 by 1994. African Americans serve as mayors and police chiefs in major cities all across the country. Contrary to Hacker's pessimistic assessment that we are "two nations," the Thernstroms argued that we are today less separate, less un-equal, and in their view less hostile than was the case in 1940.[16]

Where does the truth lie? Is the United States progressing, stagnating, or regressing in terms of social and economic inequality? There is a degree of truth in all three interpretations, depending on which segment of the popula-tion we are talking about. We can make sense of this complex subject by tak-ing the approach we suggested in Chapter 1: disaggregating it into distinct components and contexts.

First, different time frames lead to different interpretations. The Thern-stroms' optimistic interpretation uses 1940 as a baseline. Few can question their data on racial progress since that time. After all, 1940 was still a time of institu-tionalized racial segregation in the South and blatant discrimination in other parts of the country. However, even the Thernstroms conceded that progress has stagnated in the past twenty years. Using 1973 as a baseline leads to a far more pessimistic interpretation.

Second, the aggregate status of African Americans encompasses two diver-gent trends: the generally rising status of a new middle class and the deterio-rating status of the very poor.[17] The same is true for other minorities. Some Hispanics are also doing very well, and are integrating into the mainstream of U.S. life. Others are trapped at the bottom of society, and in many respects they are doing much worse than before. Asian Americans are also divided into those who are doing well and those who are not.

This book is concerned with crime. From that perspective, the persistence of a very poor group at the bottom of society assumes special importance. Predatory crime has always been concentrated among the very poor. In 1994 the robbery victimization rate was 11.1 per one thousand for families with in-come under $7,500 but only 4.5 per one thousand for people with family in-comes of $7,500 or higher. The burglary victimization rate for the very poorest is also almost twice that of the very wealthiest.[18] The reasons for this are ex-plained later in this chapter in the discussion of the different theories of crime.

The real point of disagreement between those who take an optimistic view, such as the Thernstroms, and those who take a more pessimistic view, is the *cause* of the stagnation over the past twenty years. Many observers blame the changes in the economy, including the disappearance of industrial-level jobs, particularly from the inner city. The Thernstroms blamed affirmative action and racial preferences in particular, arguing that the greatest gains in racial equality were made during the years when the civil rights movement emphasized color-blind policies, and that stagnation set in during the 1970s when civil rights leaders emphasized racial preferences.

We would reply by arguing that the civil rights movement eliminated the most blatant forms of discrimination (e.g., disenfranchisement of African Americans in the South, law schools not admitting African Americans). It is not surprising that the elimination of these barriers would lead to some rapid progress, primarily by those who were equipped to take advantage of the new opportunities. The growth of political and civil rights, however, did not necessarily address *economic* inequality, particularly for those not yet prepared to take advantage of expanding opportunities. The Thernstroms point out that affirmative action programs have not really helped those at the very bottom. However, they are wrong in arguing that affirmative action is the cause of the plight of the very poor.

The Debate over the Underclass

Those observers who take the most pessimistic view often use the term *underclass* to describe the very poor who are concentrated in the inner cities.[19] The question of the existence of an underclass is more than a matter of semantics. It makes a great deal of difference whether *underclass* is merely another euphemism for poor people (e.g., "the poor," "the deprived," "the impoverished," "the disadvantaged," "the at-risk," etc.), implying that the economic status of people at the bottom has not changed in any fundamental way, or whether it describes the emergence of a new kind of poverty in America.[20]

From our perspective, the crucial point about the development of an underclass is that the conditions affecting the very poor have two important effects. First, they tend to perpetuate poverty. Second, they create conditions, such as family breakdown, that lead to higher involvement in crime.

Evidence suggests that the nature of urban poverty has changed in significant ways. First, the industrial sector of the economy has eroded, eliminating the entry-level jobs that were historically available to the poor. Second, conditions in the underclass generate circumstances and behavior that perpetuate poverty.[21] Gary Orfield and Carole Ashkinaze's study of economic conditions in Atlanta during the 1980s found growing inequality amidst overall growth and prosperity. The authors found that although most people in the Atlanta metropolitan area fared better economically, "the dream of equal opportunity is fading fast for many young blacks in metropolitan Atlanta." For the African American poor in the inner city, "Many of the basic elements of the American dream—a good job, a decent income, a house, college education for the kids—are less accessible . . . than was the case in the 1970s."[22] Most of the economic growth occurred in the largely white suburbs, while opportunities declined in the predominantly African American inner city. At the same time, most of the expanding opportunities occurred in the service sector of the economy: either in white-collar, professional-level jobs or in minimum-wage service (e.g., fast food) jobs. The poor cannot realistically compete for the professional-level jobs, and many of the service sector jobs do not pay enough to support a family. A minimum-wage job paying $5.15 per hour (the federally mandated level as of 1998) yields an annual income of $10,300 ($5.15 x forty hours/week x fifty weeks). This is substantially less than the official poverty line of $15,569 for a family of four.

Patterns of residential segregation contribute to the development of the urban underclass. Job growth over the past twenty years has been strongest in suburban areas outside the central cities. Inner-city residents, regardless of race or ethnicity, find it extremely difficult both to learn about job opportunities and to travel to and from work. Public transportation systems are either weak or nonexistent in most cities, particularly with respect to suburban areas. A private car is almost a necessity for traveling to work. Yet, one of the basic facts of poverty is the lack of sufficient money to buy a reliable car. Concentration of the very poor and their isolation from the rest of society erodes the social networks that are extremely important for finding employment. Studies of the job-seeking process have found that whites are more likely to be referred to jobs by friends or family who have some information about a job or connection with an employer. Racial and ethnic minorities are less likely to have such contacts. The problem is especially acute for members of the underclass, who are likely to have very few personal contacts that lead to good jobs.[23]

The pessimistic analysis of the changes in Atlanta in *The Closing Door* is fully compatible with the more optimistic aspects of the Thernstroms' analysis. Atlanta has a large and growing African American professional and middle class. These individuals and families live in the suburbs, as do their white counterparts. Their very real progress, however, coexists in the Atlanta metropolitan area with the very poor African Americans trapped in the inner city.

Crutchfield explains the economic situation in the inner city in terms of a *dual labor market*. What economists call the *primary* market consists of good, high-paying jobs, with fringe benefits (especially health care coverage) and good prospects for the future. The *secondary* market consists of low-paying jobs, with limited fringe benefits and uncertain prospects for the future. He argues that the secondary market "has an effect on individual propensity to engage in crime." Individuals are less "bonded" to their work (and, by extension, to society as a whole) and to the idea that hard work will lead to a brighter future. Additionally, the inner city involves concentrations of people in the secondary market, who then "spend time with each other, socialize with one another, and at times even victimize each other."[24]

The pattern of economic change that affected Atlanta, a growing city, had even more negative effects on declining industrial cities such as New York and Chicago. Economic expansion there was concentrated in the suburban areas, and the inner cities declined significantly. Such older industrial cities did not experience the same rate of growth in the suburbs, and the decline in industrial jobs was even more severe. The relationship of the underclass to crime becomes clearer when we look at it from the standpoint of neighborhood community social structure.

COMMUNITY SOCIAL STRUCTURE

The social structure of communities has an important impact on crime. *Community* in this respect refers to both large metropolitan communities and local neighborhoods. The social structure of a community involves the spatial distribution of the population, the composition of local neighborhoods, and patterns of interaction between and within neighborhoods.

Residential Segregation

American metropolitan communities are characterized by strong patterns of residential segregation. As already indicated, this has an impact on patterns of criminal activity. Residential segregation itself is nothing new. Historically, U.S. cities have always been segregated by race, ethnicity, and income. New arrivals to the city—either immigrants from other countries or migrants from rural areas—settled in the central city, with older immigrant groups and the middle class moving to neighborhoods farther out or to suburban communities. Racial and ethnic segregation in housing has been the result of several factors: the historic practice of *de jure* segregation, covert discrimination, and group choice. In the South and some Northern communities, local ordinances prohibited African Americans from living in white neighborhoods. Particularly in the North, many property owners adopted restrictive covenants that prohibited the sale of property to African Americans or Jews. Real estate agents maintained segregation by steering minority buyers away from white neighborhoods. Banks and savings and loan companies refused to offer mortgages in poor and minority neighborhoods, a practice known as "red-lining." Finally, segregation has been maintained by personal choice. People often prefer to live among members of their own group. Thus, European immigrants tended to form distinct ethnic neighborhoods, many of which still exist (e.g., Little Italy, Chinatown, etc.).

Despite federal and state laws outlawing housing discrimination, residential segregation persists today. Social scientists have devised an index of residential segregation that measures the proportion of neighborhoods in any city that are racially homogeneous. The data indicate that in the 1980s, 70 to 90 percent of the people in major cities lived in racially homogeneous neighborhoods. The residential segregation indexes for both Detroit and Chicago in 1980 were 88, meaning that 88 percent of all people lived in either all-white or all-African American neighborhoods. In practical terms, this means that for a white person living in Detroit, an estimated 93 percent of the "potential" contacts with other people will involve other whites. For African Americans, 80 percent of the potential contacts will involve other African Americans. In New York City and Los Angeles, the residential segregation indexes were 78 and 79, respectively.[25]

Residential Segregation and Crime   Residential segregation has a direct impact on crime. Most important, it concentrates high-rate offenders in one area, which has two important consequences. First, the law-abiding residents of those areas suffer high rates of robbery, burglary, and other predatory crimes.

The National Crime Victimization Survey consistently finds that both racial and ethnic minorities and poor people are victimized more than white and middle-class people.[26]

Second, the concentration of high-rate offenders in one area has an important effect on the propensity of individuals to engage in criminal activity. Several of the theories of crime discussed later place this phenomenon in a broader framework. Teenagers in those areas are subject to disproportionate contact with persons already involved in criminal activity. They have comparatively less contact with law-abiding peers. As Crutchfield points out, unemployed or marginally employed people in the secondary labor market "spend more time with each other," and as a result, they are more likely to influence each other in the direction of a greater propensity to commit crime.[27] Even in stable families, the sheer weight of this peer influence overwhelms positive parental influence. In the worst of situations, teenagers are coerced into joining crime-involved gangs. Thus, many individuals are socialized into crime when this would not be the case if they lived in a more diverse, lower crime neighborhood.

In one of the great ironies of recent history, some of the great gains of the civil rights movement have hurt the poorest racial minority communities. Since the 1960s the civil rights movement has opened up employment opportunities in business and the professions, creating a greatly expanded African American middle class. At the same time, the end of blatant residential segregation has created housing opportunities for families in the new African American middle class. Following the example of their white counterparts, these families move out of low-income, inner-city neighborhoods and into the suburbs.

The result is that the old neighborhoods abandoned by the African American middle class are stripped of important stabilizing elements—what Wilson referred to as a "social buffer."[28] The neighborhood loses its middle-class role models, who help socialize other children into middle-class values, and an important part of its natural leadership: the people who are active in neighborhood associations and local school issues. Skogan reported that educated, middle-class, home-owning residents are more likely to be involved in neighborhood organizations than are less educated, poorer, renting residents.[29] As we have already noted, the middle class is composed of people who can provide the social networks that lead to good jobs.

All of these factors contribute directly to neighborhood deterioration and indirectly to crime. As more of the people with better incomes move out, the overall economic level of the neighborhood declines. Houses often go from owner-occupied to rental property. As the area loses purchasing power, neighborhood stores lose business and close. Wilson and Kelling, two of the early theorists of community policing, argue that the physical deterioration of a neighborhood (abandoned buildings and cars, unrepaired houses, etc.) is a sign that people do not care and, consequently, is an "invitation" to criminal behavior.[30] As the composition of the neighborhood changes, meanwhile, an increasing number of crime-involved people move in, changing the context of peer pressure in the neighborhood.

Skogan describes the impact of fear of crime on neighborhood deterioration as a six-stage process, beginning with withdrawal. People choose to have less contact with other neighborhood residents; the ultimate form of with-drawal is to move away. This leads to a reduction in informal control over be-havior by residents: People no longer monitor and report on the behavior of, say, their neighbors' children. Then, organizational life declines: Fewer residents are active in community groups. These factors lead to an increase in delin-quency and disorder. As the neighborhood becomes poorer, commercial de-cline sets in. Local shops close and buildings are abandoned. The final stage of the process is collapse. At this point, according to Skogan, "there is virtually no 'community' remaining."[31]

The Impact of Crime and Drugs Crime has a devastating impact on neighborhoods, an impact that is intensified in very poor neighborhoods. First, it results in direct economic loss and physical harm to the crime victims. Sec-ond, the resulting high fear of crime damages the quality of life for everyone in the area. Third, persistent high rates of crime cause employed and law-abiding people to move out of the neighborhood, thereby intensifying the concentra-tion of the unemployed and high-rate offenders. Fourth, crime damages local businesses, in the form of both direct losses and inability to obtain insurance. Eventually, many of these businesses move or close, with the result that the immediate neighborhood loses jobs. Those businesses that stay frequently charge higher prices to make up for their losses.

The drug problem has hit poor neighborhoods with particularly devastat-ing effects, particularly with the advent of crack cocaine in the mid-1980s. Drug trafficking fostered the growth of gangs and led to an increase in gang-related violence, including drive-by shootings that sometimes kill innocent per-sons. Moreover, crack cocaine appears to be more damaging to family life than other drugs. Mothers addicted to crack seem more likely to lose their sense of parental responsibility. The phenomenon of pregnant women becoming ad-dicted to crack has resulted in the serious problem of crack-addicted babies.[32]

In some drug-ridden neighborhoods, the drug trade is the central feature of neighborhood life. Entire blocks have become "drug bazaars," with open drug sales. The drug trade is often a highly organized and complex activity, with people watching for the police, negotiating the sale, obtaining the drugs, and holding the main supply. The buyers are frequently outsiders, and the drug market represents what economists call *economic specialization,* with one part of society providing services to the rest of society.[33] Police departments have experimented with drug enforcement crackdowns (short-term periods of intensive arrest activity), but there is no evidence that this strategy has any long-term effect on reducing the drug trade (see Chapter 4).[34]

When drug and gang activity begins to dominate a neighborhood, it be-comes virtually impossible for law-abiding residents to shield themselves and their children from illegal activity. The peer pressure on juveniles to join gangs becomes extremely intense. Often, kids join gangs for their own protection. Because of drive-by shootings and other gang-related violence, the streets are even less safe than before. This is the stage that Skogan described as neighbor-hood "collapse."[35]

THEORETICAL PERSPECTIVES ON
INEQUALITY AND CRIME

The second important issue addressed in this chapter is the relationship between inequality and crime. We have established that significant economic inequality prevails between the white majority and racial and ethnic minorities. To what extent does this inequality contribute to the racial and ethnic disparities in crime and criminal justice? To help answer this question, we turn to the major theories of criminal behavior. In different ways, each one posits a relationship between inequality and crime that helps explain the disparities within crime and criminal justice.

Social Strain Theory

Robert Merton's social strain theory holds that each society has a dominant set of values and goals along with acceptable means of achieving them. Not everyone is able to realize these goals, however. The gap between approved goals and the means people have to achieve them creates what Merton termed *social strain.*[36]

As Steven F. Messner and Richard Rosenfeld argues in *Crime and the American Dream,* the dominant goals and values in American society emphasize success through individual achievement.[37] Success is primarily measured in terms of material goods, social status, and recognition for personal expression (e.g., artistic, athletic). The indicators of material success include a person's job, income, place of residence, clothing, cars, and other consumer goods. The accepted means of achieving these goals are also highly individualistic, emphasizing hard work, self-control, persistence, and education. The American work ethic holds that anyone can succeed if only he or she will work hard enough and keep trying long enough. Failure is regarded as a personal, not a social, failure. Yet, as we have seen, many people in the United States do not enjoy success in these terms: Unemployment rates remain high, millions of people are living in poverty, and minorities are the victims of racial and ethnic discrimination.

Merton's theory of social strain holds that people respond to the gap between society's values and their own circumstances in several different ways: rebellion, retreatism, and innovation. Some of these involve criminal activity. *Rebellion* involves a rejection of both society's goals and the established means of achieving them, along with an attempt to create a new society based on different values and goals. This stage includes revolutionary political activity, which in some instances might be politically related criminal activity such as terrorism.

Retreatism entails a rejection of both the goals and the accepted means of achieving them. A person may retreat, for example, into drug abuse, alcoholism, vagrancy, or a countercultural lifestyle. Retreatism helps explain the high rates of drug and alcohol abuse in the United States. Many forms of drug abuse, meanwhile, involve criminal behavior: the buying and selling of drugs, robbery or burglary as a means of obtaining money to purchase drugs, or involvement in a drug trafficking network that includes violent crime directed against rival drug dealers. There is considerable debate among criminologists over the relationship between drugs and crime.[38] There is no clear evidence that drug abuse causes crime directly. Studies of crime and drugs have found mixed patterns: Some individuals began their criminal activity before they started using drugs, whereas for others, drug use preceded involvement in crime. Moreover, some individuals "specialize" and either use (and/or sell) drugs but engage in no other criminal activity, or they commit crimes but do not use illegal drugs.[39]

Innovation involves an acceptance of society's goals but a rejection of the accepted means of attaining them. Crime is one mode of innovation. The person who embezzles money seeks material success but chooses an illegitimate (criminal) means of achieving it. The drug dealer or the pimp is basically an innovative business entrepreneur whose line of work happens to be illegal. The person who steals to obtain money or things is seeking the external evidence of material success through illegal means.

Applying the Theory Social strain theory helps explain the high rates of delinquency and criminal behavior among racial and ethnic minorities in the United States. Criminal activity will be higher among those groups that are denied the opportunity to fulfill the American dream of individual achievement. The theory also explains far higher rates of retreatist (e.g., drug abuse) and innovative (e.g., criminal activity) responses. The high levels of economic inequality experienced by minorities, together with continuing discrimination based on race and ethnicity, mean that minorities are far less likely to be able to achieve approved social goals through conventional means.

Differential Association Theory

Edwin Sutherland's theory of differential association holds that criminal behavior is learned behavior. The more contact a person has with people who are already involved in crime, the more likely that person is to engage in criminal activity.[40]

Applying the Theory Given the structure of American communities, differential association theory has direct relevance to the disproportionate involvement of racial and ethnic minorities in the criminal justice system. Because of residential segregation based on income and race, a person who is poor and/or a racial or ethnic minority is more likely to have personal contact with people who are already involved in crime. The concentration of persons involved in crime in underclass neighborhoods produces enormous peer pressure to become involved in crime. In neighborhoods where gangs are prevalent, young people often experience tremendous pressure to join a gang simply as a means of personal protection. In schools where drug use is prevalent, juveniles will have more contact with drug users and a greater likelihood of being socialized into drug use themselves. As noted earlier, Crutchfield argues that the secondary labor market brings together high concentrations of people with a weak attachment to their work and the future, who then socialize with each other and influence their propensity to commit crime.[41] Most parents have a basic understanding of differential association theory: They warn their children to avoid the "bad" kids in the neighborhood and encourage them to associate with the "good" kids.

Social Disorganization Theory

Followers of the so-called Chicago school of thought developed the social disorganization theory of crime.[42] Focusing on poor inner-city neighborhoods, this theory holds that the conditions of poverty undermine the institutions that socialize people into conventional, law-abiding ways of life. As a result, the values and behavior leading to delinquency and crime are passed on from one generation to another. The Chicago sociologists found that recent immigrants tended to have lower rates of criminality than the first American-born generation. They argued that immigrants were able to preserve old-world family structures that promoted stability and conventional behavior. These older values broke down in the new urban environment, however, leading to higher rates of criminality among the next generation. The Chicago sociologists noted the spatial organization of the larger metropolitan areas, with higher rates of criminal behavior in the poorer inner-city neighborhoods and lower rates in areas farther out.

The conditions of poverty contribute to social disorganization and criminality in several ways. Poverty and unemployment undermine the family, the primary unit of socialization, which leads to high rates of single-parent families. Lack of parental supervision and positive role models contributes to crime and delinquency. The concentration of the poor in certain neighborhoods means that individuals are subject to strong peer influence tending toward nonconforming behavior. Poverty is also associated with inadequate prenatal care and malnutrition, which contribute to developmental and health problems, in turn leading to poor performance in schools.

Applying the Theory   Social disorganization theory helps explain the high rates of crime and delinquency among racial and ethnic minorities. As our discussion of inequality suggests, minorities experience high rates of poverty and are geographically concentrated in areas with high rates of social disorganization.

Social disorganization theory is consistent with other theories of crime. It is consistent with social strain theory in that persons who are subject to conditions of social disorganization are far less likely to be able to achieve the dominant goals of society through conventional means and, therefore, are more likely to turn to crime. It is consistent with differential association theory in that neighborhoods with high levels of social disorganization will subject individuals, particularly young men, to strong influences tending toward delinquency and crime.

Culture Conflict Theory

Culture conflict theory holds that crime will be more likely to flourish in heterogeneous societies in which there is a lack of consensus over society's values.[43] Human behavior is shaped by norms that are instilled through socialization and embodied in the criminal law. In any society, the majority not only defines social norms, but also controls the making and the administration of the criminal law. In some instances, certain groups do not accept the dominant social values. They may reject them on religious or cultural grounds or feel alienated from the majority because of discrimination or economic inequality. Conflict over social norms and the role of the criminal law leads to certain types of law breaking.

One example of religiously based culture conflict involves peyote, a cactus that has mild hallucinogenic effects when smoked. Some Native American religions use peyote as part of their traditional religious exercises.[44] Today, many observers see national politics revolving around a "culture war" involving such issues as abortion, homosexuality, and religion in the public schools.[45] Some groups believe that abortion is murder and should be criminalized; others argue that it is a medical procedure that should be governed by the individual's private choice.

Applying the Theory Culture conflict theory helps explain some of the differential rates of involvement in U.S. society, which is extremely heterogeneous, characterized by many different races, ethnic groups, religions, and cultural lifestyles. The theory encompasses the history of racial conflict—from the time of slavery, through the Civil War, to the modern civil rights movement—as one of the major themes in U.S. history. There is also a long history of ethnic and religious conflict. Americans of white, Protestant, and English background, for instance, exhibited strong prejudice against immigrants from Ireland and southern and eastern Europe, particularly Catholics and Jews.[46]

An excellent example of cultural conflict in U.S. history is the long struggle over the consumption of alcohol that culminated in national Prohibition (1920–1933). The fight over alcohol was a bitter issue for nearly one hundred years before Prohibition. To a great extent, the struggle was rooted in ethnic and religious differences. Protestant Americans tended to take a very moralistic attitude toward alcohol, viewing abstinence as a sign of self-control and a means of rising to middle-class status. For many Catholic immigrant groups, particularly the Irish and Germans, alcohol consumption was an accepted part of their cultural lifestyle. The long crusade to control alcohol use represented an attempt by middle-class Protestants to impose their lifestyle on working-class Catholics.[47]

Conflict Theory

Conflict theory holds that the administration of criminal justice reflects the unequal distribution of power in society.[48] The more powerful groups use the criminal justice system to maintain their dominant position and to repress groups or social movements that threaten it.[49] As Hawkins argued, conflict theory was developed primarily with reference to social class, with relatively little attention to race and ethnicity.[50]

The most obvious example of conflict theory in action was the Segregation Era in the South (1890s–1960s) when white supremacists instituted *de jure* segregation in public schools and other public accommodations.[51] The criminal justice system was used to maintain the subordinate status of African Americans. Because African Americans were disenfranchised as voters, they had no control or influence over the justice system. As a result, crimes by whites against African Americans went unpunished, and crimes by African Americans against whites—including alleged or even completely fabricated offenses—were treated very harshly.[52] Meanwhile, outside of the South, discrimination also limited the influence of minorities over the justice system.

The civil rights movement eliminated *de jure* segregation and other blatant forms of discrimination, but pervasive discrimination in society and the criminal justice system continues.

Applying the Theory Conflict theory explains the overrepresentation of racial and ethnic minorities in the criminal justice system in several ways. The criminal law singles out certain behavior engaged in primarily by the poor. Vagrancy laws are the classic example of the use of the criminal law to control the poor and other perceived "threats" to the social order. Criminal law has also been used against political movements challenging the established order: from sedition laws against unpopular ideas to disorderly conduct arrests of demonstrators. Finally, "street crimes" that are predominantly committed by the poor and disproportionately by racial and ethnic minorities are the target of more vigorous enforcement efforts than are those crimes committed by the rich. The term *crime* refers more to robbery and burglary than to white-collar crime. In these ways, conflict theory explains the overrepresentation of racial and ethnic minorities among people arrested, convicted, and imprisoned.

Routine Activity Theory

Routine activity theory shifts the focus of attention from offenders to criminal incidents. Felson explained that the theory examines "how these incidents originate in the routine activities of everyday life."[53] Particularly important, the theory emphasizes the extent to which the daily routine creates informal social control that helps to prevent crime, or undermines those informal controls and leads to higher involvement in crime. (Informal social control includes, for example, the watchfulness of family, friends, and neighbors. Formal social control is exercised by the police and the rest of the criminal justice system.) Felson offered the example of parental supervision of teenagers. He cited data indicating that between 1940 and the 1970s, American juveniles spent an increasing amount of time away from the home with no direct parental supervision.[54] These changes are rooted in the changing nature of work and family life in contemporary society (as opposed to some kind of moral failing). These circumstances increase the probability that young people will engage in crime. To cite an earlier example, in the 1920s many people were alarmed that the advent of the automobile created the opportunity for young men and women to be alone together without direct parental supervision, with a resulting increase in premarital sexual behavior.

Applying the Theory Routine activity theory is particularly useful in explaining crime when it is integrated with other theories. If parental supervision represents an important informal social control, then family breakdown and one-parent households will involve less supervision and increase the probability of involvement in crime. High rates of teenage unemployment will mean that more young people will have free time on their hands, and if unemployment is high in the neighborhood, they will have more association with other unemployed young people, including some who are already involved in crime.

The Limits of Current Theories

All the theories discussed here attempt to explain the relationship among race, ethnicity, and crime in terms of social conditions. Hawkins argues that this approach represents the liberal political orientation that has dominated American sociology and criminology through most of this century.[55] He also believes that there are important limitations to this orientation. The liberal emphasis on social conditions arose out of a reaction to racist theories of biological determinism, which sought to explain high rates of crime among recent European immigrants and African Americans in terms of genetic inferiority. Herrnstein and Murray's controversial book, *The Bell Curve,* represents a recent version of this approach. The liberal emphasis on social conditions, however, tends to become a form of social determinism, as criminologists focus on the social pathologies of both minority communities and lower class communities. Although consciously avoiding biologically based stereotypes, much of the research on social conditions has the unintended effect of perpetuating a different set of stereotypes about racial and ethnic minorities.

Hawkins suggests that if we seek a comprehensive explanation of the relationship among race, ethnicity, and crime, the most promising approach will be to combine the best insights from liberal criminology regarding social conditions, and conflict perspectives regarding both the administration of justice and intergroup relations.[56]

INEQUALITY AND SOCIAL REFORM

The most disturbing aspect of social inequality in the United States has been its persistence over thirty years despite a national effort to reduce or eliminate it. Peterson referred to this as the "poverty paradox": not just the persistence of poverty in the richest country in the world, but its persistence in the face of a major attack on it.[57] The civil rights movement fought to eliminate racial discrimination, and several different government policies sought to create economic opportunity and eliminate poverty. In the 1960s, liberals adopted the War on Poverty and other Great Society programs. In the 1980s, conservative economic programs of reducing taxes and government spending sought to stimulate economic growth and create job opportunities.

Not only has inequality persisted, but as Hacker, Orfield, and Ashkinaze argued, the gap between rich and poor and between whites and minorities has gotten worse in many respects. What happened? Did all the social and economic policies of the past generation completely fail? There are four major explanations for the persistence of inequality, poverty, and the growth of the underclass.[58] Many liberals argue that it is the result of an inadequate welfare state. Social welfare programs in the United States are not nearly as comprehensive as those in other industrialized countries, lacking guaranteed health care, paid family leaves, and comprehensive unemployment insurance. Other liberals argue that it is the result of the transformation of the national (and international) economy that has eliminated economic opportunities in the inner city and reduced earnings of many blue-collar jobs. Many conservatives argue that the persistence of poverty is the result of a "culture of poverty" that encourages attitudes and behavior patterns that keep people from rising out of poverty. Closely related to this view is the conservative argument that many government social and economic programs provide disincentives to work. These conservatives believe, for example, that the welfare system encourages people not to work and that the minimum wage causes employers to eliminate rather than create jobs.

Prominent African American social critic Cornell West argued that the traditional liberal–conservative debate on the relative importance of social structure versus individual character is unproductive. He pointed out that "structures and behavior are inseparable, that institutions and values go hand in hand."[59] In short, the problem of the persistence of inequality is extremely complex. The next sections examine some of the major forces that have reshaped American life in the past generation and their impact on inequality.

The Impact of the Civil Rights Movement

The civil rights movement of the post–World War II years has been one of the most important events in U.S. history. The years between 1954 and 1965 witnessed nothing less than a revolution in U.S. law, establishing equality as national policy.[60]

The legal assault on segregation, led by the National Association for the Advancement of Colored People, reached its apex in the landmark 1954 case of *Brown v. Board of Education*. The U.S. Supreme Court declared segregated public schools unconstitutional under the Fourteenth Amendment and invalidated the underlying doctrine of "separate but equal." Other cases invalidated other forms of race discrimination.[61] In 1967, for example, the Court declared unconstitutional a Virginia law barring interracial marriage.[62]

Legislation also attacked discrimination. The 1964 Civil Rights Act outlawed racial discrimination in employment, housing, public accommodations, and other areas of American life. In 1965, Congress passed the Voting Rights Act to eliminate racial discrimination in voting. President Lyndon Johnson issued Executive Order 11246 directing federal agencies to adopt affirmative action policies. Many states and municipalities, meanwhile, enacted their own civil rights statutes.

Some particularly important federal civil rights laws are as follows:

1964   Civil Rights Act

1965   Voting Rights Act

1972   Equal Opportunity Act

1990   Americans With Disabilities Act

Impact on American Society The civil rights revolution had a profound impact on the U.S. social structure. By outlawing overt or *de jure* racial discrimination, it "opened" society to a degree unprecedented in U.S. history. Second, it had a profound effect on the operations of every social institution, including the criminal justice system.

The most important changes occurred in the states of the South. The integration of the public schools between 1966 and 1973 was dramatic. In 1966, 80 percent of all minority students attended a school in which 90 percent or more of the students were also minorities. By 1973 the figure was only 25 percent. Public schools in the South went from being the most segregated to the most integrated in the entire country. At the same time, however, schools in the Northeast became more segregated between the 1960s and 1980s.[63]

The impact of the civil rights movement is also evident in electoral politics. African American voter registration and voter participation, as well as the election of African American officials, have dramatically increased. The change has been most profound in the South, where systematic disenfranchisement existed until the 1960s. In 1940, only 3.1 percent of voting-age African Americans were registered; it rose to 28.7 percent in 1960 and 66.9 percent in 1970.[64] The increase between 1960 and 1970 was clearly the result of the 1965 Voting Rights Act.

As a result of greater voter participation, the number of African American elected officials increased dramatically, from 33 nationwide in 1941 to 280 in 1965 and 7,984 in 1993. The number of African American members of the House of Representatives rose from one in 1940 to four in 1965, twenty in 1985, and thirty-eight in 1993. The total number of Hispanic elected officials rose from 3,174 in 1985 to 5,459 in 1994. The number of Hispanic members of the House rose from two in 1941 to seventeen in 1993.[65] Senator Carol Mosley Braun of Illinois, elected in 1992, became the first African American woman in the Senate. The number of African American judges increased from just 10 in 1941 to 58 in 1961 and 841 in 1986.[66]

By 1993, 751 African American officials were elected in Mississippi, including 8 elected sheriffs and 25 mayors. Throughout the South, the Voting Rights

Act has helped elect minorities to positions as county commissioners, school board members, sheriffs, and other important positions.[67] In Northern cities, African American mayors are common. In 1967, Carl Stokes was the first African American to be elected mayor of a major U.S. city in Cleveland. African Americans are serving or have recently served as mayors of New York, Chicago, Los Angeles, Philadelphia, Atlanta, New Orleans, Seattle, and many other cities.

The Civil Rights Movement and the Criminal Justice System The civil rights movement also transformed the criminal justice system. Again, the greatest changes occurred in the South. Under the old system of institutionalized segregation, the entire criminal justice system was an instrument for maintaining the subordination of African Americans. Disenfranchised as voters, African Americans did not serve on juries and had no voice in the election and appointment of officials who ran the criminal justice system.[68]

As a result, there were no African American police officers in the South, and in the border states, the few African American officers who were hired were confined to policing the black community and were not allowed to arrest whites, no matter what their offense. Nor were there any black sheriffs, prosecutors, judges, or correctional officials.

By the late 1970s, the South had become "integrated" into the national social structure. The distinctive racial caste system had been abolished, and the problems facing Southern criminal justice agencies were essentially the same as those facing agencies in the North and West. That is to say, problems persist with respect to police–community relations, but the situation in Atlanta or New Orleans is not fundamentally different from the situation in Boston or Seattle.[69] There is evidence of racial discrimination in criminal sentencing, but this problem has been found in states from all regions of the country.

The civil rights movement also had a profound effect on the criminal justice system outside the South. Racial discrimination was identified as a major problem in the justice system, and various reforms were undertaken to eliminate it. Police departments adopted police–community relations programs to improve relations with minority communities. The Supreme Court declared unconstitutional the practice of prosecutors or defense attorneys using peremptory challenges to exclude jurors because of race.[70] Racially segregated prisons were declared unconstitutional.[71] African Americans and Hispanics, meanwhile, experienced increased employment in justice agencies and they assumed positions of leadership in a number of instances. The percentage of all sworn police officers in city police departments who are African American increased from 3.6 percent in 1960 to 10 percent in 1993. Hispanics represented 4.1 percent of all municipal sworn officers in 1988 and 7 percent in 1993.[72]

The Attack on Economic Inequality

The economic policies of both liberal Democratic and conservative Republican presidents since the 1960s have attempted to stimulate the economy, create jobs, and eliminate poverty. The major liberal Democratic effort was the

War on Poverty, begun in 1965 with the Economic Opportunity Act. The federal attack on poverty and inequality also included major programs related to health care, education, Social Security, food stamps, and other forms of government assistance. The major conservative Republican effort in the 1980s involved "Reaganomics" or "supply-side economics," which sought to stimulate the economy by lowering taxes and government spending. Conservatives also sought to reduce or eliminate many government assistance programs, arguing that they created disincentives to work.

The impact of these different measures is a matter of great controversy. Conservatives argue that the War on Poverty and other liberal policies of the 1960s not only failed to eliminate poverty but actually made things worse by impeding economic growth and removing the incentives for poor people to seek employment.[73] Liberals, meanwhile, argue that Reaganomics increased the gap between rich and poor, benefitting the wealthy and eliminating programs for the poor.

The data suggest that neither the economic policies of the liberals nor those of the conservatives have eliminated the structural inequalities in American society. As we have already suggested, the long-term trends have had contradictory effects. Some people have been able to take advantage of the new economic opportunities, whereas others have become even more deeply trapped in poverty—with the creation of a new underclass.

These trends have affected racial and ethnic minorities as well as whites. As Thernstrom and Thernstrom argued, many African Americans have been able to move into the middle class as a result of the elimination of job discrimination and the expansion of white-collar job opportunities.[74] These individuals are much better off than were their parents. For example, 75 percent of employed African American men in 1940 were either farm laborers or factory machine operators; 68 percent of the employed African American women were either domestic servants or farm laborers. By 1982, 20 percent of all employed African American men were in professional or managerial occupations, compared with only 6 percent in 1950.[75] Many Hispanic Americans have experienced similar social and economic progress.

Other members of minority communities, however, have been hit hard by the shrinking opportunities and are worse off than their parents were, or even worse off than they themselves were fifteen or twenty years earlier. These are the people who are trapped in the underclass. The National Research Council found a noticeable "contrast between blacks who have achieved middle-class status and those who have not."[76] As we discussed earlier, the conditions of poverty inhibit the transmission of human and social capital from one generation to another, thereby perpetuating poverty across generations.

The complex changes in the economy over the past three decades have directly impacted the racial and ethnic dimensions of crime and criminal justice. The persistence of severe inequality and the growth of the underclass have created conditions conducive to high rates of crime. The different theories of crime we discussed earlier—social strain theory, differential association theory, social disorganization theory, culture conflict theory, conflict theory, and routine activity theory—all would predict high rates of crime, given the changes in the economy that have occurred. And because racial and ethnic minorities have been disadvantaged by these economic trends, these theories of crime help explain the persistently high rates of crime among minorities.

It is important to note that the economic trends have coincided with the increased opportunities for minorities over the same period of time—at least for those able to take advantage of them. As we have already stated, some minorities have been able to move into the middle class. At the same time, the civil rights movement has resulted in greater political empowerment among minorities, as measured by voter participation, election of public officials, and employment in the criminal justice system.

Political empowerment by itself, however, is not sufficient to reduce criminal behavior. African Americans were elected mayor in Cleveland, Detroit, Newark, Atlanta, Washington, D.C., and other cities at exactly the time when these cities faced the financial crisis resulting from the transformation of the economy. The financial crisis consisted of two parts: The tax base eroded as factories closed and middle-class people moved to the suburbs; at the same time, there were increased demands for public services in terms of welfare, police protection, and so forth.

In short, the civil rights movement has had a mixed effect on the inequalities in U.S. social structure. It has opened the doors of opportunity for some racial and ethnic minorities. Often forgotten, these accomplishments are very substantial. The achievements of the civil rights movement, however, have not addressed the worsening economic conditions of the urban underclass.

CONCLUSION

The U.S. social structure plays a major role in shaping the relationship among race, ethnicity, and crime. American society is characterized by deep inequalities related to race, ethnicity, and economics. There is persistent poverty, and minorities are disproportionately represented among the poor. In addition, economic changes have created a new phenomenon known as the urban underclass.

The major theories of crime explain the relationship between inequality and criminal behavior. In different ways, strain theory, differential association, social disorganization, culture conflict, conflict, and routine activity theories all predict higher rates of criminal behavior among the poor and racial and ethnic minorities.

DISCUSSION QUESTIONS

1. Do you agree with the Kerner Commission's conclusion that we are moving toward two societies, one black and one white? Explain your answer.

2. Explain how residential discrimination contributes to crime.

3. What is meant by the concepts of human and social capital? How do they affect criminal behavior?

4. What has been the impact of the civil rights movement on crime and criminal justice?

5. Which theory of crime do you think best explains the prevalence of crime in the U.S.?

NOTES

1. Kerner Commission, *Report of the National Advisory Commission on Civil Disorders* (New York: Bantam, 1968), p. 1.

2. Andrew Hacker, *Two Nations: Black and White, Separate, Hostile, Unequal* (New York: Scribner's, 1992).

3. Bureau of the Census, *Statistical Abstract of the United States, 1997* (Washington, D.C.: U.S. Government Printing Office, 1997), Table 724, p. 469.

4. Gerald David Jaynes and Robin Williams, Jr., eds., *A Common Destiny: Blacks and American Society* (Washington, D.C.: National Academy Press, 1989), p. 6.

5. Stephan Thernstrom and Abigail Thernstrom, *America in Black and White: One Nation, Indivisible* (New York: Simon & Schuster, 1997).

6. Bureau of the Census, *Statistical Abstract 1994* (Washington, D.C.: U.S. Government Printing Office, 1994), Table 742, p. 482; Jaynes and Williams, *A Common Destiny,* pp. 291–294.

7. Bureau of the Census, *Statistical Abstract 1994,* Table 621, p. 398.

8. Hacker, *Two Nations,* p. 105.

9. Bureau of the Census, *Statistical Abstract of the United States, 1997,* Table 627, p. 402.

10. Ibid., Table 738, p. 476.

11. Ibid., Table 739, p. 476.

12. Toby L. Parcel and Elizabeth G. Menaghan, *Parents' Jobs and Childrens' Lives* (New York: Aldine deGruyter, 1994), p. 1.

13. Elliott Currie, *Confronting Crime* (New York: Pantheon, 1985), p. 243. The original study is William McCord and Jose Sanchez, "The Treatment of Deviant Children: A Twenty-Five Year Follow-Up

Study," *Crime and Delinquency* 29 (March 1983): 239–251.

14. Jaynes and Williams, *A Common Destiny,* p. 4.

15. Thernstrom and Thernstrom, *America in Black and White,* p. 17.

16. Ibid., p. 534.

17. Ibid., Chap. 7, "The Rise of the Black Middle Class," pp. 183–202.

18. Bureau of Justice Statistics, *Criminal Victimization in the United States, 1994* (Washington, D.C.: U.S. Government Printing Office, 1997), pp. 19, 23.

19. William Julius Wilson, *The Truly Disadvantaged* (Chicago: University of Chicago Press, 1987); Christopher Jencks and Paul E. Peterson, eds., *The Urban Underclass* (Washington, D.C.: Brookings Institution, 1991); William Julius Wilson, ed., *The Ghetto Underclass* (Newbury Park, CA: Sage, 1993).

20. Hacker, *Two Nations,* p. 52.

21. Hacker, *Two Nations;* Andrew J. Winnick, *Toward Two Societies: The Changing Distributions of Income and Wealth in the U.S. Since 1960* (New York: Praeger, 1989); Gary Orfield and Carole Ashkinaze, *The Closing Door: Conservative Policy and Black Opportunity* (Chicago: University of Chicago Press, 1991).

22. Orfield and Ashkinaze, *The Closing Door,* p. xiii.

23. Jaynes and Williams, *A Common Destiny,* p. 321.

24. Robert D. Crutchfield, "Ethnicity, Labor Markets, and Crime," in *Ethnicity, Race, and Crime,* ed. D. F. Hawkins (Albany: State University Press of New York, 1995), p. 196.

25. Jaynes and Williams, *A Common Destiny,* pp. 78–79.

26. Bureau of Justice Statistics, *Criminal Victimization in the United States, 1994.*

27. Crutchfield, "Ethnicity, Labor Markets, and Crime," p. 196.

28. Wilson, *The Truly Disadvantaged,* pp. 137, 144. See also Bill E. Lawson, "Uplifting the Race: Middle-Class Blacks and the Truly Disadvantaged," in *The Underclass Question,* ed. Bill E. Lawson (Philadelphia: Temple University Press, 1992), pp. 90–113.

29. Wesley G. Skogan, *Disorder and Decline* (New York: Free Press, 1990), pp. 132–133.

30. James Q. Wilson and George Kelling, "Broken Windows: The Police and Neighborhood Safety," *Atlantic Monthly* 249 (March 1982): 29–38.

31. Wesley Skogan, "Fear of Crime and Neighborhood Change," in *Communities and Crime,* ed. A. Reiss and M. Tonry (Chicago: University of Chicago Press, 1986), pp. 215–220.

32. The problem has been exaggerated in much of the news media coverage but is a serious problem nonetheless. See Dale Gieringer, "How Many Crack Babies?" in *Drug Prohibition and the Conscience of Nations,* ed. Arnold Trebach and Kevin B. Zeese (Washington, D.C.: Drug Policy Foundation, 1990), pp. 71–75.

33. Peter Reuter, Robert MacCoun, and Patrick Murphy, *Money From Crime: A Study of the Economics of Drug Dealing in Washington, D.C.* (Santa Monica, CA: Rand, 1990).

34. Lawrence W. Sherman, "Police Crackdowns," in *Crime and Justice: An Annual Review of Research,* Vol. 12, ed. Michael Tonry and Norval Morris (Chicago: University of Chicago Press, 1990).

35. Skogan, "Fear of Crime," p. 220.

36. Robert K. Merton, *Social Theory and Social Structure* (New York: Free Press, 1957).

37. Steven F. Messner and Richard Rosenfeld, *Crime and the American Dream,* 2d ed. (Belmont, CA: Wadsworth, 1997).

38. Michael Tonry and James Q. Wilson, eds., *Drugs and Crime, Crime and Justice: A Review of Research,* Vol. 13 (Chicago: University of Chicago Press, 1990).

39. David N. Nurco et al., "The Drugs–Crime Connection," in *Handbook of Drug Control in the United States,* ed. James A. Inciardi (New York: Greenwood, 1990), pp. 71–90.

40. Edwin H. Sutherland, *Principles of Criminology,* 3d ed. (Philadelphia: Lippincott, 1939).

41. Crutchfield, "Ethnicity, Labor Markets, and Crime," p. 196.

42. W. I. Thomas and Florian Znaniecki, *The Polish Peasant in Europe and America* (Boston: Gorham, 1920); Clifford R. Shaw, Frederick M. Forbaugh, and Henry D. McKay, *Delinquency Areas* (Chicago: University of Chicago Press, 1929).

43. Thorsten Sellin, *Culture Conflict and Crime,* Bulletin 41 (New York: Social Science Research Council, 1938).

44. Christopher Vecsey, ed., *Handbook of American Indian Religious Freedom* (New York: Crossroad, 1991).

45. James Davison Hunter, *Culture Wars: The Struggle to Define America* (New York: Basic Books, 1991).

46. Gustavus Myers, *History of Bigotry in the United States* (New York: Random House, 1943).

47. Joseph R. Gusfield, *Symbolic Crusade* (Urbana: University of Illinois Press, 1966).

48. Austin T. Turk, *Criminality and Legal Order* (Chicago: Rand McNally, 1969); Richard Quinney, *The Social Reality of Crime* (Boston: Little, Brown, 1970).

49. Allen E. Liska, ed., *Social Threat and Social Control* (Albany: State University of New York, 1992).

50. Darnell F. Hawkins, "Beyond Anomalies: Rethinking the Conflict Perspective on Race and Criminal Punishment," *Social Forces,* 65 (March 1987): 719–745; Darnell F. Hawkins, "Ethnicity: The Forgotten Dimension of American Social Control," in *Inequality, Crime, and Social Control,* ed. George S. Bridges and Martha A. Myers (Boulder, CO: Westview, 1994), pp. 99–116.

51. C. Vann Woodward, *The Strange Career of Jim Crow,* 3d ed., rev. (New York: Oxford University Press, 1974).

52. Gunnar Myrdal, *An American Dilemma* (New York: Harper & Brothers, 1944).

53. Marcus Felson, *Crime and Everyday Life* (Thousand Oaks, CA: Pine Forge, 1994), p. xi.

54. Ibid., p. 104.

55. Darnell F. Hawkins, "Ethnicity, Race, and Crime: A Review of Selected Studies," in *Ethnicity, Race, and Crime*, pp. 31, 39–41.

56. Ibid.

57. Paul E. Peterson, "The Urban Underclass and the Poverty Paradox," in *The Urban Underclass*, pp. 3–27.

58. Summarized in Peterson, "The Urban Underclass and the Poverty Paradox," pp. 9–16.

59. Cornell West, *Race Matters* (Boston: Beacon, 1993), p. 12.

60. Donald G. Nieman, *Promises to Keep: African Americans and the Constitutional Order, 1776 to the Present* (New York: Oxford University Press, 1991), Chap. 6, "The Civil Rights Movement and American Law, 1950–1969."

61. Richard Kluger, *Simple Justice* (New York: Vintage Books, 1977).

62. *Loving v. Virginia*, 388 U.S. 1 (1967).

63. Jaynes and Williams, *A Common Destiny*, pp. 76–77.

64. Ibid., p. 233.

65. Bureau of the Census, *Statistical Abstract of the United States, 1997*, p. 286.

66. Jaynes and Williams, *A Common Destiny*, p. 243.

67. Bureau of the Census, *Statistical Abstract of the United States, 1997*, p. 286.

68. Myrdal, *An American Dilemma*, especially Chap. 28, "The Police and Other Public Contacts."

69. Samuel Walker, "A Strange Atmosphere of Consistent Illegality: Myrdal on 'The Police and Other Public Contacts,'" *Challenge*, 5 (July 1994): 38–57.

70. *Batson v. Kentucky*, 476 U.S. 79 (1986).

71. *Washington v. Lee*, 390 U.S. 266 (1968).

72. Bureau of Justice Statistics, *Law Enforcement Management and Administrative Statistics, 1993* (Washington, D.C.: U.S. Government Printing Office, 1995), p, ix; Samuel Walker, *The Police in America: An Introduction*, 3d ed. (New York: McGraw-Hill, 1999), p. 297.

73. Charles Murray, *Losing Ground: American Social Policy, 1950–1980* (New York: Basic Books, 1984).

74. Thernstrom and Thernstrom, *America in Black and White*.

75. Jaynes and Williams, *A Common Destiny*, p. 312.

76. Ibid., p. 4.

4

Justice on the Street?

The Police and Minorities

UNEQUAL JUSTICE?

Is there systematic police harassment of racial and ethnic minorities? In a survey of Cincinnati, Ohio, residents, nearly half (46.6 percent) of all African Americans said they had been personally "hassled" by the police, compared with only 9.6 percent of all whites. *Hassled* was defined as being "stopped or watched closely by a police officer, even when you had done nothing wrong."[1] Meanwhile, in Chicago 71 percent of students surveyed reported that they had been stopped by the police, and 62 percent of the African American students who had been stopped said the police had treated them with disrespect.[2]

Racial and ethnic minorities are arrested, stopped and questioned, and shot and killed by the police out of proportion to their representation in the population. African Americans represent only 12 percent of the population but 30 percent of all arrests, 35.5 percent of all index crime arrests, and 44.8 percent of all violent crime arrests (Figure 4.1). They are shot and killed three times as often as whites by police, down from a ratio of seven to one in the early 1970s. Police stop Hispanics far more often than they stop either whites or African Americans.[3]

A 1996 public opinion survey, however, found that the vast majority of both African Americans and Hispanics have "confidence" in their local police. Only 20.7 percent of African Americans and 11.7 percent of Hispanics reported having "very little" confidence.[4] These findings are consistent with other public opinion polls over the past thirty-five years.

Percentage African American, 1995

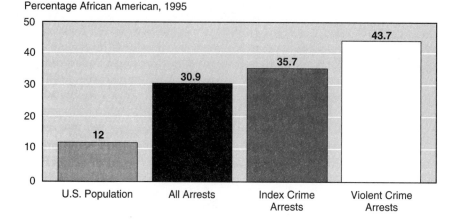

FIGURE 4.1 Disparities in Arrest

Clearly, there is much controversy and conflicting evidence about the interactions between the police and racial and ethnic minorities.

GOALS OF THE CHAPTER

This chapter explores the relationship between the police and racial and ethnic minority communities.[5] The first section outlines a contextual approach that helps to resolve the apparent contradictions in the available evidence. The second section examines public opinion about the police, comparing the attitudes of whites, African Americans, and Hispanic Americans. The third section reviews the evidence on police behavior, beginning with the most serious action, use of deadly force, and proceeding through the less serious police activities. The fourth section deals with citizen complaints against the police, reviewing the evidence on the extent of misconduct and how police departments handle citizen complaints. The final section examines police employment practices. Particular attention is given to the law of employment discrimination and the historic problem of discrimination against racial and ethnic minorities.

A CONTEXTUAL APPROACH

A contextual approach helps to understand the complex and at times contradictory evidence related to police and racial and ethnic minorities. This approach disaggregates the general subject into distinct components.

First, as we noted in Chapter 1, we cannot talk about "minorities," or even "racial and ethnic minorities" as a homogenous category. African Americans, Hispanics, Native Americans, and Asian Americans all have somewhat different experiences with the police. A 1997 national survey of police encounters with the public, for example, found that Hispanics are far less likely to call the police and far more likely to have police-initiated contact with officers than are whites or African Americans.[6] Nielsen argues that Native American involvement with criminal justice "cannot be understood without recognizing that it is just one of many interrelated issues that face Native peoples today," including "political power, land, economic development, [and] individual despair . . . ."[7]

Second, it is important to distinguish between different police departments. Some have much worse relations with minority communities than others and have long-standing reputations for brutality and corruption. Others have much better reputations. African Americans in Detroit, for example, rate the police more favorably than white residents, a fact that is probably related to the high level of African American officers in the police department.[8]

Third, we have to recognize that there are different groups *within* racial and ethnic communities.[9] Not all minorities are poor. Young men have a very different experience with the police than adults. As the Chicago survey found, young African American men are the most frequent subjects of police stops. Adults, on the other hand, are more likely to want more police protection.

Fourth, different police units and tactics have very different impacts on communities. Aggressive patrol tactics with frequent stops of citizens, for example, create resentment among young men.[10] Drug enforcement efforts are disproportionately directed at minority communities.

In short, we cannot generalize about either minorities or the police. We have to focus on particular kinds of police actions and their effects on particular minority groups.

A LONG HISTORY OF CONFLICT

Conflict between the police and racial and ethnic minorities is nothing new. There have been three major eras of riots related to police abuse: 1917–1919, 1943, and 1964–1968. The savage beating of Rodney King by Los Angeles police in 1991 and the riots that followed the acquittal of the four accused officers a year later were only the latest chapter in a long history. The background on these riots is depressingly similar. Noted African American psychologist Kenneth Clark told the Kerner Commission in 1967 that reading the reports of the earlier riots was like watching the same movie, "re-shown over and over again, the same analysis, the same recommendations, and the same inaction."[11]

Alfredo Mirandé defines the long history of conflict between Hispanics and the police in terms of "gringo justice." Taking a broad historical and political perspective, he sees a fundamental "clash between conflicting and competing cultures, world views, and economic, political and judicial systems."[12] Conflict with the police is a product of the political and economic subordination of Hispanics, their concentration in distinct neighborhoods or barrios, and stereotyping of them as criminals.

The history of relations between the police and Hispanics is also punctuated by periodic riots, often provoked by police abuse. The so-called "Zoot Suit Riot" in Los Angeles in 1943 involved attacks on Hispanic men by white Navy personnel on shore leave and by police.[13] Major conflicts between the police and the Los Angeles Hispanic community also erupted in 1970 and 1971.[14] Finally, more Hispanics were arrested in the 1992 Los Angeles riots than African Americans. A Rand report cited testimony that "both Latinos and blacks in Los Angeles feel powerless to change their position and have lost faith in the leaders and institutions of the community."[15]

THE POLICE AND A CHANGING AMERICA

The changing face of the United States presents a special challenge for the police. The constantly changing composition of the U.S. population creates potential conflict related to race, ethnicity, cultural values, lifestyles, and political power. Historically, the police have tended to aggravate rather than resolve these conflicts. They have represented the established power structure, resisted change, and reflected the prejudices of the majority community.

A paper commissioned by the Police Executive Research Forum argued that, contrary to past practice, the police can "help prevent open conflict, mitigate intergroup tensions within a community and build meaningful partnerships among the diverse populace of modern cities . . . ."[16] The police can accomplish this by openly addressing issues related to racial and ethnic conflict, and through community policing, actively establishing positive relations among all of the diverse groups that exist in the community.

One starting point is the development of language skills enabling the police to communicate effectively with all segments of the community. To serve the very diverse population of California, a private firm (Network Omni Translation) provides translation services in a number of languages under contract with several law enforcement agencies. The Minneapolis Civilian Police Review Authority, which handles complaints against the police, meanwhile, publishes brochures explaining the complaint process in seven languages (English, Spanish, Lakota, Ojibway, Vietnamese, Cambodian, and Hmong).[17]

PUBLIC ATTITUDES ABOUT THE POLICE

Race and ethnicity are consistently the most important factors in shaping attitudes about the police. Yet, as Table 4.1 indicates, public attitudes are surprising. The vast majority of white Americans have a very favorable attitude toward the police in their community. In 1998, 58 percent had a "great deal"

Table 4.1 Reported Confidence in the Police, 1998

	Great Deal/ Quite a Lot	Some	Very Little	None
White	61	30	8	X
Black	34	38	25	1
Nonwhite	40	33	24	1

Note: Racial and ethnic categories used by Gallup Organization.

or "quite a lot" of confidence in the police. Only 10 percent had "very little" confidence. Only 34 percent of African Americans, however, had a great deal or quite a lot of confidence in the police, and 25 percent had very little. In this and other surveys, Hispanic attitudes fall in between white and African American attitudes.[18]

A 1996 survey of peoples' attitudes toward their local police found very divided opinions within racial and ethnic minority groups. African Americans expressed both more strongly positive and more strongly negative attitudes than white Americans. That is, slightly more African Americans than whites (26.1 percent versus 24.5 percent) had "a great deal" of confidence in their local police. However, they were also far more likely to have "very little" confidence (20.7 percent versus 11.0 percent for whites).

The public opinion data contradict the popular image of total hostility between the police and minorities. The vast majority of African Americans and Hispanic Americans are similar to most white Americans in their experience and attitudes: They are law-abiding people who rarely have contact with the police, and their major complaint is a lack of adequate police protection. When the Justice Department asked people to suggest improvements in policing, both whites and African Americans mainly indicated that they wanted more police protection.[19]

Public opinion surveys over the past thirty years have found that public attitudes are remarkably stable.[20] In 1967 the President's Crime Commission reported that only 16 percent of nonwhites rated the police as "poor,"[21] and a 1977 survey found that only 19 percent of African Americans rated their police as "poor," compared with 9 percent of white Americans.[22] A survey of five hundred Hispanic residents of Texas found that only 15 percent rated their local police as "poor."[23]

Highly publicized controversial incidents have a short-term effect on public attitudes. In the immediate aftermath of the Rodney King beating, the percentage of white Los Angeles residents who said they "approve" of the Los Angeles police fell from more than 70 percent to 41 percent. The approval ratings by African Americans and Hispanics in the city, which were low to begin with, also fell. The approval ratings of all groups eventually returned to their previous levels, but white attitudes did so much more quickly than those of minority groups.[24]

Age is the second most important factor in shaping attitudes toward the police. Young people, regardless of race, consistently have a more negative view of the police than middle-aged and elderly people. This is not surprising. Young men are more likely to be out on the street, have contact with the police, and engage in illegal activity. At the same time, lower income people have more negative attitudes toward the police than do upper income people.[25]

Hostile relations between the police and young, low-income men are partly a result of conflict over lifestyles. Werthman and Piliavin found that juvenile gang members in the early 1960s regarded their street corner hangouts as "a sort of 'home' or 'private place.'"[26] They sought to maintain control over their space, particularly by keeping out rival gang members. Their standards of behavior for their space were different from what adults, especially middle-class adults, and the police considered appropriate for a public area.

A contextual approach, in short, indicates that the heart of the conflict between police and racial and ethnic minorities involves young people, particularly young men, and especially those in low-income neighborhoods.

POLICING MINORITY NEIGHBORHOODS

Thirty years ago, Bayley and Mendelsohn observed that "The police seem to play a role in the life of minority people out of all proportion to the role they play in the lives of the dominant white majority."[27] This is the result of several factors: income levels, reported crimes, and calls for police service.

Racial and ethnic minorities are disproportionately represented among the poor (see Chapter 3), and low-income people, regardless of race or ethnicity, are far more likely to call the police for help with family problems, medical emergencies, and other problems than are middle-class Americans.[28] They are also victimized by crime at a higher rate. The National Crime Victimization Survey (NCVS) reports that the robbery rate for African Americans is almost three times that of whites (14 versus 4.8 per 1,000). The robbery rate for Hispanics, meanwhile, is about 43 percent higher than that for non-Hispanics.[29] African Americans also report crimes to the police at a higher rate than whites. In 1994 they reported 48 percent of all violent crimes, compared with only 40 percent for whites. Hispanics, on the other hand, are slightly less likely to report crimes than non-Hispanics, 39 percent versus 41.8 percent for violent crimes.[30]

Variations Among Minorities and the Police

Our contextual approach suggests that there are significant differences between the experiences of different racial and ethnic groups and the police.

The Hispanic Community A report to the U.S. Justice Department concluded that "Latinos may have unique experiences with police which shape attitudes toward law enforcement officials."[31] The Bureau of Justice Statistics

(BJS) survey of police use of force found that Hispanics initiate contact with the police less frequently than either whites or African Americans and are far more likely to be stopped by the police.[32]

Several factors help to explain these differences. Hispanics who do not speak English have difficulty communicating with the police and may not call for that reason. Some Hispanics fear that calling the police will expose members of their community to investigation regarding immigration status. Carter, meanwhile, found that the Hispanic community's sense of family often regards intervention by an "outsider" (e.g., a police officer) as a threat to the family's integrity and, in the case of an arrest, as an attack on the father's authority.[33]

A series of focus groups in a Midwestern city found significant differences between how Hispanic, African American, and white residents would respond to an incident of police misconduct. Members of the predominantly Spanish-language-speaking group were far more fearful of the police, far less knowledgeable about the U.S. legal system, and less likely to file a complaint than either whites or African Americans. Much of the fear of the police was related to concern about possible immigration problems.[34]

Policing in Indian Country Native Americans occupy a unique legal status in the United States and this has an important effect on their relations with the police. Native American tribes are recognized as sovereign nations with broad (although not complete) powers of self-government within the boundaries of the United States. There are 510 Native American reservations recognized by the federal government, and 170 of them have separate law enforcement agencies, resulting in extremely complex problems related to the jurisdiction of tribal police, county sheriffs, and federal authorities in particular areas.[35]

Native American policing is also complex because there are five different types of tribal law enforcement agencies: (1) Some are operated by the federal Bureau of Indian Affairs (BIA); (2) others are federally funded, but are operated by the tribe under an agreement with the BIA (called PL 96-638 agencies); (3) some are operated and funded by the tribes themselves; (4) some are operated by tribes under the 1994 Indian Self-Determination Act; and (5) some are operated by state and local governments under Public Law 280.[36]

A 1996 report by the U.S. Attorney General and the Secretary of the Interior found "a public safety crisis in Indian Country." Law enforcement on Native American reservations "often fails to meet basic public safety requirements." Law enforcement is fragmented and many agencies lack adequate resources. Partly as a result, serious crime was increasing in Indian country in the mid-1990s at the same time it was falling in the rest of the country.[37]

A survey of tribal law enforcement agencies found that most were very small (ten or fewer sworn officers) and that only half had a 911 emergency telephone service. About half (42.6 percent) cross-deputize their officers with the local county sheriff's department, meaning that their officers have law enforcement powers off the reservation.[38]

Focus on an Issue

Too Much or Too Little Policing?

Much controversy exists over whether police departments overpolice or underpolice racial and ethnic minority neighborhoods. The famous African American novelist James Baldwin wrote, "The only way to police a ghetto is to be oppressive.... [The officer] moves through Harlem like an occupying soldier in a bitterly hostile country."[39] Other African Americans, however, accuse the police of providing too little protection for their neighborhoods, arguing that they assign too few officers, do not respond quickly to calls, and do not take crimes against African Americans seriously. In 1993, 74 percent of African Americans thought that police protection in their neighborhoods was "worse" than that in white neighborhoods. Surprisingly, 41 percent of whites agreed that African American neighborhoods got worse police protection. A majority of African Americans want more police protection, just as whites do. In a 1993 Gallup poll, 41 percent of African Americans and 43 percent of whites "strongly favor[ed]" putting "more police on the street."[40, 25]

Historically, the police have ignored many crimes within African American communities.[41] During the Segregation Era, Southern police reacted harshly to crimes against whites but ignored many crimes against African Americans, whether committed by whites or other African Americans.[42] Similar problems existed in other parts of the country. In 1968 the Kerner Commission found "a lack of police personnel for ghetto areas, considering the volume of calls for police."[43] Harvard law professor Randall Kennedy made the powerful argument that "Deliberately withholding protection against criminality ... is one of the most destructive forms of oppression that has been visited upon African-Americans."[44] It is worse than active discrimination (e.g., a false arrest), in his view, because it adversely affects far more people.

In the 1970s, some African American residents of Washington, D.C., sued the police department, alleging that inadequate police protection denied them equal protection of the law. A study by the Urban Institute, however, found that police services properly reflected neighborhood crime rates and calls for police service, and the suit failed.[45]

Our contextual approach helps to explain the apparent contradiction between simultaneous complaints of too much and too little policing. The police respond in different ways to different people, neighborhoods, and situations. Complaints about overpolicing or harassment are usually voiced by young men who are most likely to be stopped, questioned, frisked, and arrested on the street. Complaints of too little policing, on the other hand, are expressed by adults, especially those with families, who are worried about crime.

Unfortunately, little research has been done on actual law enforcement practices on Native American reservations. At the same time, there is no research on interactions between Native Americans and the police in urban settings, where about half of all Native Americans live.

POLICE USE OF DEADLY FORCE

On October 3, 1974, Edward Garner was shot and killed by two Memphis police officers. A fifteen-year-old African American, Garner was 5 feet, 4 inches tall, weighed 110 pounds, and was shot in the back of the head while fleeing with a stolen purse containing $10. His parents sued, and in 1985 the Supreme Court held that the fleeing felon rule, under which the Memphis police justified the shooting, was unconstitutional.[46]

The shooting of citizens by police officers has always been the most serious issue in police–community relations, particularly for African Americans. In the 1960s and early 1970s, the police fatally shot seven African Americans for every one white person. Fyfe, one of the leading experts on the subject, asked whether the police have "two trigger fingers," one for whites and one for African Americans and Hispanics.[47]

Discriminatory shooting patterns were in part the result of the old fleeing felon rule, which allowed a police officer to shoot to kill, for the purpose of arrest, any fleeing suspected felon. The rule gave police officers very broad discretion, allowing them to shoot, for example, a juvenile suspected of stealing a bicycle worth only $50. As already noted, Garner had stolen a purse containing only $10.

Police officers, of course, did not shoot every suspected fleeing felon. The data, however, suggest that they were much more likely to shoot African Americans than whites. Between 1969 and 1974, for example, Memphis, Tennessee, police officers shot and killed thirteen African Americans in the "unarmed and not assaultive" category, but only one white person (Table 4.2). In fact, half of all the African Americans shot were in that category.[48] The permissive fleeing felon rule allowed officers to act on the basis of prejudices and stereotypes. White officers were more likely to feel threatened by African American suspects than by white suspects in similar situations. The typical shooting incident occurs at night, in circumstances in which the officer has to make a split-second decision. It is often not clear whether the suspect has a weapon.

There are few studies of the shootings of Hispanics and none of Native Americans or Asian Americans. Geller and Karales found that between 1974 and 1978, Hispanics were about twice as likely to be shot and killed by the Chicago police as whites, but only half as likely to be shot as African Americans.[49] Similar patterns were found in New York City and Los Angeles.[50]

Reducing Disparities in Shootings

In the 1970s, in response to protests by civil rights groups, police departments began to adopt the defense of life rule, limiting shootings to situations that pose a threat to the life of the officer or some other person. Many departments also prohibit warning shots, shots to wound, and shots at or from moving vehicles. Officers are also now required to fill out a report any time they discharge their weapon. Meanwhile, in 1985 the Supreme Court declared the fleeing felon rule unconstitutional in *Tennessee v. Garner*. The Court ruled that

Table 4.2 Citizens Shot and Killed, Memphis

	1969–1974		1985–1989	
	White	African American	White	African American
Armed & assaultive	5	7	6	7
Unarmed & assaultive	2	6	1	5
Unarmed & not assaultive	1	13	0	0
Totals, by race	8	26	7	12
Total		34		19

SOURCE: Adapted from Jerry R. Sparger and David J. Giacopassi, "Memphis Revisited: A Reexamination of Police Shootings After the Garner Decision," *Justice Quarterly* 9 (June 1992): 211–225.

the fleeing felon rule violated the Fourth Amendment protection against unreasonable searches and seizures, holding that shooting a person was a seizure.[51]

Fyfe found that the defense of life rule reduced firearms discharges in New York City by almost 30 percent in just a few years. Across the country, the number of persons shot and killed by police declined from a peak of 559 in 1975 to 300 in 1987. Equally significant, the racial disparity between blacks and whites declined from 7 to 1 in 1970 to 2.8 to 1 in 1979.[52] Sherman and Cohn's data, moreover, suggest that virtually all of the lives "saved" by the new restrictive shooting policies were racial minorities.

Follow-up data on Memphis illustrate how the defense of life rule reduced the racial disparity in shootings. As Table 4.2 indicates, between 1985 and 1989 no people of either race were shot and killed in the fleeing felon category. The defense of life rule may not have changed police officer attitudes, but it did alter their behavior, curbing the influence of racial prejudice.

It is still difficult to obtain current and accurate data on fatal shootings by police, however. The FBI annually reports data on law enforcement officers killed and assaulted, but there is no system for collecting and reporting data on the use of either physical or deadly force by police officers.[53]

Disparity Versus Discrimination in Shootings

The data indicate that the racial disparity in persons shot and killed has been narrowed from about seven African Americans for every white to about three to one. Does either the 7:1 or the 3:1 ratio represent discrimination, or does it reflect a disparity that can be explained by factors other than race?

Geller and Karales addressed this question by controlling for the "at-risk" status of persons shot and killed by the Chicago police in the 1970s. People are not equally at risk of being shot by the police. Virtually all shooting victims are men rather than women; young men are also disproportionately represented compared with older men. Young men are more likely to engage in the behavior that places them at risk, namely use of a weapon in street crime. Geller and Karales found when they controlled for at-risk status, defined in terms of arrest for "forcible felonies" (murder, rape, armed and strong-arm robbery, aggravated battery, aggravated assault, and burglary), the racial disparity disappeared. In fact, whites were shot and killed at a slightly higher rate.[54] In short, the 7:1 ratio of persons shot and killed by the police that prevailed in the 1960s and 1970s clearly reflected racial discrimination by the police. The current ratio of 3:1 is much closer to the at-risk status based on involvement in serious crime and therefore may represent a disparity rather than systematic discrimination.

"POLICE BRUTALITY":
POLICE USE OF PHYSICAL FORCE

Q: Did you beat people up who you arrested?

A: No. We'd just beat people in general. If they're on the street, hanging around drug locations. . . .

Q: Why?

A: To show who was in charge.[55]

This exchange between the Mollen Commission and a corrupt New York City police officer documented the unrestrained character of police brutality in poor, high-crime neighborhoods in New York City. The 1991 Rodney King beating is probably the most notorious example of police use of excessive physical force. Police brutality has been a historic problem with U.S. police. In 1931 the Wickersham Commission reported that the "third degree"—the "inflicting of pain, physical or mental, to extract confessions or statements—is extensively practiced."[56] A 1998 report by Human Rights Watch concluded, "Race continues to play a central role in police brutality in the United States."[57]

The Mollen Commission defined brutality as the "threat of physical harm or the actual infliction of physical injury or pain."[58] Many people use an even broader definition. The President's Crime Commission found that 70.3 percent of African Americans defined rudeness as police brutality, compared with 54.6 percent of whites.[59] The New York City Civilian Complaint Investigative Bureau investigates eleven specific actions in the "force" category: firing a gun, pointing a gun, beating, dragging or pulling, pushing or shoving, punching or kicking, slapping, and using either mace, a nightstick, a gun, or the police radio as a club.[60]

We define *brutality* here to mean the use of excessive physical force or any force that is *more than reasonably necessary to accomplish a lawful police purpose.*[61] A police officer is legally justified in using force to protect himself or herself from physical attack or to subdue a suspect who is resisting arrest. Any amount of force in excess of that may be considered brutality.

There is much disagreement over the prevalence of police use of excessive force.[62] Critics of the police argue that it is a routine, nightly occurrence, whereas others believe that it is a very rare event. A 1996 BJS survey found that police officers used or threatened force in 1 percent of all encounters with citizens.[63] This represents an estimated annual total of 500,000 force incidents each year. The report, however, did not distinguish between justified and unjustified (or excessive) use of force. Other studies have estimated that about one third of all uses of force are excessive or unjustified. The BJS findings are roughly consistent with previous studies. In the 1960s, Reiss found that police officers used excessive force in only 37 of 3,826 encounters with citizens (or about 1 percent).[64]

A contextual approach puts this 1 percent estimate in a different perspective. Most contacts between citizens and the police involve routine order maintenance and service situations.[65] Certain situations, however, tend to be problematic. Croft and Austin found that police use force four or five times more often against persons being arrested. Police are also very likely to use force against people who challenge their authority. Some people believe that the police overreact to even legitimate questions from citizens. They refer to this police practice as "contempt of cop."[66] Reiss found that almost half of the victims of excessive force had either defied the officer's authority (39 percent of all cases) or resisted arrest (9 percent of all cases). Additionally, Reiss found that African American suspects were more likely to be disrespectful than were whites after all other variables were controlled for.[67] Police officers are also more likely to use force against people whose status or condition offends their moral beliefs, especially chronic alcoholics and homosexuals. Police officers apparently feel freer to use excessive force because they believe that these people are not likely to file a complaint about the incident.

Reiss concluded that race per se is not a determining factor in the use of excessive force: "Class rather than race determines police misconduct."[68] The typical victim of excessive force is a lower class male, regardless of race. Other observers, however, disagree with this interpretation, and see a systematic pattern of police use of force against young minority men.

The race or ethnicity of the officer has only a moderate influence on the use of physical force. The majority of excessive force incidents are intraracial: Citizens are mistreated by a police officer of the same racial or ethnic group. Reiss found that 67 percent of the people victimized by a white officer were white, and 71 percent of those victimized by African American officers were African American.[69] In New York City, white officers represented 68 percent of the department in 1997 and they received 68 percent of all complaints filed by citizens; African Americans represented 13 percent of both officers and those receiving complaints; Hispanic officers were 17 percent in both categories.[70] Worden found that African American officers were somewhat more likely than white officers to use reasonable levels of force but less likely to use improper force.[71]

The data on officer involvement in excessive use of force parallel the data on the use of deadly force. In neither case is it a simple matter of white officers shooting or beating racial minority citizens. In both cases, officer behavior is heavily determined by the contextual or situational variables: location (high-crime versus low-crime precinct); the perceived criminal involvement of the citizen; the demeanor of the citizen; and in the case of physical force, the social status of the citizen.

Our contextual approach suggests that the use of physical force has special significance for racial minority communities. Even if the overall rate of use of force is only 1 percent of all encounters, incidents are concentrated among lower class men and criminal suspects, which means they are disproportionately concentrated among racial and ethnic minorities. Moreover, incidents accumulate over time, creating a perception of systematic harassment.[72] A 1991 Gallup Poll reported that 45 percent of African Americans believed there was police brutality in their area, compared with only 33 percent of whites.[73]

Finally, police use of force has special political significance for minorities. Because the police are the symbolic representatives of the established order, incidents of excessive force are perceived as part of the broader patterns of inequality and discrimination in society.

DISCRIMINATION IN ARRESTS?

Racial minorities are arrested far more often than whites. African Americans are only 12 percent of the population, but in 1995 they represented 30.9 percent of all arrests, 35.7 percent of arrests for index crimes, and 43.7 percent of arrests for violent index crimes (Figure 4.1). Tillman found that in California, 66 percent of all African American men were likely to be arrested before the age of thirty, compared with only 34 percent of white men.[74] The FBI does not report data on ethnicity, so there are no national data on arrest rates for Hispanic Americans. Native Americans represent 0.8 percent of the U.S. population but 1.1 percent of all persons arrested.[75]

There is much controversy over whether these data indicate a pattern of systematic racial discrimination or a disparity that is related to other factors such as involvement in crime (see Chapter 1, Box 1.1). In his study of arrest discretion, Black found that police officers consistently underenforce the law, arresting only 58 percent of felony suspects and only 44 percent of misdemeanor suspects. The decision to arrest is primarily influenced by situational factors. Officers are more likely to arrest when (1) the evidence is strong; (2) the crime is of a more serious nature; (3) the complainant or victim requests an arrest; (4) the relationship between the victim and offender is distant (e.g., strangers rather than acquaintances or spouses); and (5) the suspect is disrespectful toward the officer. In Black's study, the race of the suspect was not a major determinant of arrest decisions.[76]

Black did, however, find that African Americans were arrested more often than whites, mainly because they were more often disrespectful to police officers. This phenomenon represents a vicious circle in racial discrimination. Because of the broader patterns of racial inequality in U.S. society, young African

American men have more negative attitudes toward the police (see our earlier discussion in this chapter). Expressing their hostility toward police officers results in higher arrest rates, which only heightens their feelings of alienation and hostility. Klinger, however, questioned Black's interpretation of the impact of demeanor. He argued that the study did not specify when the hostile demeanor occurred. If it occurred after the actual arrest was made—and it is understandable that a person would express anger at that point—it did not cause the arrest.[77]

Another factor contributing to the racial disparity in arrests is the greater involvement of African Americans in the more serious crimes. The NCVS reports that victims perceived the offender to be African American in 51.1 percent of all single-offender robberies but only 23 percent of all assaults.[78] Because robbery is generally regarded as a more serious crime than assault, and because greater seriousness increases the probability of arrest, it follows that more African Americans will be arrested than whites.

A comparison of the NCVS data with the FBI's Uniform Crime Reports (UCR) data, however, reveals some disparity in arrests for particular crimes. The NCVS reports that 51.1 percent of all robbers are perceived to be African Americans. Yet, the UCR reports that 59.5 percent of all persons arrested for robbery are African American.[79]

Smith, Visher, and Davidson concluded that race does have an effect on arrest discretion. Analyzing 5,688 police–citizen encounters in twenty-four police departments in three major metropolitan areas,[80] they found that police officers were more likely to arrest when the victim was white and the suspect was black and more likely to comply with a white victim's request that the suspect be arrested. After controlling for all relevant variables, they concluded that "race does matter" and that African American suspects were more likely to be arrested than whites.

Other studies have suggested that African Americans are more likely to be arrested on less stringent evidentiary criteria than whites.[81] Petersilia's study of racial disparities in California found that black and Hispanic arrestees were more likely to be released by the police without the case going to the prosecutor and to have the prosecutor reject the case. At first glance, it might appear that blacks and Hispanics are being treated more leniently in these two postarrest decisions. Petersilia, however, suggested that racial and ethnic minorities are arrested more often on weaker evidence than whites, particularly in "on-view" situations rather than with a warrant. The weak evidence in on-view arrests is then more likely to result in a release or rejection later in the criminal process.[82] Nonetheless, an arrest, even one that does not lead to prosecution, represents a significant form of punishment and is often perceived as harassment.

The race of the officer does not appear to influence arrest decisions. African American, Hispanic, and white officers arrest people at similar rates and for generally the same reasons. Black found some evidence that African American officers were slightly more likely to arrest African American suspects, in part because they appeared to be more willing to comply with re-

Focus on an Issue
Police and the War on Drugs

Many observers believe that the war on drugs represents the most blatant example of race discrimination in the entire criminal justice system. As Figure 4.1 indicates, African Americans are arrested, prosecuted, and imprisoned for drug offenses to an extent that far exceeds their reported use of illegal drugs. Jerome G. Miller characterized recent crime policy as a "search and destroy" mission directed at African American men.[86]

The National Criminal Justice Commission argued that the enormous racial disparity in drug arrests is due to the fact that police "focus almost exclusively on low-level dealers in minority neighborhoods."[87] The race discrimination here involves policy decisions by command officers rather than decisions by individual officers on the street. As the National Criminal Justice Commission explained, "Police found more drugs in minority communities because that is where they looked for them."[88] This analysis is consistent with our contextual approach: The worst forms of discrimination are related to a particular police activity.

Targeting African American and Hispanic youth as suspected gang members is one component of the discriminatory aspect of the war on drugs. The Los Angeles Police Department conducted several highly publicized "crackdowns" against gangs, with massive "sweep" arrests over a weekend. This tactic swept up many innocent people who simply had the misfortune to be in the wrong place at the wrong time. Most of the persons arrested were quickly released and never prosecuted, and the crackdown strategy has had no measurable effect on gang activity.[89]

Many police departments have created special gang units that maintain lists of gangs and alleged gang members. Many questions have been raised about the criteria for putting people on these lists.[90] At one point the Denver Police Department had about 7,000 names on its gang list. More than 90 percent were either African American or Hispanic. The numbers suggested that more than two thirds of all the young African American men in the city of Denver were gang members. After a series of protests, the size of the Denver police department's gang list was trimmed substantially.[91]

---

quests for arrests made by African American citizens. He admitted, however, that the subject has not been researched as thoroughly as it needs to be.[83]

Quality of Life Policing

One of the important new developments in law enforcement is "quality of life" policing. Under this approach the police concentrate on relatively minor crimes, such as public urination or loitering. In New York City there was particular emphasis on "fare-beaters," individuals who try to cheat the subway system by jumping over the turnstile. Many people in New York City claim that quality of life policing has reduced serious crime, because people arrested for a minor crime often turn out to have an illegal gun in their possession or are wanted on outstanding warrants.[84] Other people, however, argue that the aggressive style of quality of life policing results in harassment of citizens, particularly young racial and ethnic minority men.[85]

In sum, patterns of arrest by race are extremely complex. Racial minorities, especially African Americans, are arrested far more frequently than are whites. Much of this disparity, however, can be attributed to the greater involvement of minorities in serious crime. Greater disrespect for the police also contributes to arrest disparity. Even after all the relevant variables are controlled, however, some evidence of arrest discrimination against African Americans persists.

STOPPING, QUESTIONING, AND FRISKING

Stopping, questioning, and frisking people on the street is another source of police–community tensions. Young African American and Hispanic men believe they are singled out for frequent and unjustified harassment in such actions. In Chicago, 71 percent of the students surveyed reported that they had been stopped by the police, and 86 percent of them felt the police had been disrespectful.[92]

The BJS survey of police use of force found a striking difference in police stops of Hispanics compared with both whites and African Americans. Hispanics are much less likely to initiate contact with a police officer and much more likely to have a police officer initiate contact.[93]

In the San Diego Field Interrogation study, nearly half of all people stopped and questioned were African Americans, even though they represented only 17.5 percent and 4.8 percent of the population of the two precincts in the study (see Figure 4.2). All of the people stopped and questioned were male, and about 60 percent were juveniles.[94] A report by the Massachusetts attorney general found that "Boston police officers engaged in improper, and unconstitutional, conduct in the 1989–90 period with respect to stops and searches of minority individuals."[95] Interviews with more than fifty individuals revealed a pattern of African American men and women being stopped and questioned without any basis for suspicion, threatened by the officers if they asked why they were being stopped, and subjected to highly intrusive and embarrassing strip searches in public.

Stopping and questioning someone on the street is often referred to as a field interrogation (FI). It is a crime-fighting policy designed to "emphasize to potential offenders that the police are aware of" them and to "reassure the general public that the patrol officers are actively engaged in protecting law-abiding citizens."[96] Patrol officers have full discretion to conduct FIs. As we have seen with respect to deadly force, uncontrolled discretion opens the door for discriminatory practices. Some police departments employ an "aggressive preventive patrol" strategy to encourage FIs. The Kerner Commission found that such a strategy aggravated tensions with minority communities.[97]

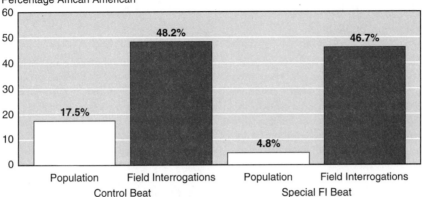

Percentage African American

FIGURE 4.2 Field Interrogations in San Diego

The San Diego Field Interrogation study found that 75 percent of all the people stopped and questioned thought the officer had a right to stop them. In some respects, this seems to be a highly positive response. On the other hand, however, if 25 percent of all people stopped and questioned did not feel that it was legitimate, there would be a significant number of unhappy or even angry people over the course of a year.[98]

An ethnographic study of a low-income, high-crime neighborhood in St. Louis found that police officers had deeply divided opinions about how to police the area. On the one hand they wanted to establish close relations with residents and help them deal with their problems. At the same time, however, many officers wanted to "kick ass," meaning they wanted to be free to use their own judgment to deal with crime in the neighborhood. It was clear that they did not engage in these tactics because of the police department's disciplinary system (being "written up").[99]

Stereotyping, Racial Prejudice, and Routine Police Work

One of the most troublesome aspects of police work is the tendency of officers to stereotype people. Skolnick argued that stereotyping is built into police work. Officers are trained to be suspicious and look for criminal activity. As a result, they develop "a perceptual shorthand to identify certain kinds of people" as suspects, relying on visual "cues": dress, demeanor, context, gender, and age. Thus, a young, low-income man in a wealthy neighborhood presents several cues that trigger an officer's suspicion in a way that a middle-aged woman or even a young woman in the same context does not.[101]

Race is also often a "cue." A young racial minority man in a white neighborhood is likely to trigger an officer's suspicion because he "looks out of place." By the same token, the presence of two middle-class white men in a

---

Focus on an Issue

"Driving While Black"

One of the most serious examples of race discrimination in policing is the so-called "driving while black" phenomenon. There is considerable evidence that the police target African Americans for traffic stops. The Maryland American Civil Liberties Union (ACLU) successfully sued the Maryland State Police in 1992, introducing evidence that 73 percent of the cars stopped and searched on Interstate 95 were driven by African Americans, although only 14 percent of all drivers were African American. The ACLU sued the State Police again in 1996 after it found that the agency was violating its previous agreement to stop the discriminatory practice. A similar pattern of disproportionate stops of African American and Hispanic drivers was found on I-95 in Florida.[100]

Representative John Conyers of Detroit introduced a bill in Congress to enact "the Traffic Stops Statistics Act of 1997," requiring all law enforcement agencies to report data on the race, ethnicity, and age of persons stopped for suspected traffic law violations.

---

minority neighborhood known to have a high level of drug trafficking is likely to trigger the suspicion that they are seeking to purchase drugs. Because racial minority men are disproportionately arrested for robbery and burglary, police officers can fall into the habit of stereotyping all young racial minority men as offenders.

Harvard law professor Randall Kennedy asks the question, "Is it proper to use a person's race as a proxy for an increased likelihood of criminal conduct?"[102] That is, can the police stop an African American man simply because the suspect in a crime is in that category, or because of statistical evidence that young African American men are disproportionately involved in crime, drug, or gang activity? He points out that the courts have frequently upheld this practice as long as race is one of several factors involved in a stop or an arrest and the stop is not done for purposes of harassment.

Kennedy then makes a strong argument that race should never be used as the basis for a police action "except in the most extraordinary of circumstances."[103] First, if the practice is strictly forbidden, it will reduce the opportunity for the police to engage in harassment under the cloak of "reasonable" law enforcement measures. Second, the current practice of using race "nourishes powerful feelings of racial grievance against law enforcement authorities."[104] Third, the resulting hostility to the police creates barriers to police–citizen cooperation in those communities "most in need of police protection."[105] Fourth, permitting the practice contributes to racial segregation, as African Americans will be reluctant to venture into white neighborhoods for fear of being stopped by the police.

VERBAL ABUSE

Verbal abuse by police officers is one of the more common complaints expressed by citizens. In 1997, 13 percent of the complaints received by the Minneapolis Civilian Review Authority involved offensive language.[106] Verbal abuse demeans the citizen and is explicitly forbidden by many police departments. The Los Angeles Police Department policy states, "The deliberate or casual use of racially or ethnically derogatory language by Department employees is misconduct and will not be tolerated under any circumstances."[107]

Despite this prohibition, the Christopher Commission found a great deal of abusive language by police officers. It recovered computer messages between Los Angeles patrol officers containing racially offensive terms: "I'm back here in the project, pissing off the natives"; "we're huntin' wabbits . . . actually Muslim wabbits"; "just got mexercise for the night"; "don't transfer me any orientals . . . I had to already."[108] The contrast between the official departmental policy and actual officer behavior in Los Angeles dramatizes the problem of controlling verbal abuse.

There is considerable disagreement over exactly what kinds of words or tones of voice constitute verbal abuse. Much depends on the specific context and how certain words are perceived by the citizen. The mildest form of abuse is simple rudeness or discourtesy. An officer may speak in a sharp tone of voice or refuse to answer a citizen's question. The New York City Civilian Complaint Review Board investigates seven specific forms of "discourtesy": curses, nasty words, profane gestures, rude gestures, rudeness, sexist remarks, and antigay slurs. Even if discourteous words do not have an explicit racial or ethnic component, they may be perceived as offensive in a certain context. Calling a citizen a name such as "asshole" or "scumbag" may not appear racially or ethnically motivated on the surface, but these words may be perceived as such in an encounter on the street between a white officer and a minority citizen.

Racial or ethnic slurs represent a more serious form of verbal abuse. They demean citizens, deny them equal treatment on the basis of their race or ethnicity, and aggravate police–community tensions.

For police officers, derogatory language is a control technique. White, Cox, and Basehart argue that profanity directed at citizens serves several functions: to get their attention; keep them at a distance; and label, degrade, dominate, and control them.[109] It is also often a moral judgment. As middle-class professionals, police officers often look down on people who do not live by their standards, including criminals, chronic alcoholics, and the homeless.

Verbal abuse is especially hard to control. The typical incident occurs on the street, often without any witnesses except other police officers or friends of the citizen, and leaves no tangible evidence (unlike a physical attack). Consequently, most complaints about verbal abuse become "swearing contests" in which the citizen says one thing and the officer says just the opposite. Only a small percentage of verbal abuse complaints are sustained. In 1990 the San Diego Police Department sustained none of the six racial or ethnic slur allegations and only nine of fifty-three (17 percent) allegations of discourtesy.[110]

POLICE OFFICER ATTITUDES
AND BEHAVIOR

Are police officers prejudiced? What is the relationship between police officer attitudes and their behavior on the street? The evidence on these questions is extremely complex. As Smith et al. explained, "Attitudes are one thing and behavior is another."[111]

Bayley and Mendelsohn compared the attitudes of Denver police officers with those of the general public and found that police officers were prejudiced "but only slightly more so than the community as a whole."[112] Eight percent of the officers indicated that they disliked Spanish-named persons, compared with 6 percent of the general public. When asked about specific social situations (e.g., "Would you mind eating together at the same table?" "Would you mind having someone in your family marry a member of a minority group?" etc.), the officers were less prejudiced against Spanish-surnamed persons than the general public but more prejudiced against African Americans.[113]

Bayley and Mendelsohn's findings are consistent with other research indicating that police officers are not significantly different from the general population in terms of psychological makeup and attitudes, including attitudes about race and ethnicity. Police departments, in other words, do not recruit a distinct group of prejudiced or psychologically unfit individuals. Bayley and Mendelsohn found that on all personality scales, Denver police officers were "absolutely average people."[114]

The attitudes of officers are often contradictory, however. Smith et al. found that the overwhelming majority of police officers (79.4 percent) agreed or strongly agreed with the statement "Most people in this community respect police officers."[115] At the same time, however, most (44.2 percent) believed that the chances of being abused by a citizen were very high. The characteristics of an officer's assignment affects perception of the community. Officers assigned to racial or ethnic minority communities, high-crime areas, and poor neighborhoods thought they received less respect from the public than officers working in other areas.

Reiss noted a significant contradiction between attitudes and behavior. About 75 percent of the officers were observed making racially derogatory remarks, yet they did not engage in systematic discrimination in arrest or use of physical force.[116] Attitudes do not translate directly into behavior for reasons related to the bureaucratic nature of police work. An arrest is reviewed first by a supervising officer and then by other criminal justice officials (prosecutor, defense attorney, judge). News media coverage is also possible. The potentially unfavorable judgments of these people serve to control the officer's behavior. Verbal abuse, however, rarely comes to the attention of other officials and is therefore much harder to control.

Much of the research on police officer attitudes was conducted in the 1960s or early 1970s. Since then, police employment practices have changed substantially. Far more African American, Hispanic, female, and college-educated officers are employed today (we discuss this more later). The earlier research, which assumed a disproportionately white male police force, may no longer be valid.[117]

Most police departments offer sensitivity or cultural diversity training programs for their officers. These programs typically cover the history of race relations, traditional racial and ethnic stereotypes, and explanations of different racial and ethnic cultural patterns. Questions have been raised about the effectiveness of these programs, however. Some critics fear that they may be counterproductive and serve only to reinforce negative attitudes, focus on attitudes rather than behavior, and fail to address departmental policies that may be the real cause of the problem.[118] Alpert, Smith, and Watters argued that "Mere classroom lectures . . . is insufficient," and that emphasis needs to be placed on actual on-the-street behavior.[119]

MINORITIES AND POLICE CORRUPTION

Police corruption has a special impact on minority communities. Most police corruption involves vice activities—particularly drugs and gambling—that historically have been segregated in low-income and racial minority neighborhoods. In the 1970s, the Knapp Commission found that payoffs to New York City police officers were about $300 per month in midtown Manhattan, the central business district, and $1,500 in Harlem, the center of the African American community.[120] In the 1990s the Mollen Commission exposed a pattern of corruption and violence in the poorest African American and Hispanic neighborhoods. Officers took bribes for protecting the drug trade, beat up drug dealers, broke into apartments, and stole drugs and money.[121]

Police corruption harms racial and ethnic minorities in several ways. First, allowing vice activities to flourish in low-income and minority communities represents an unequal and discriminatory pattern of law enforcement. Second, vice encourages secondary crime: The patrons of prostitutes are robbed; after-hours clubs are the scenes of robbery and assault; and competing drug gangs have shoot-outs with rival gangs. Third, community awareness of police corruption damages the reputation of the police. In 1993, 26 percent of African Americans thought the ethical standards of the police were "low" or "very low," compared with only 8 percent of whites.[122]

Police corruption is concentrated in poor and minority neighborhoods in large part because police officers see the residents as politically powerless, and thus unable to effectively protest and stop corrupt practices.

POLICE–COMMUNITY
RELATIONS PROGRAMS

In response to the riots of the 1960s, most big-city police departments established special police-community relations (PCR) programs to resolve racial and ethnic tensions. Most involved a separate PCR unit within the department. PCR unit officers spent most of their time to speaking in schools or to community groups.[123] Some PCR units also staffed neighborhood storefront offices to make the department more accessible to community residents who either were intimidated by police headquarters or found it difficult to travel downtown. Another popular program was the "ride-along," which allowed citizens to ride in a patrol car and view policing from an officer's perspective.

PCR programs had a troubled history. There is no evidence that they improved community relations. A Justice Department report concluded that PCR units "tended to be marginal to the operations of the police department," with little direct impact on patrol and other key operations.[124] Public education and ride-along programs reached people who already had a positive attitude toward the police. In the 1970s, most departments reduced or abolished their PCR programs.

Some of the original PCR activities have reappeared in community policing programs. The foundation of the ambitious community policing program in Chicago (Chicago Alternative Police Services) was a series of regular meetings between patrol beat officers and community residents.[125] The major difference is that under community policing, these meetings are designed to develop two-way communication, with citizens providing input into police policies. The old PCR programs mainly involved one-way communication from the police to the community.

Some police departments today maintain special programs to deal with immigrant communities in which English is not the primary language. The Santa Ana, California, police department, for example, operates a special Asian/Pacific Islander Affairs Office that "culturally cross-train[s] members of the community and police department to bridge the gap between the two." The department also has a Hispanic Affairs Officer to serve as a liaison with the Hispanic community, which comprises 65 percent of the city population.[126] The Chicago Police Department adopted a broad human rights policy in 1992, declaring that officers "will not engage in any bias or prejudice against any individual or group because of race, color, gender, age, religion, disability, national origin, ancestry, sexual orientation, marital status, parental status, military discharge status or source of income."[127]

CITIZEN COMPLAINTS
AGAINST THE POLICE

One of the greatest sources of tension between the police and minorities is the perceived failure of police departments to respond adequately to citizen complaints about police misconduct. Minorities file a disproportionate number of all complaints against the police. In Minneapolis, for example, African Americans filed 51 percent of all complaints against the police in 1997, even though they represent only 13 percent of the city's population.[128]

Racial and ethnic minorities allege that police departments fail to adequately investigate complaints and do not discipline officers who are guilty of misconduct. There is the widespread belief that the complaint review process is just a "cover-up."[129] Most people who feel they are victims of police abuse do not even file a formal complaint. One study found that only 30 percent of those people who felt they had a reason to complain about a police officer took any kind of action, and only some of them contacted the police department. Most people called someone else (a friend or some other government official).[130]

Some departments actively discourage citizen complaints. The Christopher Commission found that in Los Angeles, officers at local police stations often discouraged people from filing complaints or threatened them with arrest. Officers frequently did not complete Form 1.81, which records an official complaint.[131] In response to criticisms about how it handled complaints, the Los Angeles Police Department established a special 800-number complaint hotline. A study by the ACLU in Los Angeles, however, found that only 13 percent of the people calling local police stations were given the 800 number. Other callers (71.9 percent) were told that either there was no such number or that the officer could not give it out, or they were put on hold indefinitely.[132]

Internal affairs (IA) units have traditionally handled citizen complaints. The police subculture is very strong, however, and IA officers tend to protect their colleagues and the department against external criticism. Westley found the police subculture emphasizes "silence, secrecy, and solidarity." Under the informal "code of silence," officers are often willing to lie to cover up misconduct by fellow officers.[133] The Christopher Commission concluded that in Los Angeles "the greatest single barrier to the effective investigation and adjudication of complaints is the officers' unwritten 'code of silence.'"[134] The code "consists of one simple rule: an officer does not provide adverse information against a fellow officer."[135] The Mollen Commission investigating police corruption in New York City found the "pervasiveness" of the code of silence "alarming." The commission asked one officer, "Were you ever afraid that one of your fellow officers might turn you in?" He answered, "Never," because "cops don't tell on cops."[136]

As a result, most citizen complaints become "swearing contests": The citizen alleges one thing and the officer denies it. Few citizen complaints are sustained by police investigators. The Police Foundation found that city police departments sustain only 10.4 percent of all complaints.[137]

A study of the Minneapolis Police Department found racial and gender disparities in the sustaining of complaints. The department sustained 19 percent of all complaints filed by whites but only 11 percent of those filed by African Americans. It sustained 33 percent of those filed by young white women, compared with only 2 percent of those filed by young African American women.[138]

Citizen Review of the Police

To ensure better handling of complaints against the police, civil rights groups have demanded external or citizen review of complaints. Citizen review is based on the idea that persons who are not police officers will be more independent and objective in investigating complaints. Despite strong opposition from police unions, citizen review has spread rapidly in recent years. By early 1998 there were ninety-five procedures, a 375 percent increase since 1985. These procedures cover about 75 percent of the fifty largest cities in the country and about 25 percent of the entire U.S. population.[139]

Some citizen review procedures investigate complaints themselves (e.g., the Minneapolis Civilian Review Authority). Others provide some citizen input into investigations conducted by IA officers (e.g., the Kansas City Officer of Citizen Complaints). Some procedures systematically audit the performance of the IA unit (e.g., the Portland Police Internal Investigations Auditing Committee).

There is some evidence that citizen review enhances public confidence in the complaint process. In 1991, for example, San Francisco had five times as many complaints per officer as Los Angeles. Some observers argue that San Francisco generates more complaints because its civilian review procedure enhances citizen feelings that their complaints will receive a fair hearing, whereas the Los Angeles Police Department actively discouraged complaints.[140]

POLICE EMPLOYMENT PRACTICES

Discrimination in the employment of racial and ethnic minorities as police officers has been a long-standing problem. During the Segregation Era (1890s–1960s), Southern cities did not hire any African American officers, and police departments in Northern states engaged in systematic employment discrimination.[141] In 1967, for example, African Americans were 23 percent of the population in Oakland but only 2.3 percent of the police officers.[142] Employment discrimination occurs in three different areas of policing: recruitment, promotion to supervisory ranks, and assignment to shifts and specialized units.

Trends in Racial Minority Employment

Since the 1960s, some progress has been made in the employment of racial and ethnic minority police officers (see Figure 4.3). In 1960 an estimated 3.6 percent of all sworn officers in the United States were African Americans; by 1990 the figure had risen to 10.5 percent. Hispanic Americans, meanwhile, represented about 5.2 percent of all sworn officers in city police departments in 1990 (unfortunately, there are few data on Hispanic officers for earlier years).[148]

Focus on an Issue

Would It Make a Difference?
Assigning African American Officers to
African American Neighborhoods

Some civil rights activists argue that police departments should assign African American officers exclusively to African American neighborhoods. They believe that these officers would be more sensitive to community needs, more polite and respectful to neighborhood residents, and less likely to act in a discriminatory manner.

Is this a good idea? Would it, in fact, improve the quality of policing in minority neighborhoods? The evidence does not support this proposal.

First, as we have already seen, no evidence suggests that African American, Hispanic, and white officers behave in significantly different ways. Fyfe's research on deadly force found that officers assigned to high-crime precincts fired their weapons at similar rates, regardless of race.[143] Reiss found that white and African American officers used excessive physical force at about the same rate.[144] Black found no significant differences in the arrest patterns of white and African American officers.[145] It is worth noting that male and female officers have also been found to behave in roughly similar ways. Thus, most experts on the police argue that situational and departmental factors, not race or gender, influence police officer behavior.[146]

Second, assigning only African American officers to African American neighborhoods, or Hispanic officers to Hispanic neighborhoods, would discriminate against the officers themselves. It would "ghettoize" them and deny them the variety of assignments and experience that helps lead to promotion. The policy would also perpetuate racial stereotypes by promoting the idea that only African American officers could handle the African American community.

Finally, the proposal is based on a faulty assumption about the nature of American urban communities. Although there are all-white, all–African American, and all-Hispanic neighborhoods, there are also many mixed neighborhoods. It is impossible to draw a clear line between the "white" and the "black" communities. Under the proposed policy, which officers would be assigned to mixed neighborhoods? Moreover, the racial and ethnic composition of neighborhoods is constantly changing.[147] Today's all-white neighborhood is tomorrow's multiracial and multiethnic neighborhood. Any attempt to draw precinct boundaries based on race or ethnicity would be quickly outdated.

The aggregate figures on employment are misleading because, as noted in Chapter 1, the racial and ethnic minority groups are not evenly distributed across the country. It is more useful to look at particular police departments to see whether they represent the communities they serve. The accreditation standards for law enforcement agencies require that "the agency has minority group and female employees in the sworn law enforcement ranks in approximate proportion to the makeup of the available work force in the law enforcement agency's service community . . . ."[149]

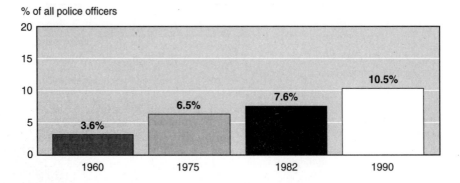

% of all police officers

FIGURE 4.3 Percentage of Police Officers Who Are African American

The Equal Employment Opportunity (EEO) Index provides a representative measure. The EEO Index compares the percentage of minority group officers with the percentage of that group in the local population. If, for example, a community is 40 percent African American and 30 percent of the officers are African American, the EEO Index is 0.75.[150]

The EEO Index offers some interesting comparisons across police departments. New York City had an EEO Index of only 0.40 for African Americans in 1992: 11.4 percent of the officers and 28.7 percent of the city population. This was one of the lowest rates for any big city. Even worse, the New York City EEO Index had been 0.40 in 1983. Thus, the department had made almost no progress in the employment of African Americans in ten years.[151] The Cleveland Police Department, on the other hand, made significant gains in the employment of African Americans. Its EEO Index rose from 0.26 in 1983 to 0.56 in 1992. This progress resulted from an active recruitment effort and was achieved despite the fact that the department shrank from 2,091 to 1,668 sworn officers.[152]

Los Angeles offers another interesting perspective on minority employment. In 1992 the police department had a perfect EEO Index (1.00) for African Americans (14 percent of both the population and the sworn officers). Yet, the Rodney King incident revealed that the department had a serious race relations problem. The Christopher Commission found a racist climate within the department, with officers making racist comments over the department's computerized message system.[153] In short, merely employing racial minority officers does not automatically eliminate police–community relations problems. The quality of policing is largely determined by the organizational culture of the department, which is the combined product of leadership by the chief, formal policies on critical issues such as the use of force, and rank-and-file officer peer culture.

In some police departments, white officers are now the minority. In Miami 47.5 percent of the officers were Hispanic in 1992, 22.4 percent were African American, and 30 percent were white. African Americans were 67.8 percent of the officers in Washington, D.C., and 53 percent of the police force in Detroit.[154]

With respect to Hispanic police officers, effectively serving Hispanic communities means having officers who can communicate in Spanish. The

Christopher Commission found that in the heavily Hispanic communities of Los Angeles, often no Spanish-speaking officers were available to take citizen complaints.[155] Similar problems arise in communities with significant Asian American populations, representing different nationalities and languages.

Relatively few Native Americans and Asian Americans are employed as sworn police officers. The Justice Department's report on *Law Enforcement Management and Administrative Statistics* provides the most systematic set of data. A few police departments do have a significant number of Asian American officers. They represent 12 percent of the officers in San Francisco, for example, and 7 percent of the Seattle police. Native Americans, on the other hand, are substantially underrepresented, even in states with the largest Native American populations. They are only 1 percent of the sworn officers in Albuquerque, New Mexico, for example.[156]

The Law of Employment Discrimination

Employment discrimination based on race or ethnicity is illegal. The Fourteenth Amendment to the U.S. Constitution provides that "No state shall . . . deny to any person . . . the equal protection of the laws." Title VII of the 1964 Civil Rights Act prohibits employment discrimination based on race, color, national origin, religion, or sex. The 1972 Equal Employment Opportunity Act extended the coverage of Title VII to state and local governments. In addition, state civil rights laws prohibit employment discrimination.

The most controversial aspect of employment discrimination is the policy of affirmative action. The Office of Federal Contract Compliance defines affirmative action as "results-oriented actions [taken] to ensure equal employment opportunity [which may include] goals to correct under-utilization . . . [and] backpay, retroactive seniority, makeup goals and timetables." Affirmative action originated in 1966 when President Lyndon Johnson issued Executive Order 11246 directing all federal contractors to have affirmative action programs. Some affirmative action programs are voluntary, whereas others are court ordered; some have general goals, whereas others have specific quotas.

An affirmative action program consists of several steps. The first is a census of employees to determine the number and percentage of racial minorities and women in different job categories. The data are then used to identify underutilization. Underutilization exists where the percentage of employees in a particular job category is less than the percentage of potentially qualified members of that group in the labor force. In a discrimination suit against the Omaha Police Department, for example, the court set a goal of 9.5 percent African American officers based on their representation in the local labor force.[157]

If underutilization exists, the employer is required to develop a plan to eliminate it. Recruitment programs typically include active outreach to potential minority applicants, mainly through meetings with community groups and leaders. The Cleveland Police Department, for example, had fourteen officers involved in recruitment; the sergeant in charge of the program said that the "key" factor in their success was "assigning recruiting officers to targeted neighborhoods by race."[158] In the past, employers often did not actively recruit

or even publicize job openings, a practice that gave the advantage to people
with personal connections and perpetuated discrimination.

An employer may voluntarily adopt an affirmative action plan with quotas.
In 1974 the Detroit Police Department adopted a voluntary quota of promoting one African American officer for each white officer promoted. As a result,
by 1992 half of all the officers at the rank of sergeant or above were African
American.[159]

Most affirmative action plans have been court ordered, as a result of discrimination suits under Title VII of the 1964 Civil Rights Act. A 1980 consent
decree settling the suit against the Omaha, Nebraska, police department, for example, established a long-term goal of having 9.5 percent African American officers in the department within seven years. At the time of the suit, African
Americans were only 4 percent of the sworn officers, and the figure had been
declining. To achieve the 9.5 percent goal, the court ordered a three-stage recruitment plan: African Americans would be 40 percent of all new recruits until they were 6 percent of the department, 33 percent of recruits until they were
8 percent, and then 25 percent of recruits until the final 9.5 percent goal was
reached.[160] The city reached the goals of the court order ahead of schedule, and
by 1992, African American officers were 11.5 percent of the police department.

Discrimination in Assignment

Discrimination also occurs in the assignment of police officers. In the South
during the Segregation Era (1890s–1960s), African American officers were not
assigned to white neighborhoods and were not permitted to arrest whites.[161]
Many Northern cities also confined minority officers to minority neighborhoods. Reiss found that some police departments dumped their incompetent
white officers on racial minority neighborhoods.[162] Seniority rules that govern the assignment in most departments today make blatant discrimination
difficult. Officers with the most seniority, regardless of race, ethnicity, or gender, have first choice for the most desirable assignments. Seniority rules can
have an indirect race effect, however. In a department that has only recently
hired a significant number of racial or ethnic minorities, these officers will be
disproportionately assigned to high-crime areas because of their lack of seniority. Fyfe found that this seniority-based assignment pattern explained why
African American officers in New York City fired their weapons more often
than white officers did (although the rates were virtually the same for all officers assigned to the high-crime areas, regardless of race).[163]

There is also discrimination in assignment to special and desirable units. The
Special Counsel to the Los Angeles County Sheriffs' Department identified two
categories of desirable positions. "Coveted" positions were those that officers
sought because they are interesting, high-paying, or convenient (in terms of
work schedule). In the Los Angeles Sheriff's Department these included the
Special Enforcement Bureau, the Narcotics Bureau, and precinct station detective assignments. "High profile" positions, on the other hand, are those likely to
lead to promotion and career advancement. These include Operations Deputy,
the Recruitment Training Bureau, and Field Training Officer positions.[164]

The assignment of African American officers to plainclothes detective work has created a new problem. In 1992 an African American transit police officer in New York City wearing plain clothes was shot and seriously wounded by a white officer who mistook him for a robber.[165] Similar incidents have occurred in other cities.

The Impact of Diversity

Civil rights leaders and police reformers have fought for increased employment of racial and ethnic minorities with three different goals in mind. First, employment discrimination is illegal and must be eliminated for that reason alone. Second, some reformers believe that minority officers will act differently on the street and be less likely to discriminate in making arrests or using physical force.[166] Third, many experts argue that police departments should reflect the communities they serve to create a positive public image.

With respect to the first objective, increased minority employment means that the agency is complying with the law of equal employment opportunity. With respect to the second objective, improved policing, there is no clear evidence that white, African American, or Hispanic police officers act differently on the job (see the earlier Focus on an Issue: Would It Make a Difference). That is, they arrest and use physical and deadly force in similar fashions. For the most part, they are influenced by situational factors: the seriousness of the offense, the demeanor of the suspect, and so forth.

With respect to the third goal, improved police–community relations, there is only limited evidence that increased minority employment improves public opinion about the police. A survey of Chicago residents found a small but significant number of people who felt that the Chicago Police Department has improved because of increased numbers of minority officers in supervisory positions. Significantly, no respondents felt that the department had gotten worse because of increased minority employment.[167] A study of Detroit, meanwhile, found that, unlike all other surveys, African American residents rated the police department more favorably than white residents. The study suggested that this more favorable rating was due to the significant African American representation in city government, including the police department.[168]

Higher minority employment has an impact on the police subculture. African American and Hispanic officers have formed their own organizations at both the local and national levels. The National Black Police Officers Association and the Guardians, for example, represent African American officers. Hispanic officers have formed the Latino Police Officers Association and the Hispanic American Command Officers Association. These organizations offer a different perspective on police issues from the one presented by white police officers. After the Rodney King incident, for example, members of the African American Peace Officers Association in Los Angeles stated, "Racism is widespread in the department."[169] This was a very different point of view than that expressed by white Los Angeles officers. In this respect, minority employment breaks down the solidarity of the police subculture.

The National Black Police Association published a brochure titled *Police Brutality: A Strategy to Stop the Violence.* In a sharp break with the traditional police subculture, it urged officers to report brutality by other officers.[170]

Minorities as Supervisors and Chief Executives

Promotion African American and Hispanic officers are also seriously underrepresented in supervisory ranks. In 1992 African Americans were 11.5 percent of all sworn officers in New York City but only 6.6 percent of the officers at the rank of sergeant and above. In Los Angeles, Hispanics were 22.3 percent of all sworn officers but only 13.4 percent of those at the rank of sergeant and above.[171]

Female African American and Hispanic officers encounter both race and gender discrimination. All women, regardless of race or ethnicity, are significantly underrepresented among all sworn officers and even more underrepresented in the supervisory ranks. A 1992 survey found that white female officers were being promoted at a faster rate than either African American or Hispanic female officers. In Chicago, for example, there were seventy-three white females, thirty-seven African American females, and two Hispanic females above the rank of sergeant in a department of 12,291 sworn officers.[172] The data contradict the popular belief that minority women enjoy a special advantage because employers count them in two affirmative action categories. Hispanic women, in fact, were almost completely unrepresented at the rank of sergeant and above.

Chief Executives Racial and ethnic minorities have been far more successful in achieving the rank of police chief executive. In recent years, African Americans have served as chief executive in many of the largest police departments in the country: New York City, Los Angeles, Chicago, Philadelphia, Atlanta, and New Orleans, among others. Several African American individuals have established distinguished careers as law enforcement chief executives. Lee P. Brown served as sheriff of Multnomah County, Oregon, and then police chief in Atlanta, Houston, and New York City. In 1993 he became President Clinton's director of the Office of Drug Control Policy. Hubert Williams served as police commissioner in Newark, New Jersey, and then became president of the Police Foundation, a private police research organization. Charles Ramsey was appointed Superintendent of the Washington, D.C., police department in 1998 after directing the Chicago police department's community policing program.

CONCLUSION

Significant problems persist in the relations between police and racial and ethnic communities in the United States. African Americans and Hispanics rate the police lower than do white Americans. There is persuasive evidence that minorities are more likely than white Americans to be shot and killed, arrested, and victimized by excessive physical force. Despite some progress in recent years in controlling police behavior, particularly with respect to the use of deadly force, significant racial and ethnic disparities remain. In addition, there is evidence of misconduct directed against racial and ethnic minorities and that police departments fail to discipline officers who are guilty of misconduct. Finally, employment discrimination by police departments continues.

With reference to the discrimination–disparity continuum we discussed in Chapter 1, the evidence about the police suggests a combination of three of the different patterns: institutionalized discrimination, contextual discrimination, and individual acts of discrimination. That is, some of the disparities are the result of the application of neutral criteria (e.g., the greater likelihood of arrest for the more serious crimes); some represent contextual discrimination (as in the greater likelihood of arrest of minorities suspected of crimes against whites); and some are individual acts of discrimination by prejudiced individuals. There is no basis for saying that a situation of pure justice exists or that racism is a "myth," as William Wilbanks argued.[173]

The evidence supports the conflict perspective regarding the police and racial and ethnic minorities. The data suggest that police actions such as arrest, use of deadly force, and verbal abuse reflect the broader patterns of social and economic inequality in U.S. society that we discussed in detail in Chapter 3. Those inequalities are both racial and economic. Thus, the injustices suffered by racial and ethnic minorities at the hands of the police are a result of both discrimination against ethnic and racial minorities and the disproportionate representation of minorities among the poor.

The evidence also supports Hawkins's call for a modified conflict perspective that takes into account evident complexities and contingencies.[174] Some of the evidence we have reviewed, for example, indicates that in certain situations, African Americans receive less law enforcement protection than do whites. Discrimination can result from too little policing as well as excessive policing. Other evidence suggests that the race of the suspect must be considered in conjunction with the race of the complainant.

Finally, the evidence indicates significant changes in some important areas of policing with respect to racial and ethnic minorities. On the positive side, the number of persons shot and killed by the police has declined. On the negative side, the war on drugs has been waged most heavily against racial and ethnic minorities. In terms of employment, some slow but steady progress has been made in the employment of African Americans and Hispanic Americans as police officers.

DISCUSSION QUESTIONS

1. What is meant by a contextual approach to examining policing, race, and ethnicity?

2. How is policing in Native American communities different than policing in the rest of the United States?

3. When does police use of force become "excessive" or "unjustified?" Give a definition of excessive force.

4. Are there any significant differences between how Hispanic Americans and African Americans interact with the police? Explain.

5. Is there racial or ethnic discrimination in arrests? What is the evidence on this question?

6. Define the concept of affirmative action. Do you support or oppose affirmative action in the employment of police officers? Do you think affirmative action is more important in policing than in other areas of life? Explain.

NOTES

1. Sandra Lee Browning, Francis T. Cullen, Liqun Cao, Renee Kopache, and Thomas J. Stevenson, "Race and Getting Hassled by the Police: A Research Note," *Police Studies* 17 (1994, No. 1): 1–11.

2. Warren Friedman and Marsha Hott, *Young People and the Police: Respect, Fear and the Future of Community Policing in Chicago* (Chicago: Chicago Alliance for Neighborhood Safety, 1995), p. iii.

3. Bureau of Justice Statistics, *Police Use of Force: Collection of National Data* (Washington, D.C.: U.S. Government Printing Office, 1997).

4. Bureau of Criminal Justice Statistics, *Sourcebook of Criminal Justice Statistics, 1996* (Washington, D.C.: U.S. Government Printing Office, 1997), p. 119.

5. A full review of the evidence on police–community relations is in Samuel Walker, *The Police in America,* 3d ed. (New York: McGraw-Hill, 1999), chap. 9.

6. Bureau of Justice Statistics, *Police Use of Force: Collection of National Data.*

7. Marianne O. Nielsen, "Contextualization for Native American Crime and Criminal Justice Involvement," in *Native Americans, Crime, and Justice,* ed. Marianne O. Nielsen and Robert A. Silverman (Boulder, CO: Westview, 1996), p. 10.

8. James Frank, Steven G. Brandl, Francis T. Cullen, and Amy Stichman, "Reassessing the Impact of Race on Citizens' Attitudes Toward the Police: A Research Note," *Justice Quarterly* 13 (June 1996, No. 2): 321–334.

9. Roger G. Dunham and Geoffrey P. Alpert, "Neighborhood Differences in Attitudes Toward Policing: Evidence for a Mixed-Strategy Model of Policing in a Multi-Ethnic Setting," *Journal of Criminal Law and Criminology* 79 (1988, No. 2): 504–523.

10. Kerner Commission, *Report of the National Advisory Commission on Civil Disorders* (New York: Bantam Books, 1968), p. 304.

11. Ibid., p. 483.

12. Alfredo Mirandé, *Gringo Justice* (Notre Dame, IN: University of Notre Dame Press, 1987).

13. Mauricio Mazon, *The Zoot-Suit Riots* (Austin: University of Texas Press, 1989).

14. Ibid., pp. 173–179.

15. Joan Petersilia and Allan Abrahamse, *The Los Angeles Riot of Spring, 1992: A Profile of Those Arrested* (Santa Monica, CA: Rand, 1993). See also U.S. Civil Rights Commission, *Mexican-Americans and the Administration of Justice* (Washington, D.C.: U.S. Government Printing Office, 1970).

16. Henry I. DeGeneste and John P. Sullivan, *Policing a Multicultural Community* (Washington, D.C.: Police Executive Research Forum, 1997), p. 15.

17. Minneapolis Civilian Review Authority, brochures (Minneapolis, MN: Author, 1998).

18. Bureau of Justice Statistics, *Sourcebook of Criminal Justice Statistics, 1997,* p. 107, Table 2.17.

19. U.S. Department of Justice, *The Police and Public Opinion* (Washington, D.C.: U.S. Government Printing Office, 1977), pp. 39–40.

20. A comprehensive overview of public opinion trends is in Steven A. Tuch and Ronald Weitzer, "Racial Differences in Attitudes Toward the Police," *Public Opinion Quarterly* 61 (1997): 643–663.

21. President's Commission on Law Enforcement and the Administration of Justice, *The Challenge of Crime in a Free Society* (Washington, D.C.: U.S. Government Printing Office, 1967), p. 99.

22. U.S. Department of Justice, *The Police and Public Opinion*, p. 13.

23. David L. Carter, "Hispanic Perceptions of Police Performance: An Empirical Assessment," *Journal of Criminal Justice* 13 (1985): 487–500.

24. Tuch and Weitzer, "Racial Differences in Attitudes Toward the Police."

25. Bureau of Justice Statistics, *Sourcebook of Criminal Justice Statistics, 1992* (Washington, D.C.: U.S. Government Printing Office, 1993), pp. 169–173.

26. Carl Werthman and Irving Piliavin, "Gang Members and the Police," in *The Police: Six Sociological Essays,* ed. David J. Bordua (New York: Wiley, 1967), p. 58.

27. David H. Bayley and Harold Mendelsohn, *Minorities and the Police: Confrontation in America* (New York: Free Press, 1969), p. 109.

28. Albert J. Reiss, *The Police and the Public* (New Haven, CT: Yale University Press, 1971).

29. Bureau of Justice Statistics, *Criminal Victimization in the United States, 1994* (Washington, D.C.: U.S. Government Printing Office, 1997), pp. 10, 12.

30. Ibid., p. 85.

31. Cynthia Perez McCluskey, *Policing the Latino Community* (East Lansing, MI: Julian Samora Research Institute, 1998), p. 3.

32. Bureau of Justice Statistics, *Police Use of Force: Collection of National Data.*

33. David L. Carter, "Hispanic Interaction With the Criminal Justice System in Texas: Experiences, Attitudes, and Perceptions," *Journal of Criminal Justice* 11 (1983, No. 3): 213–227.

34. Samuel Walker, "Complaints Against the Police: A Focus Group Study of Citizen Perceptions, Goals, and Expectations," *Criminal Justice Review* 22 (1997, No. 2): 207–225.

35. Marianne O. Nielsen and Robert Silverman, eds., *Native Americans, Crime, and Justice* (Boulder, CO: Westview, 1996).

36. Eileen Luna, "The Growth and Development of Tribal Police," *Journal of Contemporary Criminal Justice* 14 (February 1998, No. 1): 75–86.

37. Executive Committee for Indian Country Law Enforcement Improvements, *Final Report to the Attorney General and the Secretary of the Interior* (Washington, D.C.: U.S. Government Printing Office, 1997).

38. Eileen Luna and Samuel Walker, *Policing in Indian Country: A National Survey of Tribal Law Enforcement Agencies* (Omaha: University of Nebraska at Omaha, 1998).

39. James Baldwin, *Nobody Knows My Name* (New York: Dell, 1962), pp. 65–67.

40. Bureau of Justice Statistics, *Sourcebook of Criminal Justice Statistics, 1993* (Washington, D.C.: U.S. Government Printing Office, 1994), p. 167.

41. See the comprehensive discussion in Randall Kennedy, *Race, Crime, and the Law* (New York: Vintage, 1998), pp. 29–75.

42. Gunnar Myrdal, *An American Dilemma* (New York: Harper, 1944), Chap. 25, "The Police and Other Public Contacts," pp. 535–546.

43. Kerner Commission, *Report of the National Advisory Commission,* p. 308.

44. Kennedy, *Race, Crime, and the Law,* p. 29.

45. Peter B. Bloch, *Equality of Distribution of Police Services—A Case Study of Washington, D.C.* (Washington, D.C.: Urban Institute, 1974).

46. *Tennessee v. Garner,* 471 U.S. 1 (1985).

47. James J. Fyfe, "Reducing the Use of Deadly Force: The New York Experience," in U.S. Department of Justice, *Police Use of Deadly Force* (Washington, D.C.: U.S. Government Printing Office, 1978), p. 29.

48. James J. Fyfe, "Blind Justice: Police Shootings in Memphis," *Journal of Criminal Law and Criminology* 73 (1982, No. 2): 707–722.

49. William A. Geller and Kevin J. Karales, *Split-Second Decisions* (Chicago: Chicago Law Enforcement Study Group, 1981), p. 119.

50. William A. Geller and Michael S. Scott, *Deadly Force: What We Know* (Washington, D.C.: Police Executive Research Forum, 1992), pp. 149–150.

51. *Tennessee v. Garner*, 471 U.S. 1 (1985).

52. Geller and Scott, *Deadly Force*, p. 503. See also Lawrence W. Sherman and Ellen G. Cohn, *Citizens Killed by Big City Police, 1970–1984* (Washington, D.C.: Crime Control Institute, 1986).

53. Tom McEwen, *National Data Collection on Police Use of Force* (Washington, D.C.: U.S. Government Printing Office, 1996); Federal Bureau of Investigation, *Law Enforcement Officers Killed and Assaulted, 1996* (Washington, D.C.: U.S. Government Printing Office, 1997).

54. Geller and Karales, *Split-Second Decisions*, p. 119.

55. City of New York, Commission to Investigate Allegations of Police Corruption [Mollen Commission], *Commission Report* (New York: City of New York, 1994), p. 48.

56. National Commission on Law Observance and Enforcement, *Lawlessness in Law Enforcement* (Washington, D.C.: U.S. Government Printing Office, 1931), p. 4.

57. Human Rights Watch, *Shielded From Justice: Police Brutality and Accountability in the United States* (New York: Human Rights Watch, 1998), p. 39

58. Mollen Commission, *Commission Report*, p. 44, n. 4.

59. President's Commission on Law Enforcement and Administration of Justice, *Field Surveys, Vol. 5, A National Survey of Police and Community Relations* (Washington, D.C.: U.S. Government Printing Office, 1967), p. 151.

60. New York City, Civilian Complaint Investigative Bureau, 1990 *Annual Report* (New York: Author, 1990), p. 10.

61. "When making an arrest, an officer may use as much force as is reasonably necessary to carry out the arrest and for the protection of himself and others." Quoted in Lloyd L. Weinreb and James D. Whaley, *The Field Guide to Law Enforcement, 1991–1992* (Westbury, NY: Foundation, 1991), p. 13.

62. The best review of the available studies is Kenneth Adams, "Measuring the Prevalence of Police Abuse of Force," in *And Justice for All*, ed. William A. Geller and Hans Toch (Washington, D.C.: Police Executive Research Forum, 1995), pp. 61–98. See also Anthony M. Pate and Lorie Fridell, *Police Use of Force*, 2 vols. (Washington, D.C.: Police Foundation, 1993).

63. Bureau of Justice Statistics, *Police Use of Force: Collection of National Data*.

64. Albert Reiss, "Police Brutality—Answers to Key Questions," *Transaction* 5 (July–August, 1968): 10–19. A longer discussion of the data is in Reiss, *The Police and the Public*; Robert E. Worden, "The 'Causes' of Police Brutality: Theory and Evidence on Police Use of Force," in *And Justice for All*, pp. 31–60.

65. Eric J. Scott, *Calls for Service* (Washington, D.C.: U.S. Government Printing Office, 1981).

66. Human Rights Watch, *Shielded From Justice*, p. 51.

67. Reiss, "Police Brutality—Answers to Key Questions."

68. Reiss, *The Police and the Public*, pp. 149, 155.

69. Reiss, "Police Brutality—Answers to Key Questions," pp. 13–14.

70. New York City Civilian Complaint Review Board, *Semiannual Status Report, January–December 1997*, (New York: Author, 1998), p. 31.

71. Worden, "The 'Causes' of Police Brutality," pp. 52–53.

72. Reiss, *The Police and the Public*, p. 151.

73. George Gallup, Jr., *The Gallup Poll Monthly* (March 1991, No. 306).

74. Robert Tillman, "The Size of the Criminal Population: The Prevalence and Incidence of Adult Arrest," *Criminology* 25 (August 1987): 561–579.

75. Bureau of the Census, *Statistical Abstract of the United States 1994* (Washington, D.C.: U.S. Government Printing Office, 1994), p. 17.

76. Donald Black, "The Social Organization of Arrest," in *The Manners and Customs*

of the Police, ed. Donald Black (New York: Academic Press, 1980), pp. 85–108.

77. David A. Klinger, "Demeanor or Crime? Why 'Hostile' Citizens Are More Likely to Be Arrested," Criminology 32 (1994, No. 3): 475–493.

78. Bureau of Justice Statistics, Criminal Victimization in the United States, 1994, p. 40.

79. Bureau of Justice Statistics, Sourcebook of Criminal Justice Statistics, 1996, p. 382.

80. Douglas A. Smith, Christy Visher, and Laura A. Davidson, "Equity and Discretionary Justice: The Influence of Race on Police Arrest Decisions," Journal of Criminal Law and Criminology 75 (Spring 1984): 234–249; Douglas A. Smith and Christy A. Visher, "Street-Level Justice: Situational Determinants of Police Arrest Decisions," Social Problems 29 (December 1981): 167–177.

81. John R. Hepburn, "Race and the Decision to Arrest: An Analysis of Warrants Issued," Journal of Research in Crime and Delinquency 15 (1978): 54–73.

82. Joan Petersilia, Racial Disparities in the Criminal Justice System (Santa Monica, CA: Rand, 1983), pp. 21–26.

83. Black, The Manners and Customs of the Police, p. 108.

84. George L. Kelling and M. Catherine Coles, Fixing Broken Windows (New York: Free Press, 1996).

85. New York Civil Liberties Union, Deflecting Blame (New York: Author, 1998), p. 48.

86. Jerome G. Miller, Search and Destroy: African American Males in the Criminal Justice System (New York: Cambridge University Press, 1996).

87. Steven R. Donziger, ed., The Real War on Crime (New York: HarperCollins, 1996), p. 115.

88. Ibid.

89. Jerome H. Skolnick and James J. Fyfe, Above the Law: Police and the Excessive Use of Force (New York: Free Press, 1993), pp. 206–207.

90. Malcolm W. Klein, The American Street Gang (New York: Oxford University Press, 1995).

91. Miller, Search and Destroy, p. 109.

92. Friedman and Hott, Young People and the Police, p. 111.

93. Bureau of Justice Statistics, Police Use of Force: Collection of National Data, p. 11.

94. John E. Boydston, San Diego Field Interrogation: Final Report (Washington, D.C.: Police Foundation, 1975), pp. 16, 62.

95. Massachusetts Attorney General, Report of the Attorney General's Civil Rights Division on Boston Police Department Practices (Boston: Attorney General's Office, 1990).

96. Boydston, San Diego Field Interrogation, p. 7.

97. Report of the National Advisory Commission, pp. 301, 304–305.

98. Boydston, San Diego Field Interrogation, p. 62.

99. Carolyn M. Ward, "Policing in the Hyde Park Neighborhood, St. Louis: Racial Bias, Political Pressure, and Community Policing," Crime, Law and Social Change 26 (1997): 171–172.

100. David A. Harris, "'Driving While Black' and (all) Other Traffic Offenses: The Supreme Court and Pretextual Traffic Stops," Journal of Criminal Law and Criminology 87 (December 1997): 544–582.

101. Jerome Skolnick, Justice Without Trial: Law Enforcement in a Democratic Society, 3d ed. (New York: Macmillan, 1994), pp. 44–47.

102. Kennedy, Race, Crime, and the Law, p. 137.

103. Ibid., p. 151.

104. Ibid.

105. Ibid., p. 153.

106. Minneapolis Civilian Police Review Authority, 1997 Annual Report (Minneapolis, MN: Author, 1998), Exhibit F.

107. Christopher Commission, Report of the Independent Commission on the Los Angeles Police Department (Los Angeles: Author, 1991), p. 73.

108. Ibid., pp. 72–73.

109. Mervin F. White, Terry C. Cox, and Jack Basehart, "Theoretical Considerations of Officer Profanity and Obscenity in Formal Contacts With Citizens," in Police Deviance, 2d ed., ed. Thomas Barker and David L. Carter (Cincinnati, OH: Anderson, 1991), pp. 275–297; John Van Maanen, "The Asshole," in Policing: A View From the Street, ed. John Van Maanen and Peter

Manning (Santa Monica, CA: Goodyear, 1978), pp. 221–238.

110. San Diego Citizens' Review Board on Police Practices, *Annual Report 1990* (San Diego, CA: Author, 1990).

111. Douglas A. Smith, Nanette Graham, and Bonney Adams, "Minorities and the Police: Attitudinal and Behavioral Questions," in *Race and Criminal Justice,* ed. Michael J. Lynch and E. Britt Patterson (New York: Harrow & Heston, 1991), p. 31.

112. Bayley and Mendelsohn, *Minorities and the Police,* p. 144.

113. Ibid.

114. Ibid., pp. 15–18.

115. Smith et al., "Minorities and the Police," p. 28.

116. Reiss, *The Police and the Public,* p. 147.

117. Samuel Walker, "Racial-Minority and Female Employment in Policing: The Implications of 'Glacial' Change," *Crime and Delinquency* 31 (October 1985): 555–572.

118. Jerome L. Blakemore, David Barlow, and Deborah L. Padgett, "From the Classroom to the Community: Introducing Process in Police Diversity Training," *Police Studies,* 18 (1995, No. 1): 71–83.

119. Geoffrey P. Alpert, William C. Smith, and Danial Watters, "Law Enforcement: Implications of the Rodney King Beating," *Criminal Law Bulletin* 28 (September–October 1992): 477.

120. New York City, *The Knapp Commission Report on Police Corruption* (New York: Braziller, 1972), p. 1.

121. Ibid.

122. Bureau of Justice Statistics, *Sourcebook of Criminal Justice Statistics, 1993*, p. 165.

123. Fred A. Klyman and Joanna Kruckenberg, "A National Survey of Police–Community Relations Units," *Journal of Police Science and Administration* 7 (March 1979): 74.

124. U.S. Department of Justice, *Improving Police/Community Relations* (Washington, D.C.: U.S. Government Printing Office, 1973), pp. 3–4.

125. Wesley G. Skogan and Susan M. Hartnett, *Community Policing: Chicago Style* (New York: Oxford University Press, 1997).

126. Santa Ana Police Department, *Annual Report 1993* (Santa Ana, CA: The City of Santa Ana, 1993), pp. 14, 31.

127. Chicago Police Department, General Order 92-1, "Human Rights and Human Resources," July 4, 1992.

128. Minneapolis Civilian Police Review Authority, *1997 Annual Report,* Exhibit C, p. 1.

129. Human Rights Watch, *Shielded From Justice.*

130. Samuel Walker and Nanette Graham, "Citizen Complaints in Response to Police Misconduct: The Results of a Victimization Survey," *Police Quarterly,* I (1998): 65–89.

131. Christopher Commission, *Report of the Independent Commission,* pp. 153–161.

132. ACLU of Southern California, *The Call for Change Goes Unanswered* (Los Angeles: Author, 1992), p. 23.

133. William A. Westley, *Violence and the Police* (Cambridge, MA: MIT Press, 1970).

134. Christopher Commission, *Report of the Independent Commission,* p. 168.

135. Ibid.

136. New York City, *Commission Report,* p. 53.

137. Pate and Fridell, *Police Use of Force,* Vol. 1, p. 118.

138. David Pearce Demers, "The Color of Justice," *Twin Cities Reader* (March 25–31 1992): 1–2.

139. Samuel Walker, *Citizen Review of the Police: 1998 Update* (Omaha: University of Nebraska at Omaha, 1998).

140. "Police Attacks: Hard Crimes to Uncover, Let Alone Stop," *New York Times* (March 24, 1991), p. D4; Samuel Walker and Vic W. Bumphus, "The Effectiveness of Civilian Review: Observations to Recent Trends and New Issues Regarding the Civilian Review of the Police," *American Journal of Police* 11 (1992, No. 4): 1–26.

141. Marvin W. Dulaney, *Black Police in America* (Bloomington: Indiana University Press, 1996).

142. President's Commission on Law Enforcement and Administration of Justice, *Task Force Report: The Police* (Washington, D.C.: U.S. Government Printing Office, 1967), p. 168.

143. James J. Fyfe, "Who Shoots? A Look at Officer Race and Police Shooting," *Journal of Police Science and Administration* 9 (1981, No. 4): 367–382.

144. Reiss, "Police Brutality—Answers to Key Questions."

145. Black, *Manners and Customs of the Police.*

146. Lawrence W. Sherman, "Causes of Police Behavior: The Current State of Quantitative Research," *Journal of Research in Crime and Delinquency* 17 (January 1980): 69–100.

147. Reiss, *The Police and the Public,* pp. 209–210.

148. Bureau of Justice Statistics, *State and Local Police Departments, 1990* (Washington, D.C.: U.S. Government Printing Office, 1992), Table 11. For a review of the earlier data, see Samuel Walker, *The Police in America: An Introduction,* 2d ed. (New York: McGraw-Hill, 1992), pp. 303–323.

149. Commission on Accreditation for Law Enforcement Agencies, *Standards for Law Enforcement Agencies,* 3d ed. (Fairfax, VA: Author, 1994), Standard 31-2.

150. Samuel Walker and K. B. Turner, *A Decade of Modest Progress* (Omaha: University of Nebraska at Omaha, 1992).

151. Ibid.

152. Ibid.

153. Christopher Commission, *Report of the Independent Commission.*

154. Walker and Turner, *A Decade of Modest Progress,* pp. 3–4.

155. Christopher Commission, *Report of the Independent Commission,* p. 158.

156. Bureau of Justice Statistics, *Law Enforcement Management and Administrative Statistics, 1993* (Washington, D.C.: U.S. Government Printing Office, 1995), Table 4a.

157. *Brotherhood of Midwest Guardians, Inc. v. City of Omaha* (1980).

158. "Gains Despite Downsizing," *Law Enforcement News* (October 31, 1992), p. 9.

159. Samuel Walker and K. B. Turner, unpublished data.

160. *Brotherhood of Midwest Guardians, Inc. v. City of Omaha* (1980).

161. Myrdal, "Police and Other Public Contacts."

162. Reiss, *The Police and the Public,* p. 167.

163. Fyfe, "Who Shoots?"

164. Merrick J. Bobb, Special Counsel, *9th Semiannual Report* (Los Angeles: Los Angeles County, 1998), pp. 59–61.

165. "Alone, Undercover, and Black: Hazards of Mistaken Identity," *New York Times* (November 22, 1992), p. A1.

166. The Kerner Commission, for example, argued that "Negro officers can also be particularly effective in controlling disorders"; *Report of the National Advisory Commission,* p. 315.

167. Samuel E. Walker and Vincent J. Webb, "Public Perceptions of Racial and Minority Employment and Its Perceived Impact on Police Service," paper presented at the American Society of Criminology Annual Meeting, 1997.

168. Frank et al., "Reassessing the Impact of Race on Citizens' Attitudes Toward the Police."

169. "Los Angeles Force Accused From Within," *New York Times* (March 29, 1991), p. A18.

170. National Black Police Association, *Police Brutality: A Strategy to Stop the Violence* (Washington, D.C.: Author, nd.).

171. Walker and Turner, *A Decade of Modest Progress.*

172. Samuel Walker, Susan E. Martin, and K. B. Turner, "Through the Glass Ceiling? Promotion Rates for Minority and Female Police Officers," paper presented at the American Society of Criminology, November 1994.

173. William Wilbanks, *The Myth of a Racist Criminal Justice System* (Monterey, CA: Brooks/Cole, 1987).

174. Darnell F. Hawkins, "Beyond Anomalies: Rethinking the Conflict Perspective on Race and Criminal Punishment," *Social Forces* 65 (March 1987): 719–745.

5

✖

The Courts

A Quest for Justice During the Pretrial Process

In March 1931, nine African American teenage boys were accused of raping two white girls on a slow-moving freight train traveling through Alabama. They were arrested and taken to Scottsboro, Alabama, where they were indicted for rape, a capital offense. One week later, the first case was called for trial. When the defendant appeared without counsel, the judge hearing the case simply appointed all members of the local bar to represent him and his codefendants. An out-of-state lawyer also volunteered to assist in the defendants' defense, but the judge appointed no counsel of record.

The nine defendants were tried and convicted, and eight were sentenced to death. They appealed their convictions, arguing that their right to counsel had been denied. In 1932 the U.S. Supreme Court issued its ruling in the case of *Powell v. Alabama*,[1] one of the most famous Supreme Court cases in U.S. history. The Court reversed the defendants' convictions and ruled that due process of law required the appointment of counsel for young, inexperienced, illiterate, and indigent defendants in capital cases.

The Supreme Court's ruling in *Powell* provided the so-called Scottsboro Boys with only a short reprieve. They were quickly retried, reconvicted, and resentenced to death, despite the fact that one of the alleged victims had recanted and questions were raised about the credibility of the other victim's testimony. Once again, the defendants appealed their convictions, this time contending that their right to a fair trial by an impartial jury had been denied. All of the defendants had been tried by all-white juries. They argued that the jury selection procedures used in Alabama were racially biased. Although African Americans who were registered to vote were eligible for jury service, they were excluded in practice because state officials refused to place their names on the lists from which jurors were chosen. In 1935 the Supreme Court, noting that the exclusion of all African Americans from jury service deprived African American defendants of their right to the equal protection of the laws guaranteed by the Fourteenth Amendment, again reversed the convictions.[2]

The Supreme Court's decision was harshly criticized in the South. The Charleston *News and Courier*, for example, stated that racially mixed juries were "out of the question" and asserted that the Court's decision "can and will be evaded . . . ."[3] Southern sentiment also strongly favored yet another round of trials. Thomas Knight, Jr., the attorney who prosecuted the Scottsboro cases the second time, noted that "Approximately ninety jurors have been found saying the defendants were guilty of the offense with which they are charged and for which the penalty is death." Knight reported that he had been "retained by the State to prosecute the cases and [would] prosecute the same to their conclusion."[4]

Less than eight months after the Supreme Court's decision, a grand jury composed of thirteen whites and one African American returned new indictments against the nine defendants. Haywood Patterson, the first defendant to be retried, again faced an all-white jury. Although there were twelve African Americans among the one hundred potential jurors, seven of the twelve asked to be excused and the prosecutor used his peremptory challenges to remove the remaining five. In his closing argument, the prosecutor also implied that an acquittal would force the women of Alabama "to buckle six-shooters about their middles" to protect their "sacred secret parts." He pleaded with the jurors to "Get it done quick and protect the fair womanhood of this great State."[5]

Patterson was convicted and sentenced to seventy-five years in prison. The sentence, although harsh, represented "a victory of sorts."[6] As the Birmingham *Age-Herald* noted, the decision "represents probably the first time in the history of the South that a Negro has been convicted of a charge of rape upon a white woman and has been given less than a death sentence."[7]

Three of the remaining eight defendants were tried and convicted in July 1937. One of the three, Clarence Norris, was sentenced to death; the other two received prison sentences of seventy-five and ninety-nine years. Shortly thereafter, Ozie Powell pled guilty to assaulting an officer after the state agreed to dismiss the rape charge. That same day, in an unexpected and controversial move, the state dropped all charges against the remaining four defendants. In a prepared statement, Attorney General Thomas Lawson asserted that the state was "convinced beyond any question of doubt . . . that the defendants that have been tried are guilty." However, "after careful consideration of all the testimony, every lawyer connected with the prosecution is convinced that the defendants Willie Roberson and Olen Montgomery are not guilty." Regarding the remaining two defendants, who were 12 and 13 years old when the crime occurred, Lawson stated that "the ends of justice would be met at this time by releasing these two juveniles on condition that they leave the State, never to return."[8]

The state's decision to drop charges against four of the nine defendants led editorial writers for newspapers throughout the United States to call for the immediate release of the defendants who previously had been convicted. The Richmond *Times-Dispatch* stated that the state's action "serves as a virtual clincher to the argument that all nine of the Negroes are innocent," and the *New York Times* called on the state to "do more complete justice later on."[9]

Clarence Norris's death sentence was commuted to life imprisonment in 1938, but the Alabama Pardon and Parole Board repeatedly denied the five defendants' requests for parole. One of the defendants finally was granted parole in 1943 and by 1950 all of them had gained their freedom. Collectively, the nine Scottsboro Boys served 104 years in prison for a crime that many believe was "almost certainly, a hoax."[10]

THE SITUATION TODAY

The infamous Scottsboro Case illustrates overt discrimination directed against African American criminal defendants. However, those events took place in the 1930s and 1940s, and much has changed since then. Legislative reforms and Supreme Court decisions protecting the rights of criminal defendants, coupled with changes in attitudes, have made it less likely that criminal justice officials will treat defendants of different races differently. Racial minorities are no longer routinely denied bail and then tried by all-white juries without attorneys to assist them in their defense. They are no longer brought into court in chains and shackles. They no longer receive "justice" at the hands of white lynch mobs.

Despite these reforms, inequities persist. Racial minorities, and particularly those suspected of crimes against whites, remain the victims of unequal justice. In 1983, for example, Lenell Geter, an African American man, was charged with the armed robbery of a Kentucky Fried Chicken restaurant in Balch Springs, Texas. Despite the absence of any physical evidence to connect him to the crime and despite the prosecution's failure to establish his motive for the crime, Geter was convicted by an all-white jury and sentenced to life in prison.

Geter's conviction was particularly surprising given the fact that he had an ironclad alibi. Nine of his coworkers, all of whom were white, testified that Geter was at work on the day of the crime. His supervisor testified that there was no way Geter could have made the fifty-mile trip from work to the site of the crime by 3:20 P.M., the time when the robbery occurred. According to one coworker, "Unless old Captain Kirk dematerialized him and beamed him over there, he couldn't have made it back by then. He was here at work. There's no question in my mind—none at all."[11]

Prosecutors in the county where Geter was tried denied that race played a role in his conviction. As one of them put it, "To say this is a conviction based on race is as far out in left field as you can get."[12] Geter's coworkers disagreed;

they argued that Geter and his codefendant (who also was African American) would not have been charged or convicted if they had been white.

Events that occurred following the trial suggest that Geter's coworkers were right. Another man arrested for a series of armed robberies eventually was linked to the robbery of the Kentucky Fried Chicken restaurant. Geter's conviction and sentence were overturned after the employees who originally identified Geter picked this suspect out of a lineup. Geter served more than a year in prison for a crime he did not commit.

Like Lenell Geter, James Newsome, an African American sentenced to life in prison for the armed robbery and murder of a white man, also had an alibi. At his trial for the 1979 murder of Mickey Cohen, the owner of Mickey's Grocery Store in Chicago, Newsome's girlfriend and her two sisters testified that he was with them at the time of the murder. The prosecutor trying the case argued that Newsome's girlfriend, who was a convicted burglar, was not a credible witness. He also introduced the testimony of three eyewitnesses who identified Newsome as Cohen's killer.[13]

Despite the fact that there was no physical evidence linking Newsome to the crime, and in spite of the fact that Newsome's fingerprints were not found on the items in the store handled by the killer, the jury hearing the case found Newsome guilty. Although Cook County prosecutors had sought the death penalty, the jury recommended life in prison.

Newsome, who steadfastly maintained his innocence, spent the next fifteen years appealing his conviction. With the help of Norval Morris, a University of Chicago Law School Professor, and two noted Chicago defense attorneys, Newsome was able to convince the Cook County Circuit Court to order that the fingerprints obtained from the crime scene be run through the Police Department's computerized fingerprint database to see if they matched any of those on file. The tests revealed that the fingerprints matched those of Dennis Emerson, a 45-year-old Illinois death row inmate who, at the time of Cohen's murder, was out on parole after serving three years for armed robbery.

Two weeks later, Newsome was released from prison. Shortly thereafter, Illinois governor Jim Edgar pardoned Newsome and ordered his criminal record expunged. Following his release, Newsome, who spent fifteen years in prison for a crime he did not commit, said, "I finally felt vindicated. I had defeated a criminal-justice giant. Fifteen years ago, they told me that I would never walk the streets again in my life. What did I do? I slayed a giant—a criminal justice giant."[14] Like Geter, Newsome contended that race played a role in his arrest and conviction. "In the most [racially] polarized city in the world," Newsome stated, "racism was a factor. I was a suspect and I was convenient."[15]

The three cases described here, of course, do not prove that there is a pattern of *systematic* discrimination directed against racial minorities in courts throughout the United States. One might argue, in fact, that these cases are simply exceptions to the general rule of impartiality. As we explained in Chapter 1, the validity of the discrimination thesis rests not on anecdotal evidence but on the results of empirical studies of criminal justice decision making.

GOALS OF THE CHAPTER

In this chapter and in Chapter 6 we discuss the treatment of racial minorities in court. The focus in this chapter is on pretrial decision making. Our goal is to determine whether people of color are more likely than whites to be tried without adequate counsel to represent them or to be denied bail or detained in jail prior to trial. In addition, we review research on prosecutors' charging and plea bargaining decisions for evidence of differential treatment of racial minorities or whites. We argue that recent reforms adopted voluntarily by the states or mandated by court decisions have reduced, but not eliminated, racial discrimination in the criminal court system.

DECISIONS REGARDING
COUNSEL AND BAIL

As we explained in Chapter 3, racial minorities are at a disadvantage in court both because of their race and because they are more likely than whites to be poor. This "double jeopardy" makes it more difficult for minority defendants to obtain competent attorneys or secure release from jail prior to trial. This, in turn, hinders their defense and may increase the odds that they will be convicted and sentenced harshly. Given these consequences, decisions regarding provision of counsel and bail obviously are important.

Racial Minorities and the Right to Counsel

The Sixth Amendment to the U.S. Constitution states, "In all criminal prosecutions, the accused shall enjoy the right to have the assistance of counsel for his defense." Historically, this meant little more than if people had an attorney, they could bring him along to defend them. The problem, of course, was that this was of no help to the majority of defendants, and particularly minority defendants, who were too poor to hire their own attorneys. The U.S. Supreme Court, recognizing that defendants could not obtain fair trials without the assistance of counsel, began to interpret the Sixth Amendment to require the appointment of counsel for indigent defendants. The process began in 1932, when the Court ruled in *Powell v. Alabama*[16] that states must provide attorneys for indigent defendants charged with capital crimes (see discussion of the Scottsboro case). The Court's decision in a 1938 case, *Johnson v. Zerbst*,[17] required the appointment of counsel for all indigent defendants in federal criminal cases, but the requirement was not extended to the states until *Gideon v. Wainwright*[18] was decided in 1963. In that decision, Justice Black's majority opinion stated:

> [R]eason and reflection require us to recognize that in our adversary system of criminal justice, any person haled into court, who is too poor to hire a lawyer, cannot be assured a fair trial unless counsel is provided

for him . . . . The right of one charged with crime to counsel may not be deemed fundamental and essential to fair trials in some countries, but it is in ours.

In subsequent decisions, the Court ruled that "no person may be imprisoned, for any offense, whether classified as petty, misdemeanor, or felony, unless he was represented by counsel,"[19] and that the right to counsel is not limited to trial, but applies to all "critical stages" in the criminal justice process.[20] As a result of these rulings, most defendants must be provided with counsel from arrest and interrogation through sentencing and the appellate process.

At the time the *Gideon* decision was handed down, thirteen states had no statewide requirement for appointment of counsel except in capital cases.[21] Other states relied on members of local bar associations to defend indigents, often on a pro bono basis. Following *Gideon*, it became obvious that other procedures would be required if all felony defendants were to be provided with attorneys.

States moved quickly to implement the constitutional requirement articulated in *Gideon*, either by establishing public defender systems or by appropriating money for court-appointed attorneys. The number of public defender systems grew rapidly. In 1951 there were only 7 public defender organizations in the United States; in 1964 there were 136 and by 1973 the total had risen to 573.[22] A recent national survey of indigent defense services among all U.S. prosecutorial districts found that 28 percent used a public defender program, 23 percent used an assigned counsel system, and 8 percent used a contract attorney system; the remaining districts (41 percent) reported that a combination of methods was used. This survey also revealed that 76 percent of inmates in state correctional facilities reported that they were represented by a public defender or assigned counsel.[23]

Quality of Legal Representation As a result of Supreme Court decisions expanding the right to counsel and the development of federal and state policies implementing these decisions, African Americans and other racial minorities are no longer routinely denied legal representation at trial or at any other critical stage in the process. Questions have been raised, however, about the quality of legal representation provided to indigent defendants by public defenders. As Sterling noted,

> The general suspicion is that equal justice is not available to rich and poor alike. Rather, it is believed that indigents receive a lower quality of legal service, which results in their being more likely to suffer harsher penal sanctions than similarly situated defendants who can afford to buy good legal talent.[24]

One of the most oft-quoted statements about public defenders is the answer given by an unidentified prisoner in a Connecticut jail to the question of whether he had a lawyer when he went to court. "No," he replied, "I had a public defender."[25] Some social scientists have echoed this view, charging that

Box 5.1   Are Indigent Capital Defendants Represented by Incompetent Attorneys?

In "Judges and the Politics of Death," Stephen Bright and Patrick Keenan asserted that "Judges often fail to enforce the most fundamental protection of an accused, the Sixth Amendment right to counsel, by assigning an inexperienced or incompetent lawyer to represent the accused."[31] In support of their assertion, they offered the following examples:

- A capital defendant who was represented by a lawyer who had passed the bar exam only six months earlier, had not taken any classes in criminal law or criminal procedure, and had never tried a jury or a felony trial.
- An attorney who described his client as "a little old nigger boy" during the penalty phase of the trial.

- A judge in Harris County, Texas, who responded to a capital defendant's complaints about his attorney sleeping during the trial with the assertion that, "The Constitution doesn't say the lawyer has to be awake."
- A Florida attorney, who stated during the penalty phase of a capital case, "Judge, I'm at a loss. I really don't know what to do in this type of proceeding. If I'd been through one, I would, but I've never handled one except this time."
- A study of capital cases in Philadelphia that found that "even officials in charge of the system say they wouldn't want to be represented in Traffic Court by some of the people appointed to defend poor people accused of murder."

public defenders, as part of the courtroom workgroup, are more concerned with securing guilty pleas as efficiently and as expeditiously as possible than with aggressively defending their clients.[26] As Weitzer[27] noted (and as the examples in Box 5.1 confirm), "In many jurisdictions, public defenders and state-appointed attorneys are grossly underpaid, poorly trained, or simply lack the resources and time to prepare for a case—a pattern documented in cases ranging from the most minor to the most consequential, capital crimes."

Other social scientists disagree. Citing studies showing that criminal defendants represented by public defenders do not fare worse than those represented by private attorneys,[28] these researchers suggest that critics "have tended to underestimate the quality of defense provided by the public defender."[29] Wice, in fact, concluded that the public defender is able to establish a working relationship with prosecutors and judges "in which the exchange of favors, so necessary to greasing the squeaky wheel of justice, can directly benefit the indigent defendant."[30] As part of the courtroom workgroup, in other words, public defenders are in a better position than private attorneys to negotiate favorable plea bargains and mitigate punishment.

The studies cited here do not address the question of racial discrimination in the provision of counsel. Although it is true that African American defendants are more likely than white defendants to be indigent, and thus to be represented by public defenders,[32] it does not necessarily follow from this that African Americans will be treated more harshly than whites as their cases move through the criminal justice system. As noted, studies have not consistently shown that defendants represented by public defenders fare worse than defendants represented by private attorneys.

Most studies have not directly compared the treatment of African American, Hispanic, and white defendants represented by public defenders and private attorneys. It is possible that racial minorities represented by public defenders receive more punitive sentences than whites represented by public defenders, or that whites who hire their own attorneys receive more lenient sentences than racial minorities who hire their own attorneys. To put it another way, it is possible that retaining a private attorney provides more benefits to whites than to racial minorities.

Holmes and his colleagues found evidence supporting these possibilities in one of the two Texas counties where they explored the interrelationships among ethnicity, legal resources, and case outcomes.[33] The authors of this study found that in Bexar County (San Antonio) both African American and Hispanic defendants were significantly less likely than white defendants to be represented by a private attorney, even after such things as the seriousness of the crime, the defendant's prior criminal record, and the defendant's gender, age, and employment status were taken into account. The authors also found that defendants who retained a private attorney were more likely to be released prior to trial and received more lenient sentences than those represented by a public defender.[34] In this particular jurisdiction, then, African American and Hispanic defendants were less likely than whites to be represented by a private attorney and, as a result, they received more punitive treatment than whites.

An examination of the sentences imposed on defendants convicted of felonies in three large urban jurisdictions in 1993 and 1994 produced somewhat different results. Spohn and DeLone[35] compared the proportions of white, African American, and Hispanic defendants who were represented by a private attorney in Chicago, Miami, and Kansas City. As shown in Table 5.1, in all three jurisdictions whites were substantially more likely than African Americans to have private attorneys. In Chicago, in fact, 22.5 percent of white defendants, but only 6.9 percent of African American defendants, had a private attorney. In Miami, Hispanics also were less likely than whites to be represented by a private attorney.

Although the data presented in Table 5.1 reveal that smaller proportions of racial minorities than whites had access to the services of a private attorney, they do not provide evidence of differential treatment based on either type of attorney or race/ethnicity. In fact, when Spohn and DeLone examined the sentences imposed on racial minorities and whites in each jurisdiction, they found an interesting pattern of results. As shown in Figure 5.1, in Chicago and Kansas City only whites benefitted from having a private

**Table 5.1 Race/Ethnicity and Type
of Attorney in Chicago, Miami, and Kansas City**

Race of Defendant	PERCENT REPRESENTED BY A PRIVATE ATTORNEY		
	Chicago Miami	Kansas City	
White	22.5	34.5	37.8
Black	6.9	23.4	24.8
Hispanic	21.2	27.3	Na[a]

[a]There were only 47 Hispanic defendants in Kansas City.

attorney. Among African Americans, the incarceration rates for defendants represented by private attorneys were only slightly lower than the rates for defendants represented by public defenders; among Hispanics in Chicago the rate for defendants with private attorneys was actually somewhat *higher* than the rate for those with public defenders. In Miami, both whites and African Americans benefitted from representation by private counsel, but Hispanics with private attorneys were sentenced to prison at a slightly *higher* rate than Hispanics represented by the public defender.

The incarceration rates displayed in Figure 5.1 do not take into account differences in the types of cases handled by private attorneys and public defenders. It is certainly possible that the incarceration rates for defendants represented by private attorneys generally are lower than the rates for defendants represented by public defenders not because private attorneys are more experienced, more competent, and more zealous, but because the types of cases they handle are less serious or because the defendants they represent have less serious prior criminal records. If private attorneys, in other words, typically represent first offenders charged with relatively minor crimes, whereas public defenders represent recidivists as well as first offenders and violent offenders as well as nonviolent offenders, we would expect the sentences imposed on defendants with private attorneys to be less severe than those imposed on defendants with public defenders, irrespective of the quality of representation provided by the attorney.

To test this possibility, Spohn and DeLone analyzed the relationship between race/ethnicity, type of attorney, and the likelihood of incarceration, controlling for several indicators of the seriousness of the crime and for the offender's prior criminal record, age, gender, and employment status. They found that, with one exception, the type of attorney had no effect on the odds of incarceration for any racial/ethnic group in any jurisdiction. The only exception was in Miami, where African Americans represented by private attorneys faced significantly lower odds of incarceration than African Americans represented by public defenders.

These results cast doubt on assertions that racial minorities are disadvantaged by their lack of access to private counsel. At least in these three jurisdic-

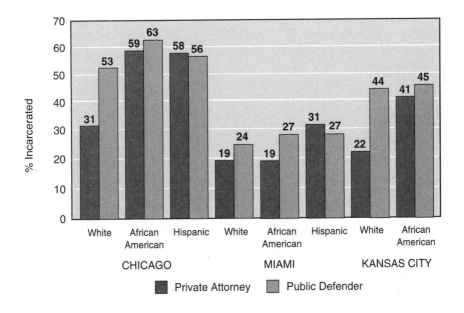

FIGURE 5.1 Race/Ethnicity, Type of Attorney, and Incarceration Rates in Chicago, Miami, and Kansas City

tions, public defenders do not appear to "provide a lower caliber defense than what private attorneys offer."[36]

In summary, although it would be premature to conclude on the basis of research conducted to date either that decisions concerning the provision of counsel are racially neutral or that the consequences of these decisions for racial minorities are unimportant, significant changes have occurred since the 1930s. It is clear that scenes from the infamous Scottsboro case will not be replayed in the future. The Supreme Court has consistently affirmed the importance of the right to counsel and has insisted that states provide attorneys to indigent criminal defendants at all critical stages in the criminal justice process. Although some critics have questioned the quality of legal services afforded indigent defendants, particularly in capital cases in which the stakes are obviously very high, the findings of a number of methodologically sophisticated studies suggest that "indigent defenders get the job done and done well."[37] In short, it is no longer true that racial minorities "are without a voice"[38] in courts throughout the United States.

Racial Minorities and Bail Decision Making

Critics of the traditional money bail system, in which defendants either pay the amount set by the judge or pay a bail bondsman to post bond for them, argue that the system discriminates against poor defendants. They also charge that the system discriminates, either directly or indirectly, against racial minorities. Critics contend that historically African American and Hispanic defendants were more likely than white defendants to be detained prior to trial, either because the judge refused bail or because the judge set bail at an unaffordable level.[39] "As a result," according to one commentator, "the country's jails are packed to overflowing with the nation's poor—with red, brown, black, and yellow men and women showing up in disproportionate numbers."[40]

Bail Reform Concerns about the rights of poor defendants and about the consequences of detention prior to trial led to the first bail reform movement, which emerged in the 1960s and emphasized reducing pretrial detention. Those who lobbied for reform argued that the purpose of bail was to ensure the defendant's appearance in court and that the amount of bail therefore should not exceed the amount necessary to guarantee that the defendant would show up for all court proceedings. Proponents of this view asserted that whether a defendant was released or detained prior to trial should not depend on his or her economic status or race. They also cited research demonstrating that the type and amount of bail imposed on the defendant and the time spent by the defendant in pretrial detention affected the likelihood of a guilty plea, the likelihood of conviction at trial, and the severity of the sentence.[41]

Arguments such as these prompted state and federal reforms designed to reduce pretrial detention. Encouraged by the results of the Manhattan Bail Project, which found that the majority of defendants released on their own recognizance did appear for trial,[42] local jurisdictions moved quickly to reduce reliance on money bail and to institute programs modeled after the Manhattan Bail Project. Many states revised their bail laws, and in 1966 Congress passed the Bail Reform Act, which proclaimed release on recognizance the presumptive bail decision in federal cases.

Then, as Walker noted, "the political winds shifted."[43] The rising crime rate of the 1970s generated a concern for crime control and led to a reassessment of bail policies. Critics challenged the traditional position that the only function of bail was to ensure the defendant's appearance in court. They argued that guaranteeing public safety was also a valid function of bail and that pretrial detention should be used to protect the community from "dangerous" offenders.

These arguments fueled the second bail reform movement, which emerged in the 1970s and emphasized preventive detention. Conservative legislators and policymakers lobbied for reforms allowing judges to consider "public safety" when making decisions concerning the type and amount of bail.[44] By 1984, thirty-four states had enacted legislation giving judges the right to deny bail to defendants deemed dangerous.[45] Also in 1984, Congress passed a law authorizing preventive detention of dangerous defendants in federal criminal cases.[46]

The Effect of Race on Bail Decision Making Proponents of bail reform argued that whether a defendant was released or detained prior to trial should not depend on his or her economic status or race. They argued that bail decisions should rest either on assessments of the likelihood that the defendant would appear in court or on predictions of the defendant's dangerousness.

The problem, of course, is that there is no way to guarantee that judges will not take race into account in making these assessments and predictions. As Mann asserted, even the seemingly objective criteria used in making these decisions "may still be discriminatory on the basis of economic status or skin color."[47] If judges stereotype African Americans and Hispanics as less reliable and more prone to violence than whites, they will be more inclined to detain people of color and release whites, irrespective of their more objective assessments of risk of flight or dangerousness.

Studies examining the effect of race on bail decisions have yielded contradictory findings. Some researchers conclude that judges' bail decisions are based primarily on the seriousness of the offense and the defendant's prior criminal record and ties to the community; race has no effect once these factors are taken into consideration.[48] Other researchers contend that the defendant's economic status, not race, determines the likelihood of pretrial release.[49] If this is the case, one could argue that bail decision making reflects *indirect* racial discrimination, as African American and Hispanic defendants are more likely than white defendants to be poor.

A number of studies document *direct* racial discrimination in bail decisions. Bynum's[50] study of bail decision making in a large western city, for example, revealed that African Americans and Native Americans were less likely than whites to be released on their own recognizance. Patterson and Lynch[51] focused on compliance with a bail schedule, which establishes a range of bail for particular offenses and is designed to structure discretion and thus to reduce disparity. They looked at whether the amount of bail required was below, above, or within the schedule amount. As shown in Table 5.2, they found differences based on both race and gender: Whites and females were much more likely than nonwhites and males to receive bail below the schedule amount.

The authors then controlled for other variables that might affect the amount of bail: the seriousness of the offense and the offender's role in the crime, prior criminal record, social class, and legal status at the time of the offense. They found that whites and nonwhites were just as likely to be given bail in excess of the schedule amount, but that whites (and particularly white females) were significantly more likely than nonwhites to be given bail below the schedule. The authors concluded that although racial minorities were not treated more harshly than whites, they were discriminated against because they were not given the same benefit of the doubt as were whites.

Other evidence of direct racial discrimination is found in an analysis of the likelihood of pretrial release in Chicago, Miami, and Kansas City. Using data on offenders convicted of felonies in 1993 and 1994, Spohn and DeLone[52] compared the odds of pretrial release for white, African American, and Hispanic defendants. They controlled for the seriousness of the charges against the defendant, the number of charges the defendant was facing, representation of the defendant by a private attorney or a public defender, and the defendant's

Table 5.2 Race, Gender, and Compliance with a Bail Schedule

	Bail Within Schedule	Bail Below Schedule	Bail Above Schedule
Race			
White	70.5%	21.3%	8.2%
Nonwhite	78.9	12.5	8.6
Gender			
Male	76.0	15.5	8.5
Female	65.4	26.9	7.7

SOURCE: Adapted from E. Britt Patterson and Michael J. Lynch, "Bias in Formalized Bail Procedures," in Michael J. Lynch and E. Britt Patterson, eds. *Race and Criminal Justice* (New York: Harrow & Heston, 1991), Table 3.2.

prior record, gender, and age. They found that in Chicago, African Americans were less likely than whites to be released pending trial, whereas in Miami, both African Americans and Hispanics were significantly less likely than whites be to released prior to trial. In Kansas City, on the other hand, the difference in the likelihood of pretrial release for whites and African Americans was not statistically significant.

These differences are illustrated by the data presented in Table 5.3. Spohn and DeLone used the results of their multivariate analysis to calculate the probability of pretrial release for "typical" white, African American, and Hispanic defendants in each jurisdiction. In Chicago, the probability of pretrial release was 50 percent for Hispanics and 48 percent for whites, but only 38 percent for African Americans. In Miami, the probabilities for African Americans and Hispanics (56 percent and 54 percent, respectively) were lower than the probability for whites (63 percent). There was, on the other hand, only a three percentage point difference in the likelihood of pretrial release for whites and African Americans adjudicated in Kansas City.

There also is evidence that defendant race interacts with other variables related to bail severity. Farnworth and Horan,[53] for example, found that the amount of bail imposed on white defendants who retained private attorneys was less than the amount imposed on African American defendants who retained private attorneys. Chiricos and Bales similarly found that the likelihood of pretrial detention was greatest for African American defendants who were unemployed.[54]

A study of bail decision making in ten federal district courts also found evidence of an indirect relationship between race/ethnicity and bail decisions. This study revealed that race did not have a direct effect on bail outcomes, but did interact with a number of other variables to produce harsher bail outcomes for some types of African American defendants.[55] More specifically, the authors found that having a prior felony conviction had a greater negative effect on bail severity for African American defendants than for white defendants, and having more education or a higher income had a greater positive effect for whites than for African Americans.

Table 5.3 Probability of Pretrial Release for Typical* White, African American, and Hispanic Defendants in Chicago, Miami, and Kansas City

| | PROBABILITY OF PRETRIAL RELEASE | | |
Race of Defendant	Chicago	Miami	Kansas City
White	.48	.63	.50
African American	.38	.56	.47
Hispanic	.50	.54	NA

*These probabilities were calculated for male defendants who were 30 years old, were charged with one count of possession of narcotics with intent, had one prior prison term of more than one year, were not on probation at the time of the current offense, and were represented by a public defender.

Bail and Case Outcomes Concerns about discrimination in bail decision making focus on two facts: African American and Hispanic defendants who are presumed to be innocent are jailed prior to trial *and* those who are detained prior to trial are more likely to be convicted and receive harsher sentences than those who are released pending trial. These concerns focus, in other words, on the possibility that discrimination in bail decision making has "spillover" effects on other case processing decisions.

A recent analysis of pretrial release of felony defendants by the Bureau of Justice Statistics (BJS) attests to the validity of these concerns.[56] Using data from 1992, BJS compared the conviction and incarceration rates for released and detained defendants in the seventy-five largest counties in the United States. As shown in Table 5.4, 79 percent of those who were detained prior to trial, but only 61 percent of those who were released, were convicted. Pretrial status also affected the likelihood of incarceration: 50 percent of the defendants who were detained pending trial were sentenced to prison, compared to only 19 percent of those who were released prior to trial. There were similar disparities for each of the four types of offenses analyzed. Among offenders charged with violent crimes, for example, the conviction rates were 72 percent for those who were detained and 47 percent for those who were released; 55 percent of the detainees, but only 20 percent of those who were released, were subsequently sentenced to prison.

Although these data suggest that pretrial release does have important spillover effects on case outcomes, the higher conviction and imprisonment rates for defendants who are detained pending trial could be due to the fact that defendants who are held in jail prior to trial tend to be charged with more serious crimes, have more serious prior criminal records, and have a past history of nonappearance at court proceedings. The BJS study, for example, found that defendants charged with murder had the lowest release rate, either because they were denied bail or because the judge set bail at a very high amount. The study also showed that defendants with more serious prior records or with a history of nonappearance were more likely to be detained prior to trial.[57] Given these findings, it is possible that the relationship between pretrial status

Table 5.4 Pretrial Status and Its Relationship to Conviction and Incarceration

	% Convicted	% Sentenced to Prison
Released Defendants		
All Offenses	61	19
Violent Offenses	47	20
Property Offenses	65	17
Drug Offenses	65	22
Public-Order Offenses	69	14
Detained Defendants		
All Offenses	79	50
Violent Offenses	72	55
Property Offenses	83	46
Drug Offenses	81	50
Public-Order Offenses	79	47

SOURCE: Adapted from Bureau of Justice Statistics, *Pretrial Release of Felony Defendants, 1992* (Washington, D.C.: U.S. Department of Justice, 1994), Tables 18 and 19.

and case outcomes would disappear once controls for case seriousness and prior criminal record are taken into consideration.

Data collected for the three-city study described earlier were used to explore this possibility.[58] Spohn and DeLone found that the offender's pretrial status was a strong predictor of the likelihood of imprisonment, even after other relevant legal and extralegal variables were taken into account. In all three cities, offenders who were released prior to trial faced substantially lower odds of a prison sentence than did offenders who were detained pending trial. Further analysis revealed that pretrial detention had a similar effect on incarceration for each of the three racial/ethnic groups. In each jurisdiction, in other words, African American, Hispanic, and white defendants who were detained prior to trial faced substantially greater odds of incarceration than African American, Hispanic, and white defendants who were released pending trial.

The results of this study, then, suggest that defendants who are detained prior to trial, regardless of their race, receive more punitive sentences than those who are released. This does not mean, however, that African American and white defendants are *equally likely* to be sentenced to prison. Earlier we noted that this study showed that African Americans were more likely than whites to be detained prior to trial in Chicago and that both African Americans and Hispanics faced a greater likelihood of pretrial detention than whites in Miami. Because they are detained more often than whites in the first place, African American and Hispanic defendants are more likely than whites to suffer both the pains of imprisonment prior to trial and the consequences of pretrial detention at sentencing.

BOX 5.2   Racial Minorities in the Legal Profession

In the early 1930s, one of the defendants in the Scottsboro case described the courtroom where he was convicted and sentenced to death as "one big smiling white face."[59] With the exception of the defendants themselves, no racial minorities were present in the courtroom.

Although the situation obviously has changed since then, racial minorities still represent a very small proportion of the lawyers and judges in the United States. Of those receiving law degrees in 1990, for example, 4.8 percent were African American, 2.9 percent were Hispanic, 1.9 percent were Asian American, and less than 1 percent were Native American.[60] In 1998, 7 percent of all lawyers but only 3 percent of all partners at law firms were racial minorities.[61]

Racial minorities comprise an even smaller proportion of the judiciary. In 1998 only 3 percent of all judges in the United States were African American or Hispanic. At the federal level, less than 10 percent of the judges were racial minorities.

Although the findings are somewhat contradictory, it thus appears that the reforms instituted since the 1960s have not resulted in racial equality in bail decision making. It is certainly true that racial minorities are no longer routinely jailed prior to trial because of judicial stereotypes of dangerousness or because they are too poor to obtain their release. Nevertheless, there is evidence that judges in some jurisdictions continue to take race into account in deciding on the type and amount of bail. There also is evidence that race interacts with factors such as prior record and employment status to produce higher pretrial detention rates for African American defendants than for white defendants. Given the consequences of pretrial detention, these findings are an obvious cause for concern.

CHARGING AND PLEA
BARGAINING DECISIONS

Thus far we have examined criminal justice decisions concerning appointment of counsel and bail for evidence of racial discrimination. We have shown that, despite reforms mandated by the Supreme Court or adopted voluntarily by the states, inequities persist. African Americans and Hispanics who find themselves in the arms of the law continue to suffer discrimination in these important court processing decisions.

In this section we examine prosecutors' charging and plea bargaining decisions for evidence of differential treatment of minority and white defendants. We argue that there is compelling evidence of racial *disparity* in charging and plea bargaining. We further contend that this disparity frequently reflects racial *discrimination*.

Prosecutors' Charging Decisions

Prosecutors exercise broad discretion in deciding whether to file formal charges against individuals suspected of crimes and in determining the number and seriousness of the charges to be filed. According to the Supreme Court, "So long as the prosecutor has probable cause to believe that the accused committed an offense defined by statute, the decision whether or not to prosecute, and what charge to file or bring before a grand jury, generally rests entirely in his discretion."[62] As Justice Jackson noted in 1940, "the prosecutor has more control over life, liberty, and reputation than any other person in America."[63]

The power of the prosecutor is reflected in the fact that in most states, from one third to one half of all felony cases are dismissed by the prosecutor prior to a determination of guilt or innocence.[64] Prosecutors can reject charges at the initial screening either because they believe the suspect is innocent or, more typically, because they believe the suspect is guilty but a conviction would be unlikely. Prosecutors also can reject charges if they feel it would not be in the "interest of justice" to continue the case because the crime is too trivial, because of a perception that the suspect has been punished enough, or because the suspect has agreed to provide information about other, more serious, cases.[65] Finally, prosecutors can reject charges as felonies but prosecute them as misdemeanors.

If a prosecutor files a formal charge, it still can be reduced to a less serious felony or to a misdemeanor during plea bargaining. It also can be dismissed by the court on a recommendation by the prosecutor. This typically happens when the case "falls apart" prior to trial. A witness may refuse to cooperate or may fail to appear at trial, or the judge may rule that a confession or other essential evidence is inadmissible. Unlike the prosecutor's initial decision to reject the charge, the decision to dismiss a charge already filed requires official court action.

The Effect of Race on Charging Decisions Although the prosecutor's discretion is broad, it is not unlimited. The Supreme Court, in fact, has ruled that the decision to prosecute may not be "deliberately based upon an unjustifiable standard such as race, religion, or other arbitrary classification."[66] The prosecutor, in other words, cannot legitimately take the race of the suspect into account in deciding whether to file charges or not or in deciding on the seriousness of the charge to be filed.

Gunnar Myrdal, a Swedish social scientist and the author of a book examining the "Negro Problem" in the United States in the late 1930s and early 1940s, found substantial discrimination against African Americans in the decision to charge or not. As Myrdal noted:

> State courts receive indictments for physical violence against Negroes in an infinitesimally small proportion of the cases. It is notorious that practically never have white lynching mobs been brought to court in the South, even when the killers are known to all in the community and are

Table 5.5 The Effect of Race and Gender on Prosecutors' Charging Decisions

| | ADJUSTED MEANS[A] | | |
Group	Rejected at Screening	Dismissed by Court	Fully Prosecuted
White Female	59%	42%	19%
White Male	54	33	26
African American Female	57	42	30
African American Male	46	34	39
Hispanic Female	54	43	31
Hispanic Male	46	33	42

[A]Means have been adjusted for the effect of four independent variables: age and prior record of the defendant, seriousness of the charge, and whether the defendant used a weapon.

SOURCE: Table adapted from Cassia Spohn, John Gruhl, and Susan Welch, "The Impact of the Ethnicity and Gender of Defendants on the Decision to Reject or Dismiss Felony Charges," *Criminology* 25 (1987): 175–191.

mentioned by name in the local press. When the offender is a Negro, indictment is easily obtained, and no such difficulty at the start will meet the prosecution of the case.[67]

Only a few studies have examined the effect of race on prosecutorial charging decisions, reaching contradictory conclusions. Some researchers found either that race did not affect charging decisions at all[68] or that race played a very minor role in the decision to prosecute or not.[69] The authors of these studies concluded that the decision to prosecute was based primarily on the strength of evidence in the case.

Several studies concluded that prosecutors' charging decisions *are* affected by race. An analysis of the decision to reject or dismiss charges against felony defendants in Los Angeles County, for example, revealed a pattern of discrimination in favor of female defendants and against African American and Hispanic defendants.[70] The authors controlled for the defendant's age and prior criminal record, the seriousness of the charge against the defendant, and whether or not the defendant used a weapon in committing the crime. As shown in Table 5.5, they found that Hispanic males were most likely to be prosecuted fully, followed by African American males, white males, and females of all ethnic groups.

The authors of this study speculated that prosecutors took both race and gender into account in deciding whether to file charges in marginal cases. They reasoned that strong cases would be prosecuted and weak cases dropped, regardless of the race or gender of the suspect. In marginal cases, on the other hand,

> prosecutors may simply feel less comfortable prosecuting the dominant rather than the subordinate ethnic groups. They might feel the dominant groups are less threatening. Or they might believe they can win convictions more often against blacks and Hispanics than against Anglos.[71]

Two studies found that race of both the suspect and the victim played a role in charging decisions. LaFree[72] found that African Americans arrested for raping white women were more likely to be charged with felonies than were either African Americans arrested for raping African American women or whites arrested for raping white women. Another study found that defendants arrested for murdering whites in Florida were more likely to be indicted for first-degree murder than those arrested for murdering blacks.[73]

A study of charging decisions in California reached a different conclusion. Petersilia found that white suspects were *more* likely than African American or Hispanic suspects to be formally charged.[74] Her analysis of the reasons given for charge rejection led her to conclude that the higher dismissal rates for nonwhite suspects reflected the fact that "blacks and Hispanics in California are more likely than whites to be arrested under circumstances that provide insufficient evidence to support criminal charges."[75] (See Chapter 4 for further discussion of this finding.) Prosecutors were more reluctant to file charges against racial minorities than against whites, in other words, because they viewed the evidence against racial minorities as weaker and the odds of convicting them as lower.

An analysis of sexual assault case processing decisions yielded similar findings. Spohn and Spears[76] used data on sexual assaults bound over for trial in Detroit Recorder's Court to examine the effect of offender race, victim race, and other case characteristics on the decision to dismiss charges against the defendant (versus the decision to fully prosecute the case). Building on previous research demonstrating that African Americans who murder or rape whites receive more punitive treatment than other victim–offender racial combinations, they hypothesized that black-on-white sexual assaults would be more likely than either black-on-black or white-on-white sexual assaults to result in the dismissal of all charges. They found just the opposite: The likelihood of charge dismissal was significantly *greater* for cases involving African American offenders and white victims than for the other two groups of offenders. They also found that African Americans prosecuted for assaulting whites were *less* likely to be convicted than whites charged with sexually assaulting whites.[77]

Spohn and Spears concluded that their "unexpected findings" suggest that black-on-white sexual assaults with weaker evidence are less likely to be screened out during the preliminary stages of the process.[78] Police and prosecutors, in other words, may regard sexual assaults involving African American men and white women as inherently more serious than intraracial sexual assaults. Consequently, they may be more willing to take a chance with a reluctant victim or a victim whose behavior at the time of the incident was questionable. According to the authors of this study,

> The police may be willing to make an arrest and the prosecutor may be willing to charge, despite questions about the procedures used to obtain physical evidence or about the validity of the defendant's confession. If this is true, then cases involving black offenders and white victims will be more likely than other types of cases to "fall apart" before or during trial.[79]

Race, Drugs, and Selective Prosecution The results of Petersilia's study in Los Angeles and Spohn and Spears' study in Detroit provide evidence suggestive of a pattern of *selective prosecution*. That is, cases involving racial minorities, or certain types of racial minorities, are singled out for prosecution, whereas similar cases involving whites are either screened out very early in the process or never enter the system in the first place.

This argument has been made most forcefully with respect to drug offenses. In *Malign Neglect*, for example, Michael Tonry[80] argued that "Urban black Americans have borne the brunt of the War on Drugs." More specifically, he charged that "the recent blackening of America's prison population is the product of malign neglect of the war's effects on black Americans."[81] Miller[82] similarly asserted that "from the first shot fired in the drug war African-Americans were targeted, arrested, and imprisoned in wildly disproportionate numbers."

There is ample evidence that the war on drugs is being fought primarily in African American and Hispanic communities. In 1997, for example, racial minorities comprised nearly 75 percent of all offenders prosecuted in federal district courts for drug trafficking: 25 percent of these offenders were white, 33 percent were African American, and 41 percent were Hispanic.[83] These figures are inconsistent with national data on use of drugs, which reveal that whites are more likely than either African Americans or Hispanics to report having ever used a variety of drugs, including cocaine, PCP, LSD, and marijuana.[84]

Some commentators cite evidence of a different type of selective prosecution in drug cases (see also Box 5.3). Noting that the penalties for use of crack cocaine mandated by the federal sentencing guidelines are substantially harsher than the penalties provided under many state statutes, these critics suggest that state prosecutors are more likely to refer crack cases involving racial minorities to the federal system for prosecution.[85] Berk and Campbell, for example, compared the racial makeup of defendants arrested for selling crack cocaine in Los Angeles to the racial makeup of defendants charged with selling crack cocaine in state and federal courts. They found that the racial makeup of arrestees was similar to the racial makeup of those charged with violating state statutes. However, African Americans were overrepresented in federal cases; in fact, over a four-year period, no whites were prosecuted in federal court for the sale of crack cocaine.

This issue was addressed by the Supreme Court in 1996. The five defendants in the case of *United States v. Armstrong et al.*[86] alleged that they were selected for prosecution in federal court (i.e., the U.S. District Court for the Central District of California) rather than in state court because they were black. They further alleged that this decision had serious potential consequences. Christopher Armstrong, for example, faced a prison term of fifty-five years to life under federal statutes, compared to three to nine years under California law. Another defendant, Aaron Hampton, faced a maximum term of fourteen years under California law but a mandatory life term under federal law.

Following their indictment for conspiring to possess with intent to distribute more than fifty grams of crack cocaine, the defendants filed a motion for

BOX 5.3   Are Black Pregnant Women Who Abuse Drugs Singled Out for Prosecution Under Child Abuse/Neglect Statutes?

Prosecution of Pregnant Women Who Abuse Drugs

In 1989 Jennifer Clarise Johnson, a 23-year-old African American crack addict, became the first woman in the United States to be convicted for exposing a baby to illegal drugs during pregnancy. The Florida court gave Johnson fifteen to twenty years probation and required her to enter drug treatment and report subsequent pregnancies to her probation officer. According to the prosecutor who filed charges against Johnson, "We needed to make sure this woman does not give birth to another cocaine baby."[90]

Other prosecutions and convictions in other state courts followed; by 1992, more than 100 women in twenty-four states had been charged with abusing an unborn child through illegal drug use during pregnancy.

Many of these cases were appealed and, until 1997, all of the appeals resulted in the dismissal of charges. Then in October 1997, the South Carolina Supreme Court became the first court in the United States to rule that a viable fetus could be considered a person under child abuse laws. Therefore, a pregnant woman who abused drugs during the third trimester of pregnancy could be charged with child abuse or other, more serious, crimes.[91] Two months later, Talitha Renee Garrick, a 27-year-old African American woman who admitted that she smoked crack cocaine an hour before she gave birth to a stillborn child, pled guilty to involuntary manslaughter in a South Carolina courtroom.

Do Prosecutors "Target" Pregnant Black Women?

A number of commentators contend that prosecutors' charging decisions in these types of cases reflect racial discrimination. Humphries et al., for example, asserted that "The overwhelming majority of prosecutions involve poor women of color."[92] Roberts[93] similarly argued that "Poor Black women are the primary targets of prosecutors, not because they are more likely to be guilty of fetal abuse, but because they are Black and poor."[94]

To support her allegations, Roberts cited evidence documenting that most of the women who have been prosecuted have been African American; she noted that the fifty-two women prosecuted through 1990 included thirty-five African Americans, fourteen whites, two Hispanics, and one Native American. Ten out of eleven cases in Florida and seventeen out of eighteen cases in South Carolina were brought against African

discovery of information held by the U.S. Attorney's office regarding the race of persons prosecuted by that office. In support of their motion, they offered a study showing that all of the defendants in the crack cocaine cases closed by the Federal Public Defender's Office in 1991 were African American.

The U.S. District Court ordered the U.S. Attorney's office to provide the data requested by the defendants. When federal prosecutors refused to do so,

BOX 5.3   Continued

American women.[95] According to Roberts, these glaring disparities create a presumption of racially selective prosecution.

Randall Kennedy, an African American professor of law at Harvard University and the author of *Race, Crime, and the Law,* acknowledged that Roberts' charges of selective prosecution and racial misconduct "are surely plausible." As he noted, "Given the long and sad history of documented, irrefutable racial discrimination in the administration of criminal law . . . no informed observer should be shocked by the suggestion that some prosecutors treat black pregnant women more harshly than identically situated white pregnant women."[96]

Kennedy asserted, however, that Roberts' contention that prosecutors target women "*because* they are black and poor,"[97] although plausible, is not persuasive. He noted that Roberts relied heavily on evidence from a study designed to estimate the prevalence of alcohol and drug abuse among pregnant women in Pinellas County, Florida. This study revealed that there were similar rates of substance abuse among African American and white women, but that African American women were ten times more likely than white women to be reported to public health authorities (as Florida law required).

Kennedy contended that the Florida study does not provide con-

clusive evidence of racial bias. He noted, in fact, that the authors of the study themselves suggested that the disparity in reporting rates might reflect either the fact that newborns who have been exposed to cocaine exhibit more severe symptoms at birth or the fact that black pregnant women are more likely than white pregnant women to be addicted to cocaine (rather than to alcohol, marijuana, or some other drug). Kennedy asserted that Roberts failed to address these alternative hypotheses and simply " insists that 'racial prejudice and stereotyping must be a factor' in the racially disparate pattern of reporting . . . ."[98]

Kennedy also contended that Roberts' analysis fails to consider the problem of underprotection of the law. Imagine, he asked, what the reaction would be if the situation were reversed and prosecutors brought child abuse charges solely against drug-abusing white women. "Would that not rightly prompt suspicion of racially selective devaluation of black babies on the grounds that withholding prosecution deprives black babies of the equal *protection* of the laws?"[99]

What do you think? Do prosecutors "target" pregnant women who are poor and black? What would the reaction be (among whites? among African Americans?) if only white women were prosecuted?

noting that there was no evidence that they had refused to prosecute white or Hispanic crack defendants, U.S. District Judge Consuelo Marshall dismissed the indictments. The Ninth Circuit U.S. Court of Appeals affirmed Judge Marshall's dismissal of the indictments. The appellate court judges stated that they began with "the presumption that people of all races commit all types of crimes—not with the premise that any type of crime is the exclusive province of any particular racial or ethnic group."[87] They stated that the defendants' evidence showing that all twenty-four crack defendants were African American required some response from federal prosecutors.

The U.S. Supreme Court disagreed. In an 8-to-1 decision that did not settle the issue of whether the U.S. Attorney's Office engaged in selective prosecution, the Court ruled that federal rules of criminal procedure regarding discovery do not require the government to provide the information requested by the defendants. Although prosecutors *are* obligated to turn over documents that are "material to the preparation of the ... defense," this applies *only* to documents needed to mount a defense against the government's "case-in-chief" (i.e., the crack cocaine charges) and not to documents needed to make a selective prosecution claim. Further, the Court ruled that "For a defendant to be entitled to discovery on a claim that he was singled out for prosecution on the basis of his race, he must make a threshold showing that the Government declined to prosecute similarly situated suspects of other races."[88]

Justice Stevens, the lone dissenter in the case, argued that the evidence of selective prosecution presented by the defendants "was sufficiently disturbing to require some response from the United States Attorney's Office." According to Stevens,

> If a District Judge has reason to suspect that [the United States Attorney for the Central District of California], or a member of her staff, has singled out particular defendants for prosecution on the basis of their race, it is surely appropriate for the Judge to determine whether there is a factual basis for such a concern.[89]

Stevens added that the severity of federal penalties imposed for offenses involving crack cocaine, coupled with documented racial patterns of enforcement, "give rise to a special concern about the fairness of charging practices for crack offenses."

Race and Plea Bargaining Decisions

There has been relatively little research focusing explicitly on the effect of race on prosecutors' plea bargaining decisions. Few studies have asked if prosecutors take the race of the defendant into consideration in deciding whether to reduce or drop charges in exchange for a guilty plea. Moreover, the studies that have been conducted have reached contradictory conclusions.

Research reveals that prosecutors' plea bargaining decisions are strongly determined by the strength of evidence against the defendant, the defendant's prior criminal record, and the seriousness of the offense.[100] Prosecutors are more willing to offer concessions to defendants who commit less serious crimes and have less serious prior records. They also are more willing to alter charges when the evidence against the defendant is weak or inconsistent.

A number of studies conclude that white defendants are offered plea bargains more frequently and get better deals than racial minorities. A study of the charging process in New York, for example, found that race did not affect charge reductions if the case was disposed of at the first presentation. Among defendants who did not plead guilty at the first opportunity, on the other hand, African Americans received less substantial reductions than whites.[101] An analysis of 683,513 criminal cases in California concluded that "Whites were more successful in getting charges reduced or dropped, in avoiding 'enhancements' or extra charges, and in getting diversion, probation, or fines instead of incarceration."[102]

A recent analysis of plea bargaining under the federal sentencing guidelines also concluded that whites receive better deals than racial minorities.[103] This study, conducted by the United States Sentencing Commission, examined sentence reductions for offenders who provided "substantial assistance" to the government. According to §5K1.1 of the *Guidelines Manual*, if an offender assists in the investigation and prosecution of another person who has committed a crime, the prosecutor can ask the court to reduce the offender's sentence. Because the guidelines do not specify either the types of cooperation that "count" as substantial assistance or the magnitude of the sentence reduction that is to be given, this is a highly discretionary decision.

The Sentencing Commission estimated the effect of race and ethnicity on both the probability of receiving a substantial assistance departure and the magnitude of the sentence reduction. They controlled for other variables such as the seriousness of the offense, use of a weapon, the offender's prior criminal record, and other factors deemed relevant under the sentencing guidelines. They found that African Americans and Hispanics were less likely than whites to receive a substantial assistance departure; among offenders who did receive a departure, whites received a larger sentence reduction than either African Americans or Hispanics.[104] According to the Commission's report, "the evidence consistently indicated that factors that were associated with either the making of a §5K1.1 motion and/or the magnitude of the departure were not consistent with principles of equity."[105]

Albonetti,[106] who examined the effect of guideline departures on sentence outcomes for drug offenders, found similar results. She found that guideline departures (most of which reflected prosecutors' motions to reduce the sentence in return for the offender's "substantial assistance") resulted in larger sentence reductions for white drug offenders than for African American or Hispanic drug offenders. A guideline departure produced a 23 percent reduction in the probability of incarceration for white offenders, compared to a 14 percent reduction for Hispanic offenders and a 13 percent reduction for African American offenders.[107] Albonetti concluded that her findings "strongly suggest that the mechanism by which the federal guidelines permit the exercise of discretion operates to the disadvantage of minority defendants."[108]

Two studies found that race did not affect plea bargaining decisions in the predicted way. An examination of the guilty plea process in nine counties in Illinois, Michigan, and Pennsylvania revealed that defendant race had no effect on four measures of charge reduction.[109] The authors of this study concluded that "the allocation of charge concessions did not seem to be dictated by blatantly discriminatory criteria or punitive motives."[110]

A study of charge reductions in two jurisdictions found that racial minorities received more *favorable* treatment than whites. In one county, African Americans received more favorable charge reductions than whites; in the other county, Hispanics were treated more favorably than whites.[111] The authors of this study speculated that these results might reflect devaluation of minority victims. As they noted, "if minority victims are devalued because of racist beliefs, such sentiments could, paradoxically, produce more favorable legal outcomes for minority defendants." The authors also suggested that the results might reflect overcharging of minority defendants by the police; prosecutors may have been forced "to accept pleas to lesser charges from black defendants because of the initial overcharging." [112]

In sum, although the evidence concerning the effect of race on prosecutors' charging and plea bargaining decisions is both scanty and inconsistent, a number of studies have found that African American and Hispanic suspects are more likely than white suspects to be charged with a crime and prosecuted fully. There is also evidence supporting charges of selective prosecution of racial minorities, especially for drug offenses. The limited evidence concerning the effect of race on plea bargaining is even more contradictory. Given the importance of these initial charging decisions, these findings "call for the kind of scrutiny in the pretrial stages that has been so rightly given to the convicting and sentencing stages."[113]

CONCLUSION

The court system that tried and sentenced the Scottsboro Boys in 1931 no longer exists, in the South or elsewhere. Reforms mandated by the U.S. Supreme Court or adopted voluntarily by the states have eliminated much of the blatant racism directed against racial minorities in court. African American and Hispanic criminal defendants are no longer routinely denied bail and then tried by all-white juries without attorneys to assist them in their defense. They are not consistently prosecuted and convicted with less-than-convincing evidence of guilt.

Implementation of these reforms, however, has not produced equality of justice. As shown in this chapter, there is evidence that defendant race/ethnicity continues to affect decisions regarding bail, charging, and plea bargaining. Some evidence suggests that race has a direct and obvious effect on these pretrial decisions; other evidence suggests that the effect of race is indirect and subtle. It is important to note, however, that discriminatory treatment during the pretrial stage of the criminal justice process can have profound consequences for racial minorities at trial and sentencing. If racial minorities are more likely than whites to be represented by incompetent attorneys or detained in jail prior to trial, they may, as a result of these differences, face greater odds of conviction and harsher sentences. Racially discriminatory charging decisions have similar spillover effects at trial.

DISCUSSION QUESTIONS

1. Some commentators have raised questions about the quality of legal representation provided to the poor. They also have suggested that racial minorities, who are more likely than whites to be poor, are particularly disadvantaged. Is this necessarily the case? Are racial minorities represented by public defenders or assigned counsel treated more harshly than those represented by private attorneys? If you were an African American, Hispanic, or Native American defendant and could choose whether to be represented by a public defender or a private attorney, which would you choose? Why?

2. Assume that racial minorities *are* more likely than whites to be detained prior to trial. Why is this a matter for concern? What are the consequences of pretrial detention? How could the bail system be reformed to reduce this disparity?

3. Randall Kennedy, the author of *Race, Crime and the Law*, argued (p. 10) that it is sometimes difficult to determine "whether, or for whom, a given disparity is harmful." Regarding the prosecution of pregnant women who abuse drugs, he stated, "Some critics attack as racist prosecutions of pregnant drug addicts on the grounds that such prosecutions disproportionately burden blacks." But, he asked, "on balance, are black communities *hurt* by prosecutions of pregnant women for using illicit drugs harmful to their unborn babies or *helped* by intervention which may at least plausibly deter conduct that will put black unborn children at risk?" How would you answer this question?

4. Assume that there is evidence that prosecutors in a particular jurisdiction offer more favorable plea bargains to racial minorities than to whites; that is, they are more willing to reduce the charges and/or to recommend a sentence substantially below the maximum permitted by law if the defendant is a racial minority. What would explain this seemingly "anomalous" finding?

5. What evidence would the defendants in *United States v. Armstrong et al.,* the Supreme Court case in which five black defendants challenged their prosecution for drug offenses in federal rather than state court, need to prove that they had been the victims of unconstitutional selective prosecution? How would they obtain this evidence? Has the Supreme Court placed an unreasonable burden on defendants alleging selective prosecution?

NOTES

1. *Powell v. Alabama*, 287 U.S. 45 (1932).

2. *Norris v. Alabama*, 294 U.S. 587 (1935).

3. Dan T. Carter, *Scottsboro: A Tragedy of the American South* (Baton Rouge: Louisiana State University Press, 1969), p. 326.

4. Ibid., p. 328.

5. Ibid., pp. 344–345.

6. Ibid., p. 347.

7. Birmingham *Age-Herald*, January 24, 1936 (quoted in Carter, *Scottsboro*, p. 347).

8. Carter, *Scottsboro,* pp. 376–377.

9. Ibid., p. 377.

10. Randall Kennedy, *Race, Crime, and the Law* (New York: Vintage Books, 1997), p. 104.

11. Peter Applebome, "Facts Perplexing in Texas Robbery," *New York Times* (December 19, 1983), p. 17.

12. Ibid.

13. Chicago *Tribune,* August 9, 1995, Section 5, pp. 1–2.

14. Ibid., p. 2.

15. Ibid.

16. *Powell v. Alabama,* 287 U.S. 45 (1932).

17. *Johnson v. Zerbst,* 304 U.S. 458 (1938).

18. *Gideon v. Wainwright,* 372 U.S. 335 (1963).

19. *Argersinger v. Hamlin,* 407 U.S. 25 (1972).

20. A defendant is entitled to counsel at every stage "where substantial rights of the accused may be affected" that require the "guiding hand of counsel" (*Mempa v. Rhay,* 389 U.S. 128, 1967). These critical stages include arraignment, preliminary hearing, entry of a plea, trial, sentencing, and the first appeal.

21. Anthony Lewis, *Gideon's Trumpet* (New York: Vintage Books, 1964).

22. Lisa J. McIntyre, *The Public Defender: The Practice of Law in the Shadows of Repute* (Chicago: University of Chicago Press, 1987).

23. Bureau of Justice Statistics, *Indigent Defense* (Washington, D.C.: U.S. Government Printing Office, 1996).

24. Joyce S. Sterling, "Retained Counsel Versus The Public Defender: The Impact of Type of Counsel on Charge Bargaining," in *The Defense Counsel,* ed. William F. McDonald (Beverly Hills, CA: Sage, 1983), p. 166.

25. Jonathan D. Casper, "Did You Have a Lawyer When You Went to Court? No, I Had a Public Defender," *Yale Review of Law and Social Action* 1 (1971): 4–9.

26. See, for example, Abraham S. Blumberg, "The Practice of Law as a Confidence Game: Organizational Cooptation of a Profession, *Law & Society Review* 1

(1967): 15–39; David Sudnow, "Normal Crimes: Sociological Features of the Penal Code in the Public Defender's Office," *Social Problems* 12 (1965): 255–277.

27. Ronald Weitzer, "Racial Discrimination in the Criminal Justice System: Findings and Problems in the Literature," *Journal of Criminal Justice* 24 (1996): 313.

28. Jonathan D. Casper, *Criminal Courts: The Defendant's Perspective* (Englewood Cliffs, NJ: Prentice-Hall, 1978); Martin A. Levin, *Urban Politics and the Criminal Courts* (Chicago: University of Chicago Press, 1977); McIntyre, *The Public Defender*; Dallin H. Oaks and Warren Lehman, "Lawyers for the Poor," in *The Scales of Justice,* ed. Abraham S. Blumberg (Chicago: Aldine, 1970); Lee Silverstein, *Defense of the Poor* (Chicago: American Bar Foundation, 1965); Gerald R. Wheeler and Carol L. Wheeler, "Reflections on Legal Representation of the Economically Disadvantaged: Beyond Assembly Line Justice," *Crime and Delinquency* 26 (1980): 319–332.

29. Jerome Skolnick, "Social Control in the Adversary System," *Journal of Conflict Resolution* 11 (1967): 67.

30. Paul B. Wice, *Chaos in the Courthouse: The Inner Workings of the Urban Municipal Courts* (New York: Praeger, 1985).

31. Stephen B. Bright and Patrick J. Keenan, "Judges and the Politics of Death: Deciding Between the Bill of Rights and the Next Election in Capital Cases," *Boston University Law Review* 75 (1995): 800.

32. The Bureau of Justice Statistics reported that among state prison inmates, 79 percent of the African Americans and 73 percent of the whites were represented by assigned counsel or public defenders. Among federal inmates, the comparable figures were 64 percent for African Americans and 48 percent for whites (Bureau of Justice Statistics, *Indigent Defense,* Table 3).

33. Malcolm D. Holmes, Harmon M. Hosch, Howard C. Daudistel, Dolores A. Perez, and Joseph B. Graves, "Ethnicity, Legal Resources, and Felony Dispositions in Two Southwestern Jurisdictions," *Justice Quarterly* 13 (1996): 11–30.

34. Ibid., p. 24.

35. The findings reported in this chapter are unpublished. See Cassia Spohn and Miriam

DeLone, "When Does Race Matter? An Examination of the Conditions Under Which Race Affects Sentence Severity," *Sociology of Crime, Law and Deviance* (in press).

36. Weitzer, "Racial Discrimination in the Criminal Justice System," p. 313.

37. Roger A. Hanson and Brian J. Ostrom, "Indigent Defenders Get the Job Done and Done Well," in *Criminal Justice: Law and Politics*, 6th ed., ed. George Cole (Belmont, CA: Wadsworth, 1993).

38. Gunnar Myrdal, *An American Dilemma: The Negro Problem and Modern Democracy* (New York: Harper, 1944), p. 547.

39. Ibid., p. 548.

40. Haywood Burns, "Black People and the Tyranny of American Law," *The Annals of the American Academy of Political and Social Sciences* 407 (1973): 161.

41. Celesta A. Albonetti, "An Integration of Theories to Explain Judicial Discretion," *Social Problems* 38 (1991): 247–266; Ronald A. Farrell and Victoria L. Swigert, "Prior Offense Record as a Self-Fulfilling Prophecy," *Law & Society Review* 12 (1978): 437–453; Caleb Foote, "Compelling Appearance in Court: Administration of Bail in Philadelphia," *University of Pennsylvania Law Review* 102 (1954): 1031–1079; Joan Petersilia, *Racial Disparities in the Criminal Justice System* (Santa Monica, CA: Rand, 1978); Wheeler and Wheeler, "Reflections on Legal Representation of the Economically Disadvantaged."

42. Wayne Thomas, *Bail Reform in America* (Berkeley: University of California Press, 1976).

43. Samuel Walker, *Taming the System: The Control of Discretion in Criminal Justice, 1950–1990* (New York: Oxford University Press, 1993).

44. J. Austin, B. Krisberg, and P. Litsky, "The Effectiveness of Supervised Pretrial Release," *Crime and Delinquency* 31 (1985): 519–537; John S. Goldkamp, "Danger and Detention: A Second Generation of Bail Reform," *Journal of Criminal Law and Criminology* 76 (1985): 1–74; Walker, *Taming the System.*

45. Goldkamp, "Danger and Detention."

46. This law was upheld by the U.S. Supreme Court in *United States v. Salerno*, 481 U.S. 739 (1987).

47. Coramae Richey Mann, *Unequal Justice: A Question of Color* (Bloomington: Indiana University Press, 1993), p. 168.

48. R. Stryker, Ilene Nagel, and John Hagan, "Methodology Issues in Court Research: Pretrial Release Decisions for Federal Defendants," *Sociological Methods and Research* 11 (1983): 460–500; Charles M. Katz and Cassia Spohn, "The Effect of Race and Gender on Bail Outcomes: A Test of an Interactive Model," *American Journal of Criminal Justice* 19 (1995): 161–184.

49. S. H. Clarke and G. G. Koch, "The Influence of Income and Other Factors on Whether Criminal Defendants Go To Prison," *Law & Society Review* 11 (1976): 57–92.

50. Tim Bynum, "Release on Recognizance: Substantive or Superficial Reform?" *Criminology* 20 (1982): 67–82.

51. E. Britt Patterson and Michael J. Lynch, "Biases in Formalized Bail Procedures," in *Race and Criminal Justice*, ed. Michael J. Lynch and E. Britt Patterson (New York: Harrow & Heston, 1991).

52. The findings reported here are unpublished. See Spohn and DeLone, "When Does Race Matter?" for a discussion of the overall conclusions of their study.

53. Margaret Farnworth and Patrick Horan, "Separate Justice: An Analysis of Race Differences in Court Processes," *Social Science Research* 9 (1980): 381–399.

54. Theodore G. Chiricos and William D. Bales, "Unemployment and Punishment: An Empirical Assessment," *Criminology* 29 (1991): 701–724.

55. Celesta A. Albonetti, Robert M. Hauser, John Hagan, and Ilene H. Nagel, "Criminal Justice Decision Making as a Stratification Process: The Role of Race and Stratification Resources in Pretrial Release," *Journal of Quantitative Criminology* 5 (1989): 57–82.

56. Bureau of Justice Statistics, *Pretrial Release of Felony Defendants, 1992* (Washington, D.C.: U.S. Department of Justice, 1994), pp. 13–14.

57. Ibid., pp. 5–6.

58. Spohn and DeLone, "When Does Race Matter?"

59. Carter, *Scottsboro.*

60. Carrell Peterson Horton and Jessie Carney Smith, eds., *Statistical Record of Black Americans* (Detroit, MI: Gale Research, 1990), Table 821.

61. "Report: Minorities not reaching top legal levels," *USA Today* (August 5, 1998), p. A1.

62. *Bordenkircher v. Hayes*, 434 U.S. 357, 364 (1978).

63. Kenneth Culp Davis, *Discretionary Justice* (Baton Rouge: Louisiana State University Press, 1969), p. 190.

64. Barbara Boland (INSLAW Inc.), *The Prosecution of Felony Arrests* (Washington, D.C.: Bureau of Justice Statistics, 1983); Kathleen B. Brosi, *A Cross-City Comparison of Felony Case Processing* (Washington, D.C.: Institute for Law and Social Research, 1979); Vera Institute of Justice, *Felony Arrests: Their Prosecution and Disposition in New York City's Courts* (New York: Longman, 1981).

65. Charles E. Silberman, *Criminal Violence, Criminal Justice* (New York, Random House, 1978), p. 271.

66. *Bordenkircher v. Hayes*, supra, 434 U.S. at 364.

67. Myrdal, *An American Dilemma*, pp. 552–553.

68. Ilene Nagel Bernstein, William R. Kelly, and Patricia A. Doyle, "Societal Reaction to Deviants: The Case of Criminal Defendants," *American Sociological Review* 42 (1977): 743–755; Malcolm M. Feeley, *The Process Is the Punishment: Handling Cases in a Lower Criminal Court* (New York: Russell Sage Foundation, 1979); John Hagan, "Parameters of Criminal Prosecution: An Application of Path Analysis to a Problem of Criminal Justice," *Journal of Criminal Law and Criminology* 65 (1975): 536–544.

69. Celesta A. Albonetti, "Criminality, Prosecutorial Screening, and Uncertainty: Toward a Theory of Discretionary Decision Making in Felony Case Processing," *Criminology* 24 (1986): 623–644; Martha A. Myers, *The Effects of Victim Characteristics in the Prosecution, Conviction, and Sentencing of Criminal Defendants*, unpublished Ph.D. dissertation (Bloomington: Indiana University, 1977).

70. Cassia Spohn, John Gruhl, and Susan Welch, "The Impact of the Ethnicity and Gender of Defendants on the Decision To Reject or Dismiss Felony Charges," *Criminology* 25 (1987): 175–191.

71. Ibid., p. 186.

72. Gary D. LaFree, "The Effect of Sexual Stratification by Race on Official Reactions to Rape," *American Sociological Review* 45 (1980): 842–854.

73. Michael L. Radelet, "Racial Characteristics and the Imposition of the Death Penalty," *American Sociological Review* 46 (1981): 918–927.

74. Joan Petersilia, *Racial Disparities in the Criminal Justice System* (Santa Monica, CA: Rand, 1983).

75. Ibid., p. 26.

76. Cassia Spohn and Jeffrey Spears, "The Effect of Offender and Victim Characteristics on Sexual Assault Case Processing Decisions," *Justice Quarterly* 13 (1996): 649–679.

77. Ibid., pp. 661–662.

78. Ibid., p. 673.

79. Ibid., p. 674.

80. Michael Tonry, *Malign Neglect: Race, Crime, and Punishment in America* (New York: Oxford University Press, 1995), p. 105.

81. Ibid., p. 115.

82. Jerome Miller, *Search and Destroy: African-American Males in the Criminal Justice System* (Cambridge: Cambridge University Press, 1996), p. 80.

83. United States Sentencing Commission, *1997 Sourcebook of Federal Sentencing Statistics* (Washington, D.C.: United States Sentencing Commission, 1998), Table 4.

84. U.S. Department of Health and Human Services, Substance Abuse and Mental Health Services Administration, *National Household Survey on Drug Abuse: Population Estimates 1994* (Rockville, MD: U.S. Department of Health and Human Services, 1995).

85. Richard Berk and Alec Campbell, "Preliminary Data on Race and Crack Charging Practices in Los Angeles," *Federal Sentencing Reporter* 6 (1993): 36–38.

86. *United States v. Armstrong et al.*, 517 U.S. 456 (1996).

87. 48 F. 3d 1508 (9th Cir. 1995).

88. *United States v. Armstrong et al.*, 517 U.S. 456 (1996).

89. Ibid. (Stevens, J., dissenting).

90. Drew Humphries, John Dawson, Valerie Cronin, Phyllis Keating, Chris Wisniewski, and Jennine Eichfeld, "Mothers and Children, Drugs and Crack: Reactions to Maternal Drug Dependency," in *The Criminal Justice System and Women*, 2nd ed., ed. Barbara Raffel Price and Natalie J. Sokoloff (New York: McGraw-Hill, 1995), p. 169.

91. *Whitner v. State of South Carolina* (1996).

92. Humphries et al., "Mothers and Children, Drugs and Crack," p. 173.

93. Dorothy Roberts, "Punishing Drug Addicts Who Have Babies: Women of Color, Equality, and the Right of Privacy," *Harvard Law Review* 104 (1991): 1419–1454.

94. Ibid., p. 1432.

95. Ibid., p. 1421, n. 6.

96. Kennedy, *Race, Crime, and the Law*, p. 354.

97. Ibid., p. 359.

98. Ibid., p. 360.

99. Ibid., p. 363.

100. Lynn M. Mather, *Plea Bargaining or Trial?* (Lexington, MA: Heath, 1979).

101. Ilene Nagel Bernstein, Edward Kick, Jan T. Leung, and Barbara Schultz, "Charge Reduction: An Intermediary State in the Process of Labelling Criminal Defendants," *Social Forces* 56 (1977): 362–384.

102. Weitzer, "Racial Discrimination in the Criminal Justice System," p. 313.

103. Linda Drazga Maxfield and John H. Kramer, *Substantial Assistance: An Empirical Yardstick Gauging Equity in Current Federal Policy and Practice* (Washington, D.C.: United States Sentencing Commission, 1998).

104. Ibid., pp. 14–19.

105. Ibid., p. 21.

106. Celesta A. Albonetti, "Sentencing Under the Federal Sentencing Guidelines: Effects of Defendant Characteristics, Guilty Pleas, and Departures on Sentence Outcomes for Drug Offenses, 1991–92," *Law & Society Review* 31 (1997): 789–822.

107. Ibid., p. 813.

108. Ibid., p. 818.

109. Peter F. Nardulli, James Eisenstein, and Roy B. Flemming, *The Tenor of Justice: Criminal Courts and the Guilty Plea Process* (Chicago: University of Chicago Press, 1988).

110. Ibid., p. 238.

111. Malcolm D. Holmes, Howard C. Daudistel, and Ronald A. Farrell, "Determinants of Charge Reductions and Final Dispositions in Cases of Burglary and Robbery," *Journal of Research in Crime and Delinquency* 24 (1987): 233–254.

112. Ibid., pp. 248–249.

113. Spohn et al., "The Impact of the Ethnicity and Gender of Defendants" p. 189.

6

✢

Justice on the Bench?

Trial and Adjudication in Adult and Juvenile Court

We began the previous chapter with a discussion of the Scottsboro Case, a case involving nine young African American males who were convicted of raping two white girls in the early 1930s. We noted that the defendants were tried by all-white juries and that the Supreme Court overturned their convictions because of the systematic exclusion of African Americans from the jury pool.

However, the Scottsboro boys were tried in the 1930s, and much has changed since then. Race relations have improved and decisions handed down by the Supreme Court have made it increasingly difficult for court systems to exclude African Americans from jury service. Nevertheless, "racial prejudice still sometimes seems to sit as a 'thirteenth juror.'"[1] All-white juries continue to convict African American defendants on less-than-convincing evidence. All-white juries continue to acquit whites who victimize African Americans despite persuasive evidence of guilt. Consider the following recent cases:

1980 Four white police officers in Miami were acquitted of all charges in the death of Arthur McDuffie, an African American insurance executive who was beaten to death following a traffic accident. The decision by an all-white jury sparked a riot that lasted several days and resulted in fourteen deaths, hundreds of injuries, and more than $100 million in property damage.

1980   An all-white jury in Texas convicted Clarence Brandley, an African American man accused of murdering Cheryl Dee Fergeson, a white high school student. The district attorney trying the case used his peremptory challenges to strike all of the prospective African American jurors. Brandley spent six years on death row before a Texas district court judge, citing misconduct on the part of police and prosecutors, threw out his conviction. The judge stated that "the color of Clarence Brandley's skin was a substantial factor which pervaded all aspects of the State's capital prosecution against him, and was an impermissible factor which significantly influenced the investigation, trial, and post-trial proceedings of [Brandley's] case."[2]

1987   A jury of ten whites and two blacks acquitted Bernie Goetz, the so-called "subway vigilante," of all but one relatively minor charge in the shooting of four young men on a New York City subway. Goetz, a white man, was accused of shooting and seriously wounding four African American youths who Goetz said had threatened him. A man outside the courtroom held up a sign reading, "Congratulations! Bernie Goetz wins one for the good guys."

1991   Four white Los Angeles police officers were charged in the beating of Rodney King, an African American man stopped for a traffic violation. A videotape of the incident, which showed the officers hitting King with their batons and kicking him in the head as he lay on the ground, was introduced as evidence at the trial. Los Angeles exploded in riots after a jury composed of ten whites, one Asian American, and one Hispanic American acquitted the officers on all charges.

GOALS OF THE CHAPTER

In this chapter we examine the jury selection process for evidence of racial discrimination. We focus on both the procedures used to select the jury pool and the process of selecting the jurors for a particular case. We also discuss the issue of "playing the race card" in a criminal trial and summarize the scholarly debate surrounding the issue of racially based jury nullification. We end the chapter with an examination of the treatment of racial minorities in the juvenile justice system.

SELECTION OF THE JURY POOL

The U.S. Supreme Court first addressed the issue of racial discrimination in jury selection in its 1879 decision of *Strauder v. West Virginia*.[3] The Court ruled that a West Virginia statute limiting jury service to white men violated the equal protection clause of the Fourteenth Amendment and therefore was unconstitutional. The Court concluded that the statute inflicted two distinct harms. The first was a harm that affected the entire African American population. According to the Court:

> The very fact that colored people are singled out and expressly denied by a statute all right to participate in the administration of the law, as jurors, because of their color . . . is practically a brand upon them affixed by the law, an assertion of their inferiority, and a stimulant to that race prejudice which is an impediment to securing to individuals of the race that equal justice which the law aims to secure to all others.[4]

The Court stated that the West Virginia statute inflicted a second harm that primarily hurt African American defendants, who were denied even the *chance* to have people of their own race on their juries. "How can it be maintained," the Justices asked, "that compelling a man to submit to trial for his life by a jury drawn from a panel from which the State has expressly excluded every man of his race, because of his color alone, however well qualified in other respects, is not a denial to him of equal legal protection?"[5] The Court added that this was precisely the type of discrimination the equal protection clause was designed to prevent.

After *Strauder v. West Virginia*, it was clear that states could not pass laws excluding African Americans from jury service. This ruling, however, did not prevent states, and particularly Southern states, from developing techniques designed to preserve the all-white jury. In Delaware, for example, local jurisdictions used lists of taxpayers to select "sober and judicious" persons for jury service. Under this system, African American taxpayers were eligible for jury service, but were seldom, if ever, selected for the jury pool. The state explained this result by noting that few of the African Americans in Delaware were intelligent, experienced, or moral enough to serve as jurors. As the Chief Justice of the Delaware Supreme Court concluded, "That none but white men were selected is in nowise remarkable in view of the fact—too notorious to be ignored—that the great body of black men residing in this State are utterly unqualified by want of intelligence, experience, or moral integrity to sit on juries."[6]

The U.S. Supreme Court refused to accept this explanation. In *Neal v. Delaware*,[7] decided two years after *Strauder*, the Court ruled that the practice had systematically excluded African Americans from jury service and was therefore a case of purposeful—and unconstitutional—racial discrimination. Justice Harlan, writing for the Court, stated that it was implausible "that such uniform exclusion of [Negroes] from juries, during a period of many years, was solely because . . . the black race in Delaware were utterly disqualified, by want of intelligence, experience, or moral integrity."[8]

These early court decisions did not eliminate racial discrimination in jury selection, particularly in the South. Gunnar Myrdal's analysis of the "Negro problem" in the United States in the late 1930s and early 1940s concluded that the typical jury in the South was composed entirely of whites.[9] He noted that some courts had taken steps "to have Negroes on the jury list and call them in occasionally for service."[10] He added, however, that many Southern courts, and particularly those in rural areas, had either ignored the constitutional requirement or had developed techniques "to fulfill legal requirements without using Negro jurors."[11] As a result, as Wishman noted, "For our first hundred years, blacks were explicitly denied the right to be jurors, which meant that if a black defendant was not lynched on the spot, an all-white jury would later decide what to do with him."[12]

Since the mid-1930s, the Supreme Court has made it increasingly difficult for court systems to exclude African Americans or Hispanics from the jury pool. It consistently has struck down the techniques used to circumvent the requirement of racial neutrality in the selection of the jury pool. The Court, for example, ruled that it was unconstitutional for a Georgia county to put the names of white potential jurors on white cards, the names of African American potential jurors on yellow cards, and then "randomly" draw cards to determine who would be summoned.[13] Similarly, the Court struck down the "random" selection of jurors from tax books in which the names of white taxpayers were in one section and the names of African American taxpayers were in another.[14] As the Justices stated in *Avery v. Georgia*, "the State may not draw up its jury lists pursuant to neutral procedures but then resort to discrimination at other stages in the selection process."[15]

Kennedy[16] noted that the states' response to the Supreme Court's increasingly vigilant oversight of the jury selection process was not always positive. The response in some Southern jurisdictions "was a new round of tokenism aimed at maintaining as much of the white supremacist status quo as possible while avoiding judicial intervention."[17] These jurisdictions, in other words, included a token number of racial minorities in the jury pool in an attempt to head off charges of racial discrimination. The Supreme Court addressed this issue as late as 1988.[18] The Court reversed the conviction of Tony Amadeo, who was sentenced to death for murder in Putnam County, Georgia, after it was revealed that the Putnam County district attorney asked the jury commissioner to limit the number of African Americans and women on the master lists from which potential jurors were chosen.

Although the Supreme Court decisions already discussed have made it more difficult for states to discriminate overtly on the basis of race, the procedures used to select the jury pool are not racially neutral. Many states obtain the names of potential jurors from lists of registered voters, automobile registrations, or property tax rolls. The problem with this seemingly objective method is that in some jurisdictions racial minorities are less likely than whites to register to vote, and they also are less likely to own automobiles or taxable property. The result is a jury pool that overrepresents white middle- and upper-class persons and underrepresents racial minorities and those who are poor (see Box 6.1).

BOX 6.1   Excerpts from Massachusetts Jury Selection Statute

Juror Service

Juror service in the participating counties shall be a duty which every person who qualifies under this chapter shall perform when selected. All persons selected for juror service on grand and trial juries shall be selected at random from the population of the judicial district in which they reside. All persons shall have equal opportunity to be considered for juror service. All persons shall serve as jurors when selected and summoned for that purpose except as hereinafter provided. No person shall be exempted or excluded from serving as a grand or trial juror because of race, color, religion, sex, national origin, economic status, or occupation. Physically handicapped persons shall serve except where the court finds such service is not feasible. This court shall strictly enforce the provisions of this section.

Disqualification from Juror Service

As of the date of receipt of the juror summons, any citizen of the United States, who is a resident of the judicial district or who lives within the judicial district more than fifty per cent of the time, whether or not he is registered to vote in any state or federal election, shall be qualified to serve as a grand or trial juror in such judicial district unless one of the following grounds for disqualification applies:

1. Such person is under the age of eighteen years.
2. Such person is seventy years of age or older and indicates on the juror confirmation form an election not to perform juror service.
3. Such person is not able to speak and understand the English language.
4. Such person is incapable by reason of a physical or mental disability of rendering satisfactory juror service.
5. Such person is solely responsible for the daily care of a permanently disabled person living in the same household and the performance of juror service would cause a substantial risk of injury to the health of the disabled person.
6. Such person is outside the judicial district and does not intend to return to the judicial district at any time during the following year.
7. Such person has been convicted of a felony within the past seven years or is a defendant in pending felony cases or is in the custody of a correctional institution.
8. Such person has served as a grand or trial juror in any state or federal court within the previous three calendar years or the person is currently scheduled to perform such service.

SOURCE: 234A M.6.L.A. § 1 et seq.

USE OF PEREMPTORY CHALLENGES

The Supreme Court consistently has ruled that the jury should be drawn from a representative cross-section of the community and that race is not a valid qualification for jury service. These requirements, however, apply only to the selection of the jury pool. They do not apply to the selection of individual jurors for a particular case. In fact, the Court has repeatedly stated that a defendant is *not* entitled to a jury "composed in whole or in part of persons of his own race."[19] Thus, prosecutors and defense attorneys can use their peremptory challenges—"challenges without cause, without explanation, and without judicial scrutiny"[20]—as they see fit, meaning they can use their peremptory challenges in a racially discriminatory manner.

It is clear that lawyers do take the race of the juror into consideration during the jury selection process. Prosecutors assume that racial minorities will side with minority defendants, and defense attorneys assume that racial minorities will be more inclined than whites to convict white defendants. As a result of these assumptions, both prosecutors and defense attorneys have used their peremptory challenges to strike racial minorities from the jury pool. Kennedy, in fact, characterized the peremptory challenge as "a creature of unbridled discretion that, in the hands of white prosecutors and white defendants, has often been used to sustain racial subordination in the courthouse."[21]

Dramatic evidence of this surfaced recently in Philadelphia. In April 1997, Lynne Abraham, Philadelphia's District Attorney, released a 1986 videotape made by Jack McMahon, a former assistant district attorney and her electoral opponent. In the hour-long training video, McMahon advised fellow prosecutors that "young black women are very bad for juries" and that "blacks from the low-income areas are less likely to convict." He also stated, "There's a resentment for law enforcement. There's a resentment for authority. And as a result, you don't want those people on your jury."[22] A Philadelphia defense attorney characterized the videotape as "an abuse of the office," noting, "It was unconstitutional then, and it's unconstitutional now. You don't teach young attorneys to exclude poor people, or black people or Hispanic people."[23]

These comments notwithstanding, there is compelling evidence that prosecutors do use their peremptory challenges to strike racial minorities. As a result, African American and Hispanic defendants are frequently tried by all-white juries. In 1964, for example, Robert Swain, a nineteen-year-old African American, was sentenced to death by an all-white jury for raping a white woman in Alabama. The prosecutor had used his peremptory challenges to strike all six African Americans on the jury panel. In 1978, two African American men accused of murdering a white man were tried by an all-white jury in California after the prosecutor struck all seven prospective African American jurors. In 1990, the state used all of its peremptory challenges to eliminate African Americans from the jury that would try Marion Barry, the African American mayor of Washington, D.C., on drug charges.

The Supreme Court initially was reluctant to restrict the prosecutor's right to use peremptory challenges to excuse jurors on the basis of race. In 1965, the Court ruled in *Swain v. Alabama*[24] that the prosecutor's use of peremptory challenges to strike all six African Americans in the jury pool did not violate the equal protection clause of the Constitution. The Court reasoned:

> The presumption in any particular case must be that the prosecutor is using the State's challenges to obtain a fair and impartial jury .... The presumption is not overcome and the prosecutor therefore subjected to examination by allegations that in the case at hand all Negroes were removed from the jury or that they were removed because they were Negroes.[25]

The Court went on to observe that the Constitution did place some limits on the use of the peremptory challenge. The Justices stated that a defendant could establish a *prima facie* case of purposeful racial discrimination by showing that the elimination of African Americans from a particular jury was part of a pattern of discrimination in that jurisdiction.

The problem, of course, was that the defendants in *Swain*, and in the cases that followed, could not meet this stringent test. As Wishman observed, "A defense lawyer almost never has the statistics to prove a pattern of discrimination, and the state under the *Swain* decision is not required to keep them."[26] The ruling, therefore, provided no protection to the individual African American defendant deprived of a jury of his peers by the prosecutor's use of racially discriminatory strikes. As Supreme Court Justice William Brennan later wrote:

> With the hindsight that two decades affords, it is apparent to me that *Swain's* reasoning was misconceived . . . . *Swain* holds that the state may presume in exercising peremptory challenges that only white jurors will be sufficiently impartial to try a Negro defendant fairly. . . . Implicit in such a presumption is profound disrespect for the ability of individual Negro jurors to judge impartially. It is the race of the juror, and nothing more, that gives rise to the doubt in the mind of the prosecutor.[27]

Despite harsh criticism from legal scholars and civil libertarians,[28] who argued that *Swain* imposed a "crushing burden . . . on defendants alleging racially discriminatory jury selection,"[29] the decision stood for twenty-one years. It was not until 1986 that the Court, in *Batson v. Kentucky*,[30] rejected *Swain's* systematic exclusion requirement and ruled "that a defendant may establish a *prima facie* case of purposeful discrimination in selection of the petit jury solely on evidence concerning the prosecutor's exercise of peremptory challenges at the defendant's trial."[31] The justices added that once the defendant makes a *prima facie* case of racial discrimination, the burden shifts to the state to provide a racially neutral explanation for excluding African American jurors.

Although *Batson* seemed to offer hope that the goal of a representative jury was attainable, an examination of cases decided since 1986 suggests otherwise. State and federal appellate courts have ruled, for example, that leaving one or two African Americans on the jury precludes any inference of purposeful racial discrimination on the part of the prosecutor[32] and that striking only one or two jurors of the defendant's race does not constitute a "pattern" of strikes.[33]

Trial and appellate courts have also been willing to accept virtually any explanation offered by the prosecutor to rebut the defendant's inference of purposeful discrimination.[34] As Kennedy[35] noted, "judges tend to give the benefit of the doubt to the prosecutor." Kennedy cited as an example *State v. Jackson*, a case in which the prosecutor used her peremptory challenges to strike four African Americans in the jury pool. According to Kennedy,

> The prosecutor said that she struck one black prospective juror because she was unemployed and had previously served as a student counselor at a university, a position that bothered the prosecution because it was

"too liberal a background." The prosecution said that it struck another black prospective juror because she, too, was unemployed, and, through her demeanor, had displayed hostility or indifference. By contrast, two whites who were unemployed were seated without objection by the prosecution.[36]

Although Kennedy acknowledged that "one should give due deference to the trial judge who was in a position to see directly the indescribable subtleties," he stated that he "still has difficulty believing that, had these prospective jurors been white, the prosecutor would have struck them just the same." Echoing these concerns, Serr and Maney concluded that "The cost of forfeiting truly peremptory challenges has yielded little corresponding benefit, as a myriad of 'acceptable' explanations and excuses cloud any hope of detecting racially based motivations."[37]

Although it is no longer true that courts "have made no pretense of putting Negroes on jury lists, much less calling or using them in trials,"[38] the jury selection process remains racially biased. Prosecutors continue to use the peremptory challenge to exclude African American jurors from cases with African American defendants,[39] and appellate courts continue to rule that their racially neutral explanations adequately meet the standards articulated in *Batson*. Supreme Court decisions notwithstanding, the peremptory challenge remains an obstacle to impartiality.

PLAYING THE "RACE CARD"
IN A CRIMINAL TRIAL

In 1994 O. J. Simpson, an African American actor and former all-American football star, was accused of murdering his ex-wife, Nicole Brown Simpson, and Ronald Goldman, a friend of hers. On October 4, 1995, a jury composed of seven African American women, two white women, one Hispanic man, and one African American man acquitted Simpson of all charges. Many commentators attributed Simpson's acquittal at least in part to the fact that his attorney, Johnnie L. Cochran, Jr., had "played the race card" during the trial. In fact, another of Simpson's attorneys, Robert Shapiro, charged that Cochran not only played the race card, but "dealt it from the bottom of the deck."[62]

Cochran was criticized for attempting to show that Mark Fuhrman, a Los Angeles police officer who found the bloody glove that linked Simpson to the crime, was a racist who planted the evidence in an attempt to frame Simpson. He also was harshly criticized for suggesting during his closing argument that the jurors would be justified in nullifying the law by acquitting Simpson. Cochran encouraged the jurors to take Fuhrman's racist beliefs into account during their deliberations. He urged them to "send a message" to society that "we are not going to take that anymore."[63]

Although appeals to racial sentiment—that is, "playing the race card"— are not unusual in U.S. courts, they are rarely used by defense attorneys

Focus on an Issue
Should We Eliminate the Peremptory Challenge?

In theory, the peremptory challenge is used to achieve a fair and impartial jury. The assumption is that each side will "size up" potential jurors and use its challenges "to eliminate real or imagined partiality or bias that may be based only on a hunch, an impression, a look, or a gesture."[40] Thus, a prosecutor may routinely strike "liberal" college professors, and a defense attorney may excuse "prosecution-oriented" business executives. The result of this process, at least in principle, is a jury that will decide the case based on the evidence alone.

The reality is that both sides use their peremptory challenges to "stack the deck."[41] The prosecutor attempts to pick a jury that will be predisposed to convict, while the defense attorney attempts to select jurors who will be inclined to acquit. Rather than choosing open-minded jurors who will withhold judgment until they have heard all of the evidence, in other words, each attorney attempts to pack the jury with sympathizers. According to one attorney, "Most successful lawyers develop their own criteria for their choices of jurors. Law professors, experienced lawyers, and a number of technical books suggest general rules to help select *favorable jurors*" [emphasis added].[42]

Do Prosecutors Use Peremptory Challenges in a Racially Discriminatory Manner?

The controversy over the use of the peremptory challenge has centered on the prosecution's use of its challenges to eliminate African Americans from juries trying African American defendants. It centers on what Justice Marshall called "the shameful practice of racial discrimination in the selection of juries."[43] Crit-

ics charge that the process reduces minority participation in the criminal justice system and makes it difficult, if not impossible, for racial minorities to obtain a "jury of their peers." They assert that peremptory challenges "can transform even a representative venire into a white, middle-class jury," thereby rendering "meaningless the protections provided to the venire selection process by *Strauder* and its progeny."[44]

There is substantial evidence that prosecutors exercise peremptory challenges in a racially discriminatory manner. A study of challenges issued in Calcasieu Parish, Louisiana, from 1976 to 1981, for example, found that prosecutors excused African American jurors at a disproportionately high rate.[45] Although the authors of the study also found that defense attorneys tended to use their challenges to excuse whites, they concluded that "Because black prospective jurors are a minority in many jurisdictions, the exclusion of most black prospective jurors by prosecution can be accomplished more easily than the similar exclusion of Caucasian prospective jurors by defense."[46]

African American defendants challenging their convictions by all-white juries also have produced evidence of racial bias. One defendant, for example, showed that Missouri prosecutors challenged 81 percent of the African American jurors available for trial in fifteen cases with African American defendants.[47] Another defendant presented evidence indicating that in fifty-three Louisiana cases involving African American defendants, federal prosecutors used more than two thirds of their challenges against African Americans, who comprised less than one fourth of the jury pool.[48] A third defendant showed that South Carolina prosecutors challenged 82 percent of the African American jurors available for thirteen trials involving African American defendants.[49] Evidence such as this supports Justice Marshall's contention (in a concurring opinion in *Batson v. Kentucky*) that "Misuse of the peremptory challenge to exclude black jurors has become both common and flagrant."[50]

Are All-White Juries Inclined to Convict African American Defendants?

Those who question the prosecutor's use of peremptory challenges to eliminate African Americans from the jury pool argue that African American defendants tried by all-white juries are disproportionately convicted. They assert that white jurors take the race of the defendant and the victim into account in deciding whether to convict the defendant.

Researchers have examined jury verdicts in actual trials and in mock jury studies for evidence of racial bias. Kalven and Zeisel, for example, asked the presiding judge in more than one thousand cases if he or she agreed with the jury's verdict. Judges who disagreed with the verdict were asked to explain the jury's behavior.[51] Judges disagreed with the jury's decision to convict the defendant in twenty-two cases; in four of these cases they attributed the jury's conviction to prejudice against African American defendants involved in interracial sex. Kalven and Zeisel also found that juries were more likely than judges to acquit African American defendants who victimized other African Americans.

Johnson argued that "Mock jury studies provide the strongest evidence that racial bias frequently affects the determination of guilt."[52] She reviewed nine mock jury studies in which the race of the defendant was varied while other factors were held constant. According to Johnson, white "jurors" in all

of the studies were more likely to convict minority-race defendants than they were to convict white defendants.[53]

One mock jury study found evidence of racial bias directed at both the defendant and the victim.[54] In this study, white college students read two transcripts of four crimes in which the race of the male defendant and the race of the female victim were varied; they then were asked to indicate which defendant was more likely to be guilty. For the crime of rape, the probability that the defendant was guilty ranged from 70 percent for crimes with black offenders and white victims to 68 percent for crimes with white offenders and white victims, 52 percent for crimes with black offenders and black victims, and 33 percent for crimes with white offenders and black victims.[55]

Should the Peremptory Challenge Be Eliminated?

Defenders of the peremptory challenge, although admitting that there is inherent tension between peremptory challenges and the quest for a representative jury, argue that the availability of peremptories ensures an *impartial* jury. Defenders of the process further argue that restricting the number of peremptory challenges or requiring attorneys to provide reasons for exercising them would make selection of an impartial jury more difficult.

Those who advocate elimination of the peremptory challenge assert that prosecutors and defense attorneys can use the challenge for cause to eliminate biased or prejudiced jurors.[56] They argue that because prosecutors exercise their peremptory challenges in a racially discriminatory manner, African American defendants are often tried by all-white juries predisposed toward conviction.

In a concurring opinion in the *Batson* case, Justice Marshall called on the Court to ban the use of peremptory challenges by the prosecutor and to allow states to ban their use by the defense.[57] Marshall argued that the remedy fashioned by the Court in *Batson* was inadequate to eliminate racial discrimination in the use of the peremptory challenge. He noted that a black defendant could not attack the prosecutor's discriminatory use of peremptory challenges at all unless the abuse was "so flagrant as to establish a prima facie case,"[58] and that prosecutors, when challenged, "can easily assert facially neutral reasons for striking a juror."[59]

Other commentators, although agreeing that the solution proposed in *Batson* is far from ideal and that reform is needed, propose more modest reforms. Arguing that the chances for abolition of the peremptory challenge are slim, they suggest that a more feasible alternative would be to limit the number of challenges available to each side. As one legal scholar noted, "Giving each side fewer challenges will make it more difficult to eliminate whole groups of people from juries."[60] Another argues that courts must "enforce the prohibition against racially discriminatory peremptory strikes more consistently and forcefully than they have done thus far."[61]

---

representing African Americans accused of victimizing whites. Much more typical are prosecutorial appeals to bias. Consider the following examples:

- An Alabama prosecutor who declared, "Unless you hang this Negro, our white people living out in the country won't be safe."[64]

- A prosecutor in North Carolina who dismissed as implausible the claim of three African American men that the white woman they were accused of raping had consented to sex with them. The prosecutor stated that "the average white woman abhors anything of this type in nature that had to do with a black man."[65]

- A prosecutor in a rape case involving an African American man and a white woman who asked the jurors, "Gentlemen, do you believe that she would have had intercourse with this black brute?"[66]

- A prosecutor in a case involving the alleged kidnapping of a white man by two African American men who said in his closing argument that "not one *white* witness has been produced" [emphasis added] to rebut the victim's testimony.[67]

- A prosecutor who stated, during the penalty phase of a capital case involving Walter J. Blair, an African American man charged with murdering a white woman, "Can you imagine [the victim's] state of mind when she woke up at 6 o'clock that morning, staring into the muzzle of a gun held by this black man?"[68]

All of these appeals to racial sentiment, with the exception of the last one, resulted in reversal of the defendants' convictions. A federal court of appeals, for example, ruled in 1978 that the North Carolina prosecutor's contention that a white woman would never consent to sex with a black man was a "blatant appeal to racial prejudice." The court added that when such an appeal involves an issue as "sensitive as consent to sexual intercourse in a prosecution for rape . . . the prejudice engendered is so great that automatic reversal is required."[69]

A federal court of appeals, on the other hand, refused to reverse Walter Blair's conviction and death sentence. Its refusal was based on the fact that Blair's attorney failed to object at trial to the prosecutor's statement. The sole dissenter in the case suggested that the court should have considered whether the defense attorney's failure to object meant that Blair had been denied effective assistance of counsel. He also vehemently condemned the prosecutor's statement, which he asserted "played upon white fear of crime and the tendency of white people to associate crime with blacks."[70]

Harvard law professor Randall Kennedy argued that playing the race card in a criminal trial is "virtually always morally and legally wrong." He maintained that doing so encourages juries to base their verdicts on irrelevant considerations and loosens the requirement that the state prove the case beyond a reasonable doubt. As he noted, "Racial appeals are not only a distraction but a menace that can distort interpretations of evidence or even seduce jurors into believing that they should vote in a certain way irrespective of the evidence."[71]

Race-Conscious Jury Nullification:
Black Power in the Courtroom?

In a provocative essay published in the *Yale Law Journal* shortly after O. J. Simpson's acquittal, Paul Butler, an African American professor of law at George Washington University Law School, argued for "racially based jury nullification."[72] That is, he urged African American jurors to refuse to convict African American defendants accused of nonviolent crimes, regardless of the strength of the evidence mounted against them. According to Butler, "it is the moral responsibility of black jurors to emancipate some guilty black outlaws."[73]

Jury nullification, which has its roots in English common law, occurs when a juror believes that the evidence presented at trial establishes the defendant's guilt, but nonetheless votes to acquit. The juror's decision may be motivated either by a belief that the law under which the defendant is being prosecuted is unfair or by an objection to the application of the law to a particular defendant. In the first instance, a juror might refuse to convict a defendant tried in federal court for possession of more than fifty grams of crack cocaine, based on her belief that the draconian penalties mandated by the law are unfair. In the second instance, a juror might vote to acquit a father charged with child endangerment after his two-year-old daughter, who was not restrained in a child safety seat, was thrown from the car and killed when he lost control of his car on an icy road. In this case, the juror does not believe that the law itself is unfair, but, rather, that the defendant has suffered enough and that nothing will be gained by additional punishment.

Jurors clearly have the power to nullify the law and to vote their conscience. If a jury votes unanimously to acquit, the double jeopardy clause of the Fifth Amendment prohibits reversal of the jury's decision. The jury's decision to acquit, even in the face of overwhelming evidence of guilt, is final and cannot be reversed by the trial judge or by an appellate court. In most jurisdictions, however, jurors do not have to be told that they have the right to nullify the law.[74]

Butler's position on jury nullification is that the "black community is better off when some nonviolent lawbreakers remain in the community rather than go to prison."[75] Arguing that there are far too many African American men in prison, Butler suggested that there should be "a presumption in favor of nullification"[76] in cases involving African American defendants charged with *nonviolent, victimless* crimes like possession of drugs. Butler contended that enforcement of these laws has a disparate effect on the African American community and does not "advance the interest of black people."[77] He also suggested that white racism, which "creates and sustains the criminal breeding ground which produces the black criminal,"[78] is the underlying cause of much of the crime committed by African Americans. He thus urged African American jurors to "nullify without hesitation in these cases."[79]

Butler did not argue for nullification in all types of cases. In fact, he asserted that defendants charged with violent crimes like murder, rape, and armed robbery should be convicted if there is proof beyond a reasonable doubt of guilt. He contended that nullification is not morally justifiable in these types of cases because "people who are violent should be separated from the community, for the sake of the nonviolent."[80] Violent African American offenders, in other words, should be convicted and incarcerated to protect potential innocent victims. Butler was willing to "write off" these offenders based on his belief that the "black community cannot afford the risks of leaving this person in its midst."[81]

The more difficult cases, according to Butler, involve defendants charged with nonviolent property offenses or with more serious drug trafficking offenses. He discussed two hypothetical cases, one involving a ghetto drug dealer and the other involving a thief who burglarizes the home of a rich family. His answer to the question, "Is nullification morally justifiable here?" is "It depends."[82] Although admitting that "encouraging people to engage in self-destructive behavior is evil," and that therefore most drug dealers should be convicted, he argued that a juror's decision in this type of case might rest on the particular facts in the case. Similarly, although he is troubled by the case of the burglar who steals from a rich family because the behavior is "so clearly wrong," he argued that the facts in the case—for example, a person who steals to support a drug habit—might justify a vote to acquit. Nullification, in other words, may be a morally justifiable option in both types of cases.

Randall Kennedy's Critique   Randall Kennedy[83] raised a number of objections to Butler's proposal, which he characterized as "profoundly misleading as a guide to action."[84] Although admitting that Butler's assertion that there is racial injustice in the administration of the criminal law is correct, Kennedy nonetheless objected to Butler's portrayal of the criminal justice system as a "one-dimensional system that is totally at odds with what black Americans need and want, a system that unequivocally represents and unrelentingly imposes 'the white man's law.'"[85] Kennedy faulted Butler for his failure to acknowledge either the legal reforms implemented as a result of struggles *against* racism or the significant presence of African American officials in policymaking positions and the criminal justice system. The problems inherent in the criminal justice system, according to Kennedy, "require judicious attention, not a campaign of defiant sabotage."[86]

Kennedy objected to the fact that Butler expressed more sympathy for non-violent African American offenders than for "the law-abiding people compelled by circumstances to live in close proximity to the criminals for whom he is willing to urge subversion of the legal system."[87] He asserted that law-abiding African Americans "desire *more* rather than *less* prosecution and punishment for *all* types of criminals,"[88] and suggested that, in any case, jury nullification "is an exceedingly poor means for advancing the goal of a racially fair administration of criminal law."[89] He contended that a highly publicized campaign of jury nullification carried on by blacks will not produce the social reforms that Butler demanded. Moreover, such a campaign might backfire. Kennedy suggested that it might lead to increased support for proposals to eliminate the requirement that the jury be unanimous to convict, restrictions on the right of African Americans to serve on juries, or widespread use of jury nullification by white jurors in cases involving white-on-black crime.

According to Kennedy, the most compelling reason to oppose Butler's call for racially based jury nullification is that it is based on "an ultimately destructive sentiment of racial kinship that prompts individuals of a given race to care more about 'their own' than people of another race."[90] He objected to the implication that it is proper for African American jurors to be more concerned about the fate of African American defendants than white defendants, more disturbed about the plight of African American communities than white communities, and more interested in protecting the lives and property of African Americans than that of white citizens. "Along that road," according to Kennedy, "lies moral and political disaster." Implementation of Butler's proposal, Kennedy insisted, would not only increase, but legitimize "the tendency of people to privilege in racial terms 'their own'."[91]

RACE/ETHNICITY AND THE JUVENILE JUSTICE SYSTEM

Although most research on the effect of race on the processing of criminal defendants has focused on adults, researchers recently have begun to examine the juvenile justice system for evidence of racial discrimination. Noting that the juvenile system, with its philosophy of *parens patriae,* is more discretionary and less formal than the adult system, researchers have suggested that there is greater potential for racial discrimination in the processing of juveniles than in the processing of adults.

There is compelling evidence that racial minorities are overrepresented in the juvenile justice system. In 1995, for example, African Americans comprised 15 percent of the general juvenile population but 34 percent of all youth in the juvenile justice system; whites constituted approximately 80 percent of the youth population but only 63 percent of all offenders in juvenile court.[92] In

Table 6.1 Juvenile Court Case Outcomes, 1993

	Whites (%)	Blacks (%)
Delinquent Cases		
Detained Prior to Juvenile Court Disposition	16.7	27.7
Petitioned to Juvenile Court	49.3	61.1
Petitioned Cases		
Adjudicated Delinquent	59.2	55.2
Waived to Adult Court	1.1	2.1
Adjudicated Cases		
Placed Out of Home	25.3	33.1
Placed on Probation	56.9	54.2
Dismissed	3.2	5.3

SOURCE: U.S. Department of Justice, Bureau of Justice Statistics, *Sourcebook of Criminal Justice Statistics 1995* (Washington, D.C.: U.S. Government Printing Office, 1996).

1991, 43 percent of the juveniles held in public detention facilities were African American, 19 percent were Hispanic, and 35 percent were white. African American youth represented 64 percent of all detained drug offenders and 40 percent of all offenders detained for offenses against a person.[93]

As shown in Table 6.1, African Americans were treated more harshly than whites at several stages in the juvenile justice process. African Americans were more likely than whites to be detained prior to juvenile court disposition, petitioned to juvenile court for further processing, and waived to adult court. Among those adjudicated delinquent, African Americans were more likely than whites to be placed in a juvenile facility and less likely than whites to be placed on probation.

The figures presented in Table 6.1 do not take racial differences in crime seriousness, prior juvenile record, or other legally relevant criteria into consideration. If racial minorities are referred to juvenile court for more serious offenses or have more serious criminal histories than whites, the observed racial disparities in case processing might diminish or disappear once these factors were taken into consideration.

Research conducted during the past twenty years suggests that the disparities revealed in Table 6.1 reflect racial discrimination, at least in some jurisdictions and for some stages of the juvenile justice process. Pope and Feyerherm, for example, reviewed forty-six studies published in the 1970s and 1980s.[94] Two thirds of the studies they examined found evidence of discriminatory treatment of racial minorities. They also noted that a number of studies revealed that small racial differences in outcomes at the initial stages of the process "accumulate and become more pronounced as minority youths are processed further into the juvenile justice system."[95]

A comprehensive review of the research on juvenile justice decision making is beyond the scope of this chapter. Instead, we summarize the findings of three recent, methodologically sophisticated studies. The first is a comparison

Table 6.2 Race and Juvenile Justice Processing in Florida

	Recommended for Formal Processing (%)	Detained (%)	Petitioned to Juvenile Court (%)	Adjudicated Delinquent (%)	Incarcerated/ Transferred (%)
Blacks	59.1	11.0	47.3	82.5	29.6
Whites	45.6	10.2	37.8	80.0	19.5
Proportion Black	34.0	30.0	32.4	33.3	43.1

SOURCE: Adapted from Donna M. Bishop and Charles E. Frazier, "The Influence of Race in Juvenile Justice Processing," *Journal of Research in Crime and Delinquency* 25 (1988): 250.

of outcomes for African Americans and whites in Florida; the second is an analysis of outcomes for African Americans, Native Americans, and whites in Iowa; and the third is an analysis of outcomes for African American, Hispanic, and white youth in Pennsylvania. We also discuss evidence concerning racial disparities in waivers to adult criminal court.

Race/Ethnicity and Juvenile Court
Outcomes in Three Jurisdictions

Processing Juveniles in Florida Bishop and Frazier examined the processing of African American and white juveniles in Florida.[96] In contrast to previous researchers, most of whom focused on a single stage of the juvenile justice process, these researchers followed a cohort of 54,266 youth through the system from intake through disposition. They examined the effect of race on five stages in the process: (1) the decision to refer the case to juvenile court for formal processing, (2) the decision to place the youth in detention prior to disposition, (3) the decision to petition the youth to juvenile court, (4) the decision to adjudicate the youth delinquent (or hold a waiver hearing in anticipation of transferring the case to criminal court), and (5) the decision to commit the youth to a residential facility or transfer the case to criminal court.

Table 6.2 displays the outcomes for African American and white youth, as well as the proportion of African Americans in the cohort at each stage in the process. These data indicate that African Americans were substantially more likely than whites to be recommended for formal processing (59.1% versus 45.6%), petitioned to juvenile court (47.3% versus 37.8%), and either incarcerated in a residential facility or transferred to criminal court (29.6% versus 19.5%).

As Bishop and Frazier noted, these differences could reflect the fact that the African American youths in their sample were arrested for more serious crimes and had more serious prior criminal records than white youths. If this were the case, the differences would reflect racial disparity but not racial discrimination.

When the authors controlled for crime seriousness, prior record, and other predictors of juvenile justice outcomes, they found that the racial differences did not disappear. Rather, African Americans were more likely than whites to be recommended for formal processing, referred to juvenile court, and adjudicated delinquent. They also received harsher sentences than whites. These findings led Bishop and Frazier to conclude that "race is a far more pervasive influence in processing than much previous research has indicated."[97]

Juvenile Justice Decision Making in Iowa Most research on the effect of race on juvenile justice decision making has been limited to a comparison of outcomes for African Americans and whites. An exception is a recent study by Leiber, who compared case processing outcomes for white, African American, and Native American youth in Iowa.[98] Like Bishop and Frazier, Leiber examined outcomes at five stages in the process.

Leiber hypothesized that racial minorities would be treated more harshly than whites and that Native Americans would receive more severe outcomes than African Americans. Regarding his prediction concerning the treatment of Native Americans, Leiber noted that he assumed that "their social and economic situation, the stereotyped perceptions of these youths as drug users and 'outsiders,' and linguistic difficulties would work against them to a greater extent than against African Americans."[99]

Leiber's hypothesis was not confirmed. He found no race differences at several stages in the process. Moreover, he found that racial minorities were less likely than whites to be petitioned to juvenile court for further processing and that Native Americans charged with serious offenses were less likely to be recommended for a petition. Native American youths, in other words, received more lenient outcomes than other groups at these two stages in the process.

Leiber attributed his finding that Native Americans were more likely to receive an informal adjustment and less likely to be referred for further processing to the juvenile court's policy of diverting Native American youth through Indian Youth of America, a tribal agency. He also noted that interviews with juvenile court personnel revealed that African American youths were released more often than whites because of a lack of diversionary programs, lack of cooperation with juvenile justice officials, and/or lack of an admission of guilt (which is required for diversion).

Processing Juveniles in Pennsylvania Leonard and Sontheimer[100] explored the effect of race and ethnicity on juvenile justice case outcomes in Pennsylvania. Although African Americans and Hispanics accounted for only 19 percent and 4 percent, respectively, of the general youth population in the fourteen counties included in the study, they comprised 46 percent (African Americans) and 7 percent (Hispanics) of all referrals to juvenile court.[101]

Like the two studies discussed earlier, this study used a multivariate model to examine the effect of race/ethnicity on a series of juvenile justice outcomes. Leonard and Sontheimer found that both African American and Hispanic youth "were more likely than whites with similar offenses, prior records, and school problems to have their cases formally processed, especially in non-rural court setting."[102] They also found that minority youth were significantly more likely than whites to be detained prior to adjudication, and that detention was a strong predictor of subsequent outcomes. African American and Hispanic youth, in other words, were detained more frequently than whites and, as a result, were more likely than whites to be adjudicated delinquent and to be placed in a residential facility following adjudication.

Leonard and Sontheimer suggested that their findings have important policy implications. In particular, they recommended:

> [The] criteria used by individual intake officers should be evaluated to determine whether factors that may more often negatively affect minorities are accorded importance. Racially neutral criteria in detention decisions should be established . . . . Cultural bias, including value judgments not based on fact (such as notions that minority parents may not provide adequate supervision for their children or that certain neighborhoods are not conducive to growing up well), must not influence detention.[103]

The studies described here suggest that the effect of race on juvenile justice outcomes may vary from one jurisdiction to another. The findings also reveal that it is important to conceptualize decision making in the juvenile justice system as a process. According to Secret and Johnson,[104] "in examining for racial bias in juvenile justice system decisions, we must scrutinize each step of the process to see whether previous decisions create a racial effect by changing the pool of offenders at subsequent steps." The importance of differentiating among racial and ethnic groups is also clear. As Leiber noted, "Circumstances surrounding the case processing of minority youths not only may be different from those for whites, but also may vary among minority groups."[105]

Transfer of Juveniles to Criminal Court

In 1994, youth under age fifteen accounted for 2 percent of all arrests for murder and manslaughter, 6 percent of all arrests for forcible rape, and 9 percent of all arrests for robbery. Youth between the ages of fifteen and seventeen comprised 17 percent of all murder and manslaughter arrests, 16 percent of all forcible rape arrests, and 32 percent of all robbery arrests.[106] More striking, juvenile arrest rates increased 100 percent between 1985 and 1994. Juvenile arrests for violent crimes increased from 66,976 in 1985 to 117,200 in 1994 (an increase of 75 percent) and arrests for murder went from 1,193 to 2,982 (an increase of 150 percent).

Statistics such as these, coupled with highly publicized cases of very young children accused of murder and other violent crimes, prompted a number of states to alter procedures for handling certain types of juvenile offenders. In 1995, for example, Illinois lowered the age for admission to prison from thirteen to ten. This change was enacted after two boys, ages ten and eleven, dropped a five-year-old boy out of a fourteenth-floor window in a Chicago public housing development. In 1996, a juvenile court judge ordered both boys, who were then twelve and thirteen, sent to a high-security juvenile penitentiary. Her decision made the twelve-year-old the nation's youngest inmate at a high-security prison.[107]

Other states responded to the increase in serious juvenile crime by either lowering the age when children can be transferred from juvenile court to criminal court and/or expanding the list of offenses for which juveniles can be waived to criminal court. A report by the U.S. General Accounting Office (GAO) indicated that between 1978 and 1995, forty-four states passed new laws regarding the waiver of juveniles to criminal court; in twenty-four of these states the new laws increased the population of juveniles that potentially could be sent to criminal court.[108] California, for example, lowered the age at which juveniles could be waived to criminal court from sixteen to fourteen (for specified offenses); Missouri reduced the age at which children could be certified to stand trial as adults from fourteen to twelve.

The GAO report also noted that the percentage of delinquency cases waived to criminal court (the judicial waiver rate) increased from 1.2 percent in 1988 to 1.6 percent in 1992; the number of cases waived increased from 7,000 to just under 12,000.[109] The 1992 judicial waiver rate was highest for drug offenses (3.1 percent), followed by person offenses (2.4 percent) and property offenses (1.3 percent).

The GAO report provided some data on the race of juveniles waived to criminal court. Nationally, 50 percent of juveniles whose cases were waived were African American, 47 percent were white, and 3 percent were of other races.[110] These figures mirror almost exactly the racial makeup of arrests of persons under age eighteen for violent crime: 50 percent were African American, 48 percent were white, and 2 percent were of other races. These similarities *suggest* that racial disparities in the judicial waiver rate do not reflect racial discrimination on the part of juvenile court judges. They suggest, in other words, that African American youth are overrepresented among those waived to criminal court because of the fact that they are overrepresented among those arrested for violent crimes.

The validity of this explanation is called into question by the data in Table 6.3, which presents judicial waiver rates by race and type of offense for six states. (Because of the small number of cases for each offense, the GAO was unable to simultaneously control for legally relevant criteria such as the type of offense, prior referrals, and age at referral.) Among offenders arrested for violent crimes, the waiver rate for African Americans was larger than the rate for whites in all six states. Among offenders arrested for drug offenses, the African American waiver rate was higher than the white rate in all but one of the six states. In four states (Arizona, Florida, Missouri, and South Carolina), African Americans were more likely to have their cases waived for each of the three types of offenses. The differences were particularly pronounced in Arizona, where black juveniles had waiver rates that were twice as high as white rates for violent offenses and property crimes and were 13.6 times higher than white rates for drug offenses.

Although additional research incorporating other legally relevant criteria obviously is needed before definitive conclusions can be drawn, the data displayed in Table 6.3 suggest that the decision to transfer a juvenile offender to adult court is not racially neutral. At least in the six states included in the GAO's analysis, African Americans faced substantially higher odds than whites of being transferred into the more punitive adult court system.

Table 6.3 Waiver Rates by Race and Type of Offense

	WAIVER RATE (%)		
	Violent Crimes	**Property Crimes**	**Drug Offenses**
Arizona			
African Americans	9.1	2.6	10.9
Whites	5.1	1.3	0.8
California			
African Americans	1.3	0.1	0.2
Whites	0.5	0.1	0.4
Florida			
African Americans	2.3	0.8	3.0
Whites	1.0	0.7	1.2
Missouri			
African Americans	7.4	1.8	7.5
Whites	2.4	1.6	3.3
Pennsylvania			
African Americans	3.0	1.6	3.9
Whites	1.4	1.6	1.6
South Carolina			
African Americans	4.4	0.4	3.8
Whites	1.6	0.2	0.0

SOURCE: United States General Accounting Office, *Juvenile Justice: Juveniles Processed in Criminal Court and Case Dispositions* (Washington, D.C.: U.S. General Accounting Office, 1995), Tables 11.3, 11.6, 11.9, 11.12, 11.15, and 11.18.

Explaining Disparate Treatment of Juvenile Offenders

The studies discussed here provide compelling evidence that African American and Hispanic juveniles are treated more harshly than similarly situated white juveniles. The question, of course, is why this occurs. Secret and Johnson[111] suggested that juvenile court judges might attribute positive or negative characteristics to offenders based on their race/ethnicity. Judges, in other words, may use extralegal characteristics like race to create "a mental map of the accused person's underlying character" and to predict his/her future behavior.[112] As Mann noted, officials' attitudes "mirror the stereotype of minorities as typically violent, dangerous, or threatening."[113] Alternatively, according to Secret and Johnson, the harsher treatment of African American and Hispanic juveniles might reflect both class and race biases on the part of juvenile court judges. As conflict theory posits, "the individual's economic and social class and the color of his skin ... determine his relationship to the legal system."[114]

These speculations regarding court officials' perceptions of minority and white youth have not been systematically tested. Researchers assume that findings of differential treatment of racial minorities signal the presence of race-linked stereotypes or racially prejudiced attitudes. However, there have been few attempts to empirically verify either the existence of differing perceptions of white and minority youth or the degree to which these perceptions can account for racial disparities in the juvenile justice system.

A recent study by Bridges and Steen[115] addressed this issue by examining 233 narrative reports written by juvenile probation officers in three counties in the state of Washington during 1990 and 1991. The narratives, used by the court in determining the appropriate disposition of the case, were based on interviews with the youth and his or her family and on written documents such as school records and juvenile court files. Each narrative included the probation officer's description of the youth's crime and assessment of the factors that motivated the crime, as well as an evaluation of the youth's background and assessment of his or her likelihood of recidivism. The information gleaned from these narratives was used "to explore the relationship between race; officials' characterizations of youths, their crimes, and the causes of their crimes; officials' assessments of the threat of future crime by youths; and officials' sentence recommendations."[116]

Bridges and Steen's review of the narratives revealed that probation officers described black and white youth and their crimes differently. They tended to attribute crimes committed by whites to negative environmental factors (poor school performance, delinquent peers, dysfunctional family, use of drugs or alcohol) but to attribute crimes committed by African Americans to negative personality traits and "bad attitudes" (refusal to admit guilt, lack of remorse, failure to take offense seriously, lack of cooperation with court officials). They also found that probation officers judged African American youth to have a significantly higher risk of reoffending than white youth.

Further analysis, which controlled for the juvenile's age, gender, and prior criminal history, and for the seriousness of the current offense, confirmed these findings. As the authors noted, "Being black significantly reduces the likelihood of negative *external* attributions by probation officers and significantly increases the likelihood of negative *internal* attributions, even after adjusting for severity of the presenting offense and the youth's prior involvement in criminal behavior."[117] To illustrate these differences, the authors discussed the narratives written for two very similar cases of armed robbery, one involving a black youth and one involving a white youth. The black youth's crime was described as "very dangerous" and as "premeditated and willful," and his criminal behavior was attributed to an amoral character, lack of remorse, and no desire to change. In contrast, the white youth was portrayed as an "emaciated little boy" whose crime was attributed to a broken home, association with delinquent peers, and substance abuse.

Bridges and Steen's examination of the factors related to probation officers' assessments of the risk of reoffending revealed that youth who committed more serious crimes or had more serious criminal histories were judged to be at higher risk of future offending. Although none of the offender's demographic characteristics, including race, was significantly related to assessments of risk, probation officers' attributions of delinquency did affect these predictions. Youth whose delinquency was attributed to negative internal causes were judged to be at higher risk of future delinquency than youth whose crimes were attributed to negative external factors. According to Bridges and Steen, "This suggests that youths whose crimes are attributed to internal causes are more likely to be viewed as 'responsible' for their crimes, engulfed in a delinquent personality and lifestyle, and prone to committing crimes in the future."[118]

The authors of this study concluded that race influenced juvenile court outcomes indirectly. Probation officers were substantially more likely to attribute negative internal characteristics and attitudes to black youth than to white youth; these attributions, in turn, shaped their assessments of dangerousness and their predictions of future offending. As Bridges and Steen stated, "Insofar as officials judge black youths to be more dangerous than white youths, they do so because they attribute crime by blacks to negative personalities or their attitudinal traits and because black offenders are more likely than white offenders to have committed serious offenses and have histories of prior involvement in crime."[119]

The results of this study illustrate the "mechanisms by which officials' perceptions of the offender as threatening develop or influence the process of legal decision-making."[120] They suggest that perceptions of threat and, consequently, predictions about future delinquency are influenced by criminal justice officials' assessments of the causes of criminal behavior. Thus, "officials may perceive blacks as more culpable and dangerous than whites in part because they believe the etiology of their crimes is linked to personal traits" that are "not as amenable to the correctional treatments the courts typically administer."[121]

CONCLUSION

In Chapter 5, we concluded that the reforms implemented during the past few decades have substantially reduced racial discrimination during the pretrial stages of the criminal justice process. Our examination of the jury selection process suggests that a similar conclusion is warranted. Reforms adopted voluntarily by the states or mandated by appellate courts have made it increasingly unlikely that African American and Hispanic defendants will be tried by all-white juries. An important caveat, however, concerns the use of racially motivated peremptory challenges. Supreme Court decisions notwithstanding, prosecutors still manage to use the peremptory challenge to eliminate African Americans from juries trying African American defendants. More troubling, prosecutors' "racially neutral" explanations for strikes alleged to be racially motivated continue to be accepted at face value. Coupled with anecdotal evidence that prosecutors are not reluctant to "play the race card" in a criminal trial, these findings regarding jury selection suggest that the process of adjudication, like the pretrial process, is not free of racial bias.

The results of studies examining the effect of race/ethnicity on juvenile justice processing decisions suggest a similar conclusion. There is compelling evidence that racial minorities are treated more harshly than whites at various points in the juvenile justice process. Most important, minority youth are substantially more likely than white youth to be detained pending disposition, adjudicated delinquent, and waived to adult court. They also are sentenced more harshly than their white counterparts, at least in part because of the tendency of criminal justice officials to attribute their crimes to internal (personality) rather than external (environmental) causes.

Based on the research reviewed in this chapter and the previous one, we conclude that contemporary court processing decisions are not characterized by *systematic* discrimination against racial minorities. This may have been true when the Scottsboro boys were tried, but it is no longer true. As noted earlier, the U.S. Supreme Court has consistently affirmed the importance of protecting the rights of criminal defendants and has insisted that the race of the defendant not be taken into consideration in making case processing decisions. Coupled with reforms adopted voluntarily by the states, these decisions make systematic racial discrimination unlikely.

We are not suggesting, however, that these reforms have produced an equitable or color-blind system of justice. We are not suggesting that contemporary court processing decisions reflect *pure justice*. Researchers have demonstrated that court processing decisions in some jurisdictions reflect racial discrimination, whereas decisions in other jurisdictions are racially neutral. Researchers also have shown that African Americans and Hispanics who commit certain types of crimes are treated more harshly than whites, and that being unemployed, having a prior criminal record, or being detained prior to trial may have a more negative effect on court outcomes for people of color than for whites.

These findings lead us to conclude that discrimination against African Americans and other racial minorities is not universal but is confined to certain types of cases, settings, and defendants. We conclude that the court system of today is characterized by *contextual discrimination*.

DISCUSSION QUESTIONS

1. Evidence suggesting the prosecutors use their peremptory challenges to preserve all-white juries in cases involving African American or Hispanic defendants has led some commentators to call for the elimination of the peremptory challenge. What do you think is the strongest argument in favor of eliminating the peremptory challenge? In favor of retaining it? Given that the Supreme Court is unlikely to rule that the peremptory challenge violates the right to a fair trial and is therefore unconstitutional, are there any remedies or reforms that could be implemented?

2. The Supreme Court has repeatedly asserted that a defendant is not entitled to a jury "composed in whole or in part of persons of his own race." Although these rulings establish that states are not *obligated* to use racially mixed juries, they do not *prohibit* states from doing so. In fact, a number of policymakers and legal scholars have proposed reforms that use racial criteria to promote racial diversity on U.S. juries. Some have suggested that the names of majority race jurors be removed from the jury list (thus ensuring a larger proportion of racial minorities); others have suggested that a certain number of seats on each jury be set aside for racial minorities. How would you justify these reforms to a state legislature? How would an opponent of these reforms respond? Overall, are these good ideas or bad ideas?

3. In this chapter, we present a number of examples of lawyers who "played the race card" in a criminal trial. Almost all of them involved prosecutors who appealed to the racist sentiments of white jurors. But what about defense attorneys representing African American defendants who attempt to appeal to the racial sentiments of African American jurors? Who urge African American jurors to nullify the law by refusing to convict African American defendants accused of certain types of crimes regardless of the evidence arrayed against them? Does this represent misconduct? How should the judge respond?

4. We suggest that preliminary evidence indicating that African American juveniles are more likely than white juveniles to be waived to adult court should be confirmed by additional research that incorporates legally relevant criteria other than the seriousness of the offense. What other variables should be taken into consideration?

5. Although studies reveal that African American, Hispanic, and Native American youth are treated more harshly than white youth at several stages of the juvenile justice process (even after the seriousness of the offense and the offender's prior juvenile record are taken into consideration), they do not tell us why these disparities occur. How would *you* explain these differences? How do Bridges and Steen account for them?

NOTES

1. James P. Levine, *Juries and Politics* (Pacific Grove, CA: Brooks/Cole, 1992).

2. Randall Kennedy, *Race, Crime, and the Law* (New York: Vintage, 1997), p. 127.

3. *Strauder v. West Virginia*, 100 U.S. 303 (1880).

4. Ibid., pp. 307–308.

5. Ibid., p. 309.

6. *Neal v. Delaware*, 103 U.S. 370, 394 (1881), at 393–394.

7. Ibid.

8. Ibid., p. 397.

9. Gunnar Myrdal, *An American Dilemma: The Negro Problem and Modern Democracy* (New York: Harper, 1944), p. 549.

10. Ibid., p. 549.

11. Ibid.

12. Seymour Wishman, *Anatomy of a Jury: The System on Trial* (New York: Times Books, 1986), p. 54.

13. *Avery v. Georgia*, 345 U.S. 559 (1953).

14. *Whitus v. Georgia*, 385 U.S. 545 (1967).

15. *Avery v. Georgia*, 345 U.S. 559 (1953), at 562.

16. Kennedy, *Race, Crime, and the Law*, p. 179.

17. Ibid.

18. *Amadeo v. Zant*, 486 U.S. 214 (1988).

19. *Strauder v. West Virginia*, 100 U.S. (1880), at 305; *Batson v. Kentucky*, 476 U.S. 79 (1986), at 85.

20. *Swain v. Alabama*, 380 U.S. 202, 212 (1965).

21. Kennedy, *Race, Crime, and the Law*, p. 214.

22. "Former Prosecutor Accused of Bias in Election Year," *New York Times* (March 31, 1997).

23. Ibid.

24. *Swain v. Alabama* 380 U.S. 202 (1965).

25. Ibid., 380 U.S. at 222.

26. Wishman, *Anatomy of a Jury*, p. 115.

27. Justice Brennan, dissenting from denial of certiorari in *Thompson v. United States*, 105 S.Ct. at 445.

28. See Comment, "*Swain v. Alabama*, A Constitutional Blueprint for the Perpetuation of the All-White Jury," *Virginia Law Review* 52 (1966): 1157; Note, "Rethinking Limitations on the Peremptory Challenge," *Columbia Law Review* 85 (1983): 1357.

29. Brian J. Serr and Mark Maney, "Racism, Peremptory Challenges, and the Democratic Jury: The Jurisprudence of a Delicate Balance," *Journal of Criminal Law and Criminology* 79 (1988): 13.

30. *Batson v. Kentucky*, 476 U.S. 79 (1986), at 93–94.

31. Ibid., at 96.

32. *United States v. Montgomery*, 819 F.2d at 851. The Eleventh Circuit, however, rejected this line of reasoning in *Fleming v. Kemp*, 794 F.2d 1478 (11th Cir. 1986), and *United States v. David*, 803 F.2d 1567 (11th Cir. 1986).

33. *United States v. Vaccaro*, 816 F.2d 443, 457 (9th Cir. 1987); *Fields v. People*, 732 P.2d 1145, 1158 n.20 (Colo. 1987).

34. Serr and Maney, "Racism, Peremptory Challenges, and the Democratic Jury," pp. 43–47.

35. Kennedy, *Race, Crime, and the Law*, p. 211.

36. Ibid., p. 213.

37. Serr and Maney, "Racism, Peremptory Challenges, and the Democratic Jury," p. 63.

38. Myrdal, *An American Dilemma*, pp. 547–548.

39. A study of peremptory challenges issued from 1976 to 1981 in Calcasieu Parish, Louisiana, for example, found that prosecutors excused African American jurors at a disproportionately high rate. See Billy M. Turner, Rickie D. Lovell, John C. Young, and William F. Denny, "Race and Peremptory Challenges During Voir Dire: Do Prosecution and Defense Agree?" *Journal of Criminal Justice* 14 (1986): 61–69.

40. H. Frank Way, *Criminal Justice and the American Constitution* (North Scituate, MA: Duxbury, 1980), p. 344.

41. Levine, *Juries and Politics*, p. 51.

42. Wishman, *Anatomy of a Jury*, p. 105.

43. *Batson v. Kentucky*, 476 U.S. 79 (1986).

44. Serr and Maney, "Racism, Peremptory Challenges, and the Democratic Jury," pp. 7–8.

45. Turner et al., "Race and Peremptory Challenges."

46. Ibid., p. 68. See also George Hayden, Joseph Senna, and Larry Siegel, "Prosecutorial Discretion in Peremptory Challenges: An Empirical Investigation of Information Use in the Massachusetts Jury Selection Process," *New England Law Review* 13 (1978): 768–790.

47. *United States v. Carter*, 528 F.2d 844, 848 (CA 8 1975).

48. *United States v. McDaniels*, 379 F.Supp. 1243 (ED La. 1974).

49. *McKinney v. Walker*, 394 F.Supp. 1015, 1017–1018 (SC 1974).

50. *Batson v. Kentucky*, 106 S.Ct. 1712, 1726 (1986) (Marshall, J., concurring).

51. Harry Kalven and Hans Zeisel, *The American Jury* (Boston: Little, Brown, 1966).

52. Sheri Lynn Johnson, "Black Innocence and the White Jury," *University of Michigan Law Review* 83 (1985): 1625.

53. Ibid., p. 1626.

54. Kitty Klein and Blanche Creech, "Race, Rape, and Bias: Distortion of Prior Odds and Meaning Changes," *Basic and Applied Social Psychology* 3 (1982): 21.

55. Ibid., p. 24.

56. Martin Howard Levin, "The Jury in a Criminal Case: Obstacles to Impartiality," *Criminal Law Bulletin*, 24 (1988): 492–520.

57. *Batson v. Kentucky*, 106 S.Ct. 1712, 1726 (1986) (Marshall, J., concurring).

58. Ibid., at 1727.

59. Ibid.

60. Note, "*Batson v. Kentucky*: Challenging the Use of the Peremptory Challenge," *American Journal of Criminal Law* 15 (1988): 298.

61. Kennedy, *Race, Crime, and the Law*, p. 230.

62. "Shapiro Lashes out at Chochran over 'Race Card,'" *USA Today* (October 4, 1995): A2.

63. Kennedy, *Race, Crime, and the Law*, pp. 286–290.

64. *Moulton v. State*, 199 Ala. 411 (1917).

65. *Miller v. North Carolina*, 583 F.2d 701 (CA 4 1978).

66. *State v. Washington*, 67 So. 930 (La. Sup. Ct. 1915).

67. *Withers v. United States*, 602 F.2d 124 (CA 6 1976).

68. *Blair v. Armontrout*, 916 F.2d 1310 (CA 8 1990).

69. *Miller v. North Carolina*, 583 F.2d 701 (CA 4 1978), at 708.

70. *Blair v. Armontrout*, 916 F.2d 1310 (CA 8 1990), at 1351.

71. Kennedy, *Race, Crime, and the Law*, pp. 256–257.

72. Paul Butler, "Racially Based Jury Nullification: Black Power in the Criminal Justice System," *Yale Law Journal* 105 (1995): 677–725.

73. Ibid., p. 679.

74. See, for example, *United States v. Dougherty*, 473 F.2d 1113 (D.C. Cir., 1972).

75. Butler, "Racially Based Jury Nullification," p. 679.

76. Ibid., p. 715.

77. Ibid., p. 714.

78. Ibid., p. 694.

79. Ibid., p. 719.

80. Ibid., p. 716.

81. Ibid., p. 719.

82. Ibid.

83. Kennedy, *Race, Crime, and the Law*, pp. 295–310.

84. Ibid., p. 299.

85. Ibid.

86. Ibid., p. 301.

87. Ibid., p. 305.

88. Ibid., pp. 305–306.

89. Ibid., p. 301.

90. Ibid., p. 310.

91. Ibid.

92. U.S. Department of Justice, Office of Juvenile Justice and Delinquency Prevention, *Delinquency Cases in Juvenile Courts, 1995* (Washington, D.C.: U.S. Department of Justice, May 1998), p. 3.

93. U.S. Department of Justice, Office of Juvenile Justice and Delinquency Prevention, *Disproportionate Minority Confinement* (Washington, D.C.: U.S. Department of Justice, April 1994), p. 1.

94. Carl E. Pope and William H. Feyerherm, "Minority Status and Juvenile Justice Processing: An Assessment of the Research Literature (Part I)," *Criminal Justice Abstracts* 22 (1990): 327–335.

95. Ibid., p. 334.

96. Donna M. Bishop and Charles E. Frazier, "The Influence of Race in Juvenile Justice Processing," *Journal of Research in Crime and Delinquency* 25 (1988): 242–263.

97. Ibid., p. 258.

98. Michael J. Leiber, "A Comparison of Juvenile Court Outcomes for Native Americans, African Americans, and Whites," *Justice Quarterly* 11 (1994): 255–279.

99. Ibid., p. 272.

100. Kimberly Kempf Leonard and Henry Sontheimer, "The Role of Race in Juvenile Justice in Pennsylvania," in *Minorities in Juvenile Justice,* ed. Kimberly Kempf Leonard, Carl E. Pope, and William H. Feyerherm (Thousand Oaks, CA: Sage, 1995).

101. Ibid., p. 108.

102. Ibid., p. 119.

103. Ibid., pp. 122–123.

104. Philip E. Secret and James B. Johnson, "The Effect of Race on Juvenile Justice Decision Making in Nebraska: Detention, Adjudication, and Disposition, 1988–1993," *Justice Quarterly* 14 (1997): 445–478.

105. Ibid., p. 274.

106. U.S. Department of Justice, Federal Bureau of Investigation, *Crime in the United States, 1994* (Washington, D.C.: U.S. Government Printing Office, 1995), pp. 227–228.

107. "Chicago Boy, 12, Will Be Youngest in U.S. Prison," *Omaha World Herald* (January 31, 1996): A2.

108. United States General Accounting Office, *Juvenile Justice: Juveniles Processed in Criminal Court and Case Dispositions* (Washington, D.C.: U.S. General Accounting Office, 1995), p. 2.

109. Ibid., p. 10.

110. Ibid., p. 12.

111. Secret and Johnson, "The Effect of Race on Juvenile Justice Decision Making in Nebraska."

112. Ibid., p. 450.

113. Coramae Richey Mann, *Unequal Justice: A Question of Color* (Bloomington: Indiana University Press, 1993), p. 255.

114. R. Lefcourt, "The Administration of Criminal Law," in *Criminal Justice in America*, ed. Richard Quinney (Boston: Little, Brown, 1974).

115. George S. Bridges and Sara Steen, "Racial Disparities in Official Assessments of Juvenile Offenders: Attributional Stereotypes as Mediating Mechanisms," *American Sociological Review* 63 (1998): 554–570.

116. Ibid., p. 558.

117. Ibid., pp. 563–564.

118. Ibid., p. 564.

119. Ibid., p. 567.

120. Ibid.

121. Ibid.

7

Race and Sentencing

In Search of Fairness
and Justice

In 1990, The Sentencing Project reported that nearly one fourth (23 percent) of all African American men age 20 to 29 were under some form of criminal justice supervision—in prison, in jail, on probation, or on parole.[1] Over the next four years, this rate, which the author of the report labeled "shockingly high," continued to increase. By 1994 almost one in three young African American men (30.2 percent) was under criminal justice supervision.[2] This figure was substantially higher than the rate for young Hispanic men (12.3 percent) and was more than four times greater than the rate for young white men (6.7 percent). The authors of the report concluded that the high rates for young African American men "attest to the gravity of the crisis facing the African American community."[3]

Explanations for the disproportionate number of African American and Hispanic men under the control of the criminal justice system are complex. As discussed in more detail in Chapter 9, a number of studies have concluded that most—but not all—of the racial disparity in incarceration rates can be attributed to racial differences in offending patterns and prior criminal records. Young African American and Hispanic men, in other words, face greater odds of incarceration than young white men primarily because they commit more serious crimes and have more serious prior criminal records. As the National Academy of Sciences Panel on Sentencing Research concluded in 1983, "factors other than racial discrimination in the sentencing process account for most of the disproportionate representation of black males in U.S. prisons."[4]

Not all of the racial disparity, however, can be explained away in this fashion. Critics contend that at least some of the overincarceration of racial minorities is due to racially discriminatory sentencing policies and practices. Michael Tonry, although acknowledging that race is at best a weak predictor of sentence outcomes, asserted that "A conclusion that black overrepresentation among prisoners is not primarily the result of racial bias does not mean that there is no racism in the system."[5] The National Academy of Sciences Panel similarly concluded that evidence of racial discrimination in sentencing may be found in some jurisdictions or for certain types of crimes.

Underlying this controversy are questions concerning discretion in sentencing. To be fair, a sentencing scheme must allow the judge or jury discretion to shape sentences to fit individuals and their crimes. The judge or jury must be free to consider all *relevant* aggravating and mitigating circumstances. To be consistent, on the other hand, a sentencing scheme requires the evenhanded application of objective standards. The judge or jury must take only relevant considerations into account and must be precluded from determining sentence severity based on prejudice or whim.

Critics of the sentencing process argue that judges and juries exercise their discretion inappropriately. Acknowledging that some degree of sentence disparity is to be expected in a system that attempts to individualize punishment, these critics suggest that there is *unwarranted* disparity in the sentences imposed on offenders convicted of similar crimes. More to the point, they assert that judges impose harsher sentences on African American and Hispanic offenders than on white offenders.

Other scholars contend that judges' sentencing decisions are not racially biased. They argue that disparity in sentencing is due to legitimate differences among individual cases, and that racial disparities disappear once these differences are taken into consideration. These scholars argue, in other words, that judges' sentencing decisions are both fair and consistent.

GOALS OF THE CHAPTER

In this chapter, we address the issue of racial disparity in sentencing. Our purpose is not simply to add another voice to the debate over the *existence* of racial discrimination in the sentencing process. Although we do attempt to determine whether racial minorities are sentenced more harshly than whites, we believe that this is a theoretically unsophisticated and incomplete approach to a complex phenomenon. It is overly simplistic to assume that racial minorities will receive harsher sentences than whites regardless of the nature of the crime, the seriousness of the offense, the culpability of the offender, or the characteristics of the victim. The more interesting question is "when does race matter?" It is this question that we attempt to answer.

RACIAL DISPARITY IN SENTENCING

There is clear and convincing evidence of racial *disparity* in sentencing. This evidence is of two types. The first is derived from national statistics on prison admissions and prison populations. These statistics, which we discuss in detail in Chapter 9, reveal that the incarceration rates for African Americans and Hispanics are much higher than the rate for whites. At the end of 1995, for example, 4,424 of every 100,000 African American men, 1,957 of every 100,000 Hispanic men, and 507 of every 100,000 white men were incarcerated in a state or federal prison. The incarceration rates for women, although much lower than the rates for men, revealed a similar pattern: 243 of 100,000 for African Americans, 112 of 100,000 for Hispanics, and 30 of 100,000 for whites.[6]

The second type of evidence of racial disparity in sentencing comes from studies of judges' sentencing decisions. These studies, which are the focus of this chapter, reveal that African American and Hispanic defendants are more likely than whites to be sentenced to prison; those who are sentenced to prison receive longer terms than whites. Consider the following statistics:

- Black and Hispanic offenders sentenced under the federal sentencing guidelines in 1989 and 1990 received harsher sentences than white offenders. The incarceration rate was 85 percent for Hispanics, 78 percent for African Americans, and 72 percent for whites. Among those sentenced to prison, the average sentence was seventy-one months for African Americans, fifty months for whites, and forty-eight months for Hispanics.[7]

- Among offenders convicted of drug offenses in federal district courts in 1991–1992, the mean sentence length was 102 months for African Americans, 80 months for Hispanics, and 72 months for whites.[8]

- Among offenders convicted of felonies in state courts nationwide in 1994, 55 percent of the African Americans and 42 percent of the whites were sentenced to prison. The average prison sentence for African Americans (seventy-five months) was longer than the average sentence for whites (sixty-six months).[9]

- African American and Hispanic offenders convicted of felonies in Chicago, Miami, and Kansas City faced greater odds of incarceration than whites. In Chicago, 66 percent of the African Americans, 59 percent of the Hispanics, and 51 percent of the whites were incarcerated. In Miami, 51 percent of the African Americans, 40 percent of the Hispanics, and 35 percent of the whites were incarcerated. In Kansas City the incarceration rates were 46 percent for African Americans, 40 percent for Hispanics, and 36 percent for whites.[10]

Three Explanations for Racial Disparities in Sentencing

Although these statistics indicate that African Americans and Hispanics receive more punitive sentences than whites, they do not tell us *why* this occurs. We

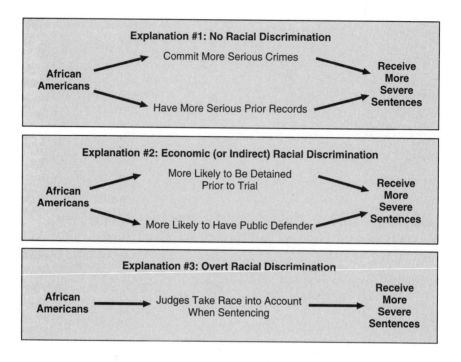

FIGURE 7.1 Three Explanations for Racial Disparity in Sentencing

suggest that there are at least three possible explanations. These explanations are diagrammed in Figure 7.1.

First, the differences in sentence severity could be due to the fact that African Americans and Hispanics commit more serious crimes and have more serious prior criminal records than whites. Studies of sentencing decisions consistently have demonstrated the importance of these two "legally relevant" factors (but see Box 7.1 for an alternative interpretation). Offenders who are convicted of more serious offenses, who use a weapon to commit the crime, or who seriously injure the victim receive harsher sentences, as do offenders who have prior felony convictions. The more severe sentences imposed on African Americans and Hispanics, then, might reflect the influence of these legally prescribed factors rather than the effect of racial prejudice on the part of judges.

The differences also could result from economic discrimination. As we discussed in Chapter 5, poor defendants are not as likely as middle-class or upper-class defendants to have a private attorney or to be released prior to trial. They also are more likely to be unemployed. All of these factors may be related to sentence severity. Defendants represented by private attorneys or released prior to trial may receive more lenient sentences than those represented by public defenders or those who are in custody prior to trial. Defendants who

---

BOX 7.1 Are Crime Seriousness and Prior Criminal Record "Legally Relevant" Variables?

Most policymakers and researchers assume that the seriousness of the conviction charge and the offender's prior criminal record are legally relevant to the sentencing decision. They assume, in other words, that judges who base sentence severity primarily on crime seriousness and prior record are making legitimate, and racially neutral, sentencing decisions. But are they?

Some scholars argue that crime seriousness and prior criminal record are "race-linked" variables. If, for example, sentencing schemes consistently mandate the harshest punishments for the offenses for which racial minorities are most likely to be arrested (e.g., robbery and drug offenses involving crack cocaine), the imposition of punishment is not necessarily racially neutral.

Similarly, if prosecutors routinely file more serious charges against racial minorities than against whites who engage in the same type of criminal conduct or offer less attractive plea bargains to racial minorities than to whites, the more serious conviction charges for racial minorities will reflect these racially biased charging and plea bargaining decisions. An African American defendant who is convicted of a more serious crime than a white defendant, in other words, may not necessarily have engaged in more serious criminal conduct than his white counterpart.

Prior criminal record also may be race-linked. If police target certain types of crimes (e.g., selling illegal drugs) or patrol certain types of neighborhoods (e.g., inner-city neighborhoods with large African American or Hispanic populations) more aggressively, racial minorities will be more likely than whites to "accumulate" a criminal history that then can be used to increase the punishment for the current offense. Racially biased charging and convicting decisions would have a similar effect.

If crime seriousness and prior criminal record are, in fact, race-linked in the ways just outlined, it is misleading to conclude that sentences based on these two variables are racially neutral.

---

are unemployed may be sentenced more harshly than those who are employed. Because African American and Hispanic defendants are more likely than white defendants to be poor, economic discrimination amounts to *indirect* racial discrimination.

Finally, the differences could be due to overt or *direct* racial discrimination on the part of judges. They could be due to the fact that judges take the race or ethnicity of the offender into account in determining the appropriate sentence. This implies that judges who are confronted with African American, Hispanic, and white offenders convicted of similar crimes and with similar prior criminal records impose harsher sentences on racial minorities than on whites. It implies that judges, the majority of whom are white, stereotype African American and Hispanic offenders as more violent, more dangerous, and less amenable to rehabilitation than white offenders.

EMPIRICAL RESEARCH ON RACE
AND SENTENCING

Researchers have conducted dozens of studies to determine which of these explanations is more correct.[11] Studies conducted from the 1930s through the 1960s often concluded that racial disparities in sentencing were due to racial discrimination. But in his review of these studies, Hagan found that most were methodologically unsound.[12] Many of them employed inadequate controls for crime seriousness and prior record or used simplistic statistical techniques. These methodological problems called the conclusions of these studies into question.

More recent and methodologically rigorous studies have produced conflicting findings regarding the effect of race on sentencing. Although a number of studies have found that African Americans are sentenced more harshly than whites,[13] others have found either that there are no significant racial differences[14] or that African Americans are sentenced more *leniently* than whites.[15] Research comparing the sentences imposed on Hispanic and white offenders is similarly equivocal.[16] These inconsistent findings have led researchers to conclude that the contemporary sentencing process, although not racially neutral, is not characterized by "a widespread systematic pattern of discrimination."[17]

A comprehensive review of the studies conducted during the "four waves of research on sentencing disparities"[19] (see Box 7.2) is beyond the scope of this book. Instead, we describe in detail the results of four recent studies: Two found that African Americans and/or Hispanics received more punitive sentences than whites, one found no racial differences, and one found that African Americans received more lenient sentences than whites for some types of offenses.

Discriminatory Sentencing in Three Urban Jurisdictions

A number of methodologically sound studies have concluded that African American and Hispanic offenders are sentenced more harshly than whites. Spohn and DeLone,[20] for example, compared the sentences imposed on African American, Hispanic, and white offenders convicted of felonies in Chicago, Kansas City, and Miami in 1993 and 1994. The study controlled for the legal and extralegal variables that affect judges' sentencing decisions: the offender's age, gender, and prior criminal record; whether the offender was on probation at the time of the current offense; the seriousness of the conviction charge; the number of conviction charges; the type of attorney representing the offender; whether the offender was detained or released prior to trial; and whether the offender pled guilty or went to trial.

The authors of this study found evidence of racial discrimination in the decision to incarcerate or not in two of the three jurisdictions. Although race had no effect on the likelihood of incarceration in Kansas City, both African Americans and Hispanics were more likely than whites to be sentenced to prison in Chicago, and Hispanics (but not African Americans) were more likely than whites to be incarcerated in Miami. These results are illustrated more clearly by the data presented in Figure 7.2. The authors used the results

---

BOX 7.2 Four Waves of Research on the Effect of Race on Sentencing

Marjorie Zatz suggested that there have been four waves of research on the effect of race on sentencing.[18]

Wave I (1930s to mid-1960s): Research conducted during this era showed "clear and consistent bias against nonwhites." These early studies, although methodologically flawed, revealed large sentence differentials, "suggesting that even with better controls they might still show evidence of discrimination."

Wave II (late 1960s through 1970s): The second wave of research was characterized by studies showing no racial discrimination in sentencing. Researchers argued either that the racially discriminatory sentencing practices of earlier years had been eliminated or that the race effect found in the early studies disappeared once crime seriousness and prior criminal record were controlled for adequately.

Wave III (1970s and 1980s): Zatz noted that "Advances in data sources and analytic techniques . . . paved the way for a new approach to the study of bias in decision making." Social scientists conducting research in the 1970s and 1980s contested the "no discrimination" thesis. They argued that discrimination had not declined or disappeared but had simply become more subtle and difficult to detect. Their research showed that race affected sentence severity indirectly through its effect on variables such as pretrial status or type of attorney, or that race interacted with other variables to affect sentence severity only for some types of crimes, in some types of settings, or for some types of defendants.

Wave IV (1980s): Researchers began to investigate the effect of race on sentence severity using data from jurisdictions that enacted determinate sentencing or sentence guidelines. Although some studies found evidence of overt racial discrimination, most found more subtle and indirect racial effects.

---

of their multivariate analyses to calculate the estimated probability of imprisonment for a "typical" white, African American, and Hispanic offender convicted of burglary in each of the three cities.[21]

These estimated probabilities confirm that offender race had no effect on the likelihood of incarceration in Kansas City; 55 percent of the whites and 54 percent of the African Americans convicted of burglary were sentenced to prison. In Chicago, on the other hand, there was about a 4 percentage-point difference between white offenders and African American offenders and between white offenders and Hispanic offenders. In Miami the difference between white offenders and Hispanic offenders was somewhat larger; even after the other legal and extralegal variables were taken into consideration, 34 percent of the Hispanics but only 26 percent of the whites received a prison sentence.

Spohn and DeLone also compared the sentences imposed on offenders who were incarcerated. They found that race or ethnicity had no effect on the length of the prison sentence in Chicago or Miami. In Kansas City, on the other hand, African Americans convicted of drug offenses received fourteen months longer than whites convicted of drug offenses; African Americans convicted of property crimes received nearly seven months more than whites convicted of these crimes.

Percentage (%)

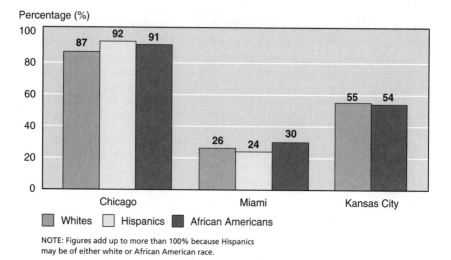

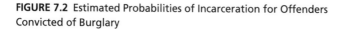

NOTE: Figures add up to more than 100% because Hispanics
may be of either white or African American race.

FIGURE 7.2 Estimated Probabilities of Incarceration for Offenders
Convicted of Burglary

Consistent with the explanations presented in Figure 7.1, Spohn and De-Lone also found evidence of economic discrimination. When they analyzed the likelihood of pretrial detention, controlling for crime seriousness, the offender's prior criminal record, and other factors associated with the type and amount of bail required by the judge, the authors found that African Americans and Hispanics faced significantly higher odds of pretrial detention than whites in Chicago and Miami, and that African Americans were more likely than whites to be detained in Kansas City. They also found that pretrial detention was a strong predictor of the likelihood of incarceration following conviction. Thus, African American and Hispanic defendants were more likely than whites to be detained prior to trial, and those who were detained were substantially more likely than those who were released to be incarcerated.

These results are diagrammed in Figure 7.3. Spohn and DeLone's research uncovered evidence of both direct and indirect racial discrimination in the critical decision to sentence the offender to prison or not. There were direct racial effects in Chicago and Miami and more subtle effects in all three jurisdictions. Discrimination was directed primarily against Hispanics in Miami, but was directed against both African Americans and Hispanics in Chicago.

The authors of this study were careful to point out that the race effects they uncovered, although statistically significant, were "rather modest"[22] and that the seriousness of the offense and the offender's prior criminal record were the primary determinants of sentence outcomes. They noted, however, that the fact that offender race/ethnicity had both direct and indirect effects, coupled with the fact that female offenders and those who were released prior to trial received substantially more lenient sentences than male offenders and those who were detained before trial, suggests that "judges' sentencing deci-

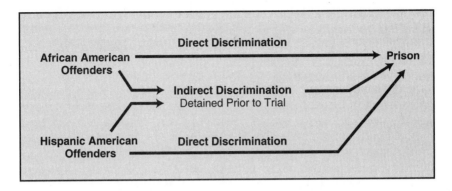

FIGURE 7.3 Direct and Indirect Racial Discrimination in Chicago, Miami, and Kansas City

sions are not guided *exclusively* by factors of explicit legal relevance."[23] In fact, the authors of this study concluded that judges' sentencing decisions reflect "stereotypes of dangerousness and culpability that rest, either explicitly or implicitly, on considerations of race, gender, pretrial status, and willingness to plead guilty."[24]

Direct and Indirect Race Effects in Two Texas Counties

A study of sentencing decisions in two Texas counties revealed a pattern of results similar to those uncovered by Spohn and DeLone.[25] Holmes and his colleagues argued that it is important to determine both the degree to which race or ethnicity directly affects sentence severity and the degree to which race or ethnicity interacts with what they referred to as "legal resources" to produce harsher sentences for racial minorities. According to the authors, "Retention of private counsel and release pending adjudication are generally thought to be legal resources, reflecting a defendant's financial status and conveying an advantage in the adjudicatory process."

Holmes and his colleagues tested their hypotheses concerning race and ethnicity, legal resources, and sentence severity using data on a sample of offenders convicted of felonies in El Paso County (El Paso) and Bexar County (San Antonio), Texas. They first analyzed the effect of race and ethnicity on the two measures of legal resources—retention of a private attorney and pretrial release—controlling for the legal and extralegal variables that have been shown to affect these outcomes. They then analyzed the effect of race and ethnicity on sentence severity; at this stage in the analysis they controlled for the gender and employment status of the offender. They also controlled for the two measures of legal resources, the seriousness of the offense, and the offender's prior criminal record.

The authors found that neither African Americans nor Hispanics were less likely than whites to be released pending trial in either county, but that both African Americans and Hispanics were less likely than whites to have a private

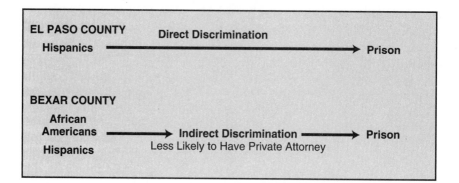

FIGURE 7.4 Direct and Indirect Discrimination in Two Texas Counties

attorney in one of the two counties (Bexar County). In both counties, defendants who were unemployed were also less likely than those who were employed to be represented by a private attorney or released prior to trial. A defendant's race/ethnicity and employment status, in other words, affected his or her ability to obtain these important legal resources.

Analysis of sentence outcomes confirmed the importance of these two measures of legal resources. In both counties, defendants who were represented by private attorneys or released prior to trial received significantly more lenient sentences than defendants who did not obtain private attorneys or pretrial release. Analysis of sentence outcomes also revealed that judges in El Paso County imposed significantly more severe sentences on Hispanic offenders than on white offenders.

Thus, consistent with the results reported by Spohn and DeLone, this study found evidence of direct discrimination against Hispanic offenders in one jurisdiction and evidence of economic or indirect discrimination against both African American and Hispanic offenders in the other jurisdiction. As diagrammed in Figure 7.4, Hispanics were sentenced more harshly than whites in El Paso County. In Bexar County, both African Americans and Hispanics were less likely than whites to have a private attorney and, as a result, were sentenced more harshly than whites. As the authors of this study concluded, these "findings do not comport with the consensus view that the harsher treatment of minorities and the poor stems *solely* from more serious and more extensive criminality."[26]

Racial Equity in Sentencing in Pennsylvania

The two studies just described concluded that African American and Hispanic offenders received harsher sentences than whites, at least in some contexts. There are a number of methodologically rigorous studies that reach a different conclusion. A study of the sentences imposed on offenders convicted of a variety of misdemeanors and felonies in Pennsylvania during the mid-1980s, for example, revealed that race had no effect on the length of the sentence imposed on offenders who were incarcerated and had only a small effect on the in-out decision.[27]

Kramer and Steffensmeier suggested that earlier findings of racial discrimination in sentencing decisions might be an artifact of the failure to control adequately for crime seriousness and prior criminal record. They argued that the Pennsylvania data are particularly well suited for a study of imprisonment decisions. Since 1982 Pennsylvania has had sentencing guidelines "designed to reduce unwarranted disparity by establishing that the severity of the convicted offense and the offender's criminal history are the major determinants of sentencing decisions."[28] The Pennsylvania guidelines incorporate standardized and very precise measures of crime seriousness and prior record; there is a guideline range for each combination of these two legally prescribed variables and the presumption is that judges will sentence within this range. Both dispositional (giving probation when the guidelines call for incarceration in jail or prison) and durational (imposing a shorter or longer term than indicated by the guidelines) departures are permitted, but the judge must provide a written justification for the departure. The Pennsylvania guidelines system, in other words, "is a relatively 'loose' one that still permits significant judicial discretion."[29]

Kramer and Steffensmeier analyzed sentencing outcomes for more than 60,000 offenders. They used the ten-point offense severity scale and the seven-point criminal history score developed by the Pennsylvania Sentencing Commission to control for these legally relevant factors. They also controlled for the offender's race, gender, and age; for the type of disposition in the case (plea versus trial), and for a number of variables designed to measure contextual differences among the Pennsylvania counties included in the study. Because their data file included offenders convicted of misdemeanors as well as those convicted of felonies, they analyzed three different in–out decisions: jail or prison versus probation, prison versus jail or probation, and prison versus jail. They also analyzed the length of sentence imposed on offenders who were imprisoned.

The question asked by the authors of this study was, "After controlling for the effects of all the other variables, how much does race contribute" to judges' sentencing decisions?[30] The answer to this question was "very little."[31] Although the incarceration (jail or prison) rate for African Americans was 8 percentage points higher than the rate for whites, there was only a 2 percentage-point difference in the likelihood of *imprisonment* for African Americans and whites. Race also played "a very small role in decisions about sentence length."[32] The average sentence for black defendants was only twenty-one days longer than the average sentence for white defendants.

Further analysis of the relationship between offender race and imprisonment decisions led the authors to conclude that most of the racial disparity was due to differences in the dispositional departure rates for African American and white offenders. Judges in Pennsylvania departed from the guidelines schema—that is, they gave a probation sentence when the guidelines called for a jail or prison sentence—more frequently if the offender was white than if the offender was African American. Examination of the reasons offered by judges to justify their departures revealed that departures for white offenders were based on such things as a nonviolent criminal history, a prior conviction in the distant past, a more stable employment history, the fact that the offense did not involve use of a weapon and was not drug related, or a belief that the offender would be amenable to rehabilitation. One judge interviewed for the study also stated that he was "reluctant to send white offenders, especially younger ones, to a prison that is largely black." Another noted that "The over-crowding and the increased violence in state prisons makes it difficult for me to send young, middle-class males to prison. That is extreme punishment."[33]

Kramer and Steffensmeier concluded that the sentence guidelines imple-mented in Pennsylvania have reduced unwarranted disparity in sentence out-comes (an issue we discuss in more detail later in this chapter). As they noted, "Today, if defendants' race affects judges' decisions in sentencing . . . it does so very weakly or intermittently, if at all."[34]

More Lenient Sentences for Nonwhite Drug Offenders

Although most studies of the effect of race on sentencing have concluded ei-ther that African Americans are sentenced more harshly than whites *or* that there are no differences in the sentences imposed on offenders in the two racial groups, a handful of studies has shown that African Americans receive more lenient sentences than whites. Typically, as Kleck[35] noted, these findings are "overlooked" or "downplayed" by criminal justice researchers, who charac-terize the findings as "anomalies."

Peterson and Hagan[36] suggested that findings of more lenient treatment of African American offenders should not necessarily be seen as anomalies. These researchers asserted that "the role of race is more variable and more compli-cated than previously acknowledged"[37] and that "both differential severity and leniency are possible."[38] They noted, for example, that African Americans who victimize whites might be sentenced more harshly, but that African Americans who victimize other African Americans might be sentenced more leniently.

Peterson and Hagan contended that race-related perceptions of victims and offenders might similarly affect the sentences imposed on individuals con-victed of *victimless* crimes. More to the point, they stated that minority drug users, at least during some time periods, might be typed or characterized as victims rather than as villains, and that this distinction might result in more le-nient sentences for minorities. If judges view minority youth as innocent tar-gets of big-time dealers or professional traffickers, in other words, they might be reluctant to impose severe sentences on minority drug users. The authors also asserted that leniency would be reserved for minority drug *users*; they ar-gued that "on those rare occasions when nonwhites do rise to the position of big dealers, the predicted leniency should . . . disappear."[39]

To test these predictions, Peterson and Hagan examined the sentences im-posed on drug offenders convicted in the Southern Federal District Court of

---

BOX 7.3 Native Americans and Sentencing Disparity

Most studies investigating the effect of race on sentence outcomes focus exclusively on African Americans and whites. There are relatively few studies that include Hispanics and even fewer that include other racial minorities, such as Native Americans.

Young[44] contended that the failure of criminal justice researchers to address issues relating to Native Americans "means that Native Americans are viewed in terms of narrow ethnocentric stereotypes (e.g., drunken savage)." Lujan[45] similarly asserted that the stereotype of the "drunken Indian" makes Native Americans more vulnerable to arrest for alcohol-related offenses and that stereotypical perceptions of reservation life as unstable and conducive to crime may lead to longer sentences for Native Americans.

The few studies that do examine sentence outcomes for Native Americans have produced mixed results. Some studies find that Native Americans and whites are sentenced similarly once crime seriousness, prior record, and other legally relevant variables are taken into account.[46] Other studies conclude that Native Americans adjudicated in federal[47] and state[48] courts are sentenced more harshly than similarly situated whites or that Native Americans serve significantly more of their prison sentence before parole or release than whites do.[49]

A recent study used data on offenders incarcerated in Arizona state correctional facilities in 1990 to compare sentence lengths for Native Americans and whites.[50] Bachman and Alvarez found that whites received longer sentences than Native Americans for homicide but Native Americans received longer sentences than whites for burglary and robbery.

Bachman and Alvarez speculated that these findings might reflect the fact that homicide tends to be intra-racial, whereas burglary and robbery are more likely to be interracial. Whites may have received longer sentences for homicide, in other words, because their victims were also likely to be white, whereas the victims of Native Americans were typically other Native Americans. As the authors noted, "Because the lives of American Indian victims may not be especially valued by U.S. society and the justice system, these American Indian defendants may receive more lenient sentences for their crime." Similarly, Native Americans convicted of burglary or robbery may have received harsher sentences than whites convicted of these crimes because their victims were more likely to be "higher-status Caucasians."[51]

Bachman and Alvarez concluded that their study demonstrates "the need for more crime-specific analyses to investigate discriminatory practices in processing and sentencing minority group members, especially American Indians."[52]

New York from 1963 through 1976. They found that nonwhite drug *users* were sentenced more leniently than white drug users, but that nonwhite drug *dealers* received substantially longer prison sentences than white dealers. Nonwhite drug users were significantly less likely than white users to be sentenced to prison; moreover, those nonwhites who were sentenced to prison received sentences that averaged about six and one-half months shorter than the sentences received by whites.[40] In contrast, the average sentence imposed on nonwhite big dealers was nineteen months longer than the sentence imposed on white dealers.[41]

Peterson and Hagan concluded that researchers should not "treat the meaning of race as a constant."[42] They asserted that it is overly simplistic to expect all African American offenders to be sentenced more harshly than all white offenders. Rather, "there are patterns of advantage and disadvantage that only contextualized analyses can reveal."[43]

WHEN DOES RACE MATTER?

As illustrated by the four studies just described, research on the effect of race on sentencing has produced conflicting results. Some of these studies support the discrimination thesis, but others do not. Indeed, some studies conclude that racial minorities are sentenced more leniently than whites.

As Peterson and Hagan noted, these inconsistent findings may result from oversimplification of conflict theory, the principal theoretical model used in studies of race and criminal punishment (see Chapter 1 for a detailed discussion of conflict theory).[53] Most researchers simply test the hypothesis that racial minorities will be sentenced more harshly than whites. These researchers assume, either explicitly or implicitly, that racial minorities will receive more severe sentences than whites regardless of the nature of the crime, the race of the victim, or the relationship between the victim and the offender.

Conflict theory, however, "does not support a simplistic expectation of greater punishment for blacks than whites under all circumstances."[54] Rather, conflict theorists argue that "the probability that criminal sanctions will be applied varies according to the extent to which the behaviors of the powerless conflict with the interests of the power segments."[55]

Crimes that threaten the power of the dominant class will therefore produce harsher penalties for African Americans who commit those crimes. Crimes that pose relatively little threat to the system of white authority, on the other hand, will not necessarily result in harsher sanctions for African Americans.[56] According to this view, African Americans who murder, rape, or rob whites will receive harsher sentences, but African Americans who victimize members of their own race will be treated more leniently. As Peterson and Hagan noted,

> When black offenders assault or kill black victims, the devalued status of the black victims and the paternalistic attitudes of white authorities can justify lenient treatment. . . . When blacks violate white victims, the high sexual property value attached to the white victims and the racial fears of authorities can justify severe treatment.[57]

Criminal justice scholars have proposed revising the conflict perspective on race and sentencing to account for the possibility of interaction between defendant race and other predictors of sentence severity. Hawkins,[58] for example, argued for the development of a more comprehensive conflict theory that embodies race-of-victim and type-of-crime effects. Similarly, Peterson and Hagan argued for research "that takes context-specific conceptions of race into account."[59]

Researchers examining the linkages between race and sentence severity have started to heed these suggestions. They have begun to conduct research designed to identify the circumstances under which African Americans will be sentenced more harshly than whites. In support of Hawkins' recommendations, their findings suggest that both the race of the victim and the seriousness of the crime are important factors.

In the sections that follow, we summarize the findings of studies that attempt to determine when race matters. We first compare the sentences imposed on offenders convicted of interracial and intraracial crimes. We focus primarily on the crime of sexual assault. (We return to this issue in Chapter 9 when we discuss the imposition of the death penalty.) We also summarize the findings of research exploring the relationship among race, unemployment, and sentence severity. We then discuss the findings of one study that examined the effect of race on sentencing for different types of crimes and the findings of a number of studies that focus explicitly on the relationship between race and sentence severity for drug offenders. We conclude with an examination of research testing the hypothesis that sentence severity reflects both the race/ethnicity and gender of the offender.

Differential Treatment of Interracial and Intraracial Crime

There is compelling historical evidence that interracial and intraracial crimes were treated differently. Gunnar Myrdal's examination of the Southern court system in the 1930s, for example, revealed that African Americans who victimized whites received the harshest punishment, whereas African Americans who victimized other African Americans were often "acquitted or given a ridiculously mild sentence."[60] Myrdal also noted that "it is quite common for a white criminal to be set free if his crime was against a Negro."[61]

These patterns are particularly pronounced for the crime of sexual assault. As Brownmiller noted, "No single event ticks off America's political schizophrenia with greater certainty than the case of a black man accused of raping a white woman."[63] Evidence of this can be found in pre-Civil War statutes that prescribed different penalties for African American and white men convicted of sexual assault. As illustrated in Box 7.4, these early laws also differentiated between the rape of a white woman and the rape of an African American woman.

Differential treatment of interracial and intraracial sexual assaults continued even after passage of the Fourteenth Amendment, which outlawed the types of explicit statutory racial discrimination already discussed. In the first half of this century, African American men accused or even suspected of sexually assaulting white women often faced white lynch mobs bent on vengeance. As Wriggens noted, "The thought of this particular crime aroused in many white people an extremely high level of mania and panic."[64] In a 1907 Louisiana case, the defense attorney stated:

> Gentlemen of the jury, this man, a nigger, is charged with breaking into the house of a white man in the nighttime and assaulting his wife, with

---

BOX 7.4　Pre-Civil War Statutes on Sexual Assault: Explicit Discrimination Against African American Men Convicted of Raping White Women

Virginia Code of 1819
The penalty for the rape or attempted rape of a white woman by a slave, African American, or mulatto was death; if the offender was white, the penalty was ten to twenty-one years.

Georgia Penal Code of 1816
The death penalty was given for rape or attempted rape of a white woman by slaves or free persons of color. A term of not more than twenty years was given for rape of a white woman by a white man. A white man convicted of raping an African American woman could be fined or imprisoned at the court's discretion.

Pennsylvania Code of 1700
The penalty for the rape of a white woman by an African American man was death; the penalty for attempted rape was castration. The penalty for a white man was one to seven years in prison.

Kansas Compilation of 1855
An African American man convicted of raping a white woman was to be castrated at his own expense. Maximum penalty for a white man convicted of raping a white woman was five years in prison.[62]

---

the intent to rape her. Now, don't you know that, if this nigger had committed such a crime, he never would have been brought here and tried; that he would have been lynched, and if I were there I would help pull on the rope.[65]

African American men who escaped the mob's wrath were almost certain to be convicted. Those who were convicted were guaranteed a harsh sentence. Many, in fact, were sentenced to death; 405 of the 453 men executed for rape in the United States were African Americans.[66] According to Brownmiller, "Heavier sentences imposed on blacks for raping white women is an incontestable historic fact."[67] As we show, it is not simply a historic fact; research conducted during the past two decades illustrates that judges continue to impose harsher sentences on African American men convicted of raping white women.

Offender–Victim Race and Sentences for Sexual Assault Researchers analyzing the impact of race on sentencing for sexual assault have argued that focusing on only the race of the defendant and ignoring the race of the victim will produce misleading conclusions about the overall effect of race on sentencing. More to the point, they contend that researchers may incorrectly conclude that race does not affect sentence severity if only the race of the defendant is taken into consideration. Table 7.1 presents a hypothetical example to illustrate how this might occur. Assume that 460 of 1,000 African American men (46

Table 7.1 Incarceration of Offenders Convicted of Sexual Assault: A Hypothetical Example of the Effect of Offender–Victim Race

Example: 2,000 men convicted of sexual assault. Analysis reveals that incarceration rate for African Americans is very similar to the rate for whites.

1,000 convicted African American offenders	460 incarcerated = 46% incarceration rate
1,000 convicted white offenders	440 incarcerated = 44% incarceration rate

Problem: Similarities are masking differences based on the race of the victim.

1,000 African American offenders	460 incarcerated (46%)
800 cases with African American victims	320 incarcerated (40%)
200 cases with white victims	140 incarcerated (70%)
1,000 White offenders	440 incarcerated (44%)
300 cases with African American victims	90 incarcerated (30%)
700 cases with white victims	350 incarcerated (50%)

Thus, the incarceration rate varies from 30% (for whites who assaulted African Americans) to 70% (for African Americans who assaulted whites).

percent) and 440 of 1,000 white men (44 percent) convicted of sexual assault in a particular jurisdiction were sentenced to prison. A researcher who focused only on the race of the offender would therefore conclude that the incarceration rates for the two groups were nearly identical.

Assume now that the 1,000 cases involving African American men included 800 cases with African American victims and 200 cases with white victims, and that 320 of the 800 cases with African American victims and 140 of the 200 cases with white victims resulted in a prison sentence. As shown in Table 7.1, although the overall incarceration rate for African American offenders is 46 percent, the rate for crimes involving African American men and white women is 70 percent, whereas the rate for crimes involving African American men and African American women is only 40 percent. A similar pattern—an incarceration rate of 50 percent for cases with white victims but only 30 percent for cases with African American victims—is found for sexual assaults involving white offenders. The nearly identical incarceration rates for African American and white offenders, in other words, mask large differences based on the race of the victim.

The findings of recent empirical research suggest that the scenario just described is not simply hypothetical. LaFree,[68] for example, examined the impact of offender-victim race on the disposition of sexual assault cases in Indianapolis. He found that African American men who assaulted white women were more likely than other offenders to be sentenced to prison. They also received longer prison sentences than any other offenders.

LaFree concluded that his results highlight the importance of examining the racial composition of the offender-victim pair. Because the law was applied *most* harshly to African Americans charged with raping white women but *least* harshly to African Americans charged with raping African American women, simply examining the overall disposition of cases with African American defendants would have produced misleading results.

Walsh[69] reached a similar conclusion. When he examined the sentences imposed on offenders convicted of sexual assault in a metropolitan Ohio county, he found that neither the offender's race nor the victim's race influenced the length of the sentence. In addition, the incarceration rate for white defendants was *higher* than the rate for African American defendants.

Further analysis, however, revealed that African Americans convicted of assaulting whites received more severe sentences than those convicted of assaulting members of their own race. This was true for those who assaulted acquaintances as well as those who assaulted strangers. As Walsh noted, "The leniency extended to blacks who sexually assault blacks provides a rather strong indication of disregard for minority victims of sexual assault."[70]

Somewhat different results were reported by Spohn and Spears,[71] who analyzed a sample of sexual assaults bound over for trial from 1970 through 1984 in Detroit Recorder's Court. Unlike previous research, which controlled only for offender–victim race and other offender and case characteristics, this study also controlled for a number of victim characteristics, including the age of the victim, the relationship between the victim and the offender, evidence of risk-taking behavior on the part of the victim, and the victim's behavior at the time of the incident. The authors compared the incarceration rates and the maximum sentences imposed on three combinations of offender–victim race: African American–African American, African American–white, and white–white.

In contrast to the results reported by LaFree and Walsh, Spohn and Spears found that the race of the offender–victim pair did not affect the likelihood of incarceration. The sentences imposed on African Americans who assaulted whites, on the other hand, were significantly longer than the sentences imposed on whites who assaulted whites or African Americans who assaulted African Americans. The average sentence for African American-on-white crimes was more than four years longer than the average sentence for white-on-white crimes and more than three years longer than the average sentence for African American-on-African American crimes. These results, according to the authors, reflected discrimination based on the offender's race and the victim's race.[72]

To explain the fact that offender–victim race affected the length of sentence but had no effect on the decision to incarcerate or not, the authors suggested that judges confronted with offenders convicted of sexual assault may have relatively little discretion in deciding whether to incarcerate. As they noted, "Because sexual assault is a serious crime . . . the 'normal penalty' may be incarceration. Judges may have more latitude, and thus more opportunities to consider extralegal factors such as offender/victim race, in deciding on the length of the sentence."[73]

Spohn and Spears also tested a number of hypotheses about the interrelationships among offender race, victim race, and the relationship between the victim and the offender. Noting that previous research has suggested that

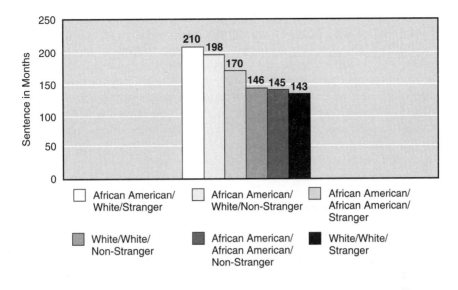

FIGURE 7.5 Offender's Race/Victim's Race/Relationship and Length of Sentence

crimes between intimates are perceived as less serious than crimes between strangers, they hypothesized that sexual assaults involving strangers would be treated more harshly than assaults involving intimates or acquaintances regardless of the race of the offender or the victim. Contrary to their hypothesis, they found that the offender–victim relationship came into play only when both the offender and the victim were African American. African Americans convicted of assaulting African American strangers received harsher sentences than African Americans convicted of assaulting African American intimates or acquaintances; they were more likely to be incarcerated, and those who were incarcerated received longer sentences.[74]

These differences are illustrated by the data presented in Figure 7.5. The authors used the results of their multivariate analysis of sentence length to calculate adjusted sentence means for each of the six offender race–victim race-relationship combinations. These adjusted rates take all of the other independent variables into account. They show that three types of offenders received substantially longer sentences than the other three types. The harshest sentences were imposed on African Americans who victimized whites (strangers or nonstrangers) and on African Americans who victimized African American strangers. More lenient sentences were imposed on African Americans who assaulted African American nonstrangers and on whites who assaulted whites (strangers or nonstrangers).

As the authors noted, these results suggest that judges take into account the offender's race, but not the relationship between the victim and offender, in determining the appropriate sentence for offenders convicted of assaulting whites. Regardless of the relationship between the victim and the offender, African Americans who victimized whites received longer sentences than whites who victimized whites. On the other hand, judges do consider the relationship between the victim and offender in determining the appropriate sentence for African Americans convicted of sexually assaulting other African Americans. Judges apparently believe that African Americans who sexually assault African American strangers deserve harsher punishment than those who sexually assault African American friends, relatives, or acquaintances.

Considered together, the results of these studies demonstrate that criminal punishment is contingent on the race of the victim as well as the race of the offender. They demonstrate that *"the meaning of race varies, and that, despite simplistic interpretations of conflict theory, both differential severity and leniency are possible."*[75] The harshest penalties will be imposed on African Americans who victimize whites and the most lenient penalties will go to African Americans who victimize other African Americans.

Race, Unemployment, and Punishment

A number of researchers have suggested that the offender's employment status may affect the severity of the sentence imposed by the judge. These researchers contend that offenders who are unemployed will be sentenced more harshly than those who are employed.

Various theoretical perspectives guide research on the relationship between unemployment and sentence severity, but most studies rest on some variant of Rusche and Kirchheimer's observation that "the poorer the masses become, the harsher the punishment in order to deter them from crime"[76] or Quinney's contention that the criminal justice system "is the modern means of controlling surplus population."[77] Arguing that "many people believe that unemployment causes crime," for example, Box and Hale suggested that judges will see the unemployed as a threat and that this "belief alone is sufficient to propel them towards stiffening their sentencing practices."[78] In a later study, Box[79] asserted that it is the *combination* of judicial anxiety about what Spitzer[80] referred to as "problem populations" and the belief that unemployment leads to crime that structures judicial decision making and leads to increased use of imprisonment.

A number of researchers contend that certain types of unemployed offenders are regarded as more problematic and thus as more in need of formal social control. Spitzer[81] used the term "social dynamite" to characterize that segment of the deviant population that is viewed as particularly threatening and dangerous. He asserted that social dynamite "tends to be more youthful, alienated and politically volatile" and contended that those who fall into this category are more likely than other offenders to be formally processed through the criminal justice system.[82] Building on this point, Box and Hale argued that unemployed offenders who are also young, male, and members of a racial minority will be perceived as particularly threatening to the social order and thus will be singled out for harsher treatment. More specifically, they suggested that "individual judges and magistrates merely have to view many young offenders, particularly if they are also black and unemployed, as likely to commit further serious criminal acts, and that would justify imposing a sentence of imprisonment."[83]

In 1991, Chiricos and Bales[84] published the first study that used individual level data explicitly to test these propositions concerning the relationship among race, unemployment, and sentence severity. They found that unemployment had a direct effect on the likelihood of imprisonment; they also found that the effect was strongest if the offender was a young black man. Chiricos and Bales concluded that their results highlighted "the growing importance of the interaction between race and economic marginality."[85]

Nobiling and her colleagues[86] conducted a similar study. They used data on offenders convicted of felonies in Chicago and Kansas City to examine the interrelationships among race/ethnicity, employment status, and sentence outcomes. Building on Blalock's[87] contention that the combination of unemployment and minority status increases perceptions of threat and dangerousness, thus leading to harsher sentences, they predicted that unemployment would have a negative effect on sentence severity for racial minorities but not for whites. Building on Melossi's[88] assertion that "dangerous classes" have come to be defined "by a mix of economic and racial references," and that, as a result, young, black men have become "a privileged target group for imprisonment,"[89] they predicted that the offender's employment status would affect sentence severity for male offenders, for black (and Hispanic in Chicago) male offenders, for young male offenders, and for young black (and Hispanic in Chicago) male offenders.

Nobiling and her associates found some support for their hypothesis that unemployment would affect sentence severity for racial minorities but not for whites. In Kansas City, unemployed African Americans were more likely than employed African Americans to be incarcerated. There were no differences in the likelihood of incarceration for unemployed and employed whites. Similarly, in Chicago, unemployment led to a longer prison sentence for African American offenders but not for white offenders. On the other hand, unemployment had no effect on the likelihood of incarceration for either African Americans or Hispanics in Chicago, and did not affect the length of the prison sentence for African Americans in Kansas City.

The authors of this study also found support for their hypothesis that unemployment would primarily affect sentence outcomes for young African American and Hispanic men. In Chicago, unemployment increased the odds of a prison sentence among young men and young Hispanic men. In this jurisdiction, unemployment also led to a longer prison sentence for men (7.29 months longer), young men (6.49 months longer), and black men (5.68 months longer). In Kansas City, unemployment led to a greater likelihood of incarceration among men and black men, but had no effect on sentence length for any of the race, gender, or age subgroups examined.

These patterns are illustrated by the data presented in Table 7.2. The authors compared the likelihood of a prison sentence for employed white offenders to the likelihood of incarceration for the five other groups of offenders. They asked

Table 7.2 The Effect of Unemployment on the Decision to Incarcerate: Employed White Offenders Versus All Other Offenders

Was There a Statistically Significant Difference in the Likelihood of Incarceration Compared to Employed Whites?

	All Offenders	Male Offenders
Chicago		
Unemployed Whites	No	No
Unemployed African Americans	Yes	Yes
Unemployed Hispanics	Yes	Yes
Employed African Americans	Yes	Yes
Employed Hispanics	No	No
Kansas City		
Unemployed Whites	No	No
Unemployed African Americans	Yes	Yes
Employed African Americans	No	No

SOURCE: Adapted from Tracy Nobiling, Cassia Spohn, and Miriam DeLone, "A Tale of Two Counties: Unemployment and Sentence Severity," *Justice Quarterly* 15 (1998): 459–485, Table 7.

the question, "Controlling for the legal and extralegal predictors of sentence severity, are employed white offenders *less likely* than unemployed whites (unemployed African Americans, unemployed Hispanics, etc.) to be incarcerated?"

As shown in Table 7.2, in each city unemployed racial minorities (as well as employed African Americans in Chicago) faced significantly greater odds of incarceration than employed whites; the incarceration rates for unemployed whites, on the other hand, were not significantly higher than the rates for employed whites.

According to Nobiling et al., these results imply that although criminal justice officials generally may not perceive unemployed offenders as more dangerous or threatening, certain types of offenders will face greater odds of incarceration as a result of their unemployment. As the authors noted, this finding is consistent with arguments that dangerous or problematic populations are defined "by a mix of economic and racial . . . references."[90] It also is consistent with Chiricos and Bales' assertion that "to the degree that prisons help to control 'social dynamite' . . . the mix of race and unemployment may be its most explosive component."[91]

The Effect of Race
on Sentencing for Various Types of Crimes

The studies just described highlight the importance of testing for interaction between offender race/ethnicity and other factors, such as the race/ethnicity of the victim and the employment status of the offender. The importance of "rethinking the conflict perspective on race and criminal punishment"[92] is also demonstrated by the results of studies examining the effect of race on sentence severity for various types of crimes. Some researchers, building on Kalven and Zeisel's "liberation hypothesis,"[93] assert that African Americans will be sentenced more harshly than whites only in less serious cases.

The liberation hypothesis suggests that jurors deviate from their fact-finding mission in cases in which the evidence against the defendant is weak or contradictory. Jurors' doubts about the evidence, in other words, liberate them from the constraints imposed by the law and free them to consider their own sentiments or values. When Kalven and Zeisel examined jurors' verdicts in rape cases, for example, they found that jurors' beliefs about the victim's behavior were much more likely to influence their verdicts if the victim was raped by an unarmed acquaintance than if the victim was raped by a stranger armed with a gun or a knife.

The liberation hypothesis suggests that in more serious cases the appropriate sentence is strongly determined by the seriousness of the crime and the defendant's prior criminal record. In these types of cases, judges have relatively little discretion and thus few opportunities to consider legally irrelevant factors such as race. In less serious cases, on the other hand, the appropriate sentence is not clearly indicated by the features of the crime or the defendant's criminal record, which may leave judges more disposed to bring extralegal factors to bear on the sentencing decision.

Consider, for example, a case of sexual assault in which the offender, who has a prior conviction for armed robbery, raped a stranger at gunpoint. In this case a severe sentence is clearly called for; all defendants who fall into this category, regardless of their race or the race of their victims, will be sentenced to prison for close to the maximum term.

The appropriate sentence for a first-time offender who assaults an acquaintance with a weapon other than a gun, on the other hand, is not necessarily obvious. Some defendants who fall into this category will be incarcerated; others will not. This opens the door for judges to consider the race of the defendant or the race of the victim in determining the appropriate sentence.

Spohn and Cederblom used data on defendants convicted of violent felonies in Detroit to test the hypothesis that racial discrimination in sentencing is confined to less serious criminal cases.[94] Although they acknowledged that all of the cases included in their data file are by definition "serious cases," they argued that some are more serious than others: Murder, rape, and robbery are more serious than assault; crimes in which the defendant used a gun are more serious than those in which the defendant did not use a gun; and crimes in which the defendant had a prior felony conviction are more serious than those in which the defendant did not have prior convictions.

As shown in Table 7.3, which summarizes the results of their analysis of the likelihood of incarceration (controlling for other variables linked to sentence severity), the authors found convincing support for their hypothesis. With only one exception, race had a significant effect on the decision to incarcerate or not only in less serious cases. African Americans convicted of assault were incarcerated at a higher rate than whites convicted of assault; there were no racial

Table 7.3 The Effect of Race on the Likelihood of Incarceration for Various Types of Cases in Detroit

	Effect of Race on Incarceration Statistically Significant?
Most serious conviction charge	
Murder	No
Robbery	No
Rape	No
Other sex offenses	No
Assault	Yes
Prior criminal record	
Violent felony conviction	No
No violent felony conviction	Yes
Relationship between offender and victim	
Strangers	No
Acquaintances	Yes
Use of a weapon	
Offender used a gun	No
Offender did not use a gun	Yes
Injury to victim	
Offender injured victim	Yes
Offender did not injure victim	Yes

SOURCE: Adapted from Cassia Spohn and Jerry Cederblom, "Race and Disparities in Sentencing: A Test of the Liberation Hypothesis," *Justice Quarterly* 8 (1991): 305–327.

differences for the three more serious offenses. Similarly, race affected the likelihood of incarceration for defendants with no violent felony convictions, but not for those with a prior conviction; for defendants who victimized acquaintances, but not for those who victimized strangers; and for defendants who did not use a gun to commit the crime, but not for those who did use a gun. Spohn and Cederblom concluded that their results provided support for Kalven and Zeisel's liberation hypothesis, at least with respect to the decision to incarcerate or not. They also concluded that their findings offered important insights into judges' sentencing decisions. According to the authors,

> When the crime is serious and the evidence strong, judges' sentencing decisions are determined primarily by factors of explicit legal relevance— the seriousness of the conviction charge, the number of conviction charges, the nature of the defendant's prior criminal record, and so on. Sentencing decisions in less serious cases, on the other hand, reflect the influence of extralegal as well as legal factors.[95]

These results demonstrate that the criteria used by judges to determine the appropriate sentence will vary depending on the nature of the crime and the defendant's prior criminal record. More to the point, they demonstrate that the effect of race on sentence severity will vary. Judges impose harsher sentences on African Americans than on whites under some circumstances and for some types of crime; they impose similar sentences under other circumstances and for other types of crime. The fact that race does not affect sentence severity for all cases, in other words, does not mean that judges do not discriminate in any cases.

Sentencing and the War on Drugs

In *Malign Neglect,* Michael Tonry[96] argued that "Urban black Americans have borne the brunt of the War on Drugs." More specifically, he charged that "the recent blackening of America's prison population is the product of malign neglect of the war's effects on black Americans."[97] Miller[98] similarly asserted that "from the first shot fired in the drug war African-Americans were targeted, arrested, and imprisoned in wildly disproportionate numbers." These allegations suggest not only that racial minorities have been arrested for drug offenses at a disproportionately high rate, but also that African American and Hispanic drug offenders have been sentenced more harshly than white drug offenders.

As demonstrated in earlier chapters and summarized in what follows, there is ample evidence in support of assertions that the war on drugs has been fought primarily in minority communities. Since 1976 the number of persons arrested for drug offenses has more than doubled. The number of whites arrested for drug offenses has increased by 85 percent, but the number of African Americans arrested for these offenses has increased fourfold.[99] The proportion of all drug arrestees who are African American also has increased, from 22 percent in 1976 to 39 percent in 1994. These racial differentials in arrest rates are reflected in prison populations, where the trend has been one of decreasing white and increasing African American percentages. Between 1986 and 1991, the proportions of African Americans and whites in state and federal prisons reversed, from 53 percent white and 46 percent African American to 53 percent African American and 46 percent white.[100] Tonry attributed this reversal to the war on drugs, noting that "At every level of the criminal justice system, empirical analyses demonstrate that an increasing black disproportion has resulted from the War on Drugs—in jail, state and federal prisons, and juvenile institutions."[101]

There are relatively few studies that focus on racial disparities in sentences imposed on drug offenders and even fewer that have been conducted since the war on drugs began. Moreover, the results of these studies are somewhat inconsistent. Some researchers find that African American and Hispanic drug offenders are sentenced more harshly than white drug offenders.[102] Other researchers conclude either that there are few if any racial differences[103] or that racial minorities convicted of certain types of drug offenses are sentenced more leniently than their white counterparts.[104]

We summarize the results of two studies comparing the sentences imposed on African American, Hispanic, and white drug offenders. Both of these studies used data on offenders sentenced since the initiation of the war on drugs.

The first study[105] used data on offenders sentenced in state courts; the second[106] analyzed data on offenders sentenced under the federal sentencing guidelines.

Sentencing of Drug Offenders in State Courts Spohn and Spears used data on offenders convicted of felony drug offenses in Chicago, Kansas City, and Miami in 1993 and 1994 to test the hypothesis that African Americans and Hispanics would be sentenced more harshly than whites. They found that Hispanics, but not African Americans, faced greater odds of incarceration than whites in Miami, but that racial minorities and whites were sentenced to prison at about the same rate in Chicago and Kansas City. Similarly, they found that African Americans received longer sentences than whites in Kansas City, but that the sentences imposed on racial minorities and whites were very similar in Chicago and Miami.

These similarities and differences are illustrated by the estimated probabilities of incarceration and the adjusted mean sentences for each racial group in each jurisdiction (see Table 7.4). The estimated probabilities of incarceration are calculated for a "typical" offender (e.g., male, thirty years old, convicted of one count of an offense involving cocaine, one prior felony conviction) and take all of the other independent variables included in the analysis into account. They reveal substantial interjurisdictional variation in the likelihood of a prison sentence. They also confirm that race/ethnicity affected the probability of a prison sentence only in Miami.

The data presented in Table 7.4 reveal that the typical drug offender faced much higher odds of imprisonment in Chicago than in Kansas City or Miami. Three of every four offenders, regardless of race, were sentenced to prison in Chicago, compared to only one of every three, again regardless of race, in Kansas City. In Miami, in contrast, the odds of a prison sentence were much lower, particularly for white drug offenders. In this jurisdiction, the typical Hispanic drug offender was twice as likely as the typical white offender to be sentenced to prison.

The authors explained that the low rate of imprisonment in Miami reflects the fact that those convicted of less serious drug offenses normally were sentenced to the Dade County Jail rather than to state prison. As shown in Table 7.4, in Miami the odds of incarceration (in either jail or prison) were very similar to the odds of imprisonment in Chicago. When the authors used overall incarceration, rather than imprisonment, they found that the predicted probabilities for African American, Hispanic, and white drug offenders were very similar. As they noted, "In Miami, then, judges appear to take the offender's ethnicity into account in deciding between prison and either jail or probation, but not in deciding between some form of incarceration and probation."[107]

The data presented in Table 7.4 also illustrate the authors' finding that judges in Kansas City imposed much longer sentences on African American drug offenders compared to white drug offenders; the mean sentence for African Americans was 73.11 months, compared to only 58.12 months for white of-

Table 7.4 Predicted Probabilities of Incarceration and Adjusted Sentences for African American, Hispanic, and White Drug Offenders in Three Cities

	Chicago	Miami	Kansas City
Probability of prison sentence			
African American	.796	.177	.370
Hispanic	.789	.227	NA
White	.765	.111	.341
Probability of a jail or prison sentence: Miami			
African American		.812	
Hispanic		.804	
White		.774	
Adjusted prison sentence (in months)			
African American	38.61	46.73	73.11
Hispanic	47.3	58.49	NA
White	41.35	56.51	58.12

SOURCE: Adapted from Cassia Spohn and Jeffrey Spears, "Sentencing of Drug Offenders in Three Cities: Does Race/Ethnicity Make a Difference?" in *Crime Control and Criminal Justice: The Delicate Balance,* eds. Darnell F. Hawkins, Samuel L. Meyers, Jr., and Randolph N. Stone (Westport, CT: Greenwood, in press), Table 4.

fenders. In Chicago and Miami, on the other hand, the mean sentences imposed on whites were very similar to those imposed on African Americans and Hispanics. There were, however, more substantial differences in the sentences imposed on African American and Hispanic offenders. Hispanics received almost fifteen months longer than African Americans in Miami and more than eight months longer than African Americans in Chicago. In all three jurisdictions, then, one group of offenders received significantly longer sentences—African Americans in Kansas City and Hispanics in Miami and Chicago.

The authors of this study admitted that they were "somewhat puzzled"[108] by their finding that Hispanics were sentenced more harshly than African Americans in Miami and Chicago. They explained that they expected the "moral panic" surrounding drug use, drug distribution, and drug-related crime[109] to produce harsher sentences for both African Americans and Hispanics, who make up the majority of drug offenders in each jurisdiction. According to Spohn and Spears,

> The fact that harsher treatment was reserved for Hispanics in *Miami*, while unexpected, is not particularly surprising; arguably, the most enduring perception about drug importation and distribution in Miami is that these activities are dominated by Hispanics of various nationalities. This explanation, however, is less convincing with regard to our finding that Hispanics received longer sentences than blacks in Chicago.[110]

Further analysis of the sentences imposed in Chicago revealed that only certain types of Hispanic offenders—those convicted of the most serious drug offenses, those with a prior felony conviction, and those who were unemployed at the time of arrest—received longer sentences than African American offenders. The authors stated that this pattern of results suggests that judges in Chicago "may be imposing more severe sentences on offenders characterized as particularly problematic."[111] It suggests, in other words, that Chicago judges use ethnicity, offense seriousness, prior record, and employment status to define what might be called a "dangerous class"[112] of drug offenders. The Hispanic drug offender who manufactures or sells large quantities of drugs, who is a repeat offender, or who has no legitimate means of financial support might be perceived as particularly dangerous, particularly likely to recidivate.

Sentencing of Drug Offenders in the Federal Courts Albonetti[113] examined sentences imposed on drug offenders under the federal sentencing guidelines for evidence of bias against racial minorities. Although the federal guidelines were designed to reduce judicial discretion in sentencing and, as a result, to eliminate "unwarranted sentencing disparity among defendants with similar records who had been found guilty of similar criminal conduct,"[114] both judges and prosecutors retain some discretion. Albonetti was particularly interested in determining the degree to which prosecutorial charging and plea bargaining decisions work to the disadvantage of racial minorities. As she noted, "Under the federal guidelines, a prosecuting attorney can circumvent the guideline-defined sentence through charging, guilty plea negotiations, and motions for a sentence that is a departure from the guideline sentence."[115]

Albonetti used 1991–1992 data on drug offenders sentenced in federal district courts to test a number of hypotheses concerning the relationship between the offender's race/ethnicity, the prosecutor's "process-related decisions,"[116] and sentence severity. She hypothesized, first, that African American and Hispanic offenders will be sentenced more harshly than similarly situated white offenders. She also hypothesized that African American and Hispanic offenders "will receive less benefit"[117] from pleading guilty and from guideline departures[118] than will white offenders. White offenders, in other words, will receive greater sentence reductions than either African American or Hispanic offenders if they plead guilty or if the judge accepts the prosecutor's motion for a departure from the guidelines.

In support of her first hypothesis, Albonetti found that both African American and Hispanic drug offenders received more severe sentences than white drug offenders. These results were obtained after all of the legally relevant variables (i.e., offense severity, criminal history, type of drug offense, and number of counts) and process-related factors (i.e., whether the defendant pled guilty and whether the defendant's sentence was a departure from the guidelines) were taken into consideration.

Focus on an Issue
Penalties for Crack and Powder Cocaine

Federal sentencing guidelines for drug offenses differentiate between crack and powder cocaine. In fact, the guidelines treat crack cocaine as being one hundred times worse than powder cocaine. Possession of 500 grams of powder cocaine, but only 5 grams of crack, triggers a mandatory minimum sentence of five years. Critics charge that this policy, although racially neutral on its face, discriminates against African American drug users and sellers, who prefer crack cocaine to powder cocaine. More than 90 percent of the offenders sentenced for crack offenses in federal courts are African American. Those who defend the policy, on the other hand, suggest that it is not racially motivated; rather, as Randall Kennedy, an African American professor at Harvard Law School, contended, the policy is a sensible response "to the desires of law-abiding people—including the great mass of black communities—for protection against criminals preying on them."[121]

In 1993 Judge Lyle Strom, the chief judge of the U.S. District Court in Nebraska, sentenced four African American crack dealers to significantly shorter prison terms than called for under the guidelines. In explanation, Strom wrote, "Members of the African American race are being treated unfairly in receiving substantially longer sentences than Caucasian males who traditionally deal in powder cocaine."[122]

Strom's decision was overturned by the Eighth Circuit Court of Appeals in 1994. The three-judge panel ruled that even if the guidelines are unfair to African Americans, that is not enough to justify a more lenient sentence than called for under the guidelines. Other federal appellate courts have upheld the hundred-to-one rule, holding that the rule does not violate the equal protection clause of the Fourteenth Amendment (see, for example, *U.S. v. Thomas*, 900 F.2d 37 [4th Cir. 1990]; *U.S. v. Frazier*, 981 F.2d 92 [3rd Cir. 1992]; and *U.S. v. Latimore*, 974 F.2d 971 [8th Cir. 1992].

In 1996 the U.S. Supreme Court ruled eight to one that African Americans who allege that they have been singled out for prosecution under the crack cocaine rule must first show that whites in similar circumstances were not prosecuted.[123] The case was brought by five African American defendants from Los Angeles, who claimed that prosecutors were systematically steering crack cocaine cases involving African Americans to federal court, where the hundred-to-one rule applied, but steering cases involving whites to state court, where lesser penalties applied. The Court stated that a defendant who claimed that he or she was a victim of selective prosecution "must demonstrate that the federal prosecutorial policy had a discriminatory effect and that it was motivated by a discriminatory purpose."

The U.S. Sentencing Commission has recommended that the penalties for crack and powder cocaine offenses be equalized. In 1995 the Commission recommended that the hundred-to-one ratio be changed to a one-to-one ratio. Both Congress and President Clinton rejected this amendment. In 1997 the Commission unanimously reiterated its earlier position that "although research and public policy may support somewhat higher penalties for crack than for powder cocaine, a 100-to-1 quantity ratio cannot be justified."[124] The Commission recommended changing the quantity levels that trigger the mandatory minimum penalties for both crack and powder cocaine. Their recommendation was that the 500-gram trigger for powder cocaine be reduced to between 125 and 375 grams and that the trigger for crack cocaine be increased from 5 grams to between 25 and 75 grams. As of the summer of 1998, Congress had not acted on this recommendation.

Regarding her second research question, Albonetti found that pleading guilty produced a similar reduction in sentence severity for all three groups of offenders. The effect of a guideline departure, on the other hand, varied among the three groups, with whites receiving a significantly greater benefit than either African Americans or Hispanics. Among white defendants, a guideline departure produced a 23 percent reduction in the probability of incarceration; the comparable figures for African Americans and Hispanics were 13 percent and 14 percent, respectively. According to the author, "These findings strongly suggest that the mechanism by which the federal guidelines permit the exercise of discretion operates to the disadvantage of minority defendants."[119]

Albonetti also found that white offenders received a larger sentence reduction than African American or Hispanic offenders as a result of being convicted for possession of drugs rather than drug trafficking, and that whites benefitted more from educational achievements than did racial minorities. She concluded that the pattern of results found in her study suggests that "the federal sentencing guidelines have not eliminated sentence disparity linked to defendant characteristics for defendants convicted of drug offenses in 1991–92."[120] (As detailed in the Focus on an Issue, there is considerable controversy regarding the sentences mandated for offenses involving crack and powder cocaine.)

The Effect of Race on Sentencing
for Male and Female Offenders

Most of the research on the effect of race on sentence severity has focused on male offenders. There are few studies that compare the sentences imposed on African American men, African American women, white men, and white women.

This is a serious shortcoming. We should not simply assume that the findings of studies of male defendants are applicable to female defendants. We should not necessarily assume, in other words, that a finding that African American men are sentenced to prison at the same rate as white men in a particular jurisdiction means that African American women are incarcerated at the same rate as white women. Although this may be true, it is also possible that judges sentence African American and white women to prison at different rates.

There are similar problems in assuming that a finding of more lenient treatment of female defendants is applicable to both African Americans and whites. Some researchers, in fact, contend that preferential treatment is reserved for

Focus on an Issue

Does It Make a Difference? A Comparison of the Sentencing Decisions of African American, Hispanic, and White Judges

Historically, most state and federal judges have been white men. Although the nation's first African American judge was appointed in 1852, by the mid-1950s there were only a handful of African Americans presiding over state or federal courts. During the 1960s and 1970s, civil rights leaders lobbied for increased representation of African Americans at all levels of government, including the courts. By 1989 there were nearly 500 African American judges on the bench nationwide.

Those who champion the appointment of racial minorities argue that African American and Hispanic judges could make a difference. They contend that increasing the proportion of African American and Hispanic judges might reduce racism in the legal system. More to the point, they assert that the appointment of African American and Hispanic judges to state and federal trial courts might result in more equitable treatment of African American, Hispanic, and white defendants.

As documented in this chapter, a number of studies have shown that, at least for some types of crimes and under some circumstances, African American and Hispanic defendants are sentenced more harshly than white defendants. If this occurs because white judges discriminate against defendants who are racial minorities, whereas African American and Hispanic judges treat racial minorities and whites alike, then African American and Hispanic judges can play more than a symbolic role in the criminal justice system. They can ensure that African American and Hispanic offenders do not receive harsher sentences than they deserve.

Statements made by African American judges suggest that they might bring a unique perspective to the courts. Smith's[131] survey of African American judges throughout the United States revealed that these judges believed that their presence on the bench reduced racial discrimination and promoted equality of justice. A Philadelphia judge, for instance, stated that the mere presence of African American judges "has done more than anything I know to reduce police brutality and to reduce illegal arrests and things of that sort."[132] Moreover, nearly half of the respondents stated that African American judges should exercise their powers to protect the rights of African American defendants. One Michigan judge remarked that African American judges should state that "everybody's going to get equal justice," by saying that, "you're going to give blacks something that they haven't been getting in the past."[133]

Decision Making by African American and White Federal Judges

As more African Americans have been appointed or elected to state and federal trial courts, it has become possible to compare their decisions with those of white judges. Two studies examined the consequences of the affirmative action policies of President Carter, who appointed a record number of African Americans to the federal courts. (Carter appointed 258 judges to the federal district courts and courts of appeals; 37, or 14 percent, of those appointed were African Americans. In contrast, only 7 of the 379 persons appointed to the federal bench by President Reagan [1.8 percent] were African American.)

Walker and Barrow[134] compared decisions handed down by the African American and white district court judges appointed by President Carter. The question they asked was, "Did it make a difference that President Carter appointed unprecedented numbers of women and minorities to the bench as opposed to filling vacancies with traditional white, male candidates?"[135] The authors found no differences in criminal cases or in four other types of cases. In criminal cases, African American judges ruled in favor of the defense 50 percent of the time; white judges ruled in favor of the defense 48 percent of the time. These similarities led the authors to conclude that black judges do not view themselves as advocates for the disadvantaged or see themselves as especially sympathetic to the policy goals of minorities.

Gottschall[136] examined decisions in the U.S. Courts of Appeals in 1979 and 1981. He compared the decisions of African American and white judges in terms of "attitudinal liberalism," which he defined as "a relative tendency to vote in favor of the legal claims of the criminally accused and prisoners in criminal and prisoner's rights cases and in favor of the legal claims of women and racial minorities in sex and race discrimination cases."[137]

In contrast to Walker and Barrow, Gottschall found that the judge's race had a "dramatic impact" on voting in cases involving the rights of criminal defendants and prisoners. African American male judges voted to support the legal claims of defendants and prisoners 79 percent of the time, as compared to only 53 percent for white male judges. African American judges, on the other hand, did not vote more liberally than white judges in race or sex discrimina-

tion cases. Gottschall concluded that "Affirmative action for blacks *does* appear to influence voting on the courts of appeals in cases involving the rights of the accused and prisoners, where black voting is markedly more liberal than is that of whites."[138]

Decision Making by African American and White State Judges

Research comparing the sentencing decisions of African American and white state court judges also has yielded mixed results. Most researchers have found few differences and have concluded that the race of the judge is not a strong predictor of sentence severity.[139] A study of the sentences imposed on offenders convicted of sexual assault, for example, found that African American judges sentenced 89 percent of the offenders to prison, and white judges sentenced 88 percent to prison. The mean sentences imposed on those who were incarcerated were also very similar.[140]

As noted previously, there is an expectation that increasing the proportion of African American judges will result in more equitable treatment of African American and white offenders. Two studies have examined the effect of judicial race on sentencing of African American and white offenders. An analysis of sentencing decisions in "Metro City" found that African American judges were more likely than white judges to send white defendants to prison.[141] Further analysis led the researchers to conclude that this difference reflected the fact that African American judges incarcerated African American and white offenders at about the same rate, whereas white judges sentenced African American offenders to prison at a higher rate than white offenders. In Metro City, in other words, African American judges imposed more equitable sentences than white judges.

A study of sentences imposed on offenders convicted of violent felonies in Detroit reached a different conclusion.[142] Spohn found that, even after relevant legal and extralegal variables were taken into account, African American offenders were sentenced to prison more often than white offenders. Moreover, both African American and white judges imposed harsher sentences on African American offenders. As the author noted, "Harsher sentencing of black offenders . . . cannot be attributed solely to discrimination by white judges."[143] The author speculated that at least part of the discriminatory treatment of African American offenders by African American judges could be attributed to concern for the welfare of African American victims. African American judges, in other words, might see themselves not as representatives of African American offenders but as advocates for African American victims.

Decision Making by Hispanic and White State Judges

Although most research examining the effect of judicial characteristics on sentencing has focused on the race of the sentencing judge, there is one study that compares the sentencing decisions of white and Hispanic judges in two Southwestern jurisdictions.[144] Holmes and his colleagues found that Hispanic judges sentenced white and Hispanic offenders similarly, whereas white judges sentenced Hispanics more harshly than whites. In fact, the sentences imposed on Hispanic offenders by Hispanic and white judges were very similar to the sentences imposed by Hispanic judges on white offenders. What was different, according to these researchers, was that white judges sentenced white offenders more leniently. Thus, "Anglo judges are not so much discriminating against Hispanic defen-

dants as they are favoring members of their ethnic groups."[145]

Reasons for Similarities in Decision Making

Although there is some evidence that African American and Hispanic judges sentence racial minorities and whites similarly, whereas white judges give preferential treatment to white offenders, the bulk of the evidence suggests that judicial race/ethnicity makes very little difference. The fact that African American, Hispanic, and white judges decide cases similarly is not particularly surprising. Although this conclusion challenges widely held presumptions about the role of African American and Hispanic criminal justice officials, it is not at odds with the results of other studies comparing African American and white decision makers. As noted in Chapter 4, studies have documented similarities in the behavior of African American and white police officers. Similarities in judicial decision making can be attributed in part to the judicial recruitment process, which produces a more or less homogeneous judiciary. Most judges recruited to state courts are middle or upper class and were born and attended law school in the state in which they serve. Even African American and white judges apparently share similar background characteristics. Studies indicate that "both the black and white benches appear to have been carefully chosen from the establishment center of the legal profession."[146] The judicial recruitment process, in other words, may screen out candidates with unconventional views.

These similarities are reinforced by the judicial socialization process, which produces a subculture of justice and encourages judges to adhere to prevailing norms, practices, and precedents. They also are reinforced by the courtroom work group—judges, prosecutors, and defense attorneys who work together day after day to process cases as efficiently as possible. Even unconventional or maverick judges may be forced to conform. As one African American jurist noted, "No matter how 'liberal' black judges may believe themselves to be, the law remains essentially a conservative doctrine, and those who practice it conform."[147]

white women and that sentences for African American women will be similar to sentences for male defendants.[125] These researchers suggest that "leniency is directed more toward white than black female defendants, on grounds that the chivalry and other protections of gender stereotyping are not accorded to low-income black women."[126]

The results of research examining the effect of race and gender on sentence severity are mixed. A study of the sentences imposed on men and women convicted in Pennsylvania, for example, found that race affected the length of prison term for women but not for men; net of all other relevant factors, African American women received sentences about three months longer than African American men.[127] A study of sentences imposed in Kentucky reached the opposite conclusion: Race affected sentence length for men but not for women.[128] The author of this study speculated that "race is not an issue for women because it is overshadowed by the effects of gender-linked, especially family, statuses."[129]

A study of male and female offenders convicted of violent felonies in Detroit reached a similar conclusion.[130] The authors controlled for the variables that have been shown to affect sentence severity. They found that black men had the highest incarceration rate (75.6 percent), followed by white men (69.0 percent), black women (61.6 percent), and white women (57.7 percent). The differences between black and white women were not statistically significant.

In sum, although the results of studies examining the effect of race and gender on sentence severity are contradictory, they do point to the importance of taking both variables into consideration. They suggest that we cannot simply assume that all black defendants, regardless of gender, will be sentenced more harshly than all white defendants.

SENTENCING REFORM: THE QUEST FOR A "JUST" PUNISHMENT SYSTEM

Concerns about disparity in sentencing led to a "remarkable burst of reform"[148] that began in the mid-1970s and continues today. Both liberal and conservative reformers challenged the principles underlying the indeterminate sentence and called for changes designed to curb discretion and reduce disparity. Liberals, in particular, were apprehensive about the potential for racial bias under indeterminate sentencing schemes. They asserted that "racial discrimination in the criminal justice system was epidemic, that judges, parole boards, and corrections officials could not be trusted, and that tight controls on officials' discretion offered the only way to limit racial disparities."[149]

After a few initial "missteps,"[150] in which jurisdictions attempted to eliminate discretion altogether, states and the federal government adopted determinate sentencing proposals designed to control the discretion of sentencing judges. Many jurisdictions adopted presumptive sentence structures that offered judges a limited number of sentencing options and included enhancements for use of a weapon, presence of a prior criminal record, or infliction of serious injury. Other states and the federal government adopted sentence guidelines that incorporated crime seriousness and prior criminal record into a sentencing "grid" that judges were to use in determining the appropriate sentence. Under both systems, judges could use aggravating and mitigating circumstances to depart from the presumptive sentence. As Zatz noted, these reforms "severely constrained the discretion of judges and parole boards, though judges were still relatively free to decide when to grant or withhold probation, hand out concurrent or consecutive sentences, and use the aggravating and mitigating circumstances loophole to alter the presumptive sentence."[151]

Sentence Reform and Sentence Disparity

One of the important goals of the reform movement was to reduce disparity, including racial disparity, in sentencing. The Minnesota sentencing guidelines, for example, explicitly state that sentences should be neutral with respect to the gender, race, and socioeconomic status of the offender. Reformers hoped that the new laws, by structuring discretion, would make it more difficult for judges to take factors like race into account when determining the appropriate sentence.

Evidence concerning the impact of the reforms on racial disparity is inconsistent. Petersilia's[152] analysis of California's determinate sentencing system found that African Americans and Hispanics were more likely than whites to be sentenced to prison; racial minorities who were incarcerated also received longer sentences and served a longer time in prison. An examination of sentences imposed by judges in Minnesota before and after the implementation of guidelines showed that the impact of race and socioeconomic status declined, but did not disappear.[153] The authors also found that race affected sentencing indirectly through its effect on prior criminal record and use of a weapon. They concluded that disparities under the guidelines "are slightly more subtle, but no less real."[154] Dixon's[155] study of sentencing under the Minnesota guidelines, on the other hand, found that offender race was unrelated to sentence severity.

A series of studies examining sentencing under Pennsylvania's guidelines demonstrates the subtle ways in which race/ethnicity can affect sentence outcomes.[156] As noted earlier, the sentencing guidelines found in Pennsylvania are "looser" than those found in Minnesota or in the federal system. Judges in Pennsylvania have considerably more discretion, and thus more opportunities to consider extralegal factors, than do judges in other jurisdictions.

One study used Pennsylvania data to explore the effect of race/ethnicity on the likelihood that the judge would depart from the guidelines.[157] Kramer and Ulmer examined both dispositional departures, in which the guidelines call for incarceration but the judge chooses an alternative to incarceration, and durational departures, in which the judge imposes a jail or prison term that is longer or shorter than the term specified by the guidelines. They found that African American offenders were less likely than white offenders to receive a dispositional departure; the downward durational departures given to African Americans also were smaller than those given to whites. The authors found similar results when they compared the sentences imposed on Hispanic and white offenders.

When Kramer and Ulmer examined the reasons given by judges for departures, they found evidence suggesting that race-linked stereotypes affected these decisions. The most common reasons given for departures were: the defendant expressed remorse or appeared to be a good candidate for rehabilitation, the defendant pled guilty, the defendant was caring for dependents, the defendant was employed, and the defendant's prior record was less serious than his or her criminal history score suggests. As the authors noted, "When these reasons are given by judges, they are given more often for women, whites, and (obviously) those who pleaded guilty."[158]

In discussing the ways in which these reasons reflected race-linked stereotypes, the authors stated:

> Although these judges do not explicitly mention factors such as race or gender, it is plausible that the process of "sizing up" a defendant's "character and attitude" in terms of whether he or she is a candidate for a departure below guidelines may involve the use of race and gender stereotypes and the behavioral expectations they mobilize.[159]

Kramer and Ulmer concluded that "departures below guidelines are an important locus of race and gender differences in sentencing."[160] Tonry suggested that sentence guidelines actually may have exacerbated the problem of racial disparity in sentencing. His critique of sentence guidelines focuses on the prohibition against consideration of offenders' "special circumstances."[161] Under sentence guidelines, the harshness of the sentence depends on the severity of the offense and the offender's prior criminal record. Judges are not supposed to consider factors such as the offender's employment status, marital status, family situation, or education.

Although Tonry acknowledged that these restrictions were designed to prevent unduly lenient sentences for affluent offenders and unduly harsh sentences for poor offenders, he argued that in reality they have harmed "disadvantaged and minority offenders, especially those who have to some degree overcome dismal life chances." Tonry characterized these restrictions as "mistakes":

> They may have been necessary mistakes that showed us how to protect against aberrantly severe penalties and exposed the injustices that result

---

BOX 7.5   The Illusion of Like-Situated Offenders

Michael Tonry suggested that those who call for proportionality in punishment mistakenly assume that it is possible to place individuals into a manageable number of categories composed of "like-situated offenders." He suggested that this is an "illusion," as "neither offenders nor punishments come in standard cases."

> Consider a minority offender charged with theft who grew up in a single-parent, welfare-supported household, who has several siblings in prison, and who was formerly drug-dependent, but who has been living in a common-law marriage for five years, has two children whom he supports, and who has worked steadily for three years at a service station—first as an attendant, then an assistant mechanic, and now a mechanic. None of these personal characteristics was supposed to influence the sentencing decision, and certainly not to justify imposing a noncustodial sentence on a presumed prison-bound offender.

Tonry also objected to the fact that sentence guidelines do not take account of the "collateral effects" of punishment.

> Incarceration for a drug crime for a woman raising children by herself may result in the breakup of her family and the placement of her children in foster homes or institutions or in homes of relatives who will not be responsible care providers. Incarceration of an employed father and husband may mean loss of the family's income and car, perhaps the breakup of a marriage.

According to Tonry, "To ignore that collateral effects of punishments vary widely among seemingly like-situated offenders is to ignore things that most people find important."

SOURCE: Michael Tonry, *Malign Neglect* (New York: Oxford University Press, 1995), pp. 155–157.

---

when sentencing shifts its focus from the offender to the offense. Mistakes they were, however, and we now know how to do better.[162]

"Doing better," according to Tonry, means allowing judges to consider factors other than the offender's crime and prior criminal record. Tonry argued that "neither offenders nor punishments come in standard cases"[163] and contended that a just punishment system would require judges to consider the offender's personal circumstances, as well as the effects of punishment on the offender and the offender's family (see Box 7.5). He argued that a just system would allow judges to mitigate sentences for disadvantaged inner-city youth, who face greater temptations to commit crimes than do affluent suburban youth. It also would allow judges to mitigate sentences for "offenders from deprived backgrounds who have achieved some personal successes."[164] The problem is that current federal and state sentence guidelines typically do not allow judges to make these distinctions.

It thus appears that reformers' hopes for determinate sentencing and sentence guidelines have not been fully realized. Although overt discrimination against African Americans is less likely, discrimination in sentencing has not disappeared. As Zatz concluded, the sentencing procedures currently being used "are less blatantly biased than were their predecessors, and are cloaked with the legitimacy accruing from formalized rules . . . . Differential processing and treatment is now veiled by legitimacy, but it is a legitimacy in which certain biases have become rationalized and institutionalized."[165]

CONCLUSION

Despite dozens of studies investigating the relationship between defendant race and sentence severity, a definitive answer to the question, "Are racial minorities sentenced more harshly than whites?" remains elusive. Although a number of studies have uncovered evidence of racial discrimination in sentencing, others have found that there are no significant racial differences.

The failure of research to produce uniform findings of racial discrimination in sentencing has led to conflicting conclusions. Some researchers assert that racial discrimination in sentencing has declined over time and contend that the predictive power of race, once relevant legal factors are taken into account, is quite low. Other researchers claim that discrimination has not declined or disappeared, but simply has become more subtle and difficult to detect. These researchers argue that discrimination against racial minorities is not universal, but is confined to certain types of cases, settings, and defendants.

We assert that the latter explanation is more convincing. We suggest that although the sentencing process in most jurisdictions today is not characterized by overt or systematic racism, racial discrimination in sentencing has not been eliminated. We argue that sentencing decisions in the 1990s reflect *contextual discrimination*. Judges in some jurisdictions continue to impose harsher sentences on racial minorities who murder or rape whites, and more lenient sentences on racial minorities who victimize members of their own racial or ethnic group. Judges in some jurisdictions continue to impose racially biased sentences in less serious cases; in these "borderline cases" racial minorities get prison, whereas whites get probation. In jurisdictions with sentencing guidelines, judges depart from the presumptive sentence less often when the offender is African American or Hispanic than when the offender is white. Judges, in other words, continue to take race into account, either explicitly or implicitly, when determining the appropriate sentence.

It thus appears that although flagrant racism in sentencing has been eliminated, equality under the law has not been achieved. It is certainly true that in the 1990s, whites who commit crimes against racial minorities are not beyond the reach of the criminal justice system, African Americans suspected of crimes against whites do not receive "justice" at the hands of white lynching mobs, and racial minorities who victimize other racial minorities are not immune from punishment. Despite these significant changes, inequities persist. Racial minorities who find themselves in the arms of the law continue to suffer discrimination in sentencing.

DISCUSSION QUESTIONS

1. How would you answer the question, "When does race make a difference in sentencing?"

2. Some researchers argue that racial stereotypes affect the ways in which decision makers, including criminal justice officials, evaluate the behavior of racial minorities. What are the stereotypes associated with African Americans? Hispanics? Native Americans? Asian Americans? How might these stereotypes affect judges' sentencing decisions?

3. Do you agree or disagree with the argument (Box 7.1) that crime seriousness and prior criminal record are not legally relevant variables?

4. Spohn and Spears' study of sentencing decisions in sexual assault cases revealed that judges imposed the harshest sentences on African Americans who sexually assaulted whites (strangers or nonstrangers) and on African Americans who sexually assaulted African American strangers. They imposed much more lenient sentences on African Americans who sexually assaulted African American friends, relatives, and acquaintances and on whites who victimized others (strangers or nonstrangers). How would you explain this pattern of results?

5. The federal sentencing guidelines currently mandate a five-year minimum prison sentence for possession of 5 grams of crack cocaine, 500 grams of powder cocaine. Is this policy racially biased? Should the hundred-to-one ratio be reduced? Eliminated?

6. What types of sentencing reforms could be implemented to eliminate racial disparities in sentencing?

NOTES

1. Marc Mauer, *Young Black Men and the Criminal Justice System: A Growing National Problem* (Washington, D.C.: The Sentencing Project, 1990).

2. Marc Mauer and Tracy Huling, *Young Black Americans and the Criminal Justice System: Five Years Later* (Washington, D.C.: The Sentencing Project, 1995).

3. Ibid., p. 2.

4. Alfred Blumstein, Jacqueline Cohen, Susan E. Martin, and Michael Tonry, *Research on Sentencing: The Search for Reform, Volume I* (Washington, D.C.: National Academy Press, 1983).

5. Michael Tonry, *Malign Neglect: Race, Crime, and Punishment in America* (New York: Oxford University Press, 1995), p. 49.

6. Bureau of Justice Statistics, *Lifetime Likelihood of Going to State or Federal Prison* (Washington, D.C.: U.S. Department of Justice, 1997), Table 6.

7. Douglas C. McDonald and Kenneth E. Carlson, *Sentencing in the Federal Courts: Does Race Matter?* (Washington, D.C.: U.S. Department of Justice, 1993).

8. Celesta A. Albonetti, "Sentencing Under the Federal Sentencing Guidelines: Effects of Defendant Characteristics, Guilty Pleas, and Departures on Sentence Outcomes for Drug Offenses, 1991-92," *Law & Society Review* 31 (1997): 789–822.

9. Bureau of Justice Statistics, *State Court Sentencing of Convicted Felons, 1994*

(Washington, D.C.: U.S. Department of Justice, 1998).

10. Cassia Spohn and Miriam DeLone, "When Does Race Matter? An Analysis of the Conditions Under Which Race Affects Sentence Severity," *Sociology of Crime, Law, and Deviance* (in press).

11. For reviews of this research see Theodore G. Chiricos and Charles Crawford, "Race and Imprisonment: A Contextual Assessment of the Evidence," in *Ethnicity, Race, and Crime: Perspectives Across Time and Place*, ed. Darnell F. Hawkins (Albany: State University of New York Press, 1995); John Hagan, "Extra-Legal Attributes and Criminal Sentencing: An Assessment of a Sociological Viewpoint," *Law & Society Review* 8 (1974): 357–383; Gary Kleck, "Racial Discrimination in Criminal Sentencing: A Critical Evaluation of the Evidence With Additional Evidence on the Death Penalty," *American Sociological Review* 46 (1981): 783–805; Marjorie S. Zatz, "The Changing Form of Racial/Ethnic Biases in Sentencing," *Journal of Research in Crime and Delinquency* 24 (1987): 69–92.

12. Hagan, "Extra-legal Attributes and Criminal Sentencing."

13. Albonetti, "Sentencing Under the Federal Sentencing Guidelines"; John H. Kramer and Jeffrey T. Ulmer, "Sentencing Disparity and Departures From Guidelines," *Justice Quarterly* 13 (1996): 81–105; Joan Petersilia, *Racial Disparities in the Criminal Justice System* (Santa Monica, CA: Rand, 1983); Spohn and DeLone, "When Does Race Matter?"; Cassia Spohn, John Gruhl, and Susan Welch, "The Effect of Race on Sentencing: A Re-Examination of an Unsettled Question," *Law & Society Review* 16 (1981–82): 71–88; Jeffrey T. Ulmer and John H. Kramer, "Court Communities Under Sentencing Guidelines: Dilemmas of Formal Rationality and Sentencing Disparity," *Criminology* 34 (1996): 383–407; and Marjorie S. Zatz, "Race, Ethnicity, and Determinate Sentencing: A New Dimension to an Old Controversy," *Criminology* 22 (1984): 147–171.

14. Stephen Klein, Joan Petersilia, and Susan Turner, "Race and Imprisonment Decisions in California," *Science* 247 (1990): 812–816; John H. Kramer and Darrell

Steffensmeier, "Race and Imprisonment Decisions," *The Sociological Quarterly* 34 (1993): 357–376; and McDonald and Carlson, *Sentencing in the Federal Courts.*

15. Ilene Nagel Bernstein, William R. Kelly, and Patricia A. Doyle, "Societal Reaction to Deviants: The Case of Criminal Defendants," *American Sociological Review* 42 (1977): 743–795; James L. Gibson, "Race as a Determinant of Criminal Sentences: A Methodological Critique and a Case Study," *Law & Society Review* 12 (1978): 455–478; and Martin A. Levin, "Urban Politics and Policy Outcomes: The Criminal Courts," in *Criminal Justice: Law and Politics*, ed. George F. Cole (Belmont, CA: Wadsworth, 1988).

16. Albonetti, "Sentencing Under the Federal Sentencing Guidelines"; Malcolm D. Holmes and Howard C. Daudistel, "Ethnicity and Justice in the Southwest: The Sentencing of Anglo, Black, and Mexican Origin Defendants," *Social Science Quarterly* 65 (1984): 265–277; Malcolm D. Holmes, Harmon M. Hosch, Howard C. Daudistel, Dolores A. Perez, and Joseph B. Graves, "Ethnicity, Legal Resources, and Felony Dispositions in Two Southwestern Jurisdictions," *Justice Quarterly* 13 (1996): 11–30; Kramer and Ulmer, "Sentencing Disparity and Departures From Guidelines"; Gary D. LaFree, "Official Reactions to Hispanics in the Southwest," *Journal of Research in Crime and Delinquency* 22 (1985): 213–237; Spohn and DeLone, "When Does Race Matter?"; James D. Unnever, "Direct and Organizational Discrimination in the Sentencing of Drug Offenders," *Social Problems* 30 (1982): 212–225; Zatz, "Race, Ethnicity, and Determinate Sentencing."

17. Blumstein et al., *Research on Sentencing.*

18. Ibid.

19. Zatz, "The Changing Forms of Racial/Ethnic Biases in Sentencing," p. 69.

20. Spohn and DeLone, "When Does Race Matter?"

21. These estimated probabilities are adjusted for the effects of the other legal and extralegal variables included in the multivariate analysis. See Spohn and DeLone, "When Does Race Matter?" for a descrip-

tion of the procedures used to calculate the probabilities.

22. Spohn and DeLone, "When Does Race Matter?," p. 29.

23. Ibid.

24. Ibid., p. 30.

25. Holmes et al., "Ethnicity, Legal Resources, and Felony Dispositions in Two Southwestern Jurisdictions."

26. Ibid., p. 27.

27. Kramer and Steffensmeier, "Race and Imprisonment Decisions."

28. Ibid., p. 360.

29. Ibid., p. 359.

30. Ibid., p. 366.

31. Ibid., p. 370.

32. Ibid., p. 368.

33. Ibid., p. 371.

34. Ibid., p. 373.

35. Kleck, "Racial Discrimination in Criminal Sentencing."

36. Ruth D. Peterson and John Hagan, "Changing Conceptions of Race: Towards an Account of Anomalous Findings of Sentencing Research," *American Sociological Review* 49 (1984): 56–70.

37. Ibid., p. 69.

38. Ibid., p. 67.

39. Ibid., p. 66.

40. Ibid., p. 64.

41. Ibid., p. 67.

42. Ibid., p. 67.

43. Ibid., p. 69.

44. Iris Marion Young *Justice and the Politics of Difference* (Princeton, N.J.: Princeton University Press, 1990), p. 59.

45. Carol Chiago Lujan, "Stereotyping by Politicians: Or 'The Only Real Indian Is the Stereotypical Indian,'" in *Images of Color, Images of Crime,* eds. Coramae Richey Mann and Marjorie Zatz (Los Angeles: Roxbury, 1998).

46. S. Feimer, F. Pommersheim, and S. Wise, "Marking Time: Does Race Make a Difference? A Study of Disparate Sentencing in South Dakota," *Journal of Crime and Justice* 13 (1990): 86–102; F. Pommersheim

and S. Wise, "Going to the Penitentiary: A Study of Disparate Sentencing in South Dakota," *Criminal Justice and Behavior* 16 (1989): 155–165.

47. B. Swift and G. Bickel, *Comparative Parole Treatment of American Indians and Non-Indians at United States Federal Prisons* (Washington, D.C.: Bureau of Social Science Research, 1974).

48. Ronet D. Bachman and Alexander Alvarez, "American Indians and Sentencing Disparity: An Arizona Test," *Journal of Criminal Justice* 24 (1996): 549–561; E. Hall and A. A. Simkus, "Inequality in the Types of Sentences Received by Native Americans and Whites," *Criminology* 13 (1975): 199–222.

49. Ronet D. Bachman, Alexander Alvarez, and C. Perkins, "The Discriminatory Imposition of the Law: Does It Affect Sentence Outcomes for American Indians?" in *Native Americans, Crime and Justice*, eds. M. Nielsen and R. Silverman (Boulder, CO: Westview, 1996); Timothy S. Bynum and Raymond Paternoster, "Discrimination Revisited: An Exploration of Frontstage and Backstage Criminal Justice Decision Making," *Sociology and Social Research* 69 (1984): 90–108.

50. Bachman and Alvarez, "American Indians and Sentencing Disparity."

51. Ibid., p. 558.

52. Ibid.

53. Darnell F. Hawkins, "Beyond Anomalies: Rethinking the Conflict Perspective on Race and Criminal Punishment," *Social Forces* 65 (1987): 719–745.

54. Ibid., p. 724.

55. Richard Quinney, *The Social Reality of Crime* (Boston: Little, Brown, 1970), p. 18.

56. Hawkins, "Beyond Anomalies," p. 736.

57. Peterson and Hagan, "Changing Conceptions of Race," p. 57.

58. Hawkins, "Beyond Anomalies."

59. Peterson and Hagan, "Changing Conceptions of Race," p. 69.

60. Gunnar Myrdal, *An American Dilemma: The Negro Problem and Modern Democracy* (New York: Harper & Brothers, 1944), p. 551.

61. Ibid., p. 553.

62. Jennifer Wriggins, "Rape, Racism, and the Law," *Harvard Women's Law Journal* 6 (1983): 103–141.

63. Susan Brownmiller, *Against Our Will: Men, Women and Rape* (New York: Bantam Books, 1975).

64. Wriggins, "Rape, Racism, and the Law."

65. Ibid., p. 109.

66. Marvin E. Wolfgang and Marc Reidel, "Race, Judicial Discretion and the Death Penalty," *Annals of the American Academy* 407 (1973): 119–133; Marvin E. Wolfgang and Marc Reidel, "Rape, Race and the Death Penalty in Georgia," *American Journal of Orthopsychiatry* 45 (1975): 658–668.

67. Brownmiller, *Against Our Will*, p. 237.

68. Gary D. LaFree, *Rape and Criminal Justice: The Social Construction of Sexual Assault* (Belmont, CA: Wadsworth, 1989).

69. Anthony Walsh, "The Sexual Stratification Hypothesis and Sexual Assault in Light of the Changing Conceptions of Race," *Criminology* 25 (1987): 153–173.

70. Ibid., p. 167.

71. Cassia Spohn and Jeffrey Spears, "The Effect of Offender and Victim Characteristics on Sexual Assault Case Processing Decisions," *Justice Quarterly* 13 (1996): 649–679.

72. Ibid., p. 663.

73. Ibid., p. 675.

74. Ibid., p. 665.

75. Peterson and Hagan, "Changing Conceptions of Race," p. 67.

76. Georg Rusche and Otto Kirchheimer, *Punishment and Social Structure* (New York: Russell & Russell, 1939), p. 18.

77. Richard Quinney, *Class, State and Crime* (New York: David McKay, 1977), p. 131.

78. Steven Box and Chris Hale, "Unemployment, Imprisonment and Prison Overcrowding," *Contemporary Crises* 9 (1985): 209–228.

79. Steven Box, *Recession, Crime and Punishment* (Totowa, NJ: Barnes & Noble, 1987).

80. Steven Spitzer, "Towards a Marxian Theory of Deviance," *Social Problems* 22 (1975): 638–651.

81. Ibid., p. 645.

82. Ibid., p. 646.

83. Box and Hale, "Unemployment, Imprisonment and Prison Overcrowding," p. 217.

84. Theodore G. Chiricos and William D. Bales, "Unemployment and Punishment: An Empirical Assessment," *Criminology* 29 (1991): 701–724.

85. Ibid., p. 719.

86. Tracy Nobiling, Cassia Spohn, and Miriam DeLone, "A Tale of Two Counties: Unemployment and Sentence Severity," *Justice Quarterly* 15 (1998): 459–485.

87. Hubert M. Blalock, *Toward a Theory of Minority-Group Relations* (New York: Wiley, 1967).

88. Dario Melossi, "An Introduction: Fifty Years Later, Punishment and Social Structure in Comparative Analysis," *Contemporary Crisis* 13 (1989): 311–326.

89. Ibid., p. 317.

90. Ibid.

91. Chiricos and Bales, "Unemployment and Punishment," p. 719.

92. Ibid., p. 719.

93. Harry Kalven, Jr. and Hans Zeisel, *The American Jury* (Boston: Little, Brown, 1966).

94. Cassia Spohn and Jerry Cederblom, "Racial Disparities in Sentencing: A Test of the Liberation Hypothesis," *Justice Quarterly* 8 (1991): 305–327.

95. Ibid., p. 323.

96. Michael Tonry, *Malign Neglect: Race, Crime, and Punishment in America* (New York: Oxford University Press, 1995), p. 105.

97. Ibid., p. 115.

98. Jerome G. Miller, *Search and Destroy: African-American Males in the Criminal Justice System* (Cambridge, England: Cambridge University Press, 1996), p. 80.

99. There were 475,209 persons arrested for drug offenses in 1976, compared to 1,117,323 in 1994. The number of whites increased from 366,081 to 677,025; the

number of African Americans increased from 103,615 to 429,479. See Tonry, *Malign Neglect,* Table 3-3, and Bureau of Justice Statistics, *Sourcebook of Criminal Justice Statistics 1995* (Washington, D.C.: U.S. Department of Justice, 1996), Table 4.10.

100. Tonry, *Malign Neglect*, p. 58.

101. Ibid., p. 113.

102. Chiricos and Bales, "Unemployment and Punishment"; Kramer and Steffensmeier, "Race and Imprisonment Decisions"; Martha Myers, "Symbolic Policy and the Sentencing of Drug Offenders," *Law & Society Review* 23 (1989): 295–315; Unnever, "Direct and Organizational Discrimination in the Sentencing of Drug Offenders." Note that Unnever found significant differences between African Americans and whites but not between Hispanics and whites.

103. Cassia Spohn and Jeffrey Spears, "Sentencing of Drug Offenders in Three Cities: Does Race/Ethnicity Make a Difference?" in *Crime Control and Criminal Justice: The Delicate Balance,* eds. Darnell F. Hawkins, Samuel L. Meyers, Jr., and Randolph N. Stone (Westport, CT: Greenwood, in press); Unnever, "Direct and Organizational Discrimination in the Sentencing of Drug Offenders."

104. See the earlier discussion of Peterson and Hagan, "Changing Conceptions of Race."

105. Spohn and Spears, "Sentencing of Drug Offenders in Three Cities."

106. Albonetti, "Sentencing Under the Federal Sentencing Guidelines."

107. Spohn and Spears, "Sentencing of Drug Offenders in Three Cities," p. 29.

108. Ibid.

109. See William J. Chambliss, "Crime Control and Ethnic Minorities: Legitimizing Racial Oppression by Creating Moral Panics," in *Ethnicity, Race, and Crime,* ed. Darnell F. Hawkins (Albany: State University of New York Press); Tonry, *Malign Neglect.*

110. Spohn and Spears, "Sentencing of Drug Offenders in Three Cities," p. 29.

111. Ibid., pp. 29–30.

112. Jeffrey S. Adler, "The Dynamite, Wreckage, and Scum in Our Cities: The Social Construction of Deviance in Industrial America," *Justice Quarterly* 11 (1994): 33–49.

113. Albonetti, "Sentencing Under the Federal Sentencing Guidelines."

114. 28 U.S.C, 991(b)(1)(B)(Supp. 1993).

115. Albonetti, "Sentencing Under the Federal Sentencing Guidelines," p. 790.

116. Ibid.

117. Ibid., p. 780.

118. Albonetti noted (p. 817) that most of the departures in these cases were "judicial decisions to comply with prosecutorial motions based on the defendant having provided substantial assistance to the government in the prosecution of others."

119. Ibid., p. 818.

120. Ibid., pp. 818–819.

121. Randall Kennedy, "Changing Images of the State: Criminal Law and Racial Discrimination: A Comment," *Harvard Law Review* 107 (1994): 1255, 1278. See also Randall Kennedy, *Race, Crime, and the Law* (New York: Vintage, 1997).

122. *Omaha World Herald* (April 17, 1993), p. 1.

123. *U.S. v. Armstrong*, 116 S.Ct. 1480 (1996).

124. United States Sentencing Commission, *Special Report to the Congress: Cocaine and Federal Sentencing Policy* (Washington, D.C.: Author, 1997), p. 2.

125. See B. Keith Crew, "Sex Differences in Criminal Sentencing: Chivalry or Patriarchy?" *Justice Quarterly* 8 (1991): 59–83; Kathleen Daly and Michael Tonry, "Gender, Race, and Sentencing," in *Crime and Justice: A Review of Research, Vol.* 22, ed. Michael Tonry (Chicago: University of Chicago Press, 1997); Candace Kruttschnitt, "Social Status and Sentencing of Female Offenders," *Law & Society Review* 15 (1980–81): 247–265; and Cassia Spohn, Susan Welch, and John Gruhl, "Women Defendants in Court: The Interaction Between Sex and Race in Convicting and Sentencing," *Social Science Quarterly* 66 (1985): 178–185.

126. Darrell Steffensmeier, John Kramer, and Cathy Streifel, "Gender and Imprisonment Decisions," *Criminology* 31 (1993): 411–443, p. 429.

127. Ibid.

128. B. Keith Crew, "Sex Differences in Criminal Sentencing."

129. Ibid., p. 79.

130. Cassia Spohn and Jeffrey Spears, "Gender and Case Processing Decisions: A Comparison of Case Outcomes for Male and Female Defendants Charged With Violent Felonies," *Women & Criminal Justice* 8 (1997): 29–59.

131. Michael David Smith, *Race Versus Robe: The Dilemma of Black Judges* (Port Washington, NY: Associated Faculty Press, 1983).

132. Cited in Smith, *Race Versus Robe*, p. 80.

133. Cited in Smith, *Race Versus Robe*, p. 81.

134. Thomas G. Walker and Deborah J. Barrow, "The Diversification of the Federal Bench: Policy and Process Ramifications," *Journal of Politics* 47 (1985): 596–617.

135. Ibid., pp. 613–614.

136. Jon Gottschall, "Carter's Judicial Appointments: The Influence of Affirmative Action and Merit Selection on Voting on the U.S. Courts of Appeals," *Judicature* 67 (1983): 165–173.

137. Ibid., p. 168.

138. Ibid., p. 173.

139. Charles Donald Engle, "Criminal Justice in the City: A Study of Sentence Severity and Variation in the Philadelphia Court System," unpublished Ph.D. dissertation, Temple University, 1971; Cassia Spohn, "Decision Making in Sexual Assault Cases: Do Black and Female Judges Make a Difference?" *Women & Criminal Justice* 2 (1990): 83–105; Thomas M. Uhlman, "Black Elite Decision Making: The Case of Trial Judges," *American Journal of Political Science* 22 (1978): 884–895.

140. Spohn, "Decision Making in Sexual Assault Cases," p. 92.

141. Susan Welch, Michael Combs, and John Gruhl, "Do Black Judges Make a Difference?" *American Journal of Political Science* 32 (1988): 126–136.

142. Cassia Spohn, "The Sentencing Decisions of Black and White Judges: Expected and Unexpected Similarities," *Law & Society Review* 24 (1990): 1197–1216.

143. Ibid., p. 1213.

144. Malcolm D. Holmes, Harmon M. Hosch, Howard C. Daudistel, Dolores A. Perez, and Joseph B. Graves, "Judges' Ethnicity and Minority Sentencing: Evidence Concerning Hispanics," *Social Science Quarterly* 74 (1993): 496–506.

145. Ibid., p. 502.

146. Uhlman, "Black Elite Decision Making," p. 893.

147. Bruce McM. Wright, "A Black Broods on Black Judges," *Judicature* 57 (1973): 22–23.

148. Samuel Walker, *Taming the System: The Control of Discretion in Criminal Justice, 1950–1990* (New York: Oxford University Press, 1993), p. 112.

149. Tonry, *Malign Neglect*, p. 164.

150. Ibid., p. 123.

151. Zatz, "The Changing Forms of Racial/Ethnic Biases in Sentencing," p. 79.

152. Petersilia, *Racial Disparities in the Criminal Justice System.*

153. Terance D. Miethe and Charles A. Moore, "Socioeconomic Disparities Under Determinate Sentencing Systems: A Comparison of Preguideline and Postguideline Practices in Minnesota," *Criminology* 23 (1985): 337–363.

154. Ibid., p. 358.

155. Jo Dixon, "The Organizational Context of Criminal Sentencing," *American Journal of Sociology* 100 (1995): 1157–1198.

156. Kramer and Steffensmeier, "Race and Imprisonment Decisions"; Kramer and Ulmer, "Sentencing Disparity and Departures From Guidelines"; Ulmer and Kramer, "Court Communities Under Sentencing Guidelines."

157. Kramer and Ulmer, "Sentencing Disparity and Departures From Guidelines."

158. Ibid., p. 99.

159. Ibid.

160. Ibid., p. 101.

161. Tonry, *Malign Neglect*, pp. 170–172.

162. Ibid., p. 190.

163. Ibid., p. 155.

164. Ibid., p. 160.

165. Zatz, "The Changing Forms of Racial/Ethnic Biases in Sentencing," p. 87

8

⚚

The Color of Death

Race and the Death Penalty

n February 1994, Supreme Court Justice Harry A. Blackmun announced that he would vote to oppose all future death sentences. In an opinion dissenting from the Court's order denying review in a Texas death penalty case, Blackmun charged the Court with coming "perilously close to murder." He also stated that the death penalty was applied in an arbitrary and racially discriminatory manner. "Rather than continue to coddle the Court's delusion that the desired level of fairness has been achieved and the need for regulation eviscerated," Blackmun wrote, "I feel morally and intellectually obligated simply to concede that the death penalty experiment has failed."[1]

Justice Blackmun is not alone is his assessment. Legal scholars, civil libertarians, and social scientists also have questioned the fairness of the process by which a small proportion of convicted murderers are sentenced to death and an even smaller proportion are eventually executed. Echoing Justice Blackmun, they have argued that "the most profound expression of racial discrimination in sentencing occurs in the use of capital punishment."[2]

GOALS OF THE CHAPTER

In this chapter, we address the issue of racial discrimination in the application of the death penalty. We begin with a discussion of Supreme Court decisions concerning the constitutionality of the death penalty. We follow this with a discussion of racial differences in attitudes toward capital punishment. We then present statistics on death sentences and executions, and summarize the results of empirical studies examining the effect of race on the application of the death penalty. We conclude with a discussion of *McCleskey v. Kemp*,[3] the Supreme Court case that directly addressed the question of racial discrimination in the imposition of the death penalty.

THE CONSTITUTIONALITY
OF THE DEATH PENALTY

The Eighth Amendment to the U.S. Constitution prohibits "cruel and unusual punishments." The determination of which punishments are cruel and unusual, and thus unconstitutional, has been left to the courts. According to the Supreme Court:

> Punishments are cruel when they involve torture or lingering death; but the punishment of death is not cruel, within the meaning of that word as used in the Constitution. It implies there something inhuman and barbarous, something more than the mere extinguishment of life.[4]
>
> Whatever the arguments may be against capital punishment, both on moral grounds and in terms of accomplishing the purposes of punishment—and they are forceful—the death penalty has been employed throughout our history, and, in a day when it is still widely accepted, it cannot be said to violate the constitutional concept of cruelty.[5]

Although the Supreme Court consistently has stated that punishments of torture violate the Eighth Amendment, the Court has never ruled that the death penalty itself is a cruel and unusual punishment.

Furman v. Georgia

In 1972 the Supreme Court ruled in *Furman v. Georgia*[6] that the death penalty, as it was being administered under then-existing statutes, was unconstitutional. The five-to-four decision, in which nine separate opinions were written, did not hold that the death penalty per se violated the Constitution's ban on cruel and unusual punishment. Rather, the majority opinions focused on the procedures by which convicted defendants were selected for the death penalty. The justices ruled that because the statutes being challenged offered no guidance to juries charged with deciding whether or not to sentence convicted murderers or rapists to death, there was a substantial risk that the death penalty would be imposed in an arbitrary and discriminatory manner.

Although all of the majority justices were concerned about the arbitrary and capricious application of the death penalty, the nature of their concerns varied. Justices Brennan and Marshall wrote that the death penalty was inherently cruel and unusual punishment. Justice Brennan argued that the death penalty violated the concept of human dignity, and Justice Marshall asserted that the death penalty served no legitimate penal purpose. These justices concluded that the death penalty would violate the Constitution under any circumstances.

The other three justices in the majority concluded that capital punishment as it was then being administered in the United States was unconstitutional. These justices asserted that the death penalty violated both the Eighth Amendment's ban on cruel and unusual punishment and the Fourteenth Amendment's requirement of equal protection under the law. Justice Douglas stated that the procedures used in administering the death penalty were "pregnant with discrimination." Justice Stewart focused on the fact that the death penalty was "so wantonly and so freakishly imposed." Justice White found "no meaningful basis for distinguishing the few cases in which [the death penalty] is imposed from the many cases in which it is not."[7]

The central issue in the *Furman* case was the meaning of the Eighth Amendment's prohibition of cruel and unusual punishment, but the issue of racial discrimination in the administration of the death penalty was raised by three of the five justices in the majority. Justices Douglas and Marshall cited evidence of discrimination against defendants who were poor, powerless, or black. Marshall, for example, noted that giving juries "untrammeled discretion" to impose a sentence of death was "an open invitation to discrimination."[8] Justice Stewart, although asserting that "racial discrimination has not been proved," stated that Douglas and Marshall "have demonstrated that, if any basis can be discerned for the selection of these few to be sentenced to die, it is the constitutionally impermissible basis of race."[9]

The Impact of *Furman* The impact of the *Furman* decision was dramatic. The Court's ruling "emptied death rows across the country," and "brought the process that fed them to a stop."[10] Many commentators argued that *Furman* reflected the Supreme Court's deep-seated concerns about the fairness of the death penalty process; they predicted that the Court's next step would be the abolition of capital punishment. Instead, the Court defied these predictions, deciding to regulate capital punishment rather than abolish it.

Also as a result of the *Furman* decision, the death penalty statutes in thirty-nine states were invalidated. Most of these states responded to *Furman* by adopting new statutes designed to narrow discretion and thus to avoid the problems of arbitrariness and discrimination identified by the justices in the majority.

These statutes were of two types. Some required the judge or jury to impose the death penalty if a defendant was convicted of first-degree murder. Others permitted the judge or jury to impose the death penalty on defendants convicted of certain crimes, depending on the presence or absence of aggravating and mitigating circumstances. These "guided-discretion" statutes typically required a bifurcated trial in which the jury first decided guilt or innocence and then decided whether to impose the death penalty or not. They also provided for automatic appellate review of all death sentences.

Post-*Furman* Decisions

The Supreme Court ruled on the constitutionality of the new death penalty statutes in 1976. The Court held that the mandatory death penalty statutes enacted by North Carolina and Louisiana were unconstitutional,[11] both because they provided no opportunity for consideration of mitigating circumstances and because the jury's power to determine the degree of the crime (conviction for first-degree murder or for a lesser included offense) opened the door to the type of "arbitrary and wanton jury discretion"[12] condemned in *Furman*. The justices stated that the central problem of the mandatory statutes was their treatment of all defendants "as members of a faceless, undifferentiated mass to be subjected to the blind infliction of the penalty of death."[13]

In contrast, the Supreme Court ruled that the guided discretion death penalty statutes adopted by Georgia, Florida, and Texas did not violate the Eighth Amendment's prohibition of cruel and unusual punishment.[14] In *Gregg v. Georgia*[15] the Court held that Georgia's statute—which required the jury to consider and weigh ten specified aggravating circumstances (see Box 8.1), allowed the jury to consider mitigating circumstances, and provided for automatic appellate review—channeled the jury's discretion and thereby reduced the likelihood that the jury would impose arbitrary or discriminatory sentences. According to the Court,

> No longer can a jury wantonly and freakishly impose the death sentence; it is always circumscribed by the legislative guidelines. In addition, the review function of the Supreme Court of Georgia affords additional assurance that the concerns that prompted our decision in *Furman* are not present to any significant degree in the Georgia procedure applied here.[16]

Since 1976 the Supreme Court has handed down additional decisions on the constitutionality of the death penalty. With the exception of *McCleskey v. Kemp,* which we address later, these decisions do not focus on the question of racial discrimination in the application of the death penalty. The Court has ruled that the death penalty cannot be imposed on a defendant convicted of the crime of rape,[18] that the death penalty can be imposed on an offender convicted of felony murder if the offender played a major role in the felony and displayed "reckless indifference to the value of human life,"[19] and that the Eighth Amendment does not prohibit the execution of the mentally retarded[20] or youths who commit crimes at age 16 or older.[21]

ATTITUDES TOWARD
CAPITAL PUNISHMENT

In *Gregg v. Georgia* the seven justices in the majority noted that both the public and state legislatures had endorsed the death penalty for murder. The Court stated that "it is now evident that a large proportion of American society continues to regard it as an appropriate and necessary criminal sanction." Public opinion data indicate that the Court was correct in its assessment of attitudes

---

BOX 8.1   Georgia's Guided Discretion Death Penalty Statute

Under Georgia law, if the jury finds at least one of the following aggravating circumstances it may, but need not, recommend death:[17]

1. The offense was committed by a person with a prior record of conviction for a capital felony or by a person who has a substantial history of serious assaultive criminal convictions.
2. The offense was committed while the offender was engaged in the commission of another capital felony, or aggravated battery, or burglary or arson in the first degree.
3. The offender knowingly created a great risk of death to more than one person in a public place by means of a weapon or device which would normally be hazardous to the lives of more than one person.
4. The offender committed the offense of murder for himself or another, for the purpose of receiving money or any other thing of monetary value.
5. The murder of a judicial officer, former judicial officer, district attorney or solicitor, or former district attorney or solicitor during or because of the exercise of his official duty.
6. The offender caused or directed another to commit murder or committed murder as an agent or employee of another person.
7. The offense was outrageously or wantonly vile, horrible, or inhuman in that it involved torture, depravity of mind, or an aggravated battery to the victim.
8. The offense was committed against any peace officer, corrections employee, or fireman while engaged in the performance of his official duties.
9. The offense was committed by a person in, or who has escaped from, the lawful custody of a peace officer or place of lawful confinement.
10. The murder was committed for the purpose of avoiding, interfering with, or preventing a lawful arrest or custody in a place of lawful confinement, of himself or another.

---

toward the death penalty. In 1976, the year that *Gregg* was decided, 66 percent of the respondents to a nationwide poll said that they favored the death penalty for persons convicted of murder; the comparable figure for 1996 was 71 percent.[22]

The reliability of these figures has not gone unchallenged. In fact, Supreme Court justices themselves have raised questions about the reliability and meaning of public opinion data derived from standard "do you favor or oppose?" polling questions. Justice Marshall observed in his concurring opinion in *Furman* that Americans were not fully informed about the ways in which the death penalty was used or about its potential for abuse. According to Marshall, the public did not realize that the death penalty was imposed in an arbitrary manner or that "the burden of capital punishment falls upon the poor, the ignorant, and the underprivileged members of society."[23] Marshall suggested that public opinion data demonstrating widespread support for the death penalty should therefore be given little weight in determining whether capital punishment is consistent with "evolving standards of decency." In what has become known as the "Marshall Hypothesis,"[24] he stated that "the average citizen" who knew "all the facts presently available regarding capital punishment would . . . find it shocking to his conscience and sense of justice."[25]

Researchers also have raised questions about the poll results,[26] suggesting that support for the death penalty is not absolute, but dependent on such things as the circumstances of the case, the character of the defendant, or the alternative punishments that are available. Bowers, for example, challenged the conclusion that "Americans solidly support the death penalty" and suggested that the poll results have been misinterpreted.[27] He argued that rather than reflecting a "deep-seated or strongly held commitment to capital punishment," expressed public support for the death penalty "is actually a reflection of the public's desire for a genuinely harsh but meaningful punishment for convicted murderers."[28]

In support of this proposition, Bowers presented evidence from surveys of citizens in a number of states and from interviews with capital jurors in three states. He found that support for the death penalty plummeted when respondents were given an alternative of life in prison without parole plus restitution to the victim's family. Moreover, a majority of the respondents in every state preferred this alternative to the death penalty. Bowers also found that about three quarters of the respondents, and 80 percent of jurors in capital cases, agreed that "the death penalty is too arbitrary because some people are executed and others are sent to prison for the very same crimes." Bowers concluded that the results of his study "could have the critical effect of changing the perspectives of legislators, judges, the media, and the public on how people think about capital punishment."[29]

It also is clear that there are significant racial differences in support for the death penalty. The results of a 1997 Harris poll, for example, found that 80 percent of whites and 72 percent of Hispanics expressed support for the death penalty, compared to only 46 percent of African Americans.[30] In fact, as shown in Figure 8.1, since 1976 the percentage of respondents who report that they support the death penalty has been significantly higher among whites than among African Americans.

Researchers have advanced a number of explanations to account for these consistent racial differences. Some attribute African American opposition to perceptions of racial bias in the application of the death penalty.[31] Others contend that white support is associated with racial prejudice.[32] One study, for example, found that antipathy to African Americans (which was measured by two items asking respondents to indicate their attitudes toward living in a majority-black neighborhood or having a family member marry an African American) and belief in racial stereotypes (believing that African Americans are lazy, unintelligent, violent, and poor) predicted white respondents' support for the death penalty.[33] As the authors noted, "Simply put, many White people are both prejudiced against Blacks and are more likely to favor capital punishment."[34] The authors concluded that their finding of an association between racial prejudice and support for the death penalty suggests "that public sentiment may be an unacceptable indicator of contemporary standards of appropriate punishment for persons convicted of homicide."[35]

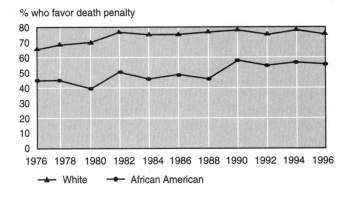

% who favor death penalty

—▲— White   —●— African American

FIGURE 8.1 African American and White Attitudes Toward Capital Punishment for Persons Convicted of Murder, 1970–1996

Data from Bureau of Justice Statistics, *Sourcebook of Criminal Justice Statistics, 1996* (Washington, D.C.: U.S. Government Printing Office, 1997).

RACE AND THE DEATH PENALTY:
THE EMPIRICAL EVIDENCE

The Supreme Court's decisions regarding the constitutionality of the death penalty have been guided by a number of assumptions. In the *Furman* decision, the five justices in the majority assumed that the absence of guidelines and procedural rules in then-existing death penalty statutes opened the door to arbitrary, capricious, and discriminatory decision making. In *Gregg,* the Court affirmed the guided discretion statutes on their face and assumed that the statutes would eliminate the problems condemned in *Furman.* The Court assumed, in other words, that racial discrimination was a potential problem under the statutes struck down in *Furman,* but would not be a problem under the statutes approved in *Gregg* and the companion cases.

In this section we address the validity of these assumptions. We begin by presenting statistics on the application of the death penalty. We then discuss the results of pre-*Furman* and post-*Furman* studies investigating the relationship between race and the death penalty.

Statistical Evidence of Racial Disparity

There is clear evidence of racial disparity in the application of the death penalty. Despite the fact that African Americans comprise only 10 to 12 percent of the U.S. population, they comprise a much larger proportion of offenders sentenced to death and executed, both historically and during the post-*Gregg* era. There also is compelling evidence that those who murder whites, and particularly African Americans who murder whites, are sentenced to death at disproportionately high rates. For example, the state of Georgia, which generated both *Furman* and *Gregg,* carried out eighteen executions between 1976 and 1994. Twelve of those executed were African Americans; six of the twelve were sentenced to death by all-white juries. Sixteen of the eighteen persons executed had killed whites.[36]

The pattern found in Georgia casts doubt on the Supreme Court's assertion in *Gregg* that the disparities that prompted their decision in *Furman* will not be present "to any significant degree"[37] under Georgia's guided discretion procedures. Other evidence also calls this into question. Consider the following statistics:

- 1,349 (41.9 percent) of the persons under sentence of death in the United States at the end of 1996 were African Americans; of the forty-eight women on death row, sixteen (33.0 percent) were African Americans.[38]

- African Americans comprise half of the death row populations in North Carolina, South Carolina, Ohio, Delaware, Mississippi, and Virginia; they constitute two thirds of those on death row in Pennsylvania, Illinois, and Louisiana. Eight of the eleven offenders under sentence of death in the federal system are African Americans.[39]

- From 1930 through 1995, 4,172 persons were legally executed in the United States. Of these, 2,187 (52.4 percent) were African Americans. Twelve of the thirty-three women executed during this period were African Americans.[40]

- Of the 358 prisoners executed from 1977 through 1996, 200 (55.9 percent) were white, 134 (37.4 percent) were African Americans, twenty-one (5.9 percent) were Hispanics, two were Native Americans, and one was Asian.[41]

- 350 (82.2 percent) of the victims of those executed between 1977 and 1996 were whites, fifty-five (12.9 percent) were African Americans, fourteen (3.3 percent) were Hispanics, and seven (1.6 percent) were Asians. During this period, approximately 50 percent of all murder victims were African Americans.[42]

- Among those executed from 1930 through 1972 for the crime of rape, 89 percent (405 of the 455) were African Americans.[43] During this period, Louisiana, Mississippi, Oklahoma, Virginia, West Virginia, and the District of Columbia executed sixty-six African American men, but not a single white man, for the crime of rape.[44]

- Among those sentenced to death for rape in North Carolina from 1909 through 1954, 56 percent of the African Americans, but only 43 percent of the whites, were eventually executed.[45]

- Twenty percent of the whites but only 11 percent of the African Americans sentenced to death for first-degree murder in Pennsylvania between 1914 and 1958 had their sentences commuted to life in prison.[46]

These statistics clearly indicate that African Americans have been sentenced to death and executed "in numbers far out of proportion to their numbers in the population."[47] The statistics document racial disparity in the application of

---

BOX 8.2   Discrimination in the Application of the
Death Penalty: A Hypothetical Example

Example 1

- 210 death-eligible homicides with African American offenders: 70 offenders (30 percent) receive the death penalty.
- 150 death-eligible homicides with white offenders: 50 offenders (30 percent) receive the death penalty.
- Conclusion: No evidence of discrimination, despite the fact that a disproportionate number of African Americans are sentenced to death.

Example 2

- 210 death-eligible homicides with African American offenders: 90 offenders (43 percent) receive the death penalty.
- 150 death-eligible homicides with white offenders: 30 offenders (20 percent) receive the death penalty.
- Conclusion: Possibility of discrimination, as African Americans are more than twice as likely as whites to be sentenced to death.

---

the death penalty, both prior to *Furman* and following *Gregg*.[48] As we have noted frequently throughout this book, however, disparities in the treatment of racial minorities and whites do not necessarily constitute evidence of racial discrimination.

Racial minorities may be sentenced to death at a disproportionately high rate, not because of discrimination in the application of the death penalty, but because they are more likely than whites to commit homicide, the crime most frequently punished by death. As illustrated by the hypothetical examples presented in Box 8.2, the appropriate comparison is not the number of African Americans and whites sentenced to death during a given year or over time. Rather, the appropriate comparison is the percentage of death-eligible homicides involving African Americans and whites that result in a death sentence.

The problem with the hypothetical example presented in Box 8.2 is that there are no national data on the number of death-eligible homicides or on the race of those who commit or who are arrested for such crimes. Kleck,[49] noting that most homicides are intraracial, used the number of African American and white homicide victims as a surrogate measure. He created an indicator of "execution risk" by dividing the number of executions (for murder) of persons of a given race in a given year by the number of homicide victims of that race who died in the previous year.[50] Using data from 1930 through 1967, Kleck found that the risk of execution was somewhat greater for whites (10.43 executions per 1,000 homicides) than for African Americans (9.72 executions per 1,000 homicides) in the United States as a whole. However, African Americans faced a greater likelihood of execution than whites in the South (10.47 for African Americans versus 8.39 for whites).[51] He concluded that the death penalty "has not generally been imposed for murder in a fashion discriminatory toward blacks, except in the South."[52]

None of the statistics cited here, including the execution rates calculated by Kleck, prove that the death penalty has been imposed in a racially discriminatory manner, in the South or elsewhere, either before the *Furman* decision or after the *Gregg* decision. As we pointed out earlier, conclusions of racial discrimination in sentencing rest on evidence indicating that African Americans are sentenced more harshly than whites after other legally relevant predictors of sentence severity are taken into account.

Even if it can be shown that African Americans face a greater risk of execution than whites, in other words, we cannot necessarily conclude that this reflects racial prejudice or racial discrimination. The difference might be due to legitimate legal factors—the heinousness of the crime or the prior criminal record of the offender, for example—that juries and judges consider in determining whether to sentence the offender to death. If African Americans are sentenced to death at a higher rate than whites because they commit more heinous murders than whites or because they are more likely than whites to have a prior conviction for murder, then we cannot conclude that criminal justice officials or juries are making racially discriminatory death penalty decisions.

The data presented in Table 8.1 provide some evidence in support of this possibility. Among prisoners under sentence of death in 1996, African Americans were more likely than either Hispanics or whites to have a prior felony conviction or a prior homicide conviction. African Americans also were more likely than whites to have been on parole when they were arrested for the capital offense.

Just as the presence of racial disparity does not necessarily signal the existence of racial discrimination, the absence of disparity does not necessarily indicate the absence of discrimination. Even if it can be shown that African Americans generally face the same risk of execution as whites, in other words, we cannot conclude that the capital sentencing process operates in a racially neutral manner. As we noted in our discussion of the noncapital sentencing process, it is important to consider not only the race of the offender, but the race of the victim as well. If African Americans who murder whites are sentenced to death at a disproportionately high rate and African Americans who murder other African Americans are sentenced to death at a disproportionately low rate, the overall finding of "no difference" in the death sentence rates for African American and white offenders may be masking significant differences based on the race of the victim. As Johnson wrote in 1941:

> If caste values and attitudes mean anything at all, they mean that offenses by or against Negroes will be defined not so much in terms of their intrinsic seriousness as in terms of their importance in the eyes of the dominant group. Obviously, the murder of a white person by a Negro and the murder of a Negro by a Negro are not at all the same kind of murder from the standpoint of the upper caste's scale of values . . . instead of two categories of offenders, Negro and white, we really need four offender–victim categories, and they would probably rank in seriousness from high to low as follows: (1) Negro versus white, (2) white versus white, (3) Negro versus Negro, and white versus Negro.[53]

**Table 8.1 Criminal History Profile of Prisoners
Under Sentence of Death in the United States, 1996**

	RACE OF PRISONER		
	African American N = 1,355	Hispanic N = 259	White N = 1,582
Prior felony conviction (%)	70.4	57.4	63.5
	(954)	(149)	(1005)
Prior homicide conviction (%)	9.5	7.2	7.9
	(129)	(19)	(125)
On parole at time of capital offense (%)	23.0	24.4	16.8
	(312)	(63)	(266)

SOURCE: Department of Justice, Bureau of Justice Statistics, *Capital Punishment 1996* (Washington, D.C.: U.S. Government Printing Office, 1997), Table 9.

Evidence in support of Johnson's rankings is presented in Box 8.3, which focuses on the "anomalous" cases in which whites have been executed for crimes against African Americans. According to Radelet, "the scandalous paucity of these cases, representing less than two-tenths of 1% of known executions, lends further support to the evidence that the death penalty in this country has been discriminatorily applied."[54]

There is now a substantial body of research investigating the relationship between race and the death penalty. Most—but not all—of the research tests for effects of both race of defendant and race of victim. Some of these studies are methodologically sophisticated, both in terms of the type of statistical analysis employed and in terms of the number of variables that are taken into consideration in the analysis. Other studies use less sophisticated statistical techniques and include fewer control variables.

We summarize the results of these studies—presenting the results of the pre-*Furman* studies first, then the results of the post-*Furman* studies. Our purpose is to assess the validity of the Supreme Court's assumptions that race played a role in death penalty decisions prior to *Furman,* but that the guided discretion statutes enacted since 1976 have removed arbitrariness and discrimination from the capital sentencing process.

Pre-*Furman* Studies

We noted in our discussion of the Supreme Court's decision in *Furman v. Georgia* that three of the five justices in the majority mentioned the problem of racial discrimination in the application of the death penalty. Even two of the dissenting justices—Chief Justice Burger and Justice Powell—acknowledged the existence of historical evidence of discrimination against African Americans. Justice Powell also stated, "If a Negro defendant, for instance, could demonstrate that members of his race were being singled out for more severe

BOX 8.3   Executions of Whites for Crimes Against African Americans: Exceptions to the Rule?

Since 1608, there have been about 16,000 executions in the United States.[55] Of these, only thirty, or about two-tenths of 1 percent, were executions of whites for crimes against African Americans. Historically, in other words, there has been one execution of a white for a crime against an African American for every 533 recorded executions.

Michael Radelet believes that these white offender–black victim cases, which would appear to be theoretically anomalous based on the proposition that race is an important determinant of sentencing, are not really "exceptions to the rule."[56] Although acknowledging that each case is in fact anomalous if race alone is used to predict the likelihood of a death sentence, Radelet suggests that these cases are consistent with a more general theoretical model that uses the relative social status of defendants and victims to explain case outcomes. These cases, in other words, are consistent with "the general rule that executions almost always involve lower status defendants who stand convicted for crimes against victims of higher status."[57]

Radelet's examination of the facts in each case revealed that ten of the thirty cases involved white men who murdered slaves and eight of those ten involved men convicted of murdering a slave who belonged to someone else. The scenario of Case 13, for example, read as follows:

> June 2, 1854. Texas. James Wilson (a.k.a. Rhode Wilson). Wilson had been on bad terms with a powerful white farmer, and had threatened to kill him on several occasions. One day Wilson arrived at the farm with the intention of carrying out the threats. The farmer was not home, so Wilson instead murdered the farmer's favorite slave (male).[58]

punishment than others charged with the same offense, a constitutional violation might be established."[62]

Several studies suggest that African Americans, and particularly African Americans who murdered or raped whites, were "singled out for more severe punishment" in the pre-*Furman* era.[63] Most of these studies were conducted in the South. Researchers found, for example, that African Americans indicted for murdering whites in North Carolina from 1930 to 1940 faced a disproportionately high risk of a death sentence,[64] that whites sentenced to death in nine Southern and border states during the 1920s and 1930s were less likely than African Americans to be executed,[65] and that African Americans sentenced to death in Pennsylvania were less likely than whites to have their sentences commuted to life in prison and were more likely than whites to be executed.[66]

Garfinkel's[67] study of the capital sentencing process in North Carolina during the 1930s revealed the importance of taking both the race of the offender and the race of the victim into account. Garfinkel examined three separate decisions: the

BOX 8.3 Continued

According to Radelet, cases such as this are really economic crimes in which the true victim is not the slave himself, but the slave's owner. As he noted, "Slaves are property, the wealth of someone else, and their rank should be measured accordingly." James Wilson, in other words, was sentenced to death not because he killed a slave, but because he destroyed the property of someone of higher status than himself. Similarly, the death sentences imposed on the two men who killed their own slaves were meant to discourage such brutality, which might threaten the legitimacy of the institution of slavery.

The twenty remaining cases of whites who were executed for crimes against African Americans involved one of the following:[59]

- An African American victim of higher social status than his white murderer (five cases).
- A defendant who was a marginal member of the white community—a tramp, a recent immi-

grant, or a hard drinker (four cases).
- A defendant with a long record of serious criminality (seven cases).
- Murders that were so heinous that they resulted in "an unqualified disgust and contempt for the offender unmitigated by the fact of his or the victim's race."

Based on his analysis of these thirty cases, Radelet concluded that "it was not primarily outrage over the violated rights of the black victim or the inherent value of the victim's life that led to the condemnation."[60] Rather, the thirty white men executed for crimes against African Americans were sentenced to death because the crimes threatened the institution of slavery, involved a victim of higher social status than the defendant, or involved a defendant who was a very marginal member of the community. As Radelet noted, "The data show that the criminal justice system deems the executioner's services warranted not simply for those who do something, but who also are someone."[61]

grand jury's decision to indict for first-degree murder, the prosecutor's decision to go to trial on a first-degree murder charge (in those cases in which the grand jury returned an indictment for first-degree murder), and the judge or jury's decision to convict for first-degree murder (and thus to impose the mandatory death sentence).

As shown in Figure 8.2, which summarizes the movement of death-eligible cases from one stage to the next, there were few differences based on the race of the offender. In fact, among defendants charged with first-degree murder, white offenders were more likely than African American offenders to be convicted of first-degree murder, and thus to be sentenced to death; 14 percent of the whites, but only 9 percent of the African Americans, received a death sentence.

In contrast, there were substantial differences based on the race of the victim, particularly in the decision to convict the defendant for first-degree murder. Only 5 percent of the defendants who killed African Americans were convicted of first-degree murder and sentenced to death, compared to 24 percent of the defendants who killed whites.

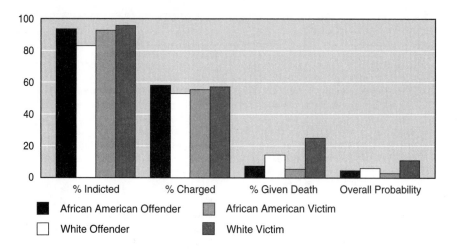

FIGURE 8.2 Death Penalty Decisions in North Carolina, by Race of Offender and Victim, 1930–1940

Data obtained from Harold Garfinkel, "Research Note on Inter- and Intra-Racial Homicides," *Social Forces* 27 (1949), Tables 2 and 3.

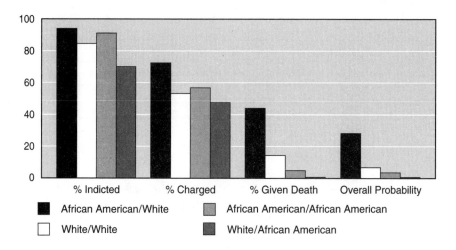

FIGURE 8.3 Death Penalty Process in North Carolina, by Race of Offender and Victim

Data obtained from Harold Garfinkel, "Research Note on Inter- and Intra-Racial Homicides," *Social Forces* 27 (1949), Tables 2 and 3.

The importance of considering both the race of the offender and the race of the victim is further illustrated by the data presented in Figure 8.3. Garfinkel's analysis revealed that African Americans who killed whites were more likely than any of the other race of offender–race of victim groups to be indicted for,

**Table 8.2 Race and the Death
Penalty for Rape in the South, 1945–1965**

	SENTENCED TO DEATH		NOT SENTENCED TO DEATH	
	N	%	*N*	%
Race of offender				
African American	110	13	713	87
White	9	2	433	98
Race of offender/victim				
African American/White	113	36	204	64
All other combinations	19	2	902	98

SOURCE: Marvin E. Wolfgang and Marc Reidel, "Race, Judicial Discretion, and the Death Penalty," *Annals of the American Academy* 407 (1973): 119–133, p. 129, Tables 1 and 2.

charged with, or convicted of first-degree murder. Again, the differences were particularly pronounced at the trial stage of the process. Among offenders charged with first-degree murder, the rate of conviction for this offense ranged from 43 percent for African Americans who killed whites, to 15 percent for whites who killed whites, to 5 percent for blacks who killed blacks, to 0 percent for whites who killed blacks. The overall probability of a death sentence (i.e., the probability that an indictment for homicide would result in a death sentence) revealed similar disparities.

The results of Garfinkel's study suggest that there were pervasive racial differences in the administration of capital punishment in North Carolina during the 1930s. Although Garfinkel did not control for the possibility that the crimes committed by African Americans and the crimes committed against whites were more serious, and thus more likely to deserve the death penalty, the magnitude of the differences "cast[s] doubt on the possibility that legally relevant factors are responsible for these differences."[68]

Studies of the use of capital punishment for the crime of rape also reveal overt and pervasive discrimination against African Americans. These studies reveal that "the death penalty for rape was largely used for punishing blacks who had raped whites."[69] One analysis of sentences for rape in Florida from 1940 through 1964, for example, revealed that 54 percent of the African Americans convicted of raping whites received the death penalty, compared to only 5 percent of the whites convicted of raping whites. Moreover, none of the eight whites convicted of raping African Americans were sentenced to death.[70]

Wolfgang and Reidel's[71] study of the imposition of the death penalty for rape in twelve Southern states from 1945 through 1965 uncovered a similar pattern. As shown in Table 8.2, they found that 13 percent of the African Americans but only 2 percent of the whites were sentenced to death. Further analysis revealed that cases in which African Americans were convicted of raping whites were eighteen times more likely to result in the death penalty than were cases with any other racial combinations.

These differences did not disappear when Wolfgang and Reidel controlled for commission of a contemporaneous felony or for other factors associated with the imposition of the death penalty. According to the authors, "All the nonracial factors in each of the states analyzed 'wash out,' that is, they have no bearing on the imposition of the death penalty in disproportionate numbers upon blacks. The only variable of statistical significance that remains is race."

Critics of the pre-*Furman* research note that most researchers did not control for the defendant's prior criminal record, the heinousness of the crime, or other predictors of sentence severity. Kleck, for example, although admitting that additional controls probably would not eliminate "the huge racial differentials in use of the death penalty" for rape, asserted that the more modest differences found for homicide might disappear if these legal factors were taken into consideration.[72]

A handful of more methodologically sophisticated studies of capital sentencing in the pre-*Furman* era control for these legally relevant factors. An analysis of death penalty decisions in Georgia, for example, found that African American defendants and defendants who murdered whites received the death penalty more often than other equally culpable defendants.[73] These results were limited, however, to borderline cases in which the appropriate sentence (life in prison or death) was not obvious.

An examination of the capital sentencing process in pre-*Furman* Texas also found significant racial effects.[74] Ralph and her colleagues controlled for legal and extralegal factors associated with sentence severity. They found that offenders who killed during a felony had a higher probability of receiving the death penalty, as did nonwhite offenders and offenders who killed whites. In fact, their analysis revealed that the race of the victim was the most important extralegal variable; those who killed whites were 25.2 percent more likely to be sentenced to death than those who killed nonwhites. The authors concluded, "Overall we found a significant race-linked bias in the death sentencing of non-Anglo-American murderers; the victim's race, along with legal factors taken together, emerged as the pivotal element in sentencing."[75]

The results of these studies, then, reveal that the Supreme Court was correct in its assumption of the potential for racial discrimination in the application of the death penalty in the pre-*Furman* era. The death penalty for rape was primarily reserved for African Americans who victimized whites. The evidence with respect to homicide, although less consistent, also suggests that African Americans, and particularly African Americans who murdered whites, were sentenced to death at a disproportionately high rate. We now turn to an examination of the capital sentencing process in the post-*Furman* period.

Post-*Furman* Studies

In *Gregg v. Georgia* the Supreme Court upheld Georgia's guided discretion death penalty statute and stated that "the concerns that prompted our decision in *Furman* are not present to any significant degree in the Georgia procedure

---

**BOX 8.4   Discrimination in the Georgia Courts:
The Case of Wilburn Dobbs**

Statistical evidence of racial disparities in the use of the death penalty,
although important, cannot illustrate
the myriad ways in which racial sentiments influence the capital sentencing process.

Consider the case of Wilburn
Dobbs, an African American on death
row in Georgia for the murder of a
white man.[78] The judge trying his case
referred to him in court as "colored"
and "colored boy," and two of the jurors who sentenced him to death admitted after trial that they used the
racial epithet "nigger." Moreover, the
court-appointed lawyer assigned to his
case, who also referred to Dobbs as
"colored," stated on the morning of
the trial that he was "not prepared to
go to trial" and that he was "in a better position to prosecute the case than
defend it." He also testified before the
federal court hearing Dobbs' appeal

that he believed that African Americans were uneducated and less intelligent than whites and admitted that
he used the word "nigger" jokingly.[79]

The federal courts that heard
Dobbs' appeals ruled that neither the
racial attitudes of the trial judge or
the defense attorney nor the racial
prejudice of the jurors required that
Dobbs' death sentence be set aside.
The Court of Appeals, for instance,
noted that although several of the jurors made statements reflecting racial
prejudice, none of them "viewed
blacks as more prone to violence than
whites or as morally inferior to
whites."[80]

The Court's reasoning in this case
led Stephen Bright to conclude that
"racial discrimination which would
not be acceptable in any other area
of American life today is tolerated in
criminal courts."[81]

---

applied here."[76] The Court, in essence, predicted that race would not affect the
capital sentencing process in Georgia or in other states with similar statutes.
Critics of the Court's ruling were less optimistic. Wolfgang and Reidel, for example, noted that the post-*Furman* statutes narrowed, but did not eliminate,
discretion. They suggested that "it is unlikely that the death penalty will be applied with greater equity when substantial discretion remains in these post-
Furman statutes.[77]

Other commentators predicted that the guided discretion statutes would
simply shift discretion, and thus the potential for discrimination, to earlier
stages in the capital sentencing process. They suggested that discretion would
be transferred to charging decisions made by the grand jury and the prosecutor. Thus, according to Bowers and Pierce, "under post-*Furman* capital statutes,
the extent of arbitrariness and discrimination, if not their distribution over
stages of the criminal justice process, might be expected to remain essentially
unchanged."

Compelling evidence supports this hypothesis. Studies conducted during
the past two decades document substantial discrimination in the application of
the death penalty under post-*Furman* statutes. In fact, a recent report by the

U.S. General Accounting Office (GAO) concluded that there was "a pattern of evidence indicating racial disparities in the charging, sentencing, and imposition of the death penalty after the *Furman* decision."[82]

The GAO evaluated the results of twenty-eight post-*Furman* empirical studies of the capital sentencing process. They found that the race of the victim had a statistically significant effect in twenty-three of the twenty-eight studies. Those who murdered whites were more likely to be charged with capital murder and to be sentenced to death than those who murdered African Americans. The authors of the report noted that the race of the victim affected decisions made at all stages of the criminal justice process. They concluded that these differences could not be explained by the defendant's prior criminal record, the heinousness of the crime, or other legally relevant variables.

With respect to the effect of the race of the defendant, the GAO report concluded that the evidence was "equivocal."[83] The report noted that about half of the studies found that the race of the defendant affected the likelihood of being charged with a capital crime or receiving the death penalty. Most, but not all, of these studies found that African Americans were more likely than whites to be sentenced to death. The authors also reported that although some studies found that African Americans who murdered whites faced the highest odds of receiving the death penalty, "the extent to which the finding was influenced by race of victim rather than race of defendant was unclear."[84]

A comprehensive review of the post-*Furman* research is beyond the scope of this book.[85] Instead we summarize the results of two studies. The first, a study of the capital sentencing process in Georgia,[86] is one of the most sophisticated studies conducted to date. It also figured prominently in the Supreme Court's decision in *McCleskey v. Kemp.* The second is a study of capital sentencing patterns in eight states.[87]

Race and the Death Penalty in Georgia David Baldus and his colleagues analyzed the effect of race on the outcomes of more than 600 homicide cases in Georgia from 1973 through 1979.[88] Their examination of the raw data revealed that the likelihood of receiving a death sentence varied by the race of both the offender and the victim. As shown in the first column of Table 8.3, 35 percent of the African Americans charged with killing whites were sentenced to death, compared to only 22 percent of the whites who killed whites, 14 percent of the whites who killed African Americans, and 6 percent of the African Americans who killed other African Americans.

Baldus and his co-authors also discovered that the race of the victim played an important role in both the prosecutor's decision to seek the death penalty and the jury's decision to impose the death penalty (see second and third columns, Table 8.3). The victim's race was a particularly strong predictor of the prosecutor's decision to seek or waive the death penalty. In fact, Georgia prosecutors were nearly four times more likely to request the death penalty for African American offenders convicted of killing whites than for African American offenders convicted of killing African Americans. The effect of the race of the victim was less pronounced when the offender was white: Prosecutors sought the

Table 8.3 Death Penalty Decisions in Post-*Furman* Georgia

	Overall Death-Sentencing Rate	Prosecutor's Decision to Seek Death Penalty	Jury's Decision to Impose Death Penalty
Offender and Victim Race			
Black/White	.35 (45/130)	.58 (72/125)	.58 (45/77)
White/White	.22 (51/230)	.38 (85/224)	.56 (51/91)
Black/Black	.06 (17/232)	.15 (34/231)	.40 (14/35)
White/Black	.14 (2/14)	.21 (3/14)	.67 (2/3)

SOURCE: David C. Baldus, George G. Woodworth, and Charles A. Pulaski, Jr., *Equal Justice and the Death Penalty* (Boston: Northeastern University Press, 1990), Tables 30 and 34.

death penalty in 38 percent of the cases with white offenders and white victims, but only 21 percent of the cases with white offenders and black victims.

The authors of this study then controlled for more than 200 variables that might explain these disparities; they included detailed information on the defendant's background and prior criminal record, information concerning the circumstances and the heinousness of the crime, and measures of the strength of evidence against the defendant. They found that inclusion of these controls did not eliminate the racial differences. The race of the offender was only a weak predictor of death penalty decisions once these legal factors were taken into consideration. However, the race of the victim continued to exert a strong effect on both the prosecutor's decision to seek the death penalty and the jury's decision to impose the death penalty. In fact, those who killed whites were more than four times as likely to be sentenced to death as those who killed African Americans.

Further analysis revealed that the effects of race were not uniform across the range of homicide cases included in the analysis. Not surprisingly, race had little effect on decision making in the least aggravated cases, in which virtually no one received the death penalty, or in the most heinous cases, in which a high percentage of murderers, regardless of their race or the race of their victims, were sentenced to death. Rather, race played a role primarily in the midrange of cases in which decision makers could decide either to sentence the offender to life in prison or impose the death penalty. In these types of cases, the death-sentencing rate for those who killed whites was 34 percent, compared to only 14 percent for those who killed African Americans.

These findings led Baldus and his colleagues to conclude that the race of the victim was "a potent influence in the system"[89] and that the state of Georgia was operating a "dual system" for processing homicide cases. According to the authors, "Georgia juries appear to tolerate greater levels of aggravation without imposing the death penalty in black victim cases; and, as compared to white victim cases, the level of aggravation in black victim cases must be substantially greater before the prosecutor will even seek a death sentence."[90]

% sentenced to death

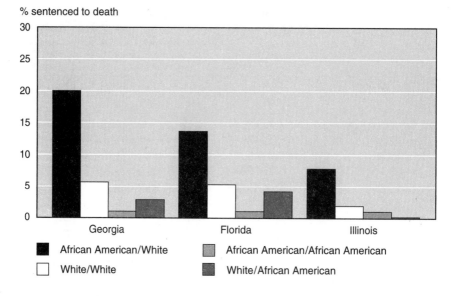

FIGURE 8.4 Death Sentence Rates in Post-*Furman* Era, by Race of Offender and Victim

Data obtained from Samuel R. Gross and Robert Mauro, *Death and Discrimination: Racial Disparities in Capital Sentencing* (Boston: Northeastern University Press, 1989).

Anthony Amsterdam's[91] analysis was even more blunt. Noting that nine of the eleven murderers executed by Georgia between 1973 and 1988 were black and that ten of the eleven had white victims, Amsterdam asked, "Can there be the slightest doubt that this revolting record is the product of some sort of racial bias rather than a pure fluke?"[92]

Some commentators would be inclined to answer this question in the affirmative. They would argue that the statistics included in the Baldus study are not representative of death penalty decisions in the United States as a whole, but rather are peculiar to Southern states like Georgia, Florida, and Mississippi. A recent study by Gross and Mauro addressed this possibility. The authors examined death penalty decisions in eight states: Arkansas, Florida, Georgia, Illinois, Mississippi, North Carolina, Oklahoma, and Virginia.

Death Penalty Decisions in Eight States Gross and Mauro found that the risk of a death sentence was much lower for defendants charged with killing African Americans than for defendants charged with killing whites in each of the eight states included in their study. In Georgia, for example, those who killed whites were nearly ten times as likely to be sentenced to death as those who killed African Americans. The ratios for the other states included in the study were ten to one (Mississippi), eight to one (Florida), seven to one (Arkansas), six to one (Illinois, Oklahoma, and North Carolina), and five to one (Virginia).

The authors also discovered that African Americans who killed whites faced the greatest odds of a death sentence. Figure 8.4 presents the percentages of death sentences by race of suspect and race of victim for the three states with the largest number of death-eligible cases. In Georgia, 20.1 percent of the African Americans who killed whites were sentenced to death, compared to only 5.7 percent of the whites who killed whites, 2.9 percent of the whites who killed African Americans, and less than 1 percent (0.8 percent) of the African Americans who killed African Americans. There were similar disparities in Florida and Illinois. In fact, in these three states, only 32 of the 4,731 cases with African American defendants and African American victims resulted in a death sentence, compared to 82 of the 621 cases involving African American defendants and white victims.

These racial disparities did not disappear when Gross and Mauro controlled for other legally relevant predictors of sentence severity. According to the authors,

> The major factual finding of this study is simple: there has been racial discrimination in the imposition of the death penalty under post-*Furman* statutes in the eight states that we examined. The discrimination is based on the race of the victim, and it is a remarkably stable and consistent phenomenon . . . The data show "a clear pattern, unexplainable on grounds other than race."[93]

Explanations for Disparate Treatment

Researchers have advanced two interrelated explanations for the higher death penalty rates for homicides involving African American offenders and white victims and the lower rates for homicides involving African American offenders and African American victims.

The first explanation builds on conflict theory's premise that the law is applied to maintain the power of the dominant group and to control the behavior of individuals who threaten that power.[94] It suggests that crimes involving African American offenders and white victims are punished most harshly because they pose the greatest threat to "the system of racially stratified state authority."[95] Some commentators further suggest that in the South the death penalty may be imposed more often on African Americans who kill whites "because of a continuing adherence to traditional southern norms of racial etiquette."[96]

The second explanation for the harsher penalties imposed on those who victimize whites emphasizes the race of the victim rather than the racial composition of the victim-offender dyad. This explanation suggests that crimes involving African American victims are not taken seriously and that crimes involving white victims are taken very seriously. It also suggests that the lives of African American victims are devalued relative to the lives of white victims. Thus, crimes against whites are punished more severely than crimes against African Americans regardless of the offender's race.

Focus on an Issue

The Death Penalty and Wrongful Convictions

Opponents of the death penalty consistently note the possibility that an individual will be sentenced to death for a crime that he or she did not commit. Bedau and Radelet[102] identified 350 cases in which defendants were wrongfully convicted of a homicide for which they could have received the death penalty or of a rape in which the death penalty was imposed. One hundred thirty-nine of these individuals were sentenced to die; twenty-three eventually were executed. Another twenty-two persons came within seventy-two hours of being executed.

These wrongful convictions include a number of persons sentenced to death in the post-*Furman* era. In 1987, for example, Walter McMillian, an African American man who was dating a white woman, was charged with the death of an eighteen-year-old white female store clerk in Alabama. In spite of testimony from a dozen witnesses, who swore he was at home on the day of the murder, and despite the lack of any physical evidence, McMillian was convicted after a one-and-a-half-day trial. His conviction hinged on the testimony of Ralph Myers, a thirty-year-old with a long criminal record. The jury recommended life in prison without parole, but the judge hearing the case, citing the "vicious and brutal killing of a young lady in the full flower of adulthood,"[103] sentenced McMillian to death.

Six years later, Myers recanted his testimony. He said he had been pressured by law enforcement officials to accuse McMillian and to testify against him in court. McMillian was freed in March 1993, after prosecutors conceded that his conviction was based on perjured testimony and that evidence had been withheld from his lawyers. He had

spent six years on death row for a crime he did not commit.

A similar fate awaited Rolando Cruz, a Hispanic American who, along with co-defendant Alejandro Hernandez, was convicted of the 1983 kidnapping, rape, and murder of ten-year-old Jeanine Nicarico in DuPage County (Illinois) Circuit Court. Cruz was twice convicted and condemned to death for the crime, but both verdicts were overturned by appellate courts because of procedural errors at trial. He spent nearly ten years on death row before he was acquitted at a third trial in November 1995. Hernandez also was convicted twice and sentenced to death once before his case was dropped following the acquittal of Cruz.[104]

This case attracted national attention for what many believed was the "railroading" of Cruz and Hernandez. Prosecutors presented no physical evidence or eyewitness testimony linking the two to the crime, but relied almost exclusively on the testimony of jailhouse informants who stated that the defendants had admitted the crime and on questionable testimony regarding a dream about the crime that Cruz allegedly described to sheriff's deputies. They also ignored compelling evidence that another man, Brian Dugan, had committed the crime. According to one commentator, "The crime had been 'solved' by cobbling together a shabby case against Rolando Cruz and Alex Hernandez of Aurora and presenting it to a jury that convicted them and sent them to Death Row."[105]

On November 3, 1995, Judge Ronald Mehling, who was presiding at Cruz's third trial, acquitted Cruz of the charges. In a strongly worded address from the bench, Mehling stated that the murder investigation was "sloppy" and that the government's case against Cruz was "riddled with lies and mistakes." He also sharply criticized prosecutors for their handling of the "vision statement" and suggested that investigators had lied about the statement and about other evidence. "What troubles me in this case," Mehling said, "is what the evidence does not show."[106] Cruz was set free that day; Hernandez was released several weeks later.

One year later, a grand jury handed down a forty-seven-count indictment against three of the prosecutors and four of the sheriff's deputies involved in the case. The indictment charged the deputies with repeated acts of perjury and alleged that prosecutors knowingly presented perjured testimony and buried the notes of an interview with Dugan that could have exonerated Cruz. The seven men were scheduled to be tried in early 1999.[107]

Most researchers have failed to explain adequately why those who victimize whites are treated more harshly than those who victimize African Americans. Gross and Mauro[97] suggested that the explanation, at least in capital cases, may hinge on the degree to which jurors are able to identify with the victim. The authors argued that jurors take the life-or-death decision in a capital case very seriously. To condemn a murderer to death thus requires something more than sympathy for the victim. Jurors will not sentence a defendant to death unless they are particularly horrified by the crime, and they will not be particularly horrified by the crime unless they can identify or empathize with the victim. According to Gross and Mauro:

> In a society that remains segregated socially if not legally, and in which the great majority of jurors are white, jurors are not likely to identify with black victims or to see them as family or friends. Thus jurors are more likely to be horrified by the killing of a white than of a black, and more likely to act against the killer of a white than the killer of a black.[98]

Bright[99] offered a somewhat different explanation, contending that the unconscious racism and racial stereotypes of prosecutors, judges, and jurors, the majority of whom are white, "may well be 'stirred up'" in cases involving an African American offender and a white victim.[100] In these types of cases, in other words, officials' and jurors' beliefs that African Americans are violent or morally inferior, coupled with their fear of African Americans, might incline them to seek or to impose the death penalty. Bright also asserted that black-on-white murders generate more publicity and evoke greater horror than other types of crimes. As he noted, "Community outrage ... the social and political clout of the family in the community, and the amount of publicity regarding the crime are often far more important in determining whether death is sought than the facts of the crime or the defendant's record and background."[101]

McCLESKEY V. KEMP: THE SUPREME COURT AND RACIAL DISCRIMINATION IN THE APPLICATION OF THE DEATH PENALTY

Empirical evidence of racial discrimination in the capital sentencing process has been used to mount constitutional challenges to the imposition of the death penalty. African American defendants convicted of raping or murdering whites have claimed that the death penalty is applied in a racially discriminatory manner in violation of both the equal protection clause of the Fourteenth Amendment and the cruel and unusual punishment clause of the Eighth Amendment.

These claims have been consistently rejected by state and federal appellate courts. The case of the Martinsville Seven, a group of African American men who were sentenced to death for the gang rape of a white woman, was the first case in which defendants explicitly argued that the death penalty was administered in a racially discriminatory manner.[108] It also was the first case in which lawyers presented statistical evidence to prove systematic racial discrimination in capital cases. As explained in more detail in the Focus on an Issue: The Case of the Martinsville Seven, the defendants' contention that the Virginia rape statute had "been applied and administered with an evil eye and an unequal hand"[109] was repeatedly denied by Virginia appellate courts.

The question of racial discrimination in the application of the death penalty also has been addressed in federal court. In a series of decisions, the Courts of Appeals ruled, first, that the empirical studies used to document systematic racial discrimination did not take every variable related to capital sentencing into account and, second, that the evidence presented did not demonstrate that the appellant's own sentence was the product of discrimination.[121]

The Supreme Court directly addressed the issue of victim-based racial discrimination in the application of the death penalty in the case of McCleskey v. Kemp.[122] Warren McCleskey, an African American, was convicted and sentenced to death in Georgia for killing a white police officer during the course of an armed robbery. McCleskey claimed that the Georgia capital sentencing process was administered in a racially discriminatory manner. In support of his claim, he offered the results of the study conducted by Baldus and his colleagues.[123] As noted earlier, this study found that African Americans convicted of murdering whites had the greatest likelihood of receiving the death penalty.

The Supreme Court rejected McCleskey's Fourteenth and Eighth Amendment claims. Although the majority accepted the validity of the Baldus study, they nonetheless refused to accept McCleskey's argument that the disparities documented by Baldus signaled the presence of unconstitutional racial discrimination. Justice Powell, writing for the majority, argued that the disparities were "unexplained" and stated that "At most, the Baldus study indicates a discrepancy that appears to correlate with race."[124] The Court stated that the Baldus study was "clearly insufficient to support an inference that any of the decisionmakers in McCleskey's case acted with discriminatory purpose."[125]

Focus on an Issue
The Case of the Martinsville Seven

Just after dark on January 8, 1949, Ruby Floyd, a thirty-two-year-old white woman, was assaulted and repeatedly raped by several men as she walked in a predominately black neighborhood in Martinsville, Virginia.[110] Within a day and a half, seven African American men had been arrested; when confronted with incriminating statements made by their co-defendants, all of them confessed. Two months later, a grand jury composed of four white men and three African American men indicted each defendant on one count of rape and six counts of aiding and abetting a rape by the other defendants.

The defendants were tried in the Seventh Judicial Circuit Court, located in Martinsville. Before the legal proceedings began, Judge Kennon Caithness Whittle, who presided over all of the trials, called the prosecutors and defense attorneys into his chambers to remind them of their duty to protect the defendants' right to a fair trial and to plead with them to "downplay the racial overtones" of the case. He emphasized that the case "must be tried as though both parties were members of the same race."[111]

Although prosecutors took Judge Whittle's admonitions to heart and emphasized the seriousness of the crime and the defendants' evident guilt rather than the fact that the crime involved the rape of a white woman by black men, the "racial overtones" of the case inevitably surfaced. Defense attorneys, for example, moved for a change of venue, arguing that inflammatory publicity about the case, coupled with widespread community sentiment that the defendants were guilty and "ought to get the works,"[112] meant that the defendants could not get a fair trial in Martinsville. Judge Whittle, who admitted that it might be difficult to find impartial jurors and acknowledged that some jurors might be biased against the defendants because of their race, denied the motion, asserting that "no mass feeling about these defendants"[113] had surfaced. Later, prosecutors used their peremptory challenges to exclude the few African Americans who remained in the jury pool after those who opposed the death penalty had been excused for cause. As a result, each case was decided by an all-white jury. The result of each day-long trial was the same: All seven defendants were found guilty of rape and sentenced to death. On May 3, 1949, less than four months after the assault on Ruby Floyd, Judge Whittle officially pronounced sentence and announced that four of the defendants were to be executed on July 15, the remaining three on July 22. Noting that this gave the defendants more than sixty days to appeal, he stated, "If errors have been made I pray God they may be corrected."[114]

The next nineteen months witnessed several rounds of appeals challenging the convictions and death sentences of the Martinsville Seven. The initial petition submitted by attorneys for the NAACP Legal Defense Fund, which represented the defendants on appeal, charged the trial court with four violations of due process. Although none of the charges focused directly on racially discriminatory practices, allegations of racial prejudice were interwoven with a number of the arguments. Appellants noted, for example, that prior to 1866, Virginia law specified that the death penalty for rape could be imposed only on black men convicted of raping white women and that even after the law was repealed virtually all of those sentenced to death for rape had been black. They also stated that the trial judge's questioning of prospective jurors about capital punishment and subsequent exclusion of those who were opposed to the imposition of the death penalty sent the unmistakable message that "only one penalty would be appropriate for the offenders."[115]

These appeals failed at both the state and federal level. The Virginia Supreme Court of Appeals voted unanimously to affirm the convictions. Chief Justice Edward W. Hudgins, who wrote the opinion, vehemently denied appellants' assertions that the death penalty was reserved for blacks, noting that there was not "a scintilla of evidence" to support it.[116] Hudgins also chastised the defendants' attorneys for even raising the issue, contending that it was nothing more than "an abortive attempt to inject into the proceedings racial prejudice."[117]

The defendants appealed the decision to the U.S. Supreme Court, but the Court declined to review the case. This prompted the NAACP attorneys to adopt a radically different strategy for the next round of appeals. Rather than challenging the defendants' convictions and death sentences on traditional due process grounds, the attorneys mounted a direct attack on the discriminatory application of the death penalty in Virginia. Martin Martin and Samuel Tucker, the NAACP attorneys who argued in support of the defendants' *habeas corpus* petition, presented statistical evidence documenting a double standard of justice in Virginia rape cases. Noting that forty-five blacks, but not a

single white, had been executed for rape since 1908, Tucker stated that blacks were entitled to the same protection of the law as whites and concluded "if you can't equalize upward [by executing more whites], we must equalize downward."[118]

In an opinion that foreshadowed the Supreme Court's decision in *McCleskey v. Kemp* a quarter of a century later, Judge Doubles, who was presiding over the Hustings Court of the City of Richmond, denied the petition. Judge Doubles stated, first, that there was no evidence of racial discrimination in the actions of the six juries that sentenced the Martinsville Seven to death or in the performance of other juries in similar cases. He then concluded that even if one assumed that those juries had been motivated by racial prejudice, "the petitioners could not demonstrate that an official policy of discrimination, rather than the independent actions of separate juries, resulted in the death verdicts."[119] As a result, there was no Constitutional violation.

The case then was appealed to the Virginia Supreme Court and, when that appeal failed, to the U.S. Supreme Court. In January 1951, the Supreme Court again declined to review the case. Last-minute efforts to save the Martinsville Seven failed. Four of the men were executed on February 2, the remaining three on February 5. "After two years, six trials, five stays of execution, ten opportunities for judicial review, and two denials of executive clemency, the legal odyssey of the Martinsville Seven had ended."[120]

The Court also expressed its concern that accepting McCleskey's claim would open a Pandora's box of litigation. "McCleskey's claim, taken to its logical conclusion," Powell wrote, "throws into serious question the principles that underlie our entire criminal justice system . . . if we accepted McCleskey's claim that racial bias impermissibly tainted the capital sentencing decision, we would soon be faced with similar claims as to other types of penalty."[126] A ruling in McCleskey's favor, in other words, would open the door to constitutional challenges to the legitimacy, not only of the capital sentencing process, but of sentencing in general.

The four dissenting justices were outraged. Justice Brennan, who was joined in dissent by Justices Blackmun, Marshall, and Stevens, wrote, "The Court today holds that Warren McCleskey's sentence was constitutionally imposed. It finds no fault with a system in which lawyers must tell their clients that race casts a large shadow on the capital sentencing process." Brennan also characterized the majority's concern that upholding McCleskey's claim would encourage other groups—"even women"[127]—to challenge the criminal sentencing process "as a fear of too much justice" and "a complete abdication of our judicial role."[128]

Legal scholars were similarly outraged. Anthony Amsterdam, who was the lead attorney in a 1968 U.S. Court of Appeals case in which an African American man challenged his death sentence for the rape of a white woman,[129] wrote:

> I suggest that any self-respecting criminal justice professional is obliged to speak out against this Supreme Court's conception of the criminal justice system. We must reaffirm that there can be no justice in a system which treats people of color differently from white people, or treats crimes against people of color differently from crimes against white people."[130]

Randall Kennedy's analysis was similarly harsh. He challenged Justice Powell's assertion that the Baldus study indicated nothing more "than a discrepancy that appears to correlate with race," which he characterized as "a statement as vacuous as one declaring, say, that 'at most' studies on lung cancer indicate a discrepancy that appears to correlate with smoking."[131] Bright characterized the decision as "a badge of shame upon America's system of justice,"[132] and Gross and Mauro concluded that, "The central message of the *McCleskey* case is all too plain; de facto racial discrimination in capital sentencing is legal in the United States."[133]

The Execution of Warren McCleskey

The Court's decision in *McCleskey v. Kemp* did not mark the end of Warren McCleskey's odyssey through the appellate courts. He filed another appeal in 1987, alleging that the testimony of a jailhouse informant, which was used to rebut his alibi defense, was obtained illegally. Offie Evans testified at McCleskey's trial in 1978 that McCleskey admitted to and boasted about killing the police officer. McCleskey argued that the state placed Evans in the jail cell next to his and instructed Evans to try to get him to talk about the crime. He contended that because he did not have the assistance of counsel at the time he made the incriminating statements, they could not be used against him.

In 1991 the Supreme Court denied McCleskey's claim, asserting that the issue should have been raised in his first appeal.[134] The Court stated that McCleskey would have been allowed to raise a new issue if he had been able to demonstrate that the alleged violation resulted in the conviction of an innocent person. However, according to the Court, "the violation, if it be one, resulted in the admission at trial of truthful inculpatory evidence which did not affect the reliability of the guilt determination. The very statement that McCleskey now embraces confirms his guilt."[135]

After a series of last-minute appeals, requests for clemency, and requests for commutation were denied, Warren McCleskey was strapped into the electric chair at the state prison in Jacksonville, Georgia. He was pronounced dead at 3:13 A.M., September 26, 1991.

Justice Thurgood Marshall, one of three dissenters from the Supreme Court's decision not to grant a stay of execution, wrote, "In refusing to grant a stay to review fully McCleskey's claims, the court values expediency over human life. Repeatedly denying Warren McCleskey his constitutional rights is unacceptable. Executing him is inexcusable."[136]

The Aftermath of *McCleskey*

Opponents of the death penalty viewed the issues raised in *McCleskey v. Kemp* as the only remaining challenge to the constitutionality of the death penalty. They predicted that the Court's decision, which effectively closed the door to similar appeals, would speed up the pace of executions. Data on the number of persons executed since 1987 provide support for this. Although only twenty-five persons were executed in 1987, eleven in 1988, sixteen in 1989, twenty-three in 1990, and fourteen in 1991, the numbers began to increase in 1992. Thirty-one persons were put to death in 1992, thirty-three in 1993, thirty-one in 1994, fifty-six in 1995, and forty-five in 1996.

The increase in executions since 1991 no doubt reflects the impact of two recent Supreme Court decisions sharply limiting death row appeals. As noted earlier, in 1991 the Court ruled that, with few exceptions, death row inmates and other state prisoners must raise constitutional claims on their first appeals.[137] This ruling, coupled with a 1993 decision stating that "late claims of innocence" raised by death row inmates who have exhausted other federal appeals do not automatically qualify for a hearing in federal court,[138] severely curtailed the ability of death row inmates to pursue multiple federal court appeals.

The U.S. House of Representatives responded to the Supreme Court's ruling in *McCleskey v. Kemp* by adding the Racial Justice Act to the Omnibus Crime Bill of 1994. A slim majority of the House voted for the provision, which would have allowed condemned defendants to challenge their death sentences by showing a pattern of racial discrimination in the capital sentencing process in their jurisdictions.

Thus, under this provision the defendant would not have to show that criminal justice officials acted with discriminatory purpose in his or her case. Rather, the defendant could use statistical evidence indicating that a disproportionate number of those sentenced to death in the jurisdiction were African Americans or had killed whites. Once this pattern of racial discrimination had

BOX 8.5 Racial Discrimination in Capital Sentencing: The Problem of Remedy

A number of commentators have suggested that the Court's reluctance to accept McCleskey's claim reflected its anxiety about the practical consequences of ruling that race impermissibly affected the capital sentencing process.[140] The Court's decision, in other words, reflected its concern about the appropriate remedy if it found a constitutional violation.

The remedies that have been suggested include the following:

1. Abolish the death penalty and vacate all existing death sentences nationwide. The problem with this remedy, of course, is that it is impractical, given the level of public support for the death penalty and the current emphasis on crime control. As Gross and Mauro noted, "Although abolition is a perfectly practical solution to the problems of capital punishment . . . it is not a serious option in America now."[141]

2. Vacate all death sentences in each state where there is compelling evidence of racial disparities in the application of the death penalty. Although this state-by-state approach would not completely satisfy the abolitionists, according to Kennedy, it would place "a large question mark over the legitimacy of any death penalty system generating unexplained racial disparities of the sort at issue in *McCleskey*."[142]

3. Limit the class of persons eligible for the death penalty to those who commit the most heinous and the most aggravated homicides. As Justice Stevens suggested in his dissent in *McCleskey*, the Court could narrow the class of death-eligible defendants to those "categories of extremely serious crimes for which prosecutors consistently seek, and juries consistently impose, the death penalty without regard to the race of the victim or the race of the offender."[143] Although not an ideal solution for a number of reasons, this would, as Baldus and his colleagues contended, impart "a greater degree of rationality and consistency into state death-sentencing systems than any of the other procedural safeguards that the Supreme Court has heretofore endorsed."[144]

4. Reinstate mandatory death sentences for certain crimes. This remedy would, of course, require the Supreme Court to retract its invalidation of mandatory death penalty statutes. Kennedy contended that this would not solve the problem, as prosecutors could refuse to charge the killers of African Americans with a capital crime and juries could decline to convict those who killed African Americans of crimes that triggered the mandatory death sentence.[145]

5. Opt for the "level-up solution,"[146] which would require courts to purposely impose more death sentences on those who murdered African Americans. According to Kennedy, states in which there are documented racial disparities in the use of the death penalty could be given a choice: Either condemn those who kill African Americans to death at the same rate as those who kill whites or "relinquish the power to put anyone to death."[147]

been established, the state would be required to prove that its death penalty decisions were racially neutral. The state might rebut an apparent pattern of racial discrimination in a case involving an African American convicted of killing a white police officer, for example, by showing a consistent pattern of seeking the death penalty for defendants, regardless of race, who were accused of killing police officers.

Opponents of the Racial Justice Act argued that it would effectively abolish the death penalty in the United States. As Senator Orrin Hatch remarked, "The so-called Racial Justice Act has nothing to do with racial justice and everything to do with abolishing the death penalty."[139] The provision was a source of heated debate before it was eventually eliminated from the 1994 Omnibus Crime Bill.

CONCLUSION

The findings of research examining the effect of race on the capital sentencing process are consistent. Study after study has demonstrated that those who murder whites are much more likely to be sentenced to death than those who murder African Americans. Many of these studies also have shown that African Americans convicted of murdering whites receive the death penalty more often than whites who murder other whites.

These results suggest that racial disparities in the application of the death penalty reflect racial discrimination. Some might argue that these results signal contextual, rather than systematic, racial discrimination. As noted earlier, although research consistently has revealed that those who murder whites are sentenced to death at a disproportionately high rate, not all studies have found that African American offenders are more likely than white offenders to be sentenced to death.

We contend that the type of discrimination found in the capital sentencing process falls closer to the systematic end of the discrimination continuum presented in Chapter 1. Racial discrimination in the capital sentencing process is not limited to the South, where historical evidence of racial bias would lead one to expect differential treatment, but is applicable to other regions of the country as well. It is not confined to one stage of the decision-making process, but affects decisions made by prosecutors as well as juries. It also is not confined to the pre-*Furman* period, when statutes offered little or no guidance to judges and juries charged with deciding whether to impose the death penalty or not, but is found, too, under the more restrictive guided discretion statutes enacted since *Furman*. Moreover, this effect does not disappear when legally relevant predictors of sentence severity are taken into consideration.

With respect to the capital sentencing process, then, empirical studies suggest that the Supreme Court was overly optimistic in predicting that the statutory reforms adopted since *Furman* would eliminate racial discrimination. To the contrary, these studies document "a clear pattern unexplainable on grounds other than race."[148]

DISCUSSION QUESTIONS

1. Do you agree or disagree with the so-called "Marshall Hypothesis"—that is, that the average citizen who knew "all the facts presently available regarding capital punishment would . . . find it shocking to his conscience and sense of justice?"

2. In *Gregg v. Georgia*, the Supreme Court assumed that racial discrimination would not be a problem under the guided discretion statutes enacted in the wake of the *Furman* decision. Does the empirical evidence support or refute this assumption?

3. Explain why Michael Radelet believes that the handful of executions of whites for crimes against African Americans are not really "exceptions to the rule."

4. In the case of the Martinsville Seven a series of state and federal court rulings rejected the defendants' allegations regarding racial discrimination in the application of the death penalty; Judge Doubles, for instance, ruled that there was no evidence of racial discrimination in the actions of the six juries that sentenced the seven men to death. In *McCleskey v. Kemp*, the U.S. Supreme Court ruled that there was insufficient evidence "to support an inference that any of the decisionmakers in McCleskey's case acted with discriminatory purpose." Assume that you are the lawyer representing an African American offender who has been sentenced to death. What types of evidence would you need to convince the appellate courts that decision makers in your client's case had "acted with discriminatory purpose"? Is it realistic to assume that any offender can meet this burden of proof?

5. Consider the five remedies for racial discrimination in capital sentencing (see Box 8.5). Which do you believe is the appropriate remedy? Why?

6. Do you agree or disagree with our conclusion that "the type of discrimination found in the capital sentencing process falls closer to the systematic end of the discrimination continuum presented in Chapter 1"? Why?

NOTES

1. Blackmun dissented from the order, *Callins v. Collins*, No. 93–7054.

2. Clyde E. Murphy, "Racial Discrimination in the Criminal Justice System," *North Carolina Central Law Journal* 17 (1988): 171–190.

3. *McCleskey v. Kemp*, 481 U.S. 279 (1987).

4. *In re Kemmler*, 136 U.S. 436, 447 (1890).

5. *Trop v. Dulles*, 356 U.S. 86, 99 (1958).

6. *Furman v. Georgia*, 408 U.S. 238 (1972).

7. Ibid., at 257 (Douglas, J., concurring); at 310 (Stewart, J., concurring); at 313 (White, J., concurring).

8. Ibid., at 257 (Marshall, J., concurring).

9. Ibid., at 310 (Stewart, J., concurring).

10. Samuel R. Gross and Robert Mauro, *Death & Discrimination: Racial Disparities in Capital Sentencing* (Boston: Northeastern University Press, 1989), p. 215.

11. *Woodson v. North Carolina,* 428 U.S. 280 (1976); *Roberts v. Louisiana,* 428 U.S. 325 (1976).

12. *Woodson v. North Carolina,* 428 U.S. (1976) at 303.

13. Ibid., at 305.

14. *Gregg v. Georgia,* 428 U.S. 153 (1976); *Proffitt v. Florida,* 428 U.S. 242 (1976); *Jurek v. Texas,* 428 U.S. 262 (1976).

15. *Gregg v. Georgia,* 428 U.S. 153 (1976).

16. Ibid., at 206–207.

17. Georgia Code Ann., §27–2534.1 (Supp. 1975).

18. *Coker v. Georgia,* 433 U.S. 584, 592 (1977).

19. *Tison v. Arizona,* 107 S.Ct. 1676 (1987).

20. *Penry v. Lynaugh,* 109 S.Ct. 2934 (1989).

21. *Stanford v. Kentucky,* 109 S.Ct. 1969 (1989).

22. National Opinion Research Center, *General Social Surveys, 1972–94, General Social Surveys, 1996* (Storrs, CT: The Roper Center for Public Opinion Research, University of Connecticut, 1997).

23. *Furman v. Georgia,* 408 U.S. 238 (1972), at 365–366 (Marshall, J., concurring).

24. Raymond Paternoster, *Capital Punishment in America* (New York: Lexington Books, 1991), p. 72.

25. *Furman v. Georgia,* 408 U.S. 238 (1972), at 369 (Marshall, J., concurring).

26. See, for example, Robert M. Bohm, "American Death Penalty Opinion, 1936–1986: A Critical Examination of the Gallup Polls," in *The Death Penalty in America: Current Research,* ed. Robert M. Bohm (Cincinnati, OH: Anderson, 1991); William Bowers, "Capital Punishment and Contemporary Values: People's Misgivings and the Court's Misperceptions," *Law & Society Review* 27 (1993): 157–175; James Alan Fox, Michael L. Radelet, and Julie L. Bonsteel, "Death Penalty Opinion in the Post-*Furman* Years," *New York University Review of Law and Social Change* 18 (1990–91): 499–528; Philip W. Harris, "Over-Simplification and Error in Public Opinion Surveys on Capital Punishment," *Justice Quarterly* 3 (1986): 429–455; Austin Sarat and Neil Vidmar, "Public Opinion, the

Death Penalty, and the Eighth Amendment: Testing the Marshall Hypothesis," in *Capital Punishment in the United States,* eds. Hugo A. Bedau and Chester M. Pierce (New York: AMS, 1976).

27. Bowers, "Capital Punishment and Contemporary Values," p. 162.

28. Ibid.

29. Ibid., p. 172.

30. Louis Harris and Associates, Inc., *The Harris Poll* (Los Angeles: Creators Syndicate, June 11, 1997), p. 3.

31. Tom W. Smith, "A Trend Analysis of Attitudes Toward Capital Punishment, 1936–1974," in *Studies of Social Change Since 1948: Vol. 2,* ed. James E. Davis (Chicago: National Opinion Research Center, 1975), pp. 257–318.

32. Steven E. Barkan and Steven F. Cohn, "Racial Prejudice and Support for the Death Penalty by Whites," *Journal of Research in Crime and Delinquency* 31 (1994): 202–209; Robert L. Young, "Race, Conceptions of Crime and Justice, and Support for the Death Penalty," *Social Psychological Quarterly* 54 (1991): 67–75.

33. Barkan and Cohn, "Racial Prejudice and Support for the Death Penalty by Whites."

34. Ibid., p. 206.

35. Ibid., p. 207.

36. Stephen B. Bright, "Discrimination, Death and Denial: The Tolerance of Racial Discrimination in Infliction of the Death Penalty," *Santa Clara Law Review* 35 (1995): 901–950.

37. *Gregg v. Georgia,* 428 U.S. 207 (1976).

38. U.S. Department of Justice, Bureau of Justice Statistics, *Capital Punishment 1996* (Washington, D.C.: U.S. Government Printing Office, 1997), p. 6.

39. Ibid.

40. U.S. Department of Justice, Bureau of Justice Statistics, *Correctional Populations in the United States, 1995* (Washington, D.C.: U.S. Department of Justice, 1997).

41. Bureau of Justice Statistics, *Capital Punishment 1996,* p. 11.

42. NAACP Legal Defense and Educational Fund, *Death Row, USA* (New York, NY: 1997).

43. Bureau of Justice Statistics, *Capital Punishment 1991* (Washington, D.C.: U.S. Government Printing Office, 1992), p. 8.

44. Marvin E. Wolfgang and Marc Riedel, "Race, Judicial Discretion, and the Death Penalty," *The Annals of the American Academy of Political and Social Science* 407 (1973): 123.

45. Elmer H. Johnson, "Selective Factors in Capital Punishment," *Social Forces* 36 (1957): 165.

46. Marvin E. Wolfgang, Arlene Kelly, and Hans C. Nolde, "Comparisons of the Executed and the Commuted Among Admissions to Death Row," *Journal of Criminal Law, Criminology, and Police Science* 53 (1962): 301.

47. Gary Kleck, "Racial Discrimination in Criminal Sentencing: A Critical Evaluation of the Evidence With Additional Evidence on the Death Penalty" *American Sociological Review* 46 (1981): 793.

48. For example, according to Raymond Fosdick, who studied U.S. police departments shortly before the country's entry into World War I, Southern police departments had three classes of homicide. One official told Fosdick, "If a nigger kills a white man, that's murder. If a white man kills a nigger, that's justifiable homicide. If a nigger kills another nigger, that's one less nigger." See Raymond Fosdick, *American Police Systems* (Montclair, NJ: Patterson Smith Reprint Series, 1972), p. 45. (Originally published in 1920.)

49. Kleck, "Racial Discrimination in Criminal Sentencing," p. 793.

50. Ibid.

51. Ibid., p. 796.

52. Ibid., p. 798.

53. Guy Johnson, "The Negro and Crime," *Annals of the American Academy* 217 (1941): 98.

54. Michael L. Radelet, "Executions of Whites for Crimes Against Blacks: Exceptions to the Rule?" *The Sociological Quarterly* 30 (1989): 535.

55. Ibid., p. 531. Radelet noted that the best source of information on executions is the archive developed by Watt Espy. Espy has obtained information on 15,978 executions carried out in U.S. jurisdictions since 1608.

56. Ibid., p. 533.

57. Ibid., p. 536.

58. Ibid., p. 538.

59. Ibid., pp. 534–535.

60. Ibid., p. 536.

61. Ibid. (emphasis in the original).

62. *Furman v. Georgia*, 408 U.S. 449 (Powell, J., dissenting).

63. Harold Garfinkel, "Research Note on Inter- and Intra-Racial Homicides," *Social Forces* 27 (1949): 369–381; Guy Johnson, "The Negro and Crime"; Charles S. Mangum, Jr. *The Legal Status of the Negro* (Chapel Hill: North Carolina Press, 1940); Paige H. Ralph, Jonathan R. Sorensen, and James W. Marquart, "A Comparison of Death-Sentenced and Incarcerated Murderers in Pre-*Furman* Texas," *Justice Quarterly* 9 (1992): 185–209; Wolfgang, Kelly, and Nolde, "Comparison of the Executed and Commuted Among Admissions to Death Row"; Marvin E. Wolfgang and Marc Reidel, "Race, Judicial Discretion, and the Death Penalty," *Annals of the American Academy* 407 (1973): 119–133; Marvin E. Wolfgang and Marc Reidel, "Rape, Race, and the Death Penalty in Georgia," *American Journal of Orthopsychiatry* 45 (1975): 658–668.

64. Guy Johnson, "The Negro and Crime."

65. Charles S. Mangum, Jr., *The Legal Status of the Negro.*

66. Wolfgang, Kelly, and Nolde, "Comparisons Among the Executed and the Commuted."

67. Garfinkel, "Research Note on Inter- and Intra-Racial Homicides."

68. William Bowers and Glenn L. Pierce, "Arbitrariness and Discrimination Under Post-*Furman* Capital Statutes," *Crime and Delinquency* 74 (1980): 1067–1100.

69. Kleck, "Racial Discrimination in Criminal Sentencing," p. 788.

70. Florida Civil Liberties Union, *Rape: Selective Electrocution Based on Race* (Miami: Florida Civil Liberties Union, 1964).

71. Wolfgang and Reidel, "Race, Judicial Discretion, and the Death Penalty."

72. Kleck, "Racial Discrimination in Criminal Sentencing," p. 788.

73. David C. Baldus, George Woodworth, and Charles A. Pulaski, *Equal Justice and the Death Penalty: A Legal and Empirical Analysis* (Boston: Northeastern University Press, 1990).

74. Ralph, Sorensen, and Marquart, "A Comparison of Death-Sentenced and Incarcerated Murderers in Pre-*Furman* Texas."

75. Ibid., p. 207.

76. Ibid., pp. 206–207.

77. Wolfgang and Reidel, "Rape, Race and the Death Penalty in Georgia," p. 667.

78. This case is described in Bright, "Death, Discrimination and Denial," pp. 912–915.

79. Ibid., pp. 912–913.

80. *Dobbs v. Zant,* 963 F.2d, 1403, 1407 (11th Cir. 1991), cited in Bright, "Death, Discrimination, Death and Denial," note 77.

81. Ibid., p. 914.

82. U.S. General Accounting Office, *Death Penalty Sentencing: Research Indicates Pattern of Racial Disparities* (Washington, D.C.: Author, 1990), p. 5.

83. Ibid., p. 6.

84. Ibid.

85. Studies that find either a race-of-victim or race-of-defendant effect include (but are not limited to): Stephen Arkin, "Discrimination and Arbitrariness in Capital Punishment: An Analysis of Post-*Furman* Murder Cases in Dade County, Florida, 1973–1976," *Stanford Law Review* 33 (1980): 75–101; William Bowers, "The Pervasiveness of Arbitrariness and Discrimination Under Post-*Furman* Capital Statutes," *Journal of Criminal Law & Criminology* 74 (1983): 1067–1100; Bowers and Pierce, "Arbitrariness and Discrimination Under Post-*Furman* Capital Statutes"; Sheldon Ekland-Olson, "Structured Discretion, Racial Bias, and the Death Penalty: The First Decade After *Furman* in Texas," *Social Science Quarterly* 69 (1988): 853–873; Thomas Keil and Gennaro Vito, "Race and the Death Penalty in Kentucky Murder Trials: An Analysis of Post-*Gregg* Outcomes," *Justice Quarterly* (1990): 189–207; Raymond Paternoster, "Prosecutorial Dis-

cretion in Requesting the Death Penalty: A Case of Victim-Based Racial Discrimination," *Law & Society Review* 18 (1984): 437–478; Michael L. Radelet, "Racial Characteristics and the Imposition of the Death Penalty," *American Sociological Review* 46 (1981): 918–927; Michael L. Radelet and Glenn L. Pierce, "Race and Prosecutorial Discretion in Homicide Cases," *Law & Society Review* 19 (1985): 587–621; Dwayne M. Smith, "Patterns of Discrimination in Assessments of the Death Penalty: The Case of Louisiana," *Journal of Criminal Justice* 15 (1987): 279–286.

86. Baldus, Woodworth, and Pulaski, *Equal Justice and the Death Penalty*.

87. Gross and Mauro, *Death & Discrimination*.

88. Baldus, Woodworth, and Pulaski, *Equal Justice and the Death Penalty*.

89. Ibid., p. 185.

90. David Baldus, Charles Pulaski, and George Woodworth, "Comparative Review of Death Sentences: An Empirical Study of the Georgia Experience," *The Journal of Criminal Law & Criminology* 74 (1983): 709–710.

91. Anthony Amsterdam, "Race and the Death Penalty," *Criminal Justice Ethics* 7 (1988): 2, 84–86.

92. Ibid., p. 85.

93. Gross and Mauro, *Death & Discrimination,* pp. 109–110.

94. Richard Quinney, *The Social Reality of Crime* (Boston: Little, Brown, 1970). Austin Turk, *Criminality and Legal Order* (New York: Rand McNally, 1969).

95. Darnell F. Hawkins, "Beyond Anomalies: Rethinking the Conflict Perspective on Race and Criminal Punishment," *Social Forces* 65 (1987): 726.

96. Keil and Vito, "Race and the Death Penalty in Kentucky Murder Trials," p. 204.

97. Gross and Mauro, *Death & Discrimination*.

98. Ibid., p. 113.

99. Bright, "Discrimination, Death and Denial," pp. 903–905.

100. Ibid., pp. 904–905.

101. Ibid., p. 921.

102. Hugo A. Bedau and Michael L. Radelt, "Miscarriages of Justice in Potentially Capital Cases," *Stanford Law Review* 40 (1987): 21–179.

103. *Omaha World Herald* (March 3, 1993).

104. Information about this case was obtained from articles appearing in the *Chicago Tribune* from 1995 to 1998.

105. Eric Zorn, "Dark Truths Buried in Nicarico Case May Yet See Light," *Chicago Tribune* (October 18, 1995), Section 2, p. 1.

106. *Chicago Tribune* (November 4, 1995), Section 1, pp. 1–2.

107. *Chicago Tribune* (April 9, 1998), DuPage section, p. 1.

108. For an excellent and detailed discussion of this case, see Eric W. Rise, *The Martinsville Seven: Race, Rape, and Capital Punishment* (Charlottesville: University Press of Virginia, 1995).

109. Ibid., p. 122.

110. Ibid.

111. Ibid., p. 30.

112. Ibid., p. 32.

113. Ibid., p. 35.

114. Ibid., p. 48.

115. Ibid., p. 85.

116. *Hampton v. Commonwealth*, 58 S.E.2d 288, 298 (Va.Sup.Ct., 1950).

117. Ibid.

118. Rise, p. 121.

119. Ibid., p. 124.

120. Ibid., p. 148.

121. See, for example, *Maxwell v. Bishop*, F.2d 138 (8th Cir. 1968) *Spinkellink v. Wainwright*, 578 F.2d 582 (5th Cir. 1978); *Shaw v. Martin*, 733 F.2d 304 (4th Cir. 1984); and *Prejean v. Blackburn*, 743 F.2d 1091 (5th Cir. 1984).

122. *McCleskey v. Kemp*, 481 U.S. 279, 107 S.Ct. 1756 (1987).

123. Baldus et al., "Monitoring and Evaluating Contemporary Death Penalty Systems: Lessons from Georgia," *University of California at Davis Law Review* 18 (1985): 1375-1407.

124. *McCleskey v. Kemp*, 107 S.Ct. at 1777.

125. Ibid., at 1769.

126. *McCleskey v. Kemp*, 481 U.S. at 315 (Brennan, J., dissenting).

127. Ibid., at 316–317.

128. Ibid.

129. *Maxwell v. Bishop*, 398 F.2d 138 (CA 8 1968).

130. Amsterdam, "Race and the Death Penalty."

131. Randall Kennedy, *Race, Crime, and the Law* (New York: Vintage Books, 1998).

132. Bright, "Discrimination, Death and Denial," p. 947.

133. Gross and Mauro, *Death & Discrimination*, p. 212.

134. *McCleskey v. Zant*, 111 S. Ct. 1454 (1991).

135. Ibid.

136. Ibid.

137. *McCleskey v. Zant*.

138. *Herrera v. Collins*, 113 S.Ct. 853 (1993).

139. *Congressional Record*, S4602 (April 21, 1994).

140. Baldus, Woodworth, and Pulaski, *Equal Justice and the Death Penalty*, pp. 384–387; Gross and Mauro, *Death & Discrimination*, chap. 11; Kennedy, *Race, Crime, and the Law*, pp. 340–345.

141. Gross and Mauro, *Death & Discrimination*, p. 216.

142. Kennedy, *Race, Crime, and the Law*, p. 341.

143. *McCleskey v. Kemp*, 107 S.Ct., at 1806 (Stevens, J., dissenting).

144. Baldus, Woodworth, and Pulaski, *Equal Justice and the Death Penalty*, p. 385.

145. Kennedy, *Race, Crime and the Law*, p. 343.

146. Ibid., p. 344.

147. Ibid.

148. Gross and Mauro, *Death & Discrimination*, pp. 109–110.

9

Corrections

A Picture in Black and White

PRISON VERSUS COLLEGE: MINORITIES IN SOCIETY

In 1996, more African Americans were under some form of correctional supervision (jail, prison, probation, and parole)[1] than were enrolled in college:[2] 2,099,500 versus 1,505,600. Among whites, the situation is just the opposite: more than ten million in college[3] and just over three million under correctional supervision.[4] These data dramatize the most compelling fact about the U.S. correctional system: African Americans are overrepresented at all levels. To put it another way, roughly 10 percent of those seeking degrees are African American, whereas half of those under correctional supervision are African American.

GOALS OF THE CHAPTER

This chapter describes various disparities in the ethnic and racial makeup of the U.S. correctional system. It examines which groups are overrepresented in situations of incarceration and supervision in the community. The extent of minority overrepresentation also is explored in relation to federal versus state populations, regional differences, historical fluctuations, gender distinctions, and juvenile populations.

This descriptive information is supplemented by a discussion of current research on discrimination in the correctional setting. Finally, the inmate social system, which reflects key aspects of prison life, is discussed. This section focuses on the influence of minority group status on prison subcultures and religion.

THE INCARCERATED:
PRISON AND JAIL POPULATIONS

Describing incarcerated populations in the United States is a complicated task. The answer to the question, Who is locked up? depends on what penal institution and which inmates we are discussing. There are a number of important distinctions between prisons and jails, federal and state institutions, and male and female inmates. In addition, important changes occur over time.

Prisons are distinct from jails because they serve different functions in the criminal justice system.[5] Federal and state prisons must be examined separately because of the differences in federal and state crime.[6] These differences result in different levels of minority overrepresentation. Male and female inmate populations also have different racial and ethnic compositions.

Minority Overrepresentation

The primary observation to be made about the prison population in the United States is that African Americans are strikingly overrepresented compared to their presence in the general population. They are less than 15 percent of the U.S. population but nearly 55 percent of all incarcerated offenders (see Table 9.1). Conversely, whites are underrepresented compared to their presence in the population: over 80 percent of the population but just under half of the prison population.

Not all racial and ethnic minorities show the same pattern of overrepresentation in prison populations. Hispanics comprise about 10 percent of the U.S. population, but are roughly 16 percent of the prison population. In recent years, Hispanics have represented the fastest growing minority group being imprisoned: In 1985 they were 10.5 percent of the prison populations, and in 1996 they were 17.7 percent. These increases reflect a rate twice as high as the increase for African American and white inmates.[7] With little information about the number of Asian and Native American prisoners, it appears their representation is not substantially greater than their representation in the general population.

The preceding numbers reflect the combined figures of state and federal prison populations. Although state prison populations account for the majority (nearly 90 percent) of incarcerated offenders, a look at the racial and ethnic percentages in state and federal populations separately is warranted. Just as state and federal laws differ, so will their prison populations, as they present different offenses and unique sentencing practices (see Chapter 6). An important

**Table 9.1 Race and Ethnic Profile
of Federal and State Prison Populations, 1996**

	Federal (%)	State (%)
Race		
White	58.7	43.4
African American	37.9	54.7
Native American	7.6	1.0
Asian	1.6	0.6
Ethnicity		
Hispanic	28.4	16.5
Non-Hispanic	71.6	83.5

SOURCE: *Correctional Populations in the United States, 1996* (Washington, D.C.: Department of Justice, 1999).

implication for federal prisoners is that they can expect to serve more of their original sentence than state inmates do (by up to 50 percent).[8]

In data from 1996, the magnitude of racial and ethnic differences in state versus federal prison populations is noticeable (see Table 9.1).[9] African Americans are more seriously overrepresented in the state prison populations than in federal prison populations (nearly 55 percent versus less than 40 percent). In contrast, when these data are disaggregated, Hispanics and Native American populations are more seriously overrepresented in federal prison populations. That is, the percentage of federal inmates who are identified as Hispanic and Native Americans is slightly higher than their representation in the general population. Thus, the representation of both Hispanics and Native Americans appears closer to their distribution in the general population when it comes to state prisons.

These differences in disparity among racial and ethnic groups are explained in large part by different patterns of offending. Whites are relatively more likely to commit and be convicted of federal offenses. African Americans, conversely, are relatively more likely to be arrested and convicted for index crimes, which are generally state offenses. Hispanics are consistently overrepresented among convicted drug offenders at the federal level and immigration law offenders.[10] Finally, Native Americans are substantially impacted by the Major Crimes Act that brings many offenders into federal courts.[11]

Differences in the magnitude of racial disparity among the various racial and ethnic groups in prison offer more support that the impact of race and ethnicity is not a constant. That is, the impact of overrepresentation in incarceration settings varies in magnitude and quality. One of the differences manifests itself in the release figures of state and federal prisons. There are important implications for those groups that spend more time in federal prison than in state prisons, given that federal prisoners can expect to serve 50 percent more of their original sentence than state inmates.[12] This differential has the most detrimental impact on Hispanics, who are a substantially larger part of the federal population than the state population.

**Table 9.2 Race and Ethnic Profile
of Federal and State Female Prison Populations, 1996**

	Federal (%)	State (%)
Race		
White	57.7	45.2
African American	39.4	52.8
Native American	1.1	1.4
Asian	1.8	0.4
Ethnicity		
Hispanic	25.2	12.7
Non-Hispanic	74.8	87.3

SOURCE: *Correctional Populations in the United States, 1996* (Washington, D.C.: Department of Justice, 1999).

Racial and Ethnic Female Prisoners

Women make up less than 10 percent of federal and state prison populations.[13] Prison populations have increased drastically in the last several years, and the increase for female inmates is almost twice that for male inmates (9.1 percent versus 4.7 percent in 1996).[14] Among female prisoners, there are similar patterns of overrepresentation in terms of the racial and ethnic makeup compared to the overall (predominately male) prison population (see Table 9.2) discussed earlier. Just over half of the female prison population is African American, with just under half identified as white females.

Comparing available demographic information from state and federal prison populations, African American females represent a higher percentage of state than federal inmates (just over one third of female federal prisoners are reported as African American).[15] However, Hispanic females account for almost one fourth of the female federal prison population, leaving the percentage of state offenders similar to the representation of Hispanic females in the general population. Once again, this aspect of differential disparity in federal and state demographic descriptions of inmates has implications for the time racial and ethnic minorities actually serve in prison. As noted, the federal inmates serve, on average, 50 percent more of their sentence than state offenders.[16] Thus, Hispanic females are not merely overrepresented in federal prison populations, but are also subject to the longer federal sentences.

Historical Trends

The overrepresentation of African Americans in state and federal prisons is not a new phenomenon. Figure 9.1 provides a graphic illustration of the changing demographic composition of the prison population from 1926 to 1996. Reviewing this figure we can document a disproportionate number of African Americans in the prison population since 1926 (the beginning of national-level data collection on prison populations). The racial disparity has increased

Percentage (%)

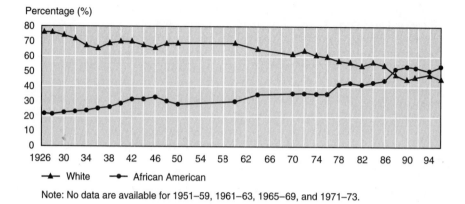

—▲— White   —●— African American

Note: No data are available for 1951–59, 1961–63, 1965–69, and 1971–73.

FIGURE 9.1 Admissions to State and Federal Prison, by Race, 1926–1996

Original, plus: BJS, *Correctional Populations in the United States, 1996* (Washington, D.C.: U. S. Department of Justice, 1999).

in recent years, however. In 1926, African Americans represented 9 percent of the population and 21 percent of the prison population.[19] Over time, the proportion of the population of African Americans increased steadily, reaching 30 percent in the 1940s, 35 percent in 1960, 44 percent in 1980, and leveling off to around 50 percent in the 1990s. The 1926 figure represented an African American prisoner population ratio of 2.5 to 1; the current ratio is 4 to 1.

Impact of the War on Drugs

Dramatic increases in the overrepresentation of African Americans in the prison population have occurred in a context of generally increasing prison population totals and rising incarceration rates since the early 1970s. Although the incarceration binge surely has multiple sources, it may reflect an impact of the war on drugs. Tonry,[20] for example, argued that the war on drugs has had a particularly detrimental effect on African American males. Evidence of this impact, he argued, can be seen by focusing on the key years affected by the war on drugs: 1980 to 1992. During this period, the number of white males incarcerated in state and federal prison increased by 143 percent; for African American males the number increased by 186 percent.[21]

Statisticians for the federal Bureau of Justice Statistics argue that the sources of growth for prison populations differ for white and African American inmates. Specifically, drug offenses and violent offenses account for the largest source of growth among state prison inmates. During the ten-year period from 1985 to 1995, "the increasing number of drug offenders accounted for 42 percent of the total growth of black inmates and 26 percent of the growth among white inmates."[22] Similarly, the number of black inmates serving time for violent offenses rose by 37 percent, whereas growth among white inmates was at a higher 47 percent.[23]

Focus on an Issue

Correctional Personnel: Similarities and Differences on the Basis of Race

Currently, federal and state prisons have fairly equitable minority representation among correctional officers and supervisors, compared to the general population.[17] The important reasons for achieving such goals are numerous. Ensuring fair employment practices in government hiring is one goal, and others champion the importance of minority decision makers as having a beneficial (and perhaps less discriminatory) impact on the treatment of minority populations.

Author's[18] review of the research in the area of attitudes and beliefs of correctional officers toward inmates and punishment ideologies suggests that respondents' views do appear to differ in many ways on the basis of race. In particular, he noted that African American officers appear to have more positive attitudes toward inmates than white officers. However, others have found that black officers expressed a preference for greater distance between officers and inmates than did white officers. Additionally, neither white nor African American correction officers reflect an ability to correctly identify the self-reported needs of prison inmates.

In relation to ideological issues, African American officers were more often supportive of rehabilitation than their white counterparts. African American officers also appear to be more ambivalent about the current punitive nature of the criminal justice system, indicating that the court system is often too harsh.

In short, current research does not offer a definitive answer to the question of whether minority correctional officers make different decisions. Assuming that differential decision making by correction officers could be both a positive and negative exercise of discretion, at what point are differential decisions beneficial to inmates versus unprofessional or unjust? What research could be done to resolve the issue of the presence or absence of differential decision making by correctional officers on the basis of race?

As we discussed in Chapters 2 and 4, the differential impact of the war on drugs may be due more to the enforcement strategies of law enforcement than higher patterns of minority drug use. Critics argue that whereas the police are *reactive* in responding to robbery, burglary, and other index offenses, they are *proactive* in dealing with drug offenses. There is evidence to suggest that they target minority communities—where drug dealing is more visible and where it is thus easier to make arrests—and tend to give less attention to drug activities in other neighborhoods.

Incarceration Rates

Another way to describe the makeup of U.S. prisons is to examine incarceration rates. The information offered by incarceration rates expands the picture of the prison inmate offered in population totals and percentages (given earlier).

**Table 9.3 Incarceration Rates
by Race/Ethnicity and Gender, 1985, 1990, 1995**

	MALE			FEMALE		
Year	White	African American	Hispanic	White	African American	Hispanic
1985	246	1,559	542	10	68	22
1990	339	2,376	817	19	125	43
1995	461	3,250	1,174	27	176	57

SOURCES: Darrell K. Gilliard and Allen J. Beck, *Prisoners, 1993* (Washington, D.C.: U.S. Department of Justice, 1994);
Christopher J. Mumola and Allen J. Beck, *Prisoners, 1995* (Washington, D.C.: U.S. Department of Justice, 1997).

Incarceration rates offer the most vivid picture of the overrepresentation of African Americans in prison populations. Rates allow for the standardization of population figures that can be calculated over a particular target population. For example, the general incarceration rate in 1995 was 615 per 100,000 population. This number can be further explored by calculating rates that reflect the number of one race group in the prison population relative to the number of that population in the overall U.S. population.

As shown in Table 9.3, over a ten-year period, African Americans and Hispanics are substantially more likely than whites to be incarcerated in state and federal prisons. Although rates for all groups are increasing, the rate for African American males remained the highest, which was six to seven times higher than that for white males. Hispanic rates were also higher than the rates for whites, but lower than the rates for African Americans. Note that rates of incarceration for females are substantially lower than male rates, but they are increasing over time, with African American female rates of incarceration nearly seven times higher than those for white females.[24]

JAILS AND MINORITIES

The Role of Jail

Jail populations are significantly different than prison populations. Because jails serve a different function in the criminal justice system, they are subject to different dynamics in terms of admissions and releases. The Annual Survey of Jails[25] reveals that approximately half of the daily population of jail inmates is convicted offenders and half are awaiting trial. Those awaiting trial are in jail because they cannot raise bail or they are denied bail altogether. The other inmates are convicted offenders who have been sentenced to serve time in jail. Although the vast majority of these inmates have been convicted of misdemeanors, some convicted felons are given a "split sentence" involving jail followed by probation.

Table 9.4 Percentage of Jail Inmates by Race and Ethnicity, 1998

Race/Ethnicity	
White/Non-Hispanic	41.3
African American/Non-Hispanic	41.2
Hispanic	15.5
Other	2.0

SOURCE: Darrell K. Gilliard, *Prison and Jail Inmates at Midyear 1998* (Washington, D.C.: U.S. Department of Justice, 1999).

Because of the jail's role as a pretrial detention center, there is a high rate of turnover among the jail population. Thus, *daily* population of jails is lower than prisons, but the *annual* total of people incarcerated in jails is higher.

Minority Overrepresentation

As Table 9.4 indicates, African Americans and Hispanics are overrepresented in jails, (41.2 and 15.5 percent, respectively), whereas whites are underrepresented (41.3 percent) in jail populations compared to the general population. The picture depicted by these numbers is similar to the reflection of race and ethnicity in prison populations. (These data represent a static one-day count, as opposed to an annual total of all people who pass through the jail system.) Although these data combine race and ethnicity into one category, as opposed to distinction of ethnicity as separate from race, limited comparisons to prison figures can be made. Keep in mind that some portion of the Hispanic population in a separate category system would fall in to the white race category, whereas others would fall in the African American or "other" categories.

Because of the jail's function as a pretrial detention center, jail population is heavily influenced by bail decisions. If more people are released on nonfinancial considerations, the number of people in jail will be lower. This raises the questions of racial discrimination in bail setting, which we discussed in Chapter 5. As noted in this chapter, there is evidence that judges impose higher bail—or are more likely to deny bail altogether—if the defendant is a racial minority.

PAROLE: EARLY RELEASE FROM PRISON

Parole is a form of early release from prison under supervision in the community. Not surprisingly, therefore, parole populations are similar in racial and ethnic distribution to federal and state prison populations. In 1997, 54 percent of the inmates released on parole were white, 45 percent were African American, and less than 1 percent were of other races.[27] Similarly, about 21 percent of the parole entrants were designated as Hispanic (see Figure 9.2).

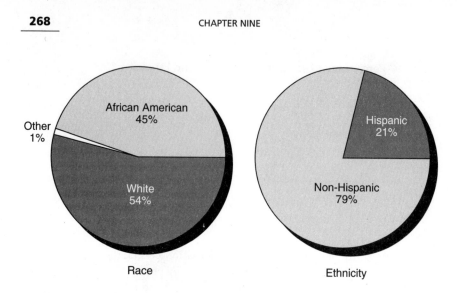

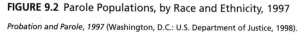

FIGURE 9.2 Parole Populations, by Race and Ethnicity, 1997

Probation and Parole, 1997 (Washington, D.C.: U.S. Department of Justice, 1998).

BOX 9.1   International Comparisons

In the international arena, the United States has one of the highest incarceration rates in the world. According to the Sentencing Project,[26] in 1993 we had 519 people incarcerated in jails and prisons for every 100,000 people in the general population, second only to Russia (558 persons per 100,000 population). The next closest country was South Africa with the substantially lower rate of 368 per 100,000 people. European countries have much lower rates: England/Wales at 93, Germany at 80, and Sweden at 69.

The Sentencing Project also calculated that the incarceration rate for African American males in the United States is more than four times the rate for South Africa in the last years of apartheid. That is, in 1993, the incarceration rate for African American males was 3,822 per 100,000 compared to the rate of 815 per 100,000 for South African black males.

The data represented in Table 9.3 also illustrate that African American males have been incarcerated at higher rates than white males. Specifically since 1985, the incarceration rates for African American males have increased at a more rapid pace than incarceration rates for white males.

The racial disparity in the nation's prison populations is revealed even more dramatically by data from the Sentencing Project that estimate that on any given day 42 percent of the young African American men in Washington, D.C. were under some form of correctional supervision. In contrast, the U.S. Department of Justice estimates that less than 3 percent of the adult U.S. population is under correctional supervision.

BOX 9.2   Supervision in the Community: An Uneven Playing Field?

Both parole and probation involve supervision in the community under a set of specific provisions for client behavior. One of the most common provisions is the requirement of employment. Not being able to attain or retain employment may lead to a violation of supervision conditions and unsuccessful discharge of an individual from probation or parole. Essentially, a person could be sent to prison for being unemployed. It is possible that the employment provision creates uneven hardships for minorities. In 1993, unemployment rates were 6 percent for whites, 12.5 percent for African Americans, and 10.5 percent for Hispanics.[30] That is, ethnic- and race-specific unemployment rates vary substantially, showing the disadvantaged status of minorities in the labor market. Does this aspect of the general economy adversely affect minorities on probation and parole? If yes, what should be done?

The benevolent side of this observation is that African Americans and Hispanics are making the transition to parole (arguably a positive move) in proportions similar to prison population figures. However, parole revocation figures require a closer look.

Success and Failure on Parole

A parolee "succeeds" on parole if he or she completes the terms of supervision without violations. A parolee can "fail" in one of two ways: by either being arrested for another crime or by violating one of the conditions of parole release (using drugs, possessing a weapon, violating curfew, etc.). In either case, parole authorities can revoke parole and send the person back to prison.

Parole revocation, therefore, is nearly equivalent to the judge's power to sentence an offender in the first place, because it can mean that the offender will return to prison. The decision to revoke parole is discretionary; parole authorities may choose to overlook a violation and not send the person back to prison. This opens the door for possible discrimination.

The revocation data reveal more disparity at this stage of decision making than at the entrance to parole.[28] Overall, 37 percent of all parolees at the state level successfully completed parole in 1990. The success rate varied somewhat by racial and ethnic groups: 39 percent of whites, 34 percent of African Americans, 35 percent of other races, and 31 percent of Hispanics. The percentage of parolees returning to prison compliments these proportions, with Hispanics having the highest return rates and whites the lowest.

Recent data on federal parole revocations[29] reveal that approximately 69 percent of federal parole discharges were from successful completion of parole conditions. Once again, these rates vary by minority group status. Whites and other races had the highest successful completion rate of 76 percent, followed by Hispanics at 68 percent, and African Americans with the lowest at 53 percent. Similarly, African Americans had the highest return to prison rates (36 percent), with all other groups exhibiting a return rate of less than 20 percent.

PROBATION: A CASE OF SENTENCING DISCRIMINATION?

Probation is an alternative to incarceration, a sentence to supervision in the community. The majority of all the people under correctional supervision are on probation, totaling over three million people.

The racial demographics in Figure 9.3 indicate that African Americans are overrepresented (35 percent) in the probation population relative to their presence in the general population.[31] Correspondingly, whites are underrepresented at 64 percent of all probationers.[32] The ethnic breakdown of those under sentence of probation reveals Hispanics are again overrepresented compared to non-Hispanics (16 percent versus 84 percent).[33]

It is immediately apparent that the racial disparity for probation is not as great as it is for the prison population, however. Given that probation is a less severe sentence than prison, this difference may indicate that the advantage of receiving the less severe sentence of probation is reserved for whites. In a study of sentencing in California, Petersilia found that 71 percent of whites convicted of a felony were granted probation, compared with 67 percent of African Americans and 65 percent of Hispanics.[34] Similarly, Spohn and colleagues found that in "borderline cases" in which judges could impose either a long probation sentence or a short prison sentence, whites were more likely to get probation and African Americans were more likely to get prison. (We discuss the issue of discrimination in sentencing in Chapter 6.)

PERSPECTIVES ON THE RACIAL DISTRIBUTION OF CORRECTIONAL POPULATIONS

Several theoretical arguments are advanced to explain the overwhelming overrepresentation of African Americans in the correctional system. The most fundamental question is whether prison populations reflect discrimination in the criminal justice system or other factors. One view is that the overrepresentation reflects widespread discrimination; the alternative view is that the overrepresentation results from a disproportionate involvement in criminal activity on the part of minorities. Mann[35] argued that there is systematic discrimination based on color, whereas Wilbanks[36] contended that the idea of systematic discrimination is a "myth."

The work of Alfred Blumstein offers a benchmark to explore the results of such research. Focusing on 1979 prison population data, Blumstein sought to isolate the impact of discrimination from other possible factors. The key element of his research is the following formula:[37]

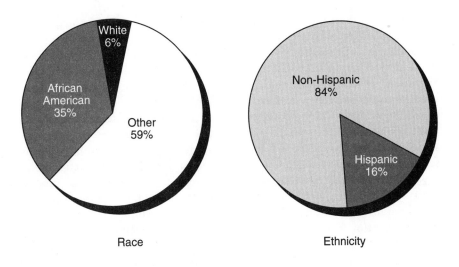

FIGURE 9.3 Probation Populations, by Race and Ethnicity, 1997

Probation and Parole, 1997 (Washington, D.C.: U.S. Department of Justice, 1998).

X = ratio of expected black-to-white incarceration rates based
only on arrest disproportionality/ratio of black-to-white
incarceration rates actually observed.

Essentially, this formula compares the expected black–white disparity (X) in state prison populations based on recorded black–white disparity in arrest rates (numerator) over the observed black–white disparity in incarceration rates (denominator). Thus, accepting the argument that arrest rates are not a reflection of discrimination, Blumstein's formula calculates the portion of the prison population left unexplained by the disproportionate representation of African Americans at the arrest stage. In short, this figure is the amount of actual racial disproportionality in incarceration rates that is open to an explanation or charge of discrimination.

Overall, Blumstein found that 20 percent of the racial disparity in incarceration rates is left unexplained by the overrepresentation of African Americans at the arrest stage. Crime-specific rates indicate that results vary by crime type:[38]

All offenses	20.0 percent
Homicide	2.8 percent
Aggravated assault	5.2 percent
Robbery	15.6 percent
Rape	26.3 percent
Burglary	33.1 percent
Larceny/auto theft	45.6 percent
Drugs	48.9 percent

Arguably, the main implication of this list is that the level of unexplained disproportionality is "directly related to the discretion permitted or used in handling each of the offenses, which tends to be related to offense seriousness—the less serious the offenses (and the greater discretion), the greater the amount of the disproportionality in prison that must be accounted for on grounds other than differences in arrest."[39]

This observation is particularly salient in the context of drug offenses. Recall the arguments from Chapter 4 that contend that drug arrest decisions are subject to more proactive enforcement than most offenses. Combine this observation with the fact that during the recent surge of incarceration rates (1980–1996), drug offenses have had the greatest impact on new commitments to prison. In short, the offense category indicated to suffer from the broad use of discrimination and the most opportunity for discrimination is the fastest growing portion of new commitments to prison. Thus, Blumstein's findings, although generally not an indictment of the criminal justice system, suggest an ominous warning for the presence of discrimination during the era of the war on drugs.

Langan[40] reexamined Blumstein's argument, contending that he relied on an inappropriate data set. Langan argued that prison admissions offered a more appropriate comparison to arrest differentials than prison populations. Langan also incorporated victim identification data as a substitute for arrest data to circumvent the biases associated with arrest. In addition to altering Blumstein's formula, he looked at three years of data (1973, 1979, 1982) across five offense types (robbery, aggravated assault, simple assault, burglary, and larceny). Even after making these modifications, Langan confirmed Blumstein's findings: About 20 percent of the racial overrepresentation in prison admissions was left unexplained.

In an updated analysis with 1990 prison population data, Blumstein found that the amount of unexplained variation in racially disproportionate prison populations on the basis of arrest data increased from 20 to 24 percent. In addition, the differentials discussed earlier on the basis of discretion and seriousness increased for drug crimes and less serious crimes, decreasing only for homicide and robbery.[41] This seems to confirm the argument that the war on drugs has increased the racial disparities in prison populations.

Tonry challenged Blumstein's work on several grounds.[42] He argued, first, that it is a mistake to assume that official UCR arrest statistics accurately reflect offending rates. As discussed in Chapter 4, there is evidence of race discrimination in arrests. This is particularly true with respect to drug arrests, which account for much of the dramatic increase in the prison populations in recent years. Second, Tonry pointed out that Blumstein's analysis used national-level data. Aggregating in this fashion can easily mask evidence of discrimination in certain areas of the country.

Tonry's third criticism is that Blumstein's approach could easily hide "offsetting forms of discrimination that are equally objectionable but not observable in the aggregate."[43] One example would be sentencing African American offenders with white victims more harshly, at the same time punishing African

American offenders with African American victims less harshly (see Chapter 6 for a more detailed discussion). The former represents a bias against African American offenders and the latter a bias against African American victims. If we aggregate the data, as Blumstein did, neither pattern is evident.

Hawkins and Hardy spoke to the possibility of regional differences by looking at state-specific imprisonment rates.[44] They found a wide variation across the fifty states in the differential in African American imprisonment rates left unexplained by disproportionate African American arrest rates. The "worst" state was New Mexico with only 2 percent of the difference explained by the expected impact of arrest. At the other end of the continuum, Missouri was the "best" state with 96 percent of the incarceration rates of African Americans explained by differential arrest rates. Hawkins and Hardy concluded, "Blumstein's figure of 80 percent would not seem to be a good approximation for all states."[45]

In an attempt to look past systematic racial discrimination in the criminal justice system, researchers have begun to explore the intricacies of contextual discrimination. A review by Chiricos and Crawford[46] reveals that researchers have started to study the social context's impact on the racial composition of imprisonment rates by investigating such issues as the population's racial composition, the percentage of unemployed African Americans, and the region.

The first two issues reflect the theoretical argument that communities and thus decision makers will be apprehensive under certain conditions and become more punitive. Specific conditions of apprehension (or threat) are related to racial mass. For example, large concentrations of African Americans will be associated with a higher fear of crime and a need to be more punitive. Michalowski and Pearson[47] found that racial composition of blacks in a state was positively associated with general incarceration rates. However, the impact of racial composition on race-specific incarceration rates is less clear. Hawkins and Hardy[48] discovered that states with smaller percentages of African Americans were associated with more racial disparity in incarceration rates than could be accounted for by arrest rates. In contrast, Bridges and Crutchfield[49] found that states with higher percentages of African Americans in the general population were associated with lower levels of racial disparity in incarceration rates. DeLone and Chiricos[50] argued that this inconsistency is due to an improper level of analysis. They argued that looking at state-level imprisonment and racial composition rates can be deceiving. The proper level of analysis is the level of the sentencing court. In their study of county-level incarceration rates, they found that higher levels of African Americans led to higher levels of general incarceration and African American incarceration rates.

Race-specific unemployment rates reflect the idea that idle (or surplus) populations are crime-prone and in need of deterrence. This line of reasoning requires more punitive response, with higher incarceration rates when the perceived crime-prone population is idle.[51] Generally, this "threat" is measured by the unemployment rate of the perceived crime-prone population—young, African American males. DeLone and Chiricos have found that at the county level, high unemployment rates among young African American males are not

BOX 9.3   Additional Explanations for the Racial Distribution of U.S. Prison Populations

Historically, some have argued that prison replaced the social control of slavery in the South after the end of the Civil War. Given the criminalization of vagrancy and the operation of the convict lease system, a *de facto* slavery system was invoked on those African Americas who did not leave the South and who refused to offer their labor to former plantation owners who needed it.[53]

Others have argued that prison has always been used to supplement the needs of capitalism as a mechanism to control surplus populations in times of high unemployment. Specifically, African American males, who have the highest unemployment rates, have been viewed as socially dangerous surplus populations.[54]

In the context of the war on drugs, some have argued that the rising African American male prison populations are a response to a moral panic about drugs that stems from the association of crime and drug use with this population almost exclusively.[55]

associated with higher general incarceration rates but are predictive of higher incarceration rates for young, African American males.[52]

Adjustment to Prison

Research on the adjustment of men to life in prison has been available for many years, beginning with Clemmer's *The Prison Community*[56] and including Sykes's *Society of Captives*[57] and Irwin and Cressey's "Thieves, Convicts and Inmate Culture."[58] Jacobs[59] argued that without exception these studies disregarded the issue of race, even though the prison populations in the institutions under study were racially diverse.[60] Consequently, according to Jacobs, the prevailing concept of the "prison subculture" needs to be revised. Jacobs argued that race is the defining factor of the prison experience. Racial and ethnic identity defines the social groupings in prisons, the operation of informal economic systems, the organization of religious activities, and the reasons for inmate misconduct. In other words, white inmates tend to associate with white inmates, African American inmates with African Americans, and so on. In this respect, the racial and ethnic segregation in prison mimics society on the outside.

Goodstein and MacKenzie support Jacobs's observations and argued that their own "exploratory study of race and inmate adjustment to prison demonstrates that the experience of imprisonment differs for African Americans and whites."[62] They reported that although African Americans may develop more anti-authoritarian attitudes and are more likely to challenge prison officials, they appear to have fewer conflicts with fellow inmates.

Wright[63] explored the relationship between "race and economic marginality" to explain adjustment to prison. He explored the apparently common-

Focus on an Issue

Life in Prison: Segregation: By Law or Choice?

A series of court decisions have declared *de jure* racial segregation in prisons to be unconstitutional. As late as the 1970s, prisons in the South and even some in Northern states such as Nebraska segregated prisoners according to race as a matter of official policy. Even though such policies have been outlawed, inmates often self-segregate along racial and ethnic lines as a matter of choice.

This poses a difficult problem for correctional administrators. Should inmates be forced to have integrated work, housing, and education assignments? Or should administrators allow them to make decisions on the basis of personal preference, even if those decisions result in self-segregation? Racial tensions are a serious problem in most prisons; forcing white and African American inmates to share cells when they are actively hostile to each other could bring these tensions to a boil. In one instance, a white inmate felt so threatened by the politicized racial atmosphere in his prison that he filed suit asking a federal court to reverse the integration requirement and return to segregation.[61]

On the other hand, if correctional administrators bowed to the wishes of inmates on this matter they would create two problems. First, they would be actively promoting racial segregation, which is illegal. Second, they would undermine their own authority by acknowledging that inmates could veto policy they did not like.

What is the best strategy for administrators in this difficult situation? You decide.

sense assumption that African Americans, because of their experience in the "modern urban ghetto" (see underclass, Chapter 3) will be more "resilient" to the pains of imprisonment. In short, "ghetto life supposedly socializes the individual to engage in self-protection against the hostile social environment of the slum and the cold and unpredictable prison setting."[64] Using multiple indicators of adaptation to the prison environment, Wright found that although economic marginality does appear to influence the ease of adjustment to prison, this appears to be the case regardless of race.

Other research on male prison populations also indicates that race may not always explain institutional behavior. Research on the effects of race on levels of institutional misconduct reveals an inconsistent picture. Although some researchers find nonwhites overrepresented in inmate misconduct, Petersilia and Honig's[65] study of three state prison systems found three different patterns in relationships between race and rule infractions. In Michigan there was no relationship between race and rule infractions; in California whites had significantly higher rule infractions; and in Texas, African Americans had significantly higher rule infractions. Flanagan[66] found similarly inconsistent results. He argued that inmates' age at commitment, history of drug use, and current incarceration offense are most predictive of general misconduct rates. He did, however, find that race is an important predictor for older inmates with no drug history sentenced for an offense other than homicide. Flanagan recommended that race (among other predictors) is a variable that is inappropriate to use in assisting with the security classification of inmates due to its low predictive power in relation to institutional misconduct.

Recent research of federal prison inmates by Harer and Steffensmeier[67] offers support for the importation model of prison violence, indicating that African American inmates are significantly more likely to receive disorderly conduct reports for violence than white inmates, but lower levels of alcohol and drug misconduct reports than whites.[68] This picture reflects the differential levels of violence and drug behavior between African Americans and whites reflected in arrest figures and assumed to characterize the general behavior patterns of these groups in U.S. society (see Chapter 2).

Many correctional observers say that even with the numerical dominance of African Americans in correctional facilities they are still at a disadvantage in terms of the allocation of resources. For example, Thomas argued that race operates in prison culture to guide behavior, allocate resources, and elevate white groups to a privileged status even when they are not numerically dominant.[69]

Race and Religion

Religion often emerges as a source of solidarity among prison inmates, as well as a mechanism for inmates to adjust to the frustrations of the prison environment. Although religion may be seen as a benign or even a rehabilitative influence, some religious activities in prison have been met with criticism by correctional officials and have been accepted only with federal court intervention. Concern arises when religious tenets seem to espouse the supremacy of one racial group over another.

Jacobs argued that the Black Muslim movement in U.S. prisons was a response to active external proselytizing by the church. Prison administrators overtly resisted the movement for several years. The American Correctional Association issued a policy statement in 1960 refusing to recognize the legitimacy of the Muslim religion, based on arguments that it was a "cult" that disrupted prison operations. Jacobs noted that "prison officials saw in the Muslims not only a threat to prison authority, but also a broader revolutionary challenge to American society"[70] that led to challenges of the white correctional authority.

Consequently, prison officials tried to suppress Muslim religious activities by such actions as banning the Koran. This led to lawsuits asserting the Muslims' right to the free exercise of religion. In 1962, however, the U.S. Supreme Court (*Fulwood v. Clemmer*) ordered the District of Columbia Department of Corrections to "stop treating the Muslims differently from other religious groups."[71] This decision paved the way for the Black Muslim movement to be seen as a legitimate religion and to be taken seriously as a vehicle of prison change through such avenues as litigation.

One example of the rise and subsequent influence of Native American religious groups can be found in Nebraska. The Native American Cultural and Spiritual Awareness group is composed of Native American inmates who seek to build solidarity and appreciation of Native American values.[72] This group also pursues change in the prison environment through litigation. The element of inmate-on-inmate violence and guard assaults characteristic of other groups are not apparent here.

As the direct result of litigation, Native American inmates won the right to have a sweat lodge on prison grounds and to have medicine men and women visit to perform religious ceremonies. The significance of this concession is that it happened four years before federal legislation dictated the recognition and acceptance of Native American religions.

Other religious movements have come to concern prison officials and social commentators due to their apparent assertions of racial supremacy. The impact of such values in a closed environment like a prison is obvious, but concerns have surfaced that the impact of these subcultures may reach outside prison walls. Are groups emerging, under the guise of religions, that promote tenets of racial hatred?

The Five Percent and Asatru movements are two groups that have prison officials concerned. The former group is made up of African Americans and the latter of whites, each emphasizing tenets of racial purity. Currently, six states censor the teachings of the Five Percenters and other states label all followers as gang members.[73] The movement began in Harlem in 1964 and has spread across the country, claiming thousands of followers. Teachings include the rejection of "history, authority and organized religion" and members call themselves a nation of Gods (men) and Earths (women).[74] Although the group advocates peace and rejects drinking and drugs, correctional officials have linked Five Percenters to violence in some state institutions. Similar to the Nation of Islam, their beliefs stress that "blacks were the original beings and must separate from white society."[75]

The Asatru followers practice a form of pagan religion based on principles of pre-Christian Nordic traditions. This religion was officially recognized in Iceland in 1972 and professes nine noble virtues, including courage, honor, and perseverance. However, prison officials claim that as this group has grown in popularity in U.S. prisons, so has racial violence. Some critics charge "that while Asatru is a genuine religion to some followers, these modern pagan groups have been a breeding ground for right-wing extremists"[76] and they attract white supremacists. Some state prison systems have taken steps to ban Asatru groups, stating security concerns. Some Asatru followers have surfaced in connection with acts of racial violence. Most notably perhaps, is the recent case of John William King, a white male convicted of the dragging death of an African American man in Jasper, Texas. While serving a prison sentence prior to this crime, King is said to have joined an Odinist group, an Asatru variant. From this affiliation he has tattoos depicting an African American man lynched on a cross and the words "Aryan Pride."[77]

Focus on an Issue
Indigenous Justice Paradigm

In "Traditional and Contemporary Tribal Justice," Melton observed that in many contemporary tribal communities "a dual justice system exists, one based on an American paradigm of justice and the other based on an indigenous paradigm."[78] The American justice paradigm is characterized by an adversarial system and it stands apart from most religious tenets. Crimes are viewed as actions against the state, with little attention to the needs of the victim or community. The focus is on the defendant's individual rights during adjudication. Punishing the offender is generally governed by a retributive philosophy and removal from society.

In contrast, tribal justice is based on a holistic philosophy and not easily divorced from the religious and spiritual realms of everyday life. Melton[79] attempted to distill the characteristic elements of a number of diverse American tribal justice ideologies into an Indigenous Justice Paradigm. The holistic philosophy is the key element of this paradigm and supports a "circle of justice," where "the center of the circle represents the underlying problems and issues that need to be resolved to attain peace and harmony for the individuals and the community."[80] The corresponding values of restorative and reparative justice prescribe the actions the offender must perform to be forgiven. These values reflect the importance of the victim and the community in restoring harmony.

The influence of the American paradigm of justice on Native American communities has a long and persistent history.[81] However, the values of restorative and reparative justice are emerging in a number of programs off the reservation. In particular, the restorative justice practices of the Navajo Nation have influenced a number of new offender rehabilitation programs, including many supported by the Presbyterian Church.

Prison Gangs

Currently, prison gangs are an integral part of understanding the prison environment and the inmate social system. Little systematic information on prison gangs (or security threat groups) is available. However, from the states that do document such subcultures, evidently they cover the racial and ethnic spectrum. Some of these gangs have networks established between prisons, across states, and most recently, with street gangs.

The Texas prison system offers an example of the variety of prison gangs present in prisons today. As of 1999, the Texas prison system documented eleven well-established prison gangs.[82] Here are some representative examples:

Texas Syndicate: This group has its origins in the California Department of Corrections. Once released, these individuals returned to Texas and entered the Texas Department of Corrections as the result of continuing criminal activity. The membership is predominately Hispanic, with the occasional acceptance of white inmates. This group is structured along para-

Focus on an Issue
Civil Rights of Convicted Felons

Individuals convicted of felonies in the United States may experience a range of sentences from incarceration to probation. Such sentences in effect limit the civil rights of the convicted. No longer do we live in a society that views the convicted felon from the legal status of civil death, literally a slave of the state, but some civil rights restrictions endure after the convicted serves a judicially imposed sentence. *Collateral consequences* is a term used to refer to the statutory restrictions imposed by a legislative body on a convicted felon's rights. Such restrictions vary by state, but they include restrictions on employment, carrying firearms, holding public office, and voting.

Forty-six states have some restriction on the rights of convicted felons to vote. In most states the right to vote can be restored (automatically or by petition) after completion of the sentence (or within a fixed number of years). However, in fourteen states the legal prohibition on voting is permanent.

Given the current increases in incarceration rates across the country, the additional penalty of disenfranchisement for convicted felons becomes an increasing concern. In short, the permanence of this measure may have unanticipated consequences.

Given the overrepresentation of African American males in our prisons, "significant proportions of the black population in some states have been locked out of the voting booth."[87] For example, in the state of Florida, which denies voting rights permanently to convicted felons, nearly one third of the African American male population is not eligible to vote. Arguably, laws such as these, which have the effect of barring a substantial portion of the minority population from voting, fail to promote a racially diverse society. Should convicted offenders be allowed to earn back their right to vote as recognition of their efforts at rehabilitation? Should we change laws that have a racial impact, even if the intent is not racially motivated?

---

military lines, has a documented history of prison violence, and will enforce rule breaking with death.[83]

Texas Mafia: The membership of this group is predominantly white with occasional acceptance of Hispanic members. These inmates have ties to motorcycle gangs and are implicated in the production and sale of illicit drugs.[84]

Aryan Brotherhood of Texas: This group emerged in the early 1980s, and its membership is dominated by white racist inmates. The group is implicated in prison violence as well as illegal activities on the outside.[85]

Mandingo Warriors: This group is made up of African Americans. It came into existence after most of the Hispanic and white groups. These members are involved in prison violence and the sub rosa economic system, but appear to be less organized than the other race and ethnic groups.[86]

Women in Prison

Studies addressing the "prisonization" of women are less numerous than those for men, but they are increasing in number. Within this growing body of research, the issue of race is not routinely addressed, either. When race is assessed the comparisons are generally limited to African Americans and whites. The evidence is mixed on the issue of whether race affects the adjustment of women to prison life.

MacKenzie[88] explained the behaviors (conflicts and misconduct reports) of women in prison on the basis of age and attitudes (anxiety, fear of victimization). She commented that the four prisons she examined are similar in racial composition, but she failed to comment on whether she explored differences by race in relation to attitudes and aggressive behavior. Such research ignores the possibility that race may influence one's perception of prison life, tendencies toward aggression, age of inmate, or length of time in prison.

MacKenzie and others[89] did, in later works, address race in the demographic description of the incarcerated women. In a study of one women's prison in Louisiana, for example, they found that nonwhite women were severely overrepresented among all prisoners and even more likely to be serving long sentences. Their findings indicate unique adjustment problems for long-term inmates, but they failed to incorporate race into their explanatory observations about institutional misconduct. This omission seems contrary to the observation that nonwhite women are more likely to have longer sentences.

Race has specifically been recognized as a factor in research addressing the issue of sexual deprivation among incarcerated women. Leger[90] identified racial dimensions to several key explanatory factors in the participation of female prisoners in lesbianism. First, the demographic information reveals that most lesbian relationships are intraracial and that no distinctions emerged by race in participation in the gay or straight groups. Second, once dividing the group by the characteristics of previous confinements (yes or no) and age at first gay experience, the pattern of even representation of whites and African Americans changed. African American females were overrepresented in the group indicating previous confinement, and the information about age at first arrest indicates that African American females are more likely to have engaged in their first lesbian act prior to their first arrest.

Juveniles Under Correctional Supervision

Juvenile court statistics reveal that the racial makeup of juveniles at key stages of the system varies by decision type. Generally, nonwhite youth (the majority of whom are African American) are overrepresented at every stage of decision making. They are also at greater risk of receiving harsher sanctions than white youth. At the stage of deciding whether to detain a juvenile before the hearing, nonwhite youth are detained in secure custody prior to their hearing at rates that exceed those for white youth, regardless of delinquency offense. Specifically, 26 percent of nonwhite youth were detained, whereas 17 percent of whites were in custody in 1993.[91]

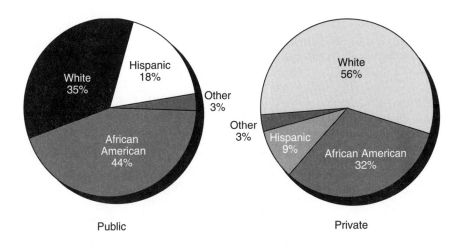

FIGURE 9.4 Juveniles Taken Into Custody, by Race and Ethnicity in Private and Public Facilities, 1993

Juveniles Taken Into Custody, 1993 (Washington, D.C.: U.S. Department of Justice).

A look at national juvenile populations under correctional supervision for those placed on probation and for those placed in secure and nonsecure facilities after adjudication reveal familiar disparities as well. Whites are more likely to receive the benevolent sanction of probation,[92] and nonwhites are at greater risk of receiving the harsher sanction of confinement.[93]

Juvenile offenders are confined in both private and public facilities. More than half of the juveniles in public facilities are minorities, with the largest category of these juveniles identified as African Americans (Figure 9.4). Hispanics are overrepresented also, but other races are not. More African Americans and Hispanics are detained in public juvenile correctional facilities, whereas the private populations are predominately white. African Americans are still overrepresented in private facilities, compared to their distribution in the general population (Figure 9.4). Both Hispanics and juveniles of other races are evenly represented in private facilities compared to their distribution in the general population. One probable explanation for the discrepancies in the nature of admissions decisions to public versus private facilities involves the costs that the parents may have to assume when children are confined to the latter. Private facilities may not be an option for parents of African American and Hispanic youth, given the overrepresentation of these groups under the poverty level (see Chapter 3).

CONCLUSION

The picture of the American correctional system is most vivid in black and white. Such basic questions as who is in prison and how individuals survive in prison cannot be divorced from the issues of race. The most salient observation about minorities and corrections is the striking overrepresentation of African Americans in prison populations. In addition, this overrepresentation is gradually increasing in new court commitments and population figures. Explanations for this increasing overrepresentation are complex.

The most obvious possibility is that African American criminality is increasing. This explanation has been soundly challenged by Tonry's work, which compares the stability of African American arrest rates since the mid-1970s to the explosive African American incarceration rates of the same period.[94] He argued that a better explanation may be the racial impact of the war on drugs.

Blumstein's analysis offers another clue to the continuing increase in the African American portion of the prison population that links discretion and the war on drugs. His work suggests that the racial disparities in incarceration rates for drug offenses are not well-explained by racial disparities in drug arrest rates. Thus, the war on drugs and its impact on imprisonment may be fostering the "malign neglect" Tonry charged.

DISCUSSION QUESTIONS

1. What must a researcher do to advance a description of disparity to an argument of discrimination? In the case of prison populations, how do you advance from the demographic description of the overrepresentation of African Americans in prison to a causal analysis of discrimination by criminal justice decision?

2. In what way are Blumstein's findings about the wide variation of unexplained racial disparity in prison populations according to type of offense similar to the liberation hypothesis discussed in the chapter on sentencing (Chapter 6)?

3. Why do we expect that correctional personnel of different races will make different decisions in regards to minority inmates? If this argument is supported by research, is it an example of contextual discrimination?

4. What policies can be created from the principles of restorative justice (based on indigenous justice principles)? Are these values more compatible with some types of offenses than others? More appropriate for some types of offenders than others?

NOTES

1. Estimates calculated from Christopher J. Mumola and Allen J. Beck, *Prisoners, 1996* (Washington, D.C.: U.S. Department of Justice, 1997) and *Correctional Populations in the US, 1995* (Washington, D.C.: U.S. Department of Justice, 1997).

2. *Chronicle of Higher Education,* August 28, 1998.

3. Ibid.

4. Estimates calculated from Mumola and Beck, *Prisoners, 1996* and *Correctional Populations in the US, 1995.*

5. Harry E. Allen and Clifford E. Simonson, *Corrections in America: An Introduction,* 7th ed. (Englewood Cliffs, NJ: Prentice-Hall, 1995).

6. Ibid.

7. Mumola and Beck, *Prisoners, 1996.*

8. Bureau of Justice Statistics, *Comparing State and Federal Inmates, 1991* (Washington, D.C.: U.S. Government Printing Office, 1993).

9. Bureau of Justice Statistics, *Correctional Populations in the United States, 1996* (Washington, D.C.: U.S. Department of Justice, 1999).

10. Bureau of Justice Statistics, *Comparing State and Federal Inmates, 1991.*

11. For a review of these issues, see Marjorie S. Zatz, Carol Chiago Lujan, and Zoann K. Snyder-Joy, "American Indians and Criminal Justice: Some Conceptual and Methodological Considerations," in *Race and Criminal Justice,* ed. Michael Lynch and E. Britt Paterson (New York: Harrow & Heston, 1995).

12. Bureau of Justice Statistics, *Comparing State and Federal Inmates, 1991.*

13. Bureau of Justice Statistics, *Correctional Populations, 1996.*

14. Bureau of Justice Statistics, *Prisoners, 1996.*

15. Bureau of Justice Statistics, *Correctional Populations, 1996.*

16. Bureau of Justice Statistics, *Comparing State and Federal Inmates, 1991.*

17. *1993 Directory of Juvenile and Adult Correctional Departments, Institutions, Agencies and Paroling Authorities* (Laurel, MD: American Correctional Association, 1993).

18. John A. Author, "Correctional Ideology of Black Correctional Officers," *Federal Probation,* 58 (1994): 57–65.

19. Margaret Werner Cahalan, *Historical Corrections Statistics in the United States, 1850–1984* (Washington, D.C.: U.S. Government Printing Office, 1986), pp. 65–66.

20. Michael Tonry, *Malign Neglect* (New York: Oxford University Press, 1995).

21. Ibid.

22. Ibid., p. 21.

23. Ibid.

24. Ibid.

25. Darrell K. Gilliard, *Prison and Jail Inmates at Midyear 1998* (Washington, D.C.: U.S. Department of Justice, 1999).

26. Marc Maur, *Americans Behind Bars: A Comparison of International Rates of Incarceration* (Washington, D.C.: The Sentencing Project, 1991).

27. *Probation and Parole, 1997* (Washington, D.C.: U.S. Department of Justice, 1998).

28. Louis W. Jankowski, *Correctional Populations in the U.S., 1990* (Washington, D.C.: U.S. Department of Justice, 1992).

29. Ibid.

30. Ibid.

31. Ibid.

32. Ibid.

33. Ibid.

34. Joan Petersilia, *Racial Disparities in the Criminal Justice System* (Santa Monica, CA: Rand, 1983), p. 28.

35. Coramae Richey Mann, *Unequal Justice: A Question of Color* (Bloomington: Indiana University Press, 1993).

36. William Wilbanks, *The Myth of the Racist Criminal Justice System* (Monterey, CA: Brooks/Cole, 1987).

37. Alfred Blumstein, "On the Disproportionality of United States' Prison Populations," *Journal of Criminal Law and Criminology* 73 (1982): 1259–1281.

38. Ibid., p. 1274.

39. Ibid.

40. Patrick Langan, "Racism on Trial: New Evidence to Explain the Racial Composition of Prisons in the United States," *Journal of Criminal Law and Criminology* 76 (1985): 666–683.

41. Alfred Blumstein, "Racial Disproportionality in U.S. Prisons Revisited," *University of Colorado Law Review* 64 (1993): 743–760.

42. Tonry, *Malign Neglect,* pp. 67–68.

43. Ibid.

44. Darnell F. Hawkins and Kenneth A. Hardy, "Black–White Imprisonment Rates: A State-by-State Analysis," *Social Justice* 16 (1989): 75–94.

45. Ibid., p. 79.

46. Theodore G. Chiricos and Charles Crawford, "Race and Imprisonment: A Contextual Assessment of the Evidence," in *Ethnicity, Race and Crime*, ed. Darnell F.

Hawkins (Albany: State University of New York Press, 1995).

47. Raymond J. Michalowski and Michael A. Pearson, "Punishment and Social Structure at the State Level: A Cross-Sectional Comparison of 1970 and 1980," *Journal of Research in Crime and Delinquency* 27 (1990): 52–78.

48. Hawkins and Hardy, "Black–White Imprisonment Rates."

49. George S. Bridges and Robert D. Crutchfield, "Law, Social Standing and Racial Disparities in Imprisonment," *Social Forces* 66 (1988): 699–724.

50. Miriam A. DeLone and Theodore G. Chiricos, "Young Black Males and Incarceration: A Contextual Analysis of Racial Composition," paper presented at the Annual Meeting of the American Society of Criminology, 1994.

51. Dario Melossi, "An Introduction: Fifty Years Later, Punishment and Social Structure in Comparative Analysis," *Contemporary Crises* 13 (1989): 311–326.

52. DeLone and Chiricos, "Young Black Males and Incarceration."

53. W. E. B. DuBois, "The Spawn of Slavery: The Convict-Lease System in the South," *The Missionary Review of the World*, 14 (1901): 737–745; Martha A. Myers, *Race, Labor and Punishment in the South* (Columbus: Ohio State University Press, 1999).

54. For a review of this literature see Theodore G. Chiricos and Miriam A. DeLone, "Labor Surplus and Punishment: A Review and Assessment of Theory and Evidence," *Social Problems* 39 (1992): 421–446.

55. Theodore G. Chiricos, "The Moral Panic of the Drug War," in *Race and Criminal Justice,* ed. Michael J. Lynch and E. Britt Patterson (New York: Harrow & Heston, 1995).

56. D. Clemmer, *The Prison Community* (New York: Holt, Reinhart & Winston, 1940).

57. Gresham M. Sykes, *The Society of Captives* (Princeton, NJ: Princeton University Press, 1958).

58. John Irwin and Donald Cressey, "Thieves, Convicts and Inmate Culture," *Social Problems* 10 (1962): 142–155.

59. James Jacobs, *New Perspectives on Prison and Imprisonment* (Ithaca, NY: Cornell University Press, 1983).

60. Ibid.

61. Ibid.

62. Lynne Goodstein and Doris Layton MacKenzie, "Racial Differences in Adjustment Patterns of Prison Inmates—Prisonization, Conflict, Stress and Control," in *The Criminal Justice System and Blacks,* ed. Daniel Georges-Abeyie (New York: Clark Boardman, 1984).

63. Kevin N. Wright, "Race and Economic Marginality," *Journal of Research in Crime and Delinquency*, 26 (1989): 67–89.

64. Ibid., p. 67.

65. Joan Petersilia and P. Honig, *The Prison Experiences of Career Criminals* (Santa Monica, CA: Rand, 1980).

66. Timothy Flanagan, "Correlates of Institutional Misconduct Among Prisoners," *Criminology* 21 (1983): 29–39.

67. Miles D. Harer and Darrell J. Steffensmeier, "Race and Prison Violence," *Criminology* 34 (1996): 323–355.

68. Ibid.

69. Jim Thomas, "Racial Codes in Prison Culture: Snapshots in Black and White," in *Race and Criminal Justice*, ed. Michael Lynch and E. Britt Patterson (New York: Harrow & Heston, 1995).

70. Jacobs, *New Perspectives,* p. 65.

71. Ibid.

72. Elizabeth S. Grobsmith, *Indians in Prison* (Lincoln: University of Nebraska Press, 1994).

73. *Omaha World Herald* (December 6, 1998), p. 19-A.

74. Ibid.

75. Ibid.

76. *Omaha World Herald* (February 28, 1999), p. 1.

77. Ibid.

78. Ada Pecos Melton, "Crime and Punishment: Traditional and Contemporary Tribal Justice," in *Images of Color, Images of Crime,* ed. Coramae Richey Mann and Marjorie S. Zatz (Los Angeles: Roxbury, 1998).

79. Ibid.

80. Ibid., p. 66.

81. See Zatz et al., "American Indians and Criminal Justice," for a review of these issues.

82. *USA Today*, April 5, 1999.

83. Salvador Buentello, "Combatting Gangs in Texas," *Corrections Today* (July 1992), pp. 58–60.

84. Ibid.

85. Ibid.

86. Fong, Vogel, and Buentello, "Prison Gang Dynamics."

87. *Omaha World Herald* (March 3, 1999), p. 22.

88. Doris L. MacKenzie, "Age and Adjustment to Prison: Interactions With Attitudes and Anxiety." *Criminal Justice and Behavior* 14 (1987): 427–447.

89. Doris L. MacKenzie, James Robinson, and Carol Campbell, "Long-Term Incarceration of Female Offenders: Prison Adjustment and Coping," *Criminal Justice and Behavior* 16 (1989): 223–238.

90. Robert G. Leger, "Lesbianism Among Women Prisoners: Participants and Nonparticipants," *Criminal Justice and Behavior* 14 (1987): 448–467.

91. National Center for Juvenile Justice, *Juvenile Court Statistics, 1993* (Washington, D.C.: National Center for Juvenile Justice, 1996).

92. Ibid.

93. U.S. Department of Justice, *National Juvenile Custody Trends, 1979–1989* (Washington, D.C.: U.S. Government Printing Office, 1992).

94. Tonry, *Malign Neglect*.

10

⚘

The Color of Justice

There is no escaping the fact that race, crime, and justice are inextricably linked in the minds of most Americans. Perceptions of the nature of this linkage vary, however. Many Americans view crime and the criminal justice system through a lens distorted by racial stereotypes and prejudice. They equate crime with African American crime but refuse to acknowledge that this perception might produce racially discriminatory criminal justice practices and policies. Although admitting that some individuals within the criminal justice system make racially biased decisions, they insist that there is no evidence of widespread or systematic racial discrimination.

Other Americans take a different but equally extreme position. They believe that it is inaccurate and misleading to suggest that crime is synonymous with African American crime and argue that our current crime control policies—which emphasize more police, higher bail, harsher sentences, and increased use of the death penalty—have a disparate effect on African Americans and Hispanics. These critics also believe that those who argue that the solution to the crime problem is to "lock 'em up and throw away the key" typically visualize the faces behind the bars as black, brown, and red. They suggest that racism permeates the criminal justice system and insist that racially biased decisions are the norm, not the exception to the general rule of impartiality.

It is our position that the truth lies somewhere between these two extremes. The first position ignores many of the complexities of crime in the United States and presents an overly optimistic view of the treatment of racial minorities who find themselves in the arms of the law. The second position glosses over some of the realities of crime in the United States and paints an unrealistically pessimistic picture of the treatment of racial minorities.

We believe that the criminal justice system is characterized by obvious disparities based on race and ethnicity. It is impossible to ignore the disproportionate number of minorities arrested, imprisoned, and on death row. Some of the decisions that produce these results involve discrimination. The question with which we have wrestled in this book, however, is whether there is *systematic* racial and ethnic discrimination. After considering all of the evidence, we conclude that the U.S. criminal justice system is characterized by *contextual* discrimination.

RACE, CRIME, AND JUSTICE

The overriding goal of this book is to separate fact from fiction and myth from reality. We have shown that it is inaccurate and misleading to equate crime with African American crime and to characterize the typical victim as white, the typical offender as African American, and the typical crime as an interracial act of violence. Victimization data consistently reveal that African Americans and Hispanics are more likely than whites to fall victim to household and personal crime. The racial differences are particularly pronounced for crimes of violence, especially murder and robbery. Crime statistics also reveal that intraracial crimes occur more often than interracial crimes.

It is less clear that the picture of the typical offender as African American is inaccurate. Certainly more whites than racial minorities are arrested each year, but this is a consequence of the fact that whites comprise 80 percent of the U.S. population and people of color only 20 percent, rather than a reflection of a more pronounced propensity toward crime among whites. If we examine arrest rates, the picture changes: African Americans are arrested at a disproportionately high rate.

Although criminal justice scholars and policymakers continue to debate the meaning of the disproportionately high African American arrest rate—some arguing that it reflects a higher offending rate and others that it signals selective enforcement of the law—there is no denying the fact that African Americans are arrested more often than one would expect, particularly for crimes of violence such as murder, rape, and robbery. The explanation for this overrepresentation is complex, incorporating social, economic, and political factors.

It thus seems clear that one cannot paint an accurate picture of crime in the United States without relying to some extent on race and ethnicity. Race and crime are linked, although not necessarily in the ways that most Americans assume.

We also have shown that the criminal justice system is neither completely free of racial bias nor systematically racially biased. In Chapter 1 we suggested that there are different types and degrees of racial discrimination (see Figure 10.1). At one end of the "discrimination continuum" is pure justice, which means that there is no discrimination at any time, place, or point in the criminal

FIGURE 10.1 Discrimination Continuum

justice system. At the other end is systematic discrimination, which means that discrimination prevails at all stages of the criminal justice system, in all places, and at all times.

We suggest that the U.S. criminal justice system falls between the two ends of the continuum. More specifically, we suggest that the system is characterized by contextual discrimination. Racial minorities are treated more harshly than whites at some stages of the criminal justice process (e.g., the decision to seek or impose the death penalty) and no differently than whites at other stages of the process (e.g., the selection of the jury pool). The treatment accorded racial minorities is more punitive than that accorded whites in some regions or jurisdictions, but is no different than that accorded whites in other regions or jurisdictions. For example, some police departments tolerate excessive force directed at racial minorities, whereas others do not. Racial minorities who commit certain types of crimes (e.g., drug offenses or violent crimes against whites) or who have certain characteristics (e.g., they are young, male, and unemployed) are treated more harshly than whites who commit these crimes or have these characteristics.

We are not arguing that the U.S. criminal justice system *never* has been characterized by systematic racial discrimination. In fact, the evidence discussed in earlier chapters suggests just the opposite. The years preceding the civil rights movement (pre-1960s) were characterized by blatant discrimination directed against African Americans and other racial minorities at all stages of the criminal justice process. This pattern of widespread discrimination was not limited to the South but was found throughout the United States.

Until fairly recently, crimes against African Americans and calls for help from minority communities often were ignored by the police. Racial minorities suspected of crimes, and particularly those suspected of crimes against whites, were more likely than whites to be harassed by the police. They also were more likely than whites to be arrested, subjected to excessive force, and the victims of deadly force.

Also until rather recently, racial minorities who were arrested were routinely denied bail, tried by all-white juries without attorneys to assist them in their defense, and prosecuted and convicted on less than convincing evidence. Racial minorities convicted of crimes were sentenced more harshly than whites. They were more likely than whites to be incarcerated and more likely than whites to be sentenced to death and executed.

Our analysis of current research on race and the criminal justice system leads us to conclude that the situation today is somewhat different. Although the contemporary criminal justice system is not characterized by pure justice, many of the grossest racial inequities have been reduced, if not eliminated. Reforms mandated by the U.S. Supreme Court or adopted voluntarily by the states have tempered the blatant racism directed against racial minorities by criminal justice officials.

The Supreme Court consistently has affirmed the importance of protecting criminal suspects' rights. The Court has ruled, for example, that searches without warrants are generally unconstitutional, that confessions cannot be coerced, that suspects must be advised of their rights and provided with attorneys to assist them in their defense, that jurors must be chosen from a representative cross-section of the population, and that the death penalty cannot be administered in an arbitrary and capricious manner.

Most of these decisions reflect the Court's concern with general procedural issues rather than racial discrimination. The Court, in other words, was attempting to safeguard the rights of all criminal defendants. Nevertheless, some observers argue that the Supreme Court's consideration of these procedural issues often was "influenced by the realization that in another case they might affect the posture of a Negro in a hostile southern court."[1]

Even when the Court did not explicitly address the question of racial discrimination in the criminal justice system, its rulings on general procedural issues did lead to improvements in the treatment of racial minorities. By insisting that the states protect the rights of all defendants—racial minorities as well as whites—the Supreme Court rulings discussed earlier led indirectly to the elimination of racially biased criminal justice practices and policies. Coupled with reforms adopted voluntarily by the states, these decisions made systematic racial discrimination unlikely.

We want to reiterate that we are not suggesting that racial discrimination has been completely eliminated from the U.S. criminal justice system. It is certainly true that in the 1990s, whites who commit crimes against African Americans are not beyond the reach of the criminal justice system, African Americans suspected of crimes against whites do not receive "justice" at the hand of white lynch mobs, and African Americans who victimize other African Americans are not immune from punishment. Despite these significant changes, racial inequities persist. As we have shown in the preceding chapters, African Americans and other racial minorities continue to suffer both overt and subtle discrimination within the criminal justice system. Persuasive evidence indicates that racial minorities suffer discrimination at the hands of the police. They are more likely than whites to be shot and killed, arrested, and victimized by excessive physical force. In addition, there is evidence of police misconduct directed at racial minorities, as well as evidence that police departments fail to discipline officers found guilty of misconduct.

Compelling evidence also points to discrimination within the court system. Supreme Court decisions and statutory reforms have not eliminated racial bias in decisions regarding bail, charging, plea bargaining, jury selection, and juvenile justice processing. Discrimination in sentencing also persists. Judges in some jurisdictions continue to impose harsher sentences on African American offenders who murder or rape whites and more lenient sentences on African Americans who victimize other African Americans. Judges also impose racially biased sentences in less serious cases; in these "borderline cases," people of color are more likely to get prison, whereas whites more typically get probation. Partly as a consequence of these discriminatory sentencing practices, the number of African Americans incarcerated in U.S. jails and prisons has swelled; African Americans now comprise a majority of those incarcerated.

We are particularly troubled by the persistence of racial discrimination at two of the most critical stages in the criminal justice process: police use of deadly force and the application of the death penalty. The effect of racial bias in these irrevocable life-or-death decisions is profound. The fact that it persists is deeply disturbing.

Court rulings and policy changes designed to regulate deadly force and death penalty decisions have made racial discrimination less likely. Studies reveal that the ratio of African Americans to whites killed by the police has dropped from approximately seven-to-one to three-to-one. Studies also reveal that the gross racial disproportions that characterized death penalty decisions earlier in this century, and particularly those that characterized decisions to impose the death penalty for the crime of rape, no longer exist.

This clearly is progress. However, we cannot ignore the fact that discrimination remains in these two critical decisions, both of which involve the ultimate decision to take the life of another person. Moreover, the fact that discrimination persists in the face of legal efforts to eradicate it suggests that decision making in these two areas reflects racial stereotypes and deeply buried racial prejudices. It suggests that police officers' definitions of dangerousness, and thus their willingness to use deadly force, depend to some degree on the race of the suspect. It suggests that judges' and jurors' assessments of the heinousness of a crime, and thus their willingness to impose the death penalty, are influenced by the race of the offender and the race of the victim.

Our analysis of race and crime in the United States suggests that those who conclude that "the criminal justice system is not racist"[2] are misinformed. Although reforms have made systematic racial discrimination—discrimination in all stages, in all places, and at all times—unlikely, the American criminal justice system has never been, and is not now, color-blind.

NOTES

1. Archibald Cox, *The Warren Court* (Cambridge, MA: Harvard University Press, 1968), p. 6.

2. William Wilbanks, *The Myth of a Racist Criminal Justice System* (Belmont, CA: Wadsworth, 1987), p. 10.

Selected Bibliography

Albonetti, Celesta A. "Criminality, Prosecutorial Screening, and Uncertainty: Toward a Theory of Discretionary Decision Making in Felony Case Processing." *Criminology* 24 (1986): 623–644.

Albonetti, Celesta A. "Sentencing Under the Federal Sentencing Guidelines: Effects of Defendant Characteristics, Guilty Pleas, and Departures on Sentencing Outcomes for Drug Offenses, 1991–1992." *Law & Society Review* 31 (1997): 789–822.

Albonetti, Celesta A., Robert M. Hauser, John Hagan, and Ilene H. Nagel. "Criminal Justice Decision Making as a Stratification Process: The Role of Race and Stratification Resources in Pretrial Release." *Journal of Quantitative Criminology* 5 (1989): 57–82.

Allen, James Paul, and Eugene James Turner. *We The People: An Atlas of America's Ethnic Diversity.* New York: Macmillan, 1988.

Amsterdam, Anthony. "Race and the Death Penalty." *Criminal Justice Ethics* 7 (1988): 84–86.

Author, John A. "Correctional Ideology of Black Correctional Officers." *Federal Probation* 58 (1994): 57–65.

Baldus, David C., Charles Pulaski, and George Woodworth. "Comparative Review of Death Sentences: An Empirical Study of the Georgia Experience." *The Journal of Criminal Law & Criminology* 74 (1983): 661–673.

Baldus, David C., George Woodworth, and Charles A. Pulaski. *Equal Justice and the Death Penalty: A Legal and Empirical Analysis.* Boston: Northeastern University Press, 1990.

Bayley, David H., and Harold Mendelsohn. *Minorities and the Police: Confrontation in America.* New York: The Free Press, 1969.

Bedau, Hugo A., and Michael L. Radelet. "Miscarriages of Justice in Potentially Capital Cases." *Stanford Law Review* 40 (1987): 21–179.

Bing, Robert. "Politicizing Black-on-Black Crime: A Critique of Terminological Preference." In *Black-on-Black Crime*, edited by P. Ray Kedia. Bristol, IN: Wyndham Hall Press, 1994.

Bishop, Donna M., and Charles E. Frazier. "The Influence of Race in Juvenile Justice Processing." *Journal of Research in Crime and Delinquency* 25 (1988): 242–263.

Blumberg, Abraham S. "The Practice of Law as a Confidence Game: Organizational Cooptation of a Profession." *Law & Society Review* 1 (1967): 15–39.

Blumstein, Alfred. "On the disproportionality of United States' Prison Populations." *The Journal of Criminal Law and Criminology* 73 (1982): 1259–1281.

Blumstein, Alfred, Jacqueline Cohen, Susan E. Martin, and Michael Tonry. *Research on Sentencing: The Search for Reform*, Vol. I. Washington, D.C.: National Academy Press, 1983.

Bowers, William. "The Pervasiveness of Arbitrariness and Discrimination Under Post-*Furman* Capital Statutes." *The Journal of Criminal Law & Criminology* 74 (1983): 1067–1100.

Bridges, George S., and Robert D. Crutchfield. "Law, Social Standing and Racial Disparities in Imprisonment." *Social Forces* 66 (1988): 699–724.

Bridges, George S., and Sara Steen. "Racial Disparities in Official Assessments of Juvenile Offending: Attributional Stereotypes as Mediating Mechanisms." *American Sociological Review* 65 (1998): 554–570.

Bright, Stephen B. "Discrimination, Death and Denial: The Tolerance of Racial Discrimination in the Infliction of the Death Penalty." *Santa Clara Law Review* 35 (1995): 901–950.

Bright, Stephen B., and Patrick J. Keenan. "Judges and the Politics of Death: Deciding Between the Bill of Rights and the Next Election in Capital Cases." *Boston University Law Review* 75 (1995): 759–835.

Browning, Sandra Lee, Francis T. Cullen, Liqun Cao, Renee Kopache, and Thomas J. Stevenson. "Race and Getting Hassled by the Police: A Research Note." *Police Studies* 17 (No. 1, 1994): 1–11.

Bureau of Justice Statistics. *Black Victims.* Washington, D.C.: Government Printing Office, 1990.

Bureau of Justice Statistics. *Capital Punishment 1991.* Washington, D.C.: U.S. Department of Justice, 1992.

Bureau of Justice Statistics. *Criminal Victimization in the United States, 1997.* Washington, D.C.: U.S. Government Printing Office, 1999.

Bureau of Justice Statistics. *Hispanic Victims.* Washington, D.C.: Government Printing Office, 1990.

Bureau of Justice Statistics. *Lifetime Likelihood of Victimization.* Washington, D.C.: U.S. Government Printing Office, 1987.

Bureau of Justice Statistics. *Police Use of Force: Collection of National Data.* Washington, DC: Government Printing Office, 1997.

Butler, Paul. "Racially Based Jury Nullification: Black Power in the Criminal Justice System." *Yale Law Journal* 105 (1995): 677–725.

Cahalan, Margaret Werner. *Historical Corrections Statistics in the United States, 1850–1984.* Washington, D.C.: Government Printing Office, 1986.

Campbell, Anne. *Girls in the Gang: A Report From New York City.* Oxford: Basil Blackwell, 1984.

Campbell, Anne. *The Girls in the Gang.* 2d ed. Cambridge, MA: Basil Blackwell, 1991.

Carter, David L. "Hispanic Interaction with the Criminal Justice System in Texas: Experiences, Attitudes, and Perceptions." *Journal of Criminal Justice* 11 (1983): 213–227.

Casper, Jonathan D. *Criminal Courts: The Defendant's Perspective.* Englewood Cliffs, NJ: Prentice Hall, 1978.

Chin, Ko-Lin, Jeffrey Fagan, and Robert J. Kelly. "Patterns of Chinese Gang Extortion." *Justice Quarterly* 9 (1992): 625–646.

Chiricos, Theodore E. "The Moral Panic of the Drug War." In *Race and Criminal Justice,* edited by Micheal J. Lynch and E. Britt Patterson. New York: Harrow and Heston, 1995.

Chiricos, Theodore G., and Charles Crawford. "Race and Imprisonment: A Contextual Assessment of the Evidence." In *Ethnicity, Race and Crime,* edited by Darnell F. Hawkins. Albany: State University of New York Press, 1995.

Chiricos, Theodore G., and Miriam A. DeLone. "Labor Surplus and Punishment: A Review and Assessment of Theory and Evidence." *Social Problems* 39 (1992): 421–446.

Chiricos, Theodore G., and William D. Bales. "Unemployment and Punishment: An Empirical Assessment." *Criminology* 29 (1991): 701–724.

Covey, Herbert C., Scott Menard, and Robert J. Franzese. *Juvenile Gangs.*

Springfield, IL: Charles C. Thomas, 1992.

Curry, David G., and Scott H. Decker. *Confronting Gangs: Crime and Community.* Los Angeles: Roxbury Publishing Company, 1998.

Decker, David L., David Shichor, and Robert M. O'Brien. *Urban Structure and Victimization.* Lexington, MA: D.C. Heath, 1982.

Decker, Scott H. "Citizen Attitudes Toward the Police: A Review of Past Findings and Suggestions for Future Policy." *Journal of Police Science and Administration* 9 (1981): 80–87.

Du Bois, W. E. B. "The Spawn of Slavery: The Convict-Lease System in the South." *The Missionary Review of the World* 14 (1901): 737–745.

Esbensen, Finn-Aage, and David Huizinga. "Gangs, Drugs and Delinquency." *Criminology* 31 (1993): 565–590.

Fagan, Jeffrey. "The Social Organization of Drug Use and Drug Dealing Among Urban Gangs." *Criminology* 27 (1989): 633–666.

Farnworth, Margaret, and Patrick Horan. "Separate Justice: An Analysis of Race Differences in Court Processes." *Social Science Research* 9 (1980): 381–399.

Flowers, Ronald Barri. *Minorities and Criminality.* Westport: Greenwood Press, 1988.

Fong, Robert, Ronald Vogel, and Salvador Buentello. "Prison Gang Dynamics: A Look Inside the Texas Department of Corrections." In *Corrections: Dilemmas and Directions*, edited by Peter J. Benekos and Alida V. Merlo. Highland Heights, KY: Anderson Publishing Co. and Academy of Criminal Justice Sciences, 1992.

Fyfe, James J. "Who Shoots? A Look at Officer Race and Police Shooting." *Journal of Police Science and Administration* 9 (1981): 367–382.

Fyfe, James J. "Blind Justice: Police Shootings in Memphis." *Journal of Criminal Law and Criminology* 73 (1982): 707–722.

Garfinkel, Harold. "Research Notes on Inter- and Intra-Racial Homicides." *Social Forces* 27 (1949): 369–381.

Geller, William A., and Hans Toch, eds. *And Justice For All.* Washington, D.C.: Police Executive Research Forum, 1995.

Geller, William A., and Michael S. Scott. *Deadly Force: What We Know.* Washington, D.C.: Police Executive Research Forum, 1992.

Gilliard, Darrell K. *Prison and Jail Inmates at Midyear, 1998.* Washington, D.C.: Department of Justice, 1999.

Gilliard, Darrell K., and Allen Beck. *Prisoners, 1993.* Washington, D.C.: U.S. Department of Justice, 1994.

Goodstein, Lynne, and Doris Layton MacKenzie. "Racial Differences in Adjustment Patterns of Prison Inmates—Prisonization, Conflict, Stress and Control." In *The Criminal Justice System and Blacks*, edited by Daniel Georges-Abeyie. New York: Clark Boardman Company, Ltd., 1984.

Greenfeld, Lawrence A., and Steven K. Smith. *American Indians and Crime.* Washington, D.C.: Bureau of Justice Statistics, 1999.

Grobsmith, Elizabeth S. *Indians in Prison.* Lincoln: University of Nebraska Press, 1994.

Gross, Samuel R., and Robert Mauro. *Death & Discrimination: Racial Disparities in Capital Sentencing.* Boston: Northeastern University Press, 1989.

Hacker, Andrew. *Two Nations: Black and White, Separate, Hostile, Unequal.* New York: Scribners, 1992.

Hagan, John. "Extra-Legal Attributes and Criminal Sentencing: An Assessment of a Sociological Viewpoint." *Law & Society Review* 8 (1974): 357–383.

Hagedorn, John M. *People and Folks.* Chicago: Lake View Press, 1989.

Hamm, Mark S. *American Skinheads.* Westport, CT: Praeger, 1994.

Harer, Miles D., and Darrell J. Steffensmeier. "Race and Prison Violence" *Criminolgy* 34 (1996): 323–355.

Harris, Mary G. *Cholas: Latino Girls in Gangs.* New York: AMS Press, 1988.

Hawkins, Darnell F. "Beyond Anomalies: Rethinking the Conflict Perspective on Race and Criminal Justice." *Social Forces* 65 (1987): 719–45.

Hawkins, Darnell F. "Ethnicity: The Forgotten Dimension of American Social Control." In *Inequality, Crime, and Social Control,* edited by George S. Bridges and Martha A. Myers. Boulder, CO: Westview Press, 1994.

Hawkins, Darnell F., ed. *Ethnicity, Race, and Crime.* Albany, NY: State University of New York Press, 1995.

Hawkins, Darnell F., and Kenneth A. Hardy. "Black-White Imprisonment Rates: A State-by-State Analysis." *Social Justice* 16 (1989): 75–94.

Hindelang, Michael J. "Race and Involvement in Common Law Personal Crimes." *American Sociological Review* 43 (1978): 93–109.

Holmes, Malcolm D., Harmon M. Hosch, Howard C. Daudistel, Dolores A. Perez, and Joseph B. Graves, "Ethnicity, Legal Resources, and Felony Dispositions in Two Southwestern Jurisdictions," *Justice Quarterly* 13 (1996): 11–30.

Huff, C. Ronald, ed. *Gangs in America.* Newbury Park, CA: Sage, 1990.

Huizinga, David, and Delbert S. Elliot. "Juvenile Offenders: Prevalence, Offender Incidence, and Arrest Rates by Race." *Crime and Delinquency* 33 (1987): 206–223.

Human Rights Watch. *Shielded From Justice: Police Brutality and Accountability in the United States.* New York: Human Rights Watch, 1998.

Jacobs, James. *New Perspectives on Prison and Imprisonment.* Ithaca: Cornell University Press, 1983.

Jacobs, James. "Should Hate Be a Crime?" *Public Interest* (1993): 3–14.

Jaynes, Gerald David, and Robin M. Williams, Jr., eds. *A Common Destiny: Blacks and American Society.* Washington, D.C.: National Academy Press, 1992.

Johnson, Elmer H. "Selective Factors in Capital Punishment." *Social Forces* 36 (1957): 165.

Johnson, Guy. "The Negro and Crime." *Annals of the American Academy* 217 (1941): 93–104.

Johnson, Sheri Lynn. "Black Innocence and the White Jury." *University of Michigan Law Review* 83 (1985): 1611–1708.

Johnstone, J. W. C. "Youth Gangs and Black Suburbs." *Pacific Sociological Review* 24 (1981): 355–375.

Kalven, Harry Jr., and Hans Zeisel. *The American Jury.* Boston: Little, Brown, 1966.

Keil, Thomas, and Gennaro Vito. "Race and the Death Penalty in Kentucky Murder Trials: An Analysis of Post-Gregg Outcomes." *Justice Quarterly* (1990): 189–207.

Kempf, Kimberly Leonard, and Henry Sontheimer. "The Role of Race in Juvenile Justice in Pennsylvania." In *Minorities and Juvenile Justice,* edited by Kimbery Kempf Leonard, Carl E. Pope, and William H. Feyerherm. Thousand Oaks, CA: Sage, 1995.

Kennedy, Randall. *Race, Crime, and the Law*. New York: Vintage Books, 1997.

Kerner Commission. Report of the National Advisory Commission on Civil Disorders. New York: Bantam Books, 1968.

Kleck, Gary. "Racial Discrimination in Criminal Sentencing: A Critical Evaluation of the Evidence with Additional Evidence on the Death Penalty." *American Sociological Review* 46 (1981): 783–805.

Klein, Malcomb W., Cheryl Maxson, and Lea C. Cunningham, et al. "'Crack,' Street Gangs and Violence." *Criminology* 29 (1991): 623–650.

Klein, Stephen, Joan Petersilia, and Susan Turner. "Race and Imprisonment Decisions in California." *Science* 247 (1990): 812–816.

Klinger, David. "Demeanor or Crime? Why 'Hostile' Citizens Are More Likely to be Arrested." *Criminology* 32 (1994): 475–493.

Knepper, Paul. "Race, Racism and Crime Statistics." *Southern Law Review* 24 (1996): 71–112.

Kramer, John H. and Jeffery T. Ulmer. "Sentencing Disparity and Departures From Guidelines." *Justice Quarterly* 13 (1996): 81–105.

LaFree, Gary D. "The Effect of Sexual Stratification by Race on Official Reactions to Rape." *American Sociological Review* 45 (1980): 842–854.

LaFree, Gary D. *Rape and Criminal Justice: The Social Construction of Sexual Assault*. Belmont, CA: Wadsworth, 1989.

Leiber, Michael J. "A Comparison of Juvenile Court Outcomes for Native Americans, African Americans, and Whites." *Justice Quarterly* 11 (1994): 255–279.

Lynch, Michael J., and E. Britt Patterson, eds. *Race and Criminal Justice*. New York: Harrow and Heston, 1991.

Mann, Coramae Richey. *Unequal Justice: A Question of Color*. Bloomington, IN: University of Indiana Press, 1993.

Mann, Coramae Richey, and Marjorie S. Zatz. *Images of Color, Images of Crime*. Los Angeles: Roxbury Publishing Company, 1998.

Melossi, Dario. "An Introduction: Fifty Years Later, Punishment and Social Structure in Comparative Analysis." *Contemporary Crises* 13 (1989): 311–326.

Melton, Ada Pecos. "Crime and Punishment: Traditional and Contemporary Tribal Justice." In *Images of Color, Images of Crime*, edited by Coramae Richey Mann and Marjorie S. Zatz. Los Angeles: Roxbury Publishing Company, 1998.

Michalowski, Raymond J., and Michael A. Pearson. "Punishment and Social Structure at the State Level: A Cross-Sectional Comparison of 1970 and 1980." *Journal of Research in Crime and Delinquency* 27 (1990): 52–78.

Miethe, Terance D., and Charles A. Moore. "Socioeconomic Disparities Under Determinate Sentencing Systems: A Comparison of Preguideline and Postguideline Practices in Minnesota." *Criminology* 23 (1985): 337–363.

Miller, Jerome. *Search and Destroy: African-American Males in the Criminal Justice System*. Cambridge: Cambridge University Press, 1996.

Moore, J. D., and Vigil R. Garcia. "Residence and Territoriality in Chicano Gangs." *Social Problems* 31 (1983): 182–194.

Mumola, Christopher J., and Allen J. Beck. *Prisoners, 1996*. Washington, D.C.: Department of Justice, 1997.

Myers, Martha A. Race. *Labor and Punishment in the South.* Columbus: Ohio State University Press, 1999.

Myrdal, Gunnar. *An American Dilemma: The Negro Problem and Modern Democracy.* New York: Harper and Brothers, 1944.

Nobiling, Tracy, Cassia Spohn, and Miriam DeLone. "A Tale of Two Counties: Unemployment and Sentence Severity." *Justice Quarterly* 15 (1998): 459–485.

O'Brien, Robert M. "The Interracial Nature of Violent Crimes: A Reexamination." *American Journal of Sociology* 92 (1987): 817–835.

Pate, Anthony M., and Lorie Fridell. *Police Use of Force* (2 Vols.). Washington, D.C.: The Police Foundation, 1993.

Paternoster, Raymond. "Prosecutorial Discretion in Requesting the Death Penalty: A Case of Victim-Based Racial Discrimination." *Law & Society Review* 18 (1984): 437–478.

Peak, K., and J. Spencer. "Crime in Indian Country: Another Trail of Tears." *Journal of Criminal Justice* 15 (1987): 485–494.

Petersilia, Joan. *Racial Disparities in the Criminal Justice System.* Santa Monica, CA: Rand, 1983.

Peterson, Ruth D., and John Hagan. "Changing Conceptions of Race: Towards an Account of Anomalous Findings of Sentencing Research." *American Sociological Review* 49 (1984): 56–70.

Radelet, Michael L. "Racial Characteristics and the Imposition of the Death Penalty." *American Sociological Review* 46 (1981): 918–927.

Radelet, Michael L., and Glenn L. Pierce. "Race and Prosecutorial Discretion in Homicide Cases." *Law & Society Review* 19 (1985): 587–621.

Ralph, Paige H., Jonathan R. Sorensen, and James W. Marquart. "A Comparison of Death-Sentenced and Incarcerated Murderers in Pre-*Furman* Texas." *Justice Quarterly* 9 (1992): 185–209.

Reddy, Marlita A., ed. *Statistical Record of African Americans.* Detroit: Gale Research, ___.

Reddy, Marlita A., ed. *Statistical Record of Hispanic Americans.* Detroit: Gale Research, 1993.

Reiss, Albert J. *The Police and the Public.* New Haven: Yale University Press, 1971.

Roberts, Dorothy. "Punishing Drug Addicts Who Have Babies: Women of Color, Equality, and the Right of Privacy." *Harvard Law Review* 104 (1991): 1419–1454.

Russell, Katheryn K. *The Color of Crime.* New York University Press, 1998.

Seer, Brian J. and Mark Maney. "Racism, Peremptory Challenges, and the Democratic Jury: The Jurisprudence of a Delicate Balance." *Journal of Criminal Law and Criminology* 79 (1988): 1–65.

Silberman, Charles E. Criminal Violence, Criminal Justice. New York: Random House, 1978.

Smith, Douglas A., Christy Visher, and Laura A. Davidson. "Equity and Discretionary Justice: The Influence of Race on Police Arrest Decisions." *Journal of Criminal Law and Criminology* 75 (1984): 234–249.

Snell, Tracy. *Correctional Populations in the United States, 1992.* Washington, D.C.: Department of Justice, 1995.

Song, John Huey-Long. "Attitudes of Chinese Immigrants and Vietnamese Refugees Toward Law Enforcement in the United States." *Justice Quarterly* 9 (1992) 703–719.

Spohn, Cassia. "The Sentencing Decisions of Black and White Judges: Expected and Unexpected Similarities." *Law & Society Review* 24 (1990): 1197–1216.

Spohn, Cassia. "Crime and the Social Control of Blacks: Offender/Victim Race and the Sentencing of Violent Offenders." In *Inequality, Crime & Social Control*, edited by George S. Bridges and Martha A. Myers. Boulder, CO: Westview Press, 1994.

Spohn, Cassia, and Jerry Cederblom. "Race and Disparities in Sentencing: A Test of the Liberation Hypothesis." *Justice Quarterly* 8 (1991): 305–327.

Spohn, Cassia, and Miriam DeLone. "When Does Race Matter? An Analysis of the Conditions Under Which Race Affects Sentence Severity." *Sociology of Crime, Law, and Deviance* (in press).

Spohn, Cassia, John Gruhl, and Susan Welch. "The Effect of Race on Sentencing: A Re-Examination on an Unsettled Question." *Law & Society Review* 16 (1981–82): 71–88.

Spohn, Cassia, John Gruhl, and Susan Welch. "The Impact of the Ethnicity and Gender of Defendants on the Decision to Reject or Dismiss Felony Charges." *Criminology* 25 (1987): 175–191.

Spohn, Cassia and Jeffrey Spears. "The Effect of Offender and Victim Characteristics on Sexual Assault Case Processing Decisions." *Justice Quarterly* 13 (1996): 649–679.

Steffensmeier, Darrell, John Kramer, and Cathy Streifel. "Gender and Imprisonment Decisions." *Criminology* 31 (1993): 411–443.

Sudnow, David. "Normal Crimes: Sociological Features of the Penal Code in the Public Defender's Office." *Social Problems* 12 (1965): 255–277.

Thomas, Jim. "Racial Codes in Prison Culture: Snapshots in Black and White." In *Race and Criminal Justice*, edited by Michael Lynch and Britt Patterson. New York: Harrow and Heston, 1991.

Tonry, Michael. *Malign Neglect: Race, Crime and Punishment in America.* New York: Oxford University Press, 1995.

Tonry, Michael. *Sentencing Matters.* New York: Oxford University Press, 1996.

Toy, Calvin. "A Short History of Asian Gangs in San Francisco." *Justice Quarterly* 9 (1992): 645–665.

Turner, Billy M., Rickie D. Lovell, John C. Young, and William F. Denny. "Race and Peremptory Challenges During Voir Dire: Do Prosecution and Defense Agree?" *Journal of Criminal Justice* 14 (1986): 61–69.

Uhlman, Thomas M. "Black Elite Decision Making: The Case of Trial Judges." *American Journal of Political Science* 22 (1978): 884–895.

Ulmer, Jeffery T., and John H. Kramer. "Court Communities Under Sentencing Guidelines: Dilemmas of Formal Rationality and Sentencing Disparity." *Criminology* 34 (1996): 383–407.

U.S. Department of Justice. *The Police and Public Opinion.* Washington, D.C.: Government Printing Office, 1977.

U.S. Department of Justice, Bureau of Justice Statistics. *Comparing Federal and State Inmates, 1991.* Washington, D.C.: U.S. Government Printing Office, 1993.

Vigil, James D. *Barrio Gangs.* Austin, TX: University of Texas Press, 1988.

Walker, Samuel. "Racial Minority and Female Employment in Policing: The Implications of 'Glacial' Change." *Crime and Delinquency* 31 (1985): 555–572.

Walker, Samuel. "Complaints Against the Police: A Focus Group Study of Citizen Perceptions, Goals, and Expectations." *Criminal Justice Review* 22 (No. 2, 1997): 207–225.

Walker, Samuel, and K. B. Turner. *A Decade of Modest Progress: Employment of Black and Hispanic Police Officers, 1982–1992.* Omaha: University of Nebraska Press, 1992.

Walsh, Anthony. "The Sexual Stratification Hypothesis in Light of Changing Conceptions of Race." *Criminology* 25 (1987): 153–173.

Welch, Susan, Michael Combs, and John Gruhl. "Do Black Judges Make a Difference?" *American Journal of Political Science* 32 (1988): 126–136.

Wheeler, Gerald R., and Carol L. Wheeler. "Reflections on Legal Representation of the Economically Disadvantaged: Beyond Assembly Line Justice." *Crime and Delinquency* 26 (1980): 319–332.

Wilbanks, William. "Is Violent Crime Intraracial?" *Crime and Delinquency* 31 (1985): 117–128.

Wilbanks, William. *The Myth of a Racist Criminal Justice System.* Monterey: Brooks/Cole, 1987.

Wilson, William Julius. *The Truly Disadvantaged.* Chicago: University of Chicago Press, 1987.

Wolfgang, Marvin E., and Marc Reidel. "Race, Judicial Discretion, and the Death Penalty." *The Annals of the American Academy of Political and Social Science* 407 (1973): 119–133.

Wolfgang, Marvin E., and Marc Reidel. "Rape, Race and the Death Penalty in Georgia." *American Journal of Orthopsychiatry* 45 (1975): 658–668.

Zatz, Marjorie S. "Pleas, Priors and Prison: Racial/Ethnic Differences in Sentencing." *Social Science Research* 14 (1985): 169–193.

Zatz, Marjorie S. "The Changing Form of Racial/Ethnic Biases in Sentencing." *Journal of Research in Crime and Delinquency* 25 (1987): 69–92.

Zatz, Marjorie S., Carol Chiago Lujan, and Zoann K. Snyder-Joy, "American Indians and Criminal Justice: Some Conceptual and Methodological Considerations." In *Race and Criminal Justice*, edited by Coramae Richey Mann and Marjorie Zatz. New York: Harrow and Heston, 1991.

Index